THE PATHS OF KATERI'S KIN

AMERICAN INDIAN CATHOLICS

CHRISTOPHER VECSEY

———

VOLUME II

The Paths of Kateri's Kin

THE PATHS OF KATERI'S KIN

CHRISTOPHER VECSEY

UNIVERSITY OF NOTRE DAME PRESS

NOTRE DAME, INDIANA

Copyright 1997 by
University of Notre Dame Press
Notre Dame, Indiana 46556

Manufactured in the United States of America

Library of Congress Cataloging-in-Publication Data

Vecsey, Christopher,
    The paths of Kateri's kin / Christopher Vecsey.
      p.   cm. — (American Indian Catholics ; v. 2)
    Includes bibliographical references and index.
    ISBN 0-268-03820-1 (cloth ; alk. paper)
    1. Indians of North America—Religion.   2. Indians of
North America—Missions.   3. Catholic Church—Missions—
North America—History.   4. Catholic Church—Missions—
New France—History.   5. Christianity and culture—North
America—History.   6. America—Discovery and exploration—
Religious aspects—Catholic Church.   I. Title.   II. Series.
    E98.R3V444 1997
    282′.7′08997—dc21   97-21499
                                                              CIP

The paper used in this publication meets the minimum requirements of the
American National Standard for Information Sciences—Permanence of Paper
for Printed Library Material, ANSI Z39.481984.

Book design by Will Powers
Set in Galliard CC
by Stanton Publication Services, Inc.

For my teachers,
Edmund Perry, Madeleine Hooke Rice,
Robert W. Venables, Barbara Ann Welter

*The earliest known painting of Kateri Tekakwitha is
attributed to Rev. Claude Chauchetière, S.J., c. 1690.*

Used by permission of St. Francis Xavier Mission, Kahnawake, Quebec; photograph by Bob Peters.

CONTENTS

MAPS

PREFACE

The encounter between the Catholicism of Europe and the aboriginal religions of North America has produced distinctive forms of Native American Catholic tradition over five centuries. Millions of Indians in Mexico and several hundred thousand in the United States and Canada identify themselves, or are identified by Church authorities, as participants in Catholic faith and institutions. Most of these American Indian Catholics continue to bear a special heritage that colors their Catholicism, and it is the task of this work to understand the particular Catholic life formed within the native experience.

In the first volume of *American Indian Catholics, On the Padres' Trail,* I examined the heritage of Spanish Catholicism passed down among the Indians of the Caribbean, Mexico, and the American South. This volume followed the spread of New Spain's Catholic institutions to its northern frontiers, to Florida and Texas, but more significantly to the Yaquis of northern Mexico, the O'odham (Pimas and Papagos) of the Sonoran borderland, the Pueblos of New Mexico and Arizona, and the various Indians of California. In all cases I have provided a history of missionary and colonization efforts that led to the christianization of the Native Americans; however, my primary interest has been in the practice of Indian Catholicism, especially in the twentieth century. My goal in *American Indian Catholics* is to document the ways in which American Indians of the United States—but also of Mexico and Canada—have adopted Catholic forms, adapting them to their own culture and at the same time modulating themselves to the demands of their new religious complex.

In bringing the history of American Indian Catholicism up to date, I am also concerned with evaluating the present-day reflection of Catholic Indians regarding their faith, including the processes by which they and their ancestors became connected to the Church. In the first volume I found a contemporary critique of the Catholic evangelical enterprise, even among Native Americans faithful to the one, holy, catholic and apostolic Church. This critique addresses the historical circumstances of the Spanish Catholic heritage in the Americas: the concepts of "discovery" as an ideology of conquest; the requirement of missionization as an aspect of colonization; the violent nature of Spanish expansion into Indian lands.

The present volume addresses different but related circumstances, evolving from the foundation of New France in North America. French Catholics spread their faith and institutions among Indians of the present-day United States and Canada, beginning in the early seventeenth century on the easternmost shores of Nova Scotia and Maine and traveling progressively, but with stops and starts, through the interior along the Great Lakes and the Mississippi River to the southern coast of Louisiana and eventually, by the nineteenth century, to the Pacific Ocean in Oregon and Washington. The primary carriers of the French Catholic faith were the priestly members of the Society of Jesus (although Recollects, Capuchins, Sulpicians, Hospitaliers, Ursulines, Oblates, and others have played their parts); hence, we shall begin by coming to understand the motivations, methods, and effects of the Jesuits in the seventeenth century, especially among the Montagnais and Hurons of Quebec Province. We shall follow the heritage of French Catholicism among the Eastern Algonkians of Acadia and New England, particularly the Passamaquoddies of Maine, from the seventeenth century to the present day.

The demise of the Huron mission in the 1650s, crushed by the Iroquois, forced the French Jesuits to enter Iroquois territory to regain contact with captive Hurons and to attempt the conversion of the Iroquois. We shall examine the Catholic inroads among the Iroquois, particularly the Mohawks. Succeeding chapters will analyze Catholicism among the Central Algonkian Anishinabe of the Great Lakes—the Ojibways, Ottawas, and Potawatomis—as they migrated westward to the prairies of middle America and Canada from the seventeenth to the twentieth centuries. One chapter observes the Houma Indians of Louisiana, now three centuries deep in Catholic tradition.

In the nineteenth century, European Jesuits, including Belgians, Italians, and eventually Germans, reestablished Indian missions left fallow when the Society of Jesus was banned in 1773. They were joined by other priests, including Benedictines, Franciscans, and diocesan clergy, as they encountered the Indians of the western plains, the Rocky Mountains, and the northwest coast of the continent. In western Canada in the nineteenth century the Oblates instituted missions whose impact is still felt. The last chapters of this volume document the coming of Catholicism to the northern and western Indians, concluding with a chapter on the Catholic tradition today among the Coast Salish Catholics of Washington State.

Thematically, the central figure in the narrative of this volume is Kateri Tekakwitha, the renowned Mohawk convert of the late seventeenth century. For thousands of American Indian Catholics from a panoply of tribes across North America, she serves today as a symbolic model of their two-part cultural identity. Indeed, many feel with her a profound kinship as they travel the paths of Native American Catholicism.

ACKNOWLEDGMENTS

I proffer my thanks to Msgr. Roland J. Boudreaux, Archivist, Diocese of Houma-Thibodaux; Vi Hilbert, Archivist, Lushootseed Research; Leonard Forsman, Archivist, Suquamish Museum; Msgr. David W. Stinebrickner, Archivist, Diocese of Ogdensburg; Rev. Leo Cooper, Archivist, Archdiocese of Kansas City in Kansas; Mark G. Thiel, Archivist, Marquette University Memorial Library, Department of Special Collections; Sharon Sumpter, Archivist, the University of Notre Dame; Christine Taylor, Archivist, Archdiocese of Seattle; Murphy D. Smith, Archivist, American Philosophical Society; James R. Glenn, Archivist, Smithsonian Institution, Bureau of American Ethnology Archives; Dr. Josephine L. Harper, the State Historical Society of Wisconsin; and to the many people who have shared their time and insight with me: Josephine Angus, Sister Marie-Therese Archambault, O.S.F., Babe Bell, John Bigtree, Eva Pierre Boudreaux, Joseph Norris Boudreaux, Msgr. Roland J. Boudreaux, Peg Bova, Ron Boyer, Prof. Jack Campisi, Catherine Clinton, Larry Cloud-Morgan, Elaine Cook, Cecilia Cree, Sister Therese Culhane, I.H.M., Sister Genevieve Cuny, O.S.F., Joan Dana, Julie Daniels, Mercedes Degand, Prof. Jay P. Dolan, Anna Dyer, Lydia Gregoire Duthu, Ted Duthu, Sr., the late Rev. Thomas F. Egan, S.J., Dominic Eshkakagon, John Farmer, Noah Foret, Leonard Forsman, Joe Fox, John Francis, Joseph Gabriel, Lillien Gabriel, Simon Gabriel, Cheryl Gillespie, Françes Carlos Gregoire, Mary Gregoire, Sarah Hassenplug, Rev. Gilbert F. Hemauer, O.F.M.Cap., Vi Hilbert, Donna Holstein, Ursula Jacko, Robert Joe, Peter Johnston, Nancy Kilcoyne, Sister Therese Klepac, S.C.L., Milton LaClair, Laïse Marie Ledet, Msgr. Paul A. Lenz, Rev. Thomas Lequin, Henry Lickers, Esther Lucero, Zelda Martinez, Rev. Paul McCarty, S.J., Kenneth B. Mello, Delia Mitchell, Sister Carolyn Murphy, S.N.J.M., Rev. Roch Naquin, Charles Nolan, Sarah Patterson, Joan Paul, Most Rev. Donald E. Pelotte, S.S.S., Sister Mary Hugh Placilla, I.H.M., Prof. James J. Preston, Jane Puckkee, M. Grace Roderick, Prof. Sue N. Roark-Calnek, Mary Lou Shawana, Sarah Shillinger, Mary Solet, Pierre Solet, Rev. Carl F. Starkloff, S.J., Prof. William A. Starna, Terry Steele, George Stevens, Jr., Rev. Michael Stogre, S.J.,

Laura Thackery, Rev. Norman Thibodeau, Shannon Thompson, Margaret Toulouse, Gerald Tuckwin, Rev. Patrick J. Twohy, S.J., Kirby Verret, Zoe Verret, Dennis Wawia, and Rev. Ted Zuern, S.J. The American Philosophical Society, the Cushwa Center for the Study of American Catholicism, and Colgate University have provided generous grants of money to help defray research costs. Colgate's Case Library staff has been very helpful to my study. I appreciate the support. Finally, I thank Wanda Kelly for helping me so ably in producing the manuscript, and Julia Meyerson for creating the maps.

* I *

*French Catholicism
among Native Americans*

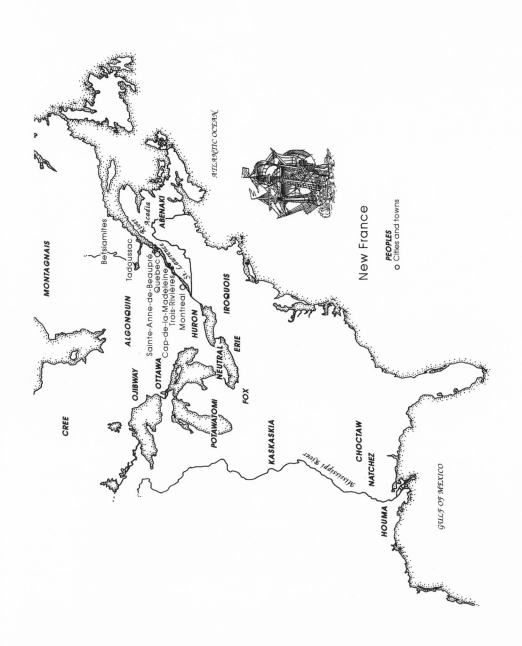

CREE

MONTAGNAIS

Betsiamites

OJIBWAY

ALGONQUIN

Tadoussac

OTTAWA

Saguenay River

Acadia

ABENAKI

Sainte-Anne-de-Beaupré

Québec

Cap-de-la-Madeleine

Trois-Rivières

Montréal

St. Lawrence River

HURON

NEUTRAL

ERIE

IROQUOIS

POTAWATOMI

FOX

KASKASKIA

Mississippi River

CHOCTAW

NATCHEZ

HOUMA

GULF OF MEXICO

ATLANTIC OCEAN

New France

PEOPLES
o Cities and towns

INTRODUCTION

Several decades elapsed between the first Columbian encounter in the Caribbean and the official French arrival in the Americas. Before Jacques Cartier made his first landing in the Gaspé Peninsula in 1534, the Spaniards had already received the blessing of the papacy for their "discovery" of the New World. They had already established the rule of Christendom in the isles and mainland of New Spain. They had conquered Montezuma's Aztec Empire, and the first legions of friars had begun the process of evangelization in central Mexico.

When Cartier sailed down the St. Lawrence River in 1535, journeying as far as present-day Montreal in search of a sea route to the Far East, he planted a Christian cross and claimed the lands of the St. Lawrence drainage for Christian France according to the "right of discovery." Visualizing the possibilities of trading for furs with the Algonkian and Iroquoian peoples he met on his voyages, he returned in 1541 with colonists, hoping to initiate an economic beachhead. The colony was short-lived, and for the remainder of the sixteenth century the French contacts with Native North Americans were sporadic. If there were any religious interchanges during these years, they went unrecorded. One might call the first French colonists "malefactors and murderers" (Axtell 1986: 32) and imagine them to be ignoble carriers of the Christian tradition, unlikely to introduce Native Americans to the ideals of Catholic faith. It is also possible that the chaplains of fishing and fur-trading vessels expended some effort in explaining their religion to the indigenes, or performing public rituals for their edification. The fact is, however, that we know nothing of French Catholic contact with North American Indians until the next century. In the 1530s Cartier received the commission to explore, "in order the better to do what is pleasing to God, our Creator and Redeemer, and what may be for the increase of his holy and sacred name, and of our holy mother, the Church" (in Shea 1855: 123). Nonetheless, permanent settlement and christianization of New France were delayed until the early 1600s.

Samuel de Champlain commenced his exploration of the North American interior in 1603, and in 1608 he chose Quebec (the place of the present city) as the site for a small settlement and fur-trading post.

In the same year the French established their first village in Acadia, at Port Royal (now Annapolis) in Nova Scotia. The first French Catholic missions among the North American Indians occurred at these locations.

The Indians who met the French already possessed religious traditions of their own making. The Algonkians (including the Micmacs and Abenakis of Acadia, the Montagnais and Algonquins north of the St. Lawrence, the Ottawas, Ojibways, and Potawatomis of the Great Lakes) and the Iroquoians (primarily the Hurons and the five nations of the Iroquois Confederacy: the Mohawks, Oneidas, Onondagas, Cayugas, and Senecas) lived their lives ever aware of a spiritual realm inhabited by powerful beings. The Algonkians referred to the spirit world with the expression *manito* (the *manitos* were the spirits); the Iroquoians spoke of *orenda* to denote the supernatural. In their dreams and visions the Indians received communication from spirit-persons. Young men and women sought protection and inspiration from these vision visitors; individuals and communities endeavored to please the spirits by following their guidance and offering them gifts. Elders passed down the stories of creation and transformation accomplished by the tribal gods and culture heroes. Religious specialists used the skills and strengths gained from the spirit world in order to cure diseases, locate animals for the kill, control weather, and (where farming existed, e.g., among the Iroquoians) protect crops. The rituals of a human life cycle—bestowing a name, marking a first menstruation, seeking adolescent direction, passing from this world to the next after death—took place with the spirits in mind. The Indians marked their seasonal activities—tapping maple syrup, gathering wild strawberries, harvesting corn, and so forth—by thanking the spiritualized world for its blessings. They consoled one another, interpreted each other's dreams, fought, tortured prisoners, and adopted their enemies, always mindful of their existence as ensouled beings, as spiritualized as the world around them. The hunting and gathering Algonkians kept their religious practice to themselves as atomized individuals; the Iroquoian agricultural communities engaged in public ceremonialism; however, all of these tribal peoples recognized their familial connections to be matters of shared spirituality. It was with this tradition of religiousness that the natives of northeast North America encountered French Catholicism.

From the beginning of French exploration there was a European notion that the Indian peoples lacked, needed, and deserved Christianity. Cartier urged missionary work, to no avail. Champlain observed that the indigenes were ignorant of Christian faith but were not opposed to learning of it. French colonial spokesmen deemed the natives uncivilized, having neither law, faith, nor king, and they hoped to rectify these failings. King Henry IV called for clerics to aid the new colonies. As a result, the French authorities hired priests, brothers, and later nuns to introduce the Indians to Christianity. Jesuits made their first contact with the Micmacs and Abenakis of Acadia between 1611 and 1613, until the English crushed their efforts. Franciscan Recollects labored among the Montagnais and Hurons from their post in Quebec City, beginning in 1615, and they attempted to revive the Acadian mission from 1619 to 1624, when that region fell into Scottish hands. In 1625 the Recollects invited the help of Jesuits, who entered Montagnais and Huron territory.

The French crown's charter to the fur-trading Company of the Hundred Associates in 1627 stipulated that "any Indian converts would be considered 'natural-born Frenchmen' and would be allowed to settle in France, acquire property, and inherit or make donations and legacies like any other citizens" (Axtell 1986: 38–39). Before the Recollects and Jesuits could convert many natives, however, the English conquered and occupied Quebec, chasing the Catholic priests from their territories until France regained the colony in 1632. From this time until the 1763 Treaty of Paris, the Jesuits were the dominant missionary order within New France. They acquired choice lands around Quebec City, Trois-Rivières, Montreal, and Tadoussac. They served as allies of the Hundred Associates in the fur trade. With the aid of Ursuline and Hospitalier nuns, they educated Indian youths, formed reductions (communities of resettled Indians) after the model of Jesuit *reducciones* in South America, and expanded the boundaries of Christendom. Within a century, over 150 Jesuit fathers and numerous lay brothers had established thirty-odd missions in what is today Nova Scotia, Maine, Quebec, Ontario, New York, Michigan, Wisconsin, Illinois, Ohio, Indiana, and Louisiana. In 1642 the twenty-nine Jesuit priests constituted a goodly portion of the French Canadian population of 356 (fifty-three of them soldiers). In 1663, when Louis XIV made New France a crown colony, there were seventy-eight priests, nuns, and brothers among the three thousand New World French colonials.

One by one, in native village and in reduction, in good health and on the bed of death, Indians (at least as many as twenty thousand) received baptism from the Jesuits in the seventeenth century and became economic and military allies of the French. These were not the mass baptisms of the Spanish, accomplished under the rights of "discovery" expressed in the Spanish Requirement and under conquistadorial sword. New France had a military force and was not shy to use it to combat the English and their Indian allies (like the Iroquois), or to crush those natives—e.g., the Fox and the Natchez—who resisted colonization. Evangelization, however, took place primarily through the personal efforts of Jesuits without the benefit of overwhelming arms. *Coureurs des bois* may have imparted some of their Christian culture to their native mates and offspring; French soldiery may have impressed Indians with the apparently supernatural underpinnings of their military might. Nevertheless, Catholicism came to the Native Americans of New France through the agency of Jesuits: Pierre Biard and Ennemond Massé among the Micmacs, Jean du Quen and Paul Le Jeune among the Montagnais, Gabriel Druillettes and Sébastian Râle among the Abenakis, Jean de Brébeuf and Antoine Daniel with the Hurons, Isaac Joques and Simon Le Moyne with the Iroquois, Claude Allouez and Charles Raymbault with the Ottawas and Ojibways, Jacques Marquette with the Kaskaskias, and many, many others.

The Jesuits evangelized as Catholics and as Frenchmen, laboring zealously for God and king. They felt themselves to be the vanguard of the Counter-Reformation, combating the enemies of true religion throughout the world. St. Ignatius Loyola, the Spanish soldier who became a warrior for Christ, founded the Society of Jesus in the sixteenth century to create a cadre of committed troops, fortified by spiritual exercises and determined to march under the papal banner. Whether they countered Protestants or pagans, the Jesuits viewed themselves as waging a holy battle against Catholicism's enemies. At the same time, the French Jesuits in North America were connected with the official interests of New France: "From the outset, evangelization was closely linked with policies of assimilation, economic exploitation and imperialism" (Jaenen 1976b: 22). The commercial powers hired, supported, and protected the missionaries; in this context the Jesuits sought to "bring the native into obedience of the faith" (ibid.).

The Jesuits of the seventeenth century, with their Catholic and

French loyalties, were confident of success. After gaining from the crown a monopoly over the spiritual welfare of New France in 1632, the priesthood attracted talented and dedicated men to the order, and they believed that the future was theirs. Father Paul Le Jeune wrote in 1640, "The faith is extending, and taking deep root among the Savages. These few words might suffice to show that we are living here in a golden age" (Thwaites 1896–1901, 18:83). This enthusiasm and optimism persisted through 1657, when the Society of Jesus was required to share clerical jurisdiction with diocesan clergy and other missionary orders, and at least until 1690, when the Jesuit impulse subsided and the French military took a greater role imposing the objectives of New France policy. In the eighteenth century the old religiosity of France slackened; libertinism and philosophic rationalism became the leading attitudes of the age. No longer were the brilliant men of France becoming Jesuits in such large numbers. At the same time, the French government no longer encouraged the Jesuits to expand their missionary operations. For all these reasons, the Jesuits lost the impetus to expand. Between 1700 and the Capitulation of Canada to England in 1760, the Jesuit mission posts held constant their number but not their former vigor.

When the British defeated the French in the Seven Years' War (or, as it was called in the English colonies, the French and Indian War) and took formal possession of French Canada in 1763, the victors expelled most of the Jesuits among the French populace of sixty-five thousand. At the same time, the Catholic thrones of Europe were in the process of curtailing Jesuit activities. In 1773 Pope Clement XIV suppressed the order worldwide, although several secularized Jesuits lived on among their Indian congregations. The last of these Jesuits, Father Joseph Huguet, died at the reduction of Caughnawaga in 1783. A contingent of former Jesuits entered the British territories in the 1790s and established a mission among the Maliseets on the Tobique River in New Brunswick, and another further west among the Ottawas along the Detroit River. However, the Society of Jesus was not restored until 1814. The nineteenth century witnessed renewed Jesuit evangelization among Indians in the United States and Canada, and these efforts persist to the present time.

THE SOCIETY OF JESUS

To understand the missionization of Indians in New France is to understand the French Jesuits. Fortunately for the scholar, the order left voluminous records: the famous Jesuit Relations (Thwaites 1896–1901; cf. Campeau 1967, 1979, 1987a, 1989, 1990, 1992). These were regular and periodic reports from missionaries to their regional superiors, who collated and edited the documents for the viewing not only of the superior generals of the order and other Church authorities (including, presumably, the popes) but also the educated public throughout France. "Designed for public consumption" (Donnelly 1967: 2), the Jesuit Relations were a witness to Catholic faith; they were devotional literature meant to edify readers for the glory of Church and God, and to raise funds for the missionary endeavor. They were also accurate accounts of the missionary enterprise: the Indians and their territories, the goals and techniques of evangelization, and the effects of that enterprise upon the Native Americans. Critics of the Jesuits in the seventeenth century, including their chief missionary rivals, the Recollects, as well as secular forces in French society, denigrated the Relations as self-promoting, falsely optimistic propaganda; however, in the twentieth century they comprise the first order of documentation regarding the culture and history of the Northeastern Indians and the progress of Christian faith among them. They tell us much of the Indians' world: its natural history, animals, fish, insects, vegetation, minerals, lakes, climate, geology, and various natural phenomena. They tell us a great deal about the Jesuits themselves and their associates: their personalities and their prayerfulness, their love of God, and their acceptance of possible martyrdom. They also depict the process by which American Indians became imbued with Catholic culture.

In their own day the Jesuit Relations inspired some French men and women to devote their lives to the cause of evangelization in New France, and convinced many others to support the cause. In the nineteenth and twentieth centuries the leitmotifs of the Relations—paganism, martyrdom, conversion—have nourished the Church's reflection on the drama of faith among the Indians (e.g., Talbot 1956, 1961). In recent decades scholars have made critical analyses of the Relations (e.g.,

Axtell 1986, Jaenen 1976a, Kennedy 1950, Moore 1982, and Pouliot 1940), primarily as a means of understanding the Jesuits. In this volume, however, the Relations are used primarily to examine the ways in which Indians first encountered and appropriated the life of the Catholic Church.

The Jesuits came to the Indians as christianizers, seeking to sanctify the land they found with the blessings and teachings of Christendom. Father Paul Le Jeune expressed this commission repeatedly (Thwaites 1896–1901, vol. 8) in the early years of his apostolate. He was eager for the French colonizers to enter an environment that would reaffirm their Christian culture rather than seduce them from it. His task was to prepare the way for his fellows by converting the landscape and the native peoples through the sacramental orderliness of the Church. Like the Spanish missionaries, Le Jeune sought to possess a heathen domain and transform it into a portion of Christendom. The French Jesuits aligned themselves not only with the pope but also with the king of France, "resolved to make of his New France a land of conquest" (ibid., 46:221). In this empire there were "Savages to convert and lands to conquer for Jesus Christ" (67). When Jacques Marquette met Indians at the Mississippi River in 1673, he orated a frenchified version of the triumphant Requirement that Spanish "discoverers" read to the natives they encountered:

> I announced to them that God, who had Created them, had pity on Them, inasmuch as, after they had so long been ignorant of him, he wished to make himself Known to all the peoples; that I was Sent by him for that purpose; and that it was for Them to acknowledge and obey him. (59:119–121)

By saying the Catholic mass, "he took possession of that land in the name of Jesus Christ, and gave to that mission the name of the Immaculate Conception of the blessed virgin" (191). To locate the overarching goal of the Jesuits among the Indians of North America, one can quote Le Jeune, who wrote, "not only shall we render our America French, but we shall also make it wholly Christian, and shall form a Sanctuary out of a vast solitude, where the divine Majesty will find worshipers of every Tongue and Nation" (47:111).

The Jesuits cooperated with the economic aims of the Hundred Associates; however, the priests proclaimed their mission as spiritual. Therefore, they "resolved to preach publicly to all, and to acquaint them with the reasons of our coming into their Country, which is not for their furs, but to declare to them the true God and son Jesus Christ, the universal savior of our souls" (8:143). With this divine fire kindling their motives, the priests embraced hardships and even a martyr's death if necessary, in order to make Christians of the Indians.

How did the Jesuits conduct their mission? They studied Indian languages assiduously in order to explain the doctrines and commandments of God and Church. They engaged in debate with native religious leaders and tried to discredit and supplant them among their people. Seeking to gain the loyalty of the major lineages and personages, the clerics were willing to form Christian factions and undermine the pagan community ethos. They introduced lively and vivid forms of Christian catechesis, worship, and paraliturgical practices, and they translated French and Latin expressions into native idiom. After a suitable period of instruction, the Jesuits baptized many Indians and initiated partial participation in sacramental life.

In employing these techniques, the missionaries treated Indian cultures—as distasteful as they found them—with more than a modicum of accommodation. Their initial hope was for Indian ways to be christianized over time and with care. Perhaps the "savages," as they called them, were devoid enough of corrupting idolatry that Catholic religiousness would appeal to them without too much obstruction. Over the decades, however, the Jesuits came to acknowledge the continuing resistance of native peoples with their own religious traditions. Segregating the catechumens in reductions and instilling Christian devotionalism proved insufficient to effect thorough conversions among the majority, however spectacular were the changes wrought among many.

There was never any question among the French Jesuits regarding the full humanity of Native Americans. These were people with souls, descendants of Adam and Eve, rational beings and sinners in dire need of God's grace for eternal salvation. In order to impress upon the Indians a recognition of their sinfulness and the Church's sacramental role in providing necessary understanding and grace, the priests first sought to comprehend the ways and values of the natives. The Jesuits were keen observers of the Indians because of the approach of their mission: their desire to understand Indian culture and to suit the teachings of Catholicism to that culture.

The priests did not regard that culture highly. They believed that

Indians had souls and were truly human, but by and large they despised the natives' behavior and regarded them as hideous examples of
fallen humanity, to be tamed and civilized. The standard Jesuit view of
the "savages" was of the crudeness of their existence. These peoples—
and the clerics often blurred distinctions among the tribes—spent all
their time in pursuit of food in the alleviation of hunger and the quest
for merely physical survival. To the Jesuits this meant that the Indians
were "merely content with life" (Pompedli 1987: 277), and therefore fit
Aristotle's description of the lowest type of human evolution. These
were peoples, the Jesuits said, who lacked the time to develop a higher
culture or a true religion. Father Biard said of the Eastern Algonkians
in 1612:

> [A]s the savages have no definite religion, magistracy or government,
> liberal or mechanical arts, commercial or civil life, they have conse-
> quently no words to describe things which they have never seen or even
> conceived. Furthermore, rude and untutored as they are, all their con-
> ceptions are limited to sensible and material things; there is nothing ab-
> stract, internal, spiritual, or distinct. (Thwaites 1896–1901, 2:9–11)

Four years later he expanded upon his observation:

> It is true . . . that they are purely and absolutely wretched, as much be-
> cause they have no part in the natural happiness which is in the contem-
> plation of God, and in the knowledge of sublime things and in the
> perfection of the nobler parts of the soul, but chiefly because they are
> outside the grace of our Lord Jesus Christ, and the way of Eternal salva-
> tion. (3:135)

Because the Indians were beyond the touch of Christ's grace delivered
by the visible Church, they were incapable of sharing in the happiness of Christ; hence, their lives were miserable, according to the
missionaries.

Jesuits complained of Indian vices: their gluttony and their drunkenness under European influence, their dishonesty and vindictiveness,
their lack of compassion, and their brutality in battle. The priests
claimed the natives engaged in incest as well as polygamy. They found
them dirty. They called many of them thieves and they disapproved of
their seasonal wanderings (see 6:243–269). The missionaries were disturbed by the constant physicality of the Indians, their daily focus
upon the things of this world rather than spiritual matters. Father Le
Jeune complained in 1634:

These people do not think there is any other science in the world, except that of eating and drinking; and in this lies all their Philosophy.
They are astonished at the value we place upon books, seeing that a
knowledge of them does not give us anything with which to drive away
hunger. They cannot understand what we ask from God in our prayers.
"Ask him," they say to me, "for Moose, Bears, and Beavers; tell him that
thou wishest them to eat;" and when I tell them that those are only
trifling things, that there are still greater riches to demand, they laughingly reply, "What couldst thou wish better than to eat thy fill of these
good dishes?" In short, they have nothing but life; yet they are not always sure of that, since they often die of hunger. (7:9)

The Indians' materialism, according to the Jesuits, was matched by
their individualism. The Algonkians particularly seemed to possess little government; their state seemed to be libertarian anarchy. Indians
hated restraint, and in their egalitarianism nobody told anyone else
what to do. In such a condition it was difficult for the priests to assert
their authority, especially since their message called upon the "savages"
to look beyond their physical state to the Christian deity and the spiritual condition of their eternal souls. "Thy God," an Indian told a Jesuit, "has not come to our country, and that is why we do not believe
in him; make me see him and I will believe in him. . . . I see nothing
except with the eyes of the body, save in sleeping, and thou dost not
approve our dreams" (in 7:101).

The Jesuits decried Indian physicality; they also condemned what
they saw as superstitious behavior among the natives. The "savages"
consulted their reveries for omens, "looking upon their Dreams as
their Divinities, upon whom the happiness of their lives depends," according to one priest (23:153). The natives communicated with spirits
whose existence the missionaries either doubted or railed against. The
Jesuits were determined to infuse the Indians with Christian religiousness, and that meant a substantial alteration in the patterns of traditional spirituality.

At first the Jesuits thought of the Indians as lacking any formal religious tradition. They saw no churches, no hierarchical priesthoods,
no visible institutions. Perhaps the "savages" possessed no system beyond vague elements of superstitions—some stories of creation, some
notions of divinity, an afterlife for the soul, some occasions of prayer—
and perhaps, then, the task of conversion would be an easy one. The
Jesuits were wary of the Indians' mentality, "full of Diabolical Superstitions" (23:153). At the same time they hoped for an unimpeded

path to the unformed Indian mind: "Because—as upon a bare tablet, from which there was nothing to erase—we might without opposition impress on them Ideas of a true God, and guide them into that respect and Adoration which are due to him throughout the Earth" (151–153). These were people, the Jesuits surmised, living in a religious vacuum, with a primitive potential for accepting Christian doctrines and practices.

Over the decades, however, the Jesuits came to realize that the Indians possessed religious traditions for which Christianity was competition. The missionaries had difficulty in penetrating the veil of secrecy with which the Indians concealed their religiousness, and what information the priests did gain often remained inscrutable. "There is a mysterious something, I know not what, in this semblance of a Tortoise," wrote one Jesuit to another, "to which these people attribute their origin. We shall know in time what there is to it" (17:157), he suggested. The missionaries recognized over the years that there were indeed religious functionaries among the tribes who passed down authoritative tradition, who mediated between the community and the spirits, and who opposed the Christian inroads. There was a polytheism at work among all the Indian peoples, and as the Jesuits witnessed Indian ritualism, including seances, healings, propitiations, and exorcisms, they viewed many of the practices as demonic. There was indeed a complex of Indian religious elements confronting the process of conversion, a complex firmly embedded in a way of life, and the missionaries had to discern a strategy for overcoming it.

THE JEƒUIT PROGRAM

The Jesuit plan was to instruct the Indians in the doctrines of Christianity, and at the same time to demonstrate the tactile aspects of Christian devotion. Their hope in the short run was to create Catholic forms of religiousness—chapels, sodalities, sacraments, calendars, choirs and all manner of ceremonial display—for the natives to experience firsthand. Simultaneously the priests tried to discredit native religious authority. Over time they hoped to shape innate Indian spiritual yearnings into Catholic expressions and to gain the loyalty of Indians to the Church. The long-term goal was to make the natives normative members of the faith.

The Jesuits displayed and distributed the sacramentals that they hoped would excite Indian religious curiosity. They showed off crucifixes, medals, rings, rosaries, and relics, all which could be thought to have some magical power. They blessed Indians with holy water, emphasizing its healing potential. They decorated their churches with Indian designs, including wampum and porcupine quills. They performed not only the mass and other sacraments, but also the panoply of processions that marked the liturgical year. The priests wore colorful vestments and engaged in showy pageantry, in order to impress the natives. As Father Biard noted early on, "It comforts us to see these little Savages, though not yet christians, yet willingly, when they are here, carrying the candles, bells, holy water and other things, marching in good order in the processions and funerals which occur here. Thus they become accustomed to act as christians, to become so in reality in his time" (Thwaites 1896–1901, 2:53).

The Jesuits made use of pictography—in the dirt, on bark, and on paper—to express the tenets of Christian faith to the Indians. They also used pieces of wood to indicate lessons, giving these sticks and their catechetical meanings to prayer chiefs to employ among the Indians in the absence of clerics. Jerome Lalement, S.J., wrote in 1646 (18:151; 29:45–46, 137, 141) of five such sticks (he called them books) used to remind the natives of their lessons: black, to signify the demonic aboriginal religion; white, to indicate daily Christian prayers; red, to show the duties owed on Sundays and holy days. Those with appendages of rope symbolized delinquency to be corrected, and those with native designs signified the ways in which Indians could behave properly and thank God. Father Jean Pierron and other priests made use of paintings, engravings, and tableaux to make palpable the decisive events of the last judgment and the eternal fates of heaven and hell. These illustrations made it clear, at least in the Jesuits' minds, how momentous a decision it was for Indians to choose or reject baptism and Christian identity. In the 1670s a Jesuit among the Indians of Wisconsin

> used to call the Savages together in his little Chapel, where he had three large Pictures adapted to these People's instruction,—one representing the universal judgment, in the upper part of which the parents were glad to be shown the place that their baptized children would occupy; while below they saw, with horror, the torments suffered by the devil. (56:135)

In these pictures the priests depicted the sharp contrast between saved and condemned souls—the latter often besieged by snakes. The Jesuits hoped that the images of the Virgin Mary assumed into heaven, the angels, and other celestial presences would excite the natives' consciousness as they moved toward becoming Christians.

Music, no less than art, served as a device for instruction and inculcation of Christian pieties. By teaching the Indians Christian hymns, the missionaries might move them to express Christian thoughts. Father Louis André said that among the Ojibways,

> I could not entice the Savages to prayers with presents, but my musical instrument came to my aid. I promised them to play on it, and to let them sing my Canticles, after they had prayed. This inducement was so successful that not only did I instruct those who loved the faith, but also those who hated it; for, in their wish to hear their children sing, they learned everything with them, almost without intending to. In the space of three months, they became sufficiently versed in our Mysteries. (55:153)

When pictures and songs fell short of instruction, the Jesuits employed games, with playing cards and other devices, to show the life of redemption from birth to eternity. François Le Mercier stated that this game contained "everything a Christian needs to know," and it was easy to learn and difficult to put out of mind:

> The seven Sacraments are all seen depicted there, the three Theological Virtues, all the Commandments of God and of the Church, together

with the principal mortal sins; even the venial sins that are commonly committed are there expressed in their order, with marks of the horror that ought to be felt for them. Original sin, followed by all the ills that it has caused, appears there in a particular order. I have represented there the four ends of man, the fear of God, the Indulgences, and all the works of mercy. Grace is depicted there in a separate Cartouch, conscience in another; the freedom that we have to obtain salvation or destruction, the small number of the Elect,—in a word, all that a Christian is obliged to know is found expressed there by emblems which portray each of these things. (53:209)

When the Indians responded to these teaching devices with queries, the Jesuits engaged in discussion and disputation, even during religious services. Indians interrupted the priests' sermons to argue a point, and the clerics humored them in this practice, unheard of in France. If a native expressed doubt regarding the truthfulness or usefulness of Christian dogma, the Jesuits engaged them in theological debate, appealing to the Indians' rationality as well as their emotions.

French Catholic missioners in the seventeenth century were sharply aware of the importance of language in their work. Father Paul Le Jeune reminded his fellow Jesuits that "faith . . . enters by the ear" (in Morrison 1985: 368). The priests reported that the Indian languages of North America were "inadequate for expressing their religious message." One Frenchman wrote:

[T]hey have no words which can represent the mysteries of our religion, and it would be impossible to translate even the Lord's prayer into their language save by paraphrase. For of themselves they do not know what is sanctification, or the kingdom of Heaven, or supersubstantial bread (which we call daily), or to lead into temptation. The words glory, virtue, reason, beatitude, Trinity, Holy Spirit, angels, archangels, resurrection, paradise, hell, Church, baptism, faith, hope, charity, and an infinity of others are not in use among them. (in Jaenen 1976a: 52)

A modern linguist might not find the Algonkian and Iroquoian languages so deficient, but at first contact the task of theological translation, in order to make sense of Christian doctrine, was daunting.

The Society of Jesus contained skilled and determined linguists, who employed their Latin-based grammatical training in order to transform Indian speech into Christian expression. Their hope was to grasp the Indian tongues with a device of Latin grammar, and then to translate Christian ideas into Algonkian, Iroquoian, and other languages using latinized forms. By thus "conquering" (Hanzeli 1969: 45)

Indian languages, the Jesuits desired to conquer the Indians' paganism and bring them to Christian ideas and worship. Linguistics was for the priests an engine of war, and they became so adept at translation that by 1665 they requested from France a printing press with which they could produce in written form the Indian languages and Christian translations for New France. The Jesuits thus translated complex Christian concepts and institutional titles into Indian languages, by introducing new French terms, by constructing composites of Indian and French terms, and by using Indian words, all with the stamp of Latin grammar.

This process could not but cause some confusion for the Indians. When Father Brébeuf translated the concept of the immortal soul into Huron, he used the Huron word for the spirit that comes into being at one's death, which resides in the bones of the deceased. He used the same term, then, to name the Holy Spirit. In Iroquois the word translated as the soul was a term meaning "our medicine." The concept of sin was very difficult to convey—in Iroquois the Jesuits called it mistaking one matter for another—since there was "no word to convey the idea of sin as an offense against God" (Axtell 1986: 108). Conversionary translation was more than a matter of finding corresponding words, however; the goal was to convince the Indians of the entirety of the Christian worldview. In time, the Christian words, like that of sin, would make sense to the natives. The Jesuits hoped the Iroquois and other Indians would come to feel themselves as sinners, even without an exact word for sin. The natives "could easily be taught to feel remorse for having committed such an offense after the Jesuits convinced them that their familiar Great Spirit was in reality the Christian God—omnipotent, omniscient, and a stickler for moral details" (ibid.).

The process of conversion as conceived by the Jesuits was a means of winning hearts, minds, and bodies. They wanted the Indians to feel like Christians, think like Christians, and behave like Christians. They aimed to teach the "savages" the proper gestures and stances by which they would express Christian emotion, attitude, and adherance to Christian concepts. In order to become Christians, for example, the Indians needed to learn how to kneel. Kneeling meant submission to God and Church. It evoked the central clause of the Lord's Prayer, in which the human states to God, "Thy will be done." Kneeling was an act of humility, an admission of human sinfulness before God, a gesture that beseeched God for necessary grace, for Jesus, salvation, the Church, sacraments, and the entirety of Christianity brought by the evangelists of the Society of Jesus. To teach Indians to kneel was to direct them toward a Christian life:

> The holy awe in which they held Church rituals and priests helped the native converts to learn to kneel before the altar and during the administration of the sacraments. When the Hurons paid the first visit to the Jesuit chapel in Quebec in 1633, they all squatted down 'like monkeys' at the altar because kneeling was for them a posture 'altogether strange and extraordinary' as it was for the other tribes of New France. (Ibid.)

For the same reason the seventeenth-century Jesuits educated the Indians in the art of genuflection, they also wished the Indians to alter patterns of seasonal traveling. Particularly the Algonkian hunters, but even the village-based Iroquoians, changed their domicile several times during the year, as they made use of various food sources in their extended ecosystems. The Jesuits did not attempt to turn the fur-trapping natives from their ever-productive forests—after all, the missionaries were associates of the fur trade and did not wish to disrupt the economy—but they doubted success without making the Indians somewhat more stationary. Father Le Jeune was a spokesman for this policy, writing of four "great words" necessary to conversion:

> the settlement of the Savages, the Hospital, the Seminary for the little Savage boys, and the seminary for little Savage girls. These last three depend upon the first. Let these barbarians remain always nomads,— then their sick will die in the woods, and their children will never enter the seminary. Render them sedentary, and you will fill these three institutions, which all need to be vigorously aided. (Thwaites 1896–1901, 16:33)

By the end of their stay, the Jesuits felt that they had begun the process of producing a settled life among Indian communities.

Jesuit missionary method aimed to introduce Indians to full Catholic sacramental participation; however, the three most important sacraments for the Indians of New France were baptism, matrimony, and extreme unction. These marked the three passages most desired by the missionaries for the Native Americans: passage by way of initiation into the visible Church, passage into the familial, moral, and social life of Christianity, and passage into heaven, respectively. Each required a Catholic ritual to mark the movement.

For the seventeenth-century Jesuits, baptism was a necessary step toward salvation. The unbaptized person lacked the grace necessary for overcoming innate sinfulness and accepting the salvation offered by God. In Jesuit terms, the unbaptized "savage" lacked the sanctifying grace which he or she needed to accept salvific grace. Baptism had the power to transform persons, even without their understanding; hence, the Jesuits christened infants and dying adults whenever they could, determining to win salvation for these individuals through the sacramental force of the Catholic Church. Christian theology allowed for other means of salvation beyond the visible, sacramental baptism with water. In theory, non-Christians could attain salvation through the agency of the Mystical Body of Christ, the invisible Church— "baptism of desire," as demonstrated through a morally upright life. In practice, the Jesuits treated Indians as if they were doomed to eternal hell without the aid of sacramental baptism.

The French Jesuits were not in the habit, however, of baptizing infants *en masse*, and they were cautious about christening healthy adults without instructing them thoroughly in matters of faith and doctrine. The priests did not object to baptizing children who had an opportunity of receiving catechesis over time; after all, baptism for them was not a last step, but rather the starting point toward the reception of salvific grace. For adults, however, it would be a scandal to receive the sacrament and to know nothing substantial about the Christian life, or to live in contempt for Christ and His Church.

In times of Indian illness, especially when children were in danger of death, the Jesuits baptized as a matter of policy. At these moments of crisis the natives were least likely to resist; indeed, they might hope that the spiritual power of the rite would serve as medicine for the child. If the sick one recovered, word would spread of the miraculous efficacy of Christian initiation. If the child died, then its soul would attain heaven, and perhaps its parents would request baptism for themselves, in order to join their child in the Christian afterworld. If the parents resisted baptism for their offspring—they might regard Christian ritualism as a cause rather than a cure of disease and death— the Jesuits were not above subterfuge in order to accomplish the christening. One priest baptized an infant

> two months old, in manifest danger of death, without its parents being aware that he did so; not having succeeded in obtaining their permission, he employed the following device: Our sugar does wonders here; he made a feint of wishing to give it a little sugared water to drink, and at the same time dipped his finger in the water; and seeing that its father showed some distrust, and urgently requested him not to baptize the child, he put the spoon into the hands of a woman who was standing by, and said to her, "Give it to him thyself." She drew near and

found that the child was asleep; and at the same time the Father, under pretext of seeing if it really slept, applied his wet finger to its face and baptized it; at the end of forty-eight hours, it went to heaven. (14:41)

On other occasions the priest baptized ill youths whose parents were out of sight or unaware of what was taking place (23:229). The eternal souls of these children were too precious for the Jesuits to forsake their sacred christening duty.

Since the emphasis of Jesuit baptisms often fell upon those Indians in danger of death, this sacrament was sometimes combined with extreme unction, the sacrament for the sick and dying. The priests were concerned that the natives' transition to an eternal afterlife be blessed by the Church, and so they introduced Christian practices into burials. The clerics said requiem masses. They set up sacred burial grounds. They attempted to christianize the rituals of mourning and the remembrance of the dead, even as the Indians persisted in their aboriginal practices.

The missionaries taught the Indians to confess their sins, and over time the converts received the Eucharist. Confirmation was not common and holy orders did not take place for natives of New France. The sacrament most eagerly encouraged (besides baptism) and the most difficult to apply was matrimony. The Jesuits understood a sexual and parental union between men and women to be a matter of Church sacramentalism. Marriages were to be monogamous and permanent, in keeping with Catholic tradition, not only because the marriage relation was considered analogous to the human relation to God but also because the Christian family was the building block of the Church's future. To the Jesuits, who themselves had forsaken marriage in order to perform their heroic sacerdotal duties, marriage was a means of curbing concupiscence (by restricting sexual activity to one partner, and by placing that activity in the context of familial love, under the authority of the Church) and a means of procreating children to be raised in the faith. For these reasons the Jesuits directed the Indian converts against sexual promiscuity (in Christian terms, that is, sexual activity outside the monogamous marital bond) and against divorce. They also tried to prevent mixed marriages, that is, marriages between Catholics and non-Catholics.

The priests were astonished by the sexuality of the northeastern Indians, particularly that of females. Women and girls were active sexually, seeking and changing partners, expressing their sexual desires candidly, boasting of sexual experiences. Indian men and women enjoyed each others' bodies without a sense of "sin" or "guilt," in many cases outside the marriage bond, and the native societies encouraged sexual acts as power-laden aspects of healing rituals. From the Jesuits' point of view, sexuality suffused Indian culture and needed taming. Hence, it was the task of the priests to convince converts to live their lives according to Christian notions of marriage, and to do so was to alter individual behavior and the relationships between men and women. The lack of fidelity in Indian marriage was, to the priests, the greatest obstacle to progress in conversion and submission to Christian rule, and they aimed to overcome it.

A recent study (Anderson 1991; cf. Leacock and Goodman 1976, Devens 1992) argues that the Jesuit project of inculcating Catholic family values in seventeenth-century New France meant, perforce, the subjugating of Indian women to their husbands. In France the relations were hierarchic: men were considered superior in rationality and power; women were considered more susceptible to evil, and by nature they ought to submit to their husbands as all humans ought to submit to the Church. In the New World, outside the influence of Church authority, women seemed like firebrands of hell to the Jesuits. The women were haughty, proud, and lewd, resisting conversion more assiduously than men because they dreaded the subjugation of Christian marriage. Christianization of Indian societies meant that women needed to be "chained, beaten and even starved if they ran away; . . . publicly chastised if they didn't obey their husbands" (Anderson 1991: 4). Husbands were chided for beating their wives, but the Jesuits elicited confessions from the women for having brought their husbands to anger by uppitiness or refusal to attend Christian services (see Thwaites 1896–1901, 18:155; 20:147–149; 26:99).

If sexuality suffused Indian society, as the Jesuits said, then the priests themselves were subject to temptation, particularly from brazen women. It was necessary for the priests to resist sexual overtures. To enter sexual relations with the Indians on their terms was to fail in christianizing Indian family life. Until that life could be sanctified over time, the Jesuits hoped that Indian children would be freed from its influences by confining them to the seminaries in Quebec. Eventually, however, Christian marriages would alter the nature of Indian society, making bonds stable, providing a means for educating the young, and thus serving as the key to true and lasting conversion.

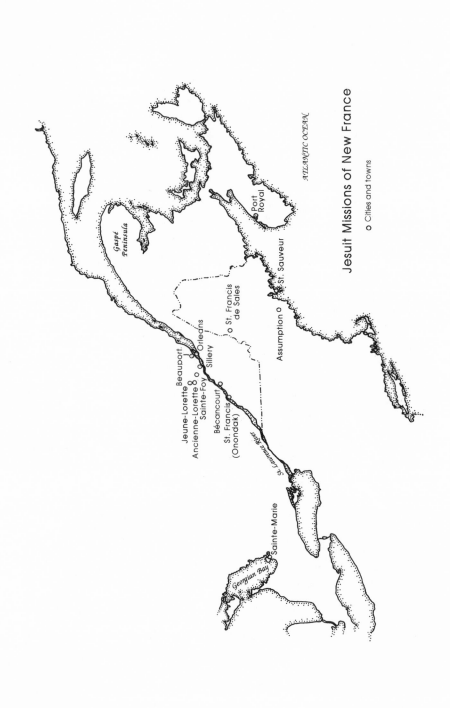

Jesuit Missions of New France

o Cities and towns

ACCOMMODATIONS TO CULTURES

The Jesuits came to realize before too long that the Indians of North America possessed not only religious structures but also a way of life that resisted Catholicism. In both Indian and Catholic cultures, ideas about the divine, ritual practices designed to set humans in harmony with the cosmos, and the institutions necessary to sustain both, were intricately connected to patterns of daily life, including speech, mode of production, and sexuality. Among the obstacles to conversion, the Jesuits learned, was that the Indians, far from having no religion, had a religion that was totally integrated with a way of life. Conversion might, in fact, require not only new beliefs and rituals but also "a completely new life" (Jaenen 1976a: 56). The priests asked the natives to change their relations with the spiritual world, to be sure, but they asked them also to "renounce all the rights and intercourse of friendship with their kinsmen and compatriots" (Thwaites 1896–1901, 17:129), so as to avoid intimacy between Christians and pagans.

Within each native community the missionaries tried to drive a wedge between the pagans and the converts, and in particular they aimed to denigrate the upholders of the pagan traditions, the religious specialists who held considerable status among their peers. The Jesuits ridiculed these "sorcerers" and "jugglers" as superstitious, and praised those Indians who chose not to consult traditional healers when ill. The priests flouted taboos that were supposed to bring harm upon the wrongdoer, and they publicized the curers' inability to treat the contagious diseases brought by Europeans. The Jesuits realized that to overthrow the traditional religious culture was to attack frontally the living embodiments of that culture: "Evangéliser, c'est donc discréditer les sorciers" (Laflèche 1980: 154).

Simultaneously, the priests took for themselves the roles and behavior of the aboriginal religious leadership. They cared for the sick and dying, thus demonstrating their compassion. They performed amazing acts—employing magnets, magnifying glasses, writing, almanacs, and the like—in order to draw the aura of the supernatural upon themselves. They claimed the power of their God over disease, drought, hunting, harvest, and war. Believing themselves that God intervened in human history, they encouraged Indian prayers to accomplish their material wishes, and they were not averse to the natives' calling Jesus the divinity of successful medicine, economy, and battle.

If Indians resisted such claims, the Jesuits reminded them of the ravaging diseases from which they suffered. One priest expressed satisfaction that God was coercing the natives to listen to the priests. It "pleased God to pull their ears through a . . . pestilence which spread over the whole country, and adjudged many to their graves" (Thwaites 1896–1901, 17:227). For him, the epidemics that decimated populations were part of God's plan for the salvation of the savages: "JESUS CHRIST wills to save certain ones of these peoples, and already sends his precursors or his forerunners,—pestilential diseases, afflictions, and death itself; these are scourges which humiliate souls, and which make them have recourse to him who has the power in hand" (28:289).

If Indians would not convert through fear of illness and death, the Jesuits reminded them of eternal fates more ghastly. Preaching from the heart of Christian theology, the priests told the natives that behavior in this world determined their future existence. The priests had to convince the Indians that they were sinful by nature, and that they desperately needed Christianity, the sacramental institution created by Christ to give grace, for their eternal salvation. To resist the Church, to resist faith in Jesus Christ, was to condemn oneself to hell forever. Said one priest of his preachings to an Indian woman, "I threatened her with hell, . . . telling her that hell was full of people who had not recognized themselves as sinners" (13:201). The Jesuits' catechetical paintings, sermons, pageants, and demonstrations of the properties of sulfur all emphasized the physical horrors of the nether regions. Christ's sacrificial act on the cross made salvation possible, and baptism in Christ's Church was the first step toward avoiding those horrors. The priests did not miss an opportunity to drive home the message. For example, when a Jesuit took leave of some catechumens,

> he made them two presents, in order to remind them of two things: the first was a Crucifix, to warn them to keep the Faith all their life, and to remember that the son of God had died for them. The second was a dry stick, which was good only to put in the fire,—adding, that it would be the same with those who should not obey God; that they would be like dead wood, and would burn forever in Hell. (24:99)

In spite of the severity of their good news and their repulsion at Indian behavior, the Jesuits found in the natives a simplicity to be admired.

The priests could not bear to live in the same houses with Indians, with their different tolerance for dirt, fleas, nakedness, and lack of privacy. Nonetheless, the natives could be held up in France as models of innocence with great potential to achieve a modicum of Christian perfection. In their Relations the Jesuits needed to represent the "savages" as subjects worthy of missionizing; simultaneously, the Indians could be employed for the purpose of social commentary back home in France. In the course of the seventeenth century the Jesuits viewed their fellow Frenchmen as evil influences over the Indians, liquor and debauchery being the worst of the contagions they spread. The Jesuits called the Indians "les sauvages," referring to their forest dwellings. These were people who lived apart from civilization, and the Jesuits wanted to keep them that way, so as to christianize them without corrupting them with civilizing influences. Although the priests noted cruelty, promiscuity, superstition, and faulty reasoning among other deficiencies common to the Indians, they also depicted them with an aura of purity that might be called "primitivism" (Clements 1994: 46–48), which led perhaps to the concept of the "noble savages" in European thought.

The Jesuits applied Christian standards to themselves and to the Indians, and for all their ability to put up with unpleasant cultural traits among the "savages," they made sharp distinctions between mere cultural customs, neutral to morals or religion, and religious beliefs and moral practices that were either right (Catholic) or wrong (not Catholic). One should not think of the Jesuits as moral relativists or romantics. Nonetheless, they had Thomistic and Arminian tendencies, regarding highly the potential of the human intellect to come to correct knowledge of God and right behavior. They did not believe that the pagans were necessarily condemned to hell simply by virtue of their culture or their lack of contact with Christianity. To the Jesuits, human nature could seek God, guided by grace, especially with missionary help. Pagan Indian life might be hideous, but the Jesuits found the converts holy, because their human potentiality was uplifted by faith and Church. In order to accomplish the transformation, the Jesuits took care not to attack every aspect of native culture unless particular customs "clearly violated the essential spirit of Christianity" (Healy 1958: 151).

Twentieth-century observers (e.g., Axtell 1986, Clements 1994, Duignan 1958, Jaenen 1976a, Kennedy 1950, Moore 1982) of the New

France Jesuits have emphasized the accommodationist tendencies of the missioners. Certainly in Asia the Jesuits were known (throughout the Rites Controversy) for the attitude that in every cultural religion there is a notion of God, a perception of an immortal soul in each human, a moral sense, and an idea of world order that must be accommodated rather than attacked. Wherever the Jesuits evangelized, they sought to identify the religiousness basic to the indigenes in order to transform it into Christianity. Each group's cultural shaping of innate spirituality could be supernaturalized through catechesis, sacramental initiation, and ecclesiastical authority. Because all men have souls, said the Jesuits, the Indians had the intellectual and spiritual capability of being educated in Catholic ways, without having to give up all aspects of aboriginal culture.

It is said (Duignan 1958: 729) that the Jesuits of the seventeenth century followed Aristotle's Nichomachean Ethics, rejecting the Platonic idea that ethics are universal, of divine origin. Rather, they saw each people trying to create the best ethics they could from their own nature and circumstance; therefore, to condemn Indians for their particular Indian morality, suited to their particular circumstances, would be wrongheaded. This evangelical philosophy, sometimes called Probabalism (Clements 1994: 47–48), caused the Jesuits to emulate the advice of Pope Gregory I, who, in A.D. 601, told the missioners Augustine and Melletus to accommodate the Christian good news to the cultures they encountered in the British Isles. The Jesuits also entertained the idea (Figurism) that God revealed Himself to all peoples, before and apart from the Mosaic revelation. This is how Indians believed in a creator God and the immortality of the soul before encountering Christians. Following the lead of the sixteenth-century Spanish Jesuit Luis de Molina, the missionaries had hopes that Indians' natural reason would lead them to virtue; indeed, it already led to virtue even before contact with the Church (Molinism).

The Jesuits' task, according to one scholar (Moore 1982: xi, 39) was to practice "accommodation" in order to "adapt" both themselves and their Christianity to the "native cultural environment." The Jesuits' principle of accommodation was grounded in their concepts of "natural revelation and natural law. For the Jesuits, *good* already existed in the native cultures and provided the foundation upon which native Christianity could be built." Indian culture was to be left "largely intact," even if this meant alterations in "the Catholic cultus itself—that amalgam of ritual and devotion at the heart of the Church's life." Thus, the Jesuits did not insist that Indians cease work on Sundays, since the natives needed to hunt, gather, or bring in firewood daily. Lenten and Friday fasts were made optional. Indians out on the hunt could not attend mass on Sundays, so it was enough for them to mark the day on their rosaries and with their own devotions: prayers before a cross, dressed in their skins, faces painted. On Easter the Indians smoked their tobacco, held feasts, and the like, in order to celebrate Christ's resurrection. In these ways, according to modern interpreters, the Jesuits accommodated the Indians' culture.

In China the Jesuits' accommodation to ancestor veneration and other rites earned the opprobrium of other missionary orders, particularly the Franciscans and Dominicans. These rivals accused the Jesuits of heresy, and in 1742 the papacy ruled decisively—at least for two centuries—against the thoroughgoing policy of missionary accommodationism. In the New World the Jesuits also had their critics, particularly the Franciscan Recollects who shared their apostolic enterprise for a while. The Recollects believed that Indians could be brought to Christianity only by French laws and mores. In the early years of the Quebec colony they wished to teach the Algonkian Indians how to farm and live in villages. Fathers Christian Le Clercq (1881), Louis Hennepin (1966), and other Recollects found the Indians so primitive—so fond of individual freedom, so lacking in the notion of ecclesiastical authority, so deficient in hierarchical institutions and dogmas, that is, so undeveloped in what Christians thought of as religion in its institutional sense—that conversion was going to require bluntly powerful techniques. "These tribes," wrote Rev. Hennepin in 1683, "must absolutely first be civilized to make them embrace Christianity, for so long as Christians are not absolutely their masters we shall see little success, without a most special grace of God, without a miracle which he does not work in regard to all nations" (Hennepin 1966: 338).

The Hundred Associates had little desire for the Recollects to alter the culture of their Indian fur trappers. The trade depended upon the natives' living in the bush and bringing in pelts. Hence, the Franciscans were retired officially from the field of New France, but they did not cease their criticism of Jesuit accommodationism, as they saw it. When the Society of Jesus made slight concessions to Indian culture, when they expressed optimism in the natural and cultural capacity of Indians to become Christians by degrees, when they gathered the

Indians into reductions, away from corrupting French influences, the Recollects found fault.

Indeed, it is primarily because of the Recollect charges that we have the image of Jesuits in New France as rabid relativists. A careful perusal of the Jesuit Relations, in fact, reveals very little of accommodationism, except insofar as the Jesuits had little or no power to insist upon radical cultural change among the savages. The Jesuits made a sharp distinction between their own, true Catholic religion and the deviltry of Indian tradition. Their goal was to convert the Indians wholeheartedly, and they used every technique available to them in order to achieve their aims. The Jesuits recognized native spirituality and native reason, but the job of missionizing was to transform these qualities. If Indians wished to celebrate feasts on Christian holidays, this could be accommodated. If they wanted to call Jesus the God of War, this was not necessarily a misunderstanding, when the enemies were the Iroquois (who seemed for a while to be the implacable foes of France and Catholicism). But if the Indians attempted to take on Christian religious forms without giving up their own traditional forms over time, the Jesuits showed little evidence of relativism or liberality. They separated family members from one another over the issue of religious allegiance; they preached hellfire; they tried to transform the practices of sexuality and marriage. If the Jesuits made small concessions to the Indians, the Indian was expected to make the major accommodation to the Jesuit.

INDIAN RE/PONSE/

The French Recollects were so unable to alter the northeastern Indians in their own locales that the missioners shipped some of their youths to France for training. Only two survived the dislocation and returned to New France. One, a Huron named Louis Amantacha, was soon captured by the Iroquois. The other, Pierre-Antoine Pastedechouen of the Montagnais, was "ruined" by six years in France. He forgot his native tongue; he had no hunting skills. He drank alcohol to excess and could not support a wife. Eventually he "died of starvation in the woods, alone" (Axtell 1986: 55–56). No wonder that the Recollects grew discouraged at making any headway among the natives of the New World.

The Jesuits persevered, but for all their accommodationism, they still made demands for radical changes among the Indians. Those who became Christians were "compelled, in effect, to commit cultural suicide. . . . Because missionaries demanded no less than 'cultural revolution,' . . . their attacks on Indian religions . . . posed a threat to the very survival of native American society" (Ronda 1977: 67).

As a result, many Indians resisted the missionaries' demands, and some even argued openly against Christianity. They rejected the notions of original sin and human depravity and the need for Christ's Church to accomplish moral regeneration and eternal salvation. They felt little guilt for their behavior and rejected Christian codes of ethics. Heaven and hell seemed unconvincing to many, or if they existed, Indians said, they must exist only for the French. Father Le Jeune's debates with the Montagnais Carigonan, depicted at length in the Jesuit Relations (Thwaites 1896–1901, vols. 6 and 7; cf. Harrod 1984), made it clear that the Indians possessed their own way of life and felt little need, at least at first, to adopt Christian worldview, habit, or authority. Indians offered critiques of all aspects of French culture. They found the French priests ugly in their beards and unmanly in their celibacy. Over time, French foods, childrearing practices, government, architecture, manners, marriage customs, and system of justice all met with Native American disparagement.

At first encounter the Indians were relatively unimpressed with

French ways. "Apart from concessions to French material civilization, technology and military force, they felt equal to, or superior to, the Europeans at the time of contact in the seventeenth century" (Jaenen 1974: 289–290). The Hurons may have shown amazement at a clock they encountered in the Jesuits' residence. The timepiece's mechanical motions and sounds caused them to think of it as a living person, "the Captain of the day" (Thwaites 1896–1901, 8:111), and the priests expressed a smug superiority to naive natives who could not fathom clockwork mechanics. At the same time, however, the Hurons were as astonished by the Frenchmen's behavior—the foreigners obeyed the commands of their automatic "Captain" when it directed them to wake, eat, or pray—as they were by the machine itself. The wonder of the clock did not lead the Hurons automatically to conversion.

In their dialogues with the Jesuits, Indians such as the Montagnais were blunt in their critiques of the Frenchmen and their religion. They rejected the authoritarianism of the Church in favor of the personal inspiration found in dreams. They decried what they perceived as economic callousness among the French traders, favoring a more communal sharing of property. They upheld their right to perform their traditional rituals and accused the priests of ill-mannered behavior (see Morrison 1985: 370–377). The Jesuits were willing to hear these blasts and they had no compunctions against returning in kind.

In the face of Jesuit evangelism, many Indians not only rejected Christianity as they understood it but also organized anti-Catholic movements. Religious specialists accused the missionaries of witchcraft. Natives employed dreams with messages from the spirit world against the invading religionists, and they imitated baptismal rites for their own cults. When asked to receive baptism, some Indians demurred, either because they thought it would kill them or because they feared that it would relegate them to a Frenchman's afterworld, where they would be bereft of Indian relatives. One Indian man said, "For my part, I have no desire to go to heaven; I have no acquaintances there, and the French who are there would not care to give me anything to eat" (in Thwaites 1896–1901, 13:127).

If becoming a Christian meant altering marital relations, it would require a significant revolution in all aspects of native life, and many Indians were unwilling to make such changes. "My heart is sad," said an Algonkian man,

for it seems to me that God does not love us, since he gives us commandments that we cannot keep; there are many sins that I do not fear,
but there are some that make me afraid. I do not fear drunkenness, nor
eat-all feasts, nor the consultation of Demons, nor our songs, nor pride,
nor theft, nor murder; but I do fear women. God commands us to
marry but one wife, and, if she leaves us, not to take another; behold
me, then, obliged to remain single, for our women have no sense. To
live among us without a wife is to live without help, without home, and
to be always wandering. (In 16:161–163)

Women offered the same objections, saying that a Christian life was
one in which they would have to forego their sexuality and their freedoms. "They would not submit themselves to the authority of their
husbands and fathers. They would not behave in a modest and gentle
fashion. They made no attempt to hide their sexuality, did not value
virginity, chastity, or sexual continence and refused to remain married
to an unsuitable spouse" (Anderson 1991: 18).

For those who rejected Christianity, one of the strongest arguments
against it was the effect it had on Indian communities who adopted its
ways and allegiances. Many believed there was a correlation between
the teaching of the faith and the disasters visited upon many tribes: the
contagious diseases, the wars, the intratribal factionalism. "How many
times have they told us," wrote Father Barthelemy Vimont, "that they
had never seen calamities like those which have appeared since we
speak of Jesus Christ! 'You tell us,' (exclaim some), 'that God is full of
goodness; and then, when we give ourselves up to him, he massacres
us.'" Christianized Indians saw their pagan enemies prospering, and
asked: "'What profit can there come to us from lending ear to the
Gospel, since death and the faith nearly always march in company?'"
(Thwaites 1896–1901, 25:35–37).

The Native Americans had many reasons for resisting Christian incursions in the seventeenth century; however, thousands of them
made motions that the Jesuits interpreted as steps toward christianization. Father Jerome Lalemant estimated there were over ten thousand
Algonkian and Iroquoian converts by the year 1650 (36:49–53). He
said that there were so many requests on the part of Indians for Jesuit
evangelization that "flying missions" (221–225) were established by necessity among isolated tribes, in addition to the regular mission posts
among the Hurons, Montagnais, Algonquins, and Abenakis. By conversions Father Lalemant meant baptisms, and a scholar (Pouliot

1940: 308, n. 1) has counted sixteen thousand indigenous christenings in the Relations between 1632 and 1672. He notes that many more baptisms took place for certain, since some Relations were lost. Of the sixteen thousand baptized, two thousand died immediately, and another eighty-six hundred died within the forty-year period of inquiry. The four most prodigious years for baptisms took place among the Hurons: in 1640, during an epidemic (a thousand baptisms), and between 1648 and 1650 (seven thousand), when the Iroquois were destroying the Huron villages.

It would appear, then, that baptisms took place often on the deathbed and in time of crisis. In these situations the Jesuits were willing to forego thorough catechetical instruction in order to save the Indians' souls from eternal damnation. It would also appear, however, that there were thousands of baptisms that took place "in full health, after having been well instructed in the principal and most necessary articles of our creed" (Thwaites 1896–1901, 16:59), according to Father Le Jeune. For all the accounts of Indians begging in their illness for the sacrament that might cure them or at least grant them protection in the afterlife from the eternal fires of hell, there were other Native Americans who received an education in Christian doctrine before receiving the sacrament, and lived their lives ostensibly as Christians. The Jesuits made note of the different kinds of baptisms (see 11:81–147), and rejoiced in them all.

So did the converts, according to the Relations. The Algonkian Manitougatche (called La Nasse by the priests) listened to instruction regarding the creation account, the incarnation, and the redemptive crucifixion of Jesus Christ, and he was "much pleased to listen to such talk. Seeing us praying to God one day after dinner," wrote Father Le Jeune, "he sighed deeply, saying: 'Oh, how unhappy I am that I am not able to pray to God as you do!'" (in 5:117). La Nasse's compatriot, Sasousmat, became interested in Christianity and asked for baptism when he became mortally ill. "We baptized him," reported Le Jeune,

> believing that he was going to die. We gave him the name François, in honor of Saint [Francis] Xavier. He regained consciousness, and, having learned what had taken place, expressed his joy at having been made a Child of God. He passed his time constantly until his death, which was two days later, in different acts that I caused him to practice, sometimes of Faith and Hope, sometimes of the Love of God, and of remorse for having offended him. He took a very obvious pleasure in

this, and repeated all alone with deep feeling what had been taught
him. (6:113)

La Nasse himself became ill, and "he urged his wife and children to
bring him back to us, hoping for the same charity he had seen us practice toward his fellow-savage. He was received with open arms, perceiving which, he cried out, 'Now I shall die happy, since I am with
you!'" (119–121). He survived his christening by twelve days. On the
other hand, as we shall see, some prominent converts like Noel Negabamat of the reduction at Sillery and Joseph Chihwatenwa of Huronia
lived for many years as devout Catholics, according to the accounts of
the Jesuits.

What attracted these Indians to Christianity? Perhaps the priests
themselves were formidable models. Despite their deficiencies—they
could not hunt; they stumbled in gaining Indian languages; they had
no status at first among the tribes—they possessed a determined bravery that may have been impressive. They were confident and committed to their faith, and largely without force of arms they claimed an
authority that could be resisted but which continued to assert itself. At
first the Jesuits seemed harmless, but the claims they made about
Christian power and glory had a force that made itself felt. It is said
that the Jesuits had virtually no soldiers at their command, very little
material wealth, and no shows of force to buttress their missionary authority (Anderson 1991: 9). However, there were some French soldiers, and over time these armies and their Indian allies made war
against the Indians who resisted them, particularly the Iroquois. Despite the Indians' early sense of self-satisfaction, they came to desire
certain French goods, and the Jesuits were part and parcel of the fur
trade that brought those goods to the tribes. The priests must have
had some panache because of their association with the lucrative trade.
As Father Le Jeune remarked, "The more the glory of the French continues to increase in these Regions, the more these Barbarians will respect them, and the more fear they will have of offending them . . . and
the Savages, coming little by little to admire the power, ingenuity and
morality of our French . . . will make much of their faith, and will
more readily embrace it" (Thwaites, 1896–1901, 9:97). At the very least,
French arms were a means of luring Indians to become Christians.
Father Vimont wrote, "The use of arquebuses, refused to the Infidels
by Monsieur the Governor, and granted to the Christian Neophytes, is

a powerful attraction to win them; it seems that our Lord intends to use this means in order to render Christianity acceptable in these regions" (25:27).

Indians were impressed by the charity paid to the sick, the hungry, and the dying, not only by the Jesuits but also by the Sisters Hospitaliers who arrived in Quebec in 1639. The very health of the French, especially their relative immunity to contagious diseases, marked them with power, and the miracles claimed by the Jesuits—their ability to cure the sick and predict the future (by use of almanacs), their magical displays of reading and writing—earned them a reputation as wonderworkers as well as sorcerers. If Christianity was the means by which these wonders were accomplished, the Indians wanted a part of the amazing source of medicines. When extraordinary events took place, e.g., the earthquake that shook the Northeast in 1663, Indians looked for protection in demonstrations of Christian faith. Following the quake, the Algonquins at Sillery confessed their sins and received the Eucharist with "feelings of genuine fear of God's judgments" (48:59). The Montagnais at Tadoussac ". . . all manifested thereafter such an unusual ardor for receiving instruction, that the Father, delighted and overwhelmed by such an exhibition of pious desire, could not refuse Holy Baptism to those poor forsaken souls" (71). At such times the Jesuits wrote:

> It was a beautiful sight to see those devout Barbarians, some of whom came from a great distance, at the risk of falling into the hands of the Iroquois and of their other enemies, in order to be instructed. It was a beautiful sight, I say, to see Jugglers break and demolish their Tabernacles; Apostates appeal for mercy, and beg with flowing tears to be admitted into the Church; little children uplift their voices in the brief Catechism and the prayers which they recited; and Old men turn Disciples of these children in order to learn of them, and follow the Father whithersoever he went, without giving him any respite, night or day, that they might lose none of his teachings. (Ibid.)

When epidemics raged, the fervor of the faith flamed all the stronger, and the Jesuits took advantage of it to accomplish baptisms and instructions.

In the face of crises engendered by the European invasion—the diseases, wars, and dislocations of the seventeenth century—many Indians, at least temporarily, found in Christianity an explanatory power that was attractive, even irresistible. A scholarly commentator observes that "Indians converted largely because they were persuaded—by the missionaries and the logic of the situation as the natives saw it—that the Christian answers to the urgent, new questions of life were intellectually and emotionally satisfying, at least more so than the outmoded explanations offered by their traditional wise men" (Axtell 1986: 285–286). The Jesuits studied the Indians carefully and offered solutions to their present difficulties—difficulties brought by the missionaries and their New France confreres. Christianity posed the problems and held attractive solutions, according to this scenario. If Indians were dying of diseases, God's power was seen as cause and cure. If they were powerless before their enemies, Jesus appeared as the deity of war, and the French offered guns to Christian Indian allies. As Indian communities fell asunder, due in part to factionalism created by evangelism, Christian cadres replaced traditional family structures. And as the aboriginal worldview came under attack by the missioners, the Christian explanations seemed more plausible. The Jesuits found the Indians superstitious and aimed to rid them of their beliefs in the spiritual world. They did this both by rationalist explanation and by expounding upon the spiritual realities inherent in Christian faith. It is ironic in this regard that ". . . the missionaries unwittingly represented a society in process of secularization. Even while they sought to propagate a new religion, their rationalistic assumptions tended to brush away a little of the mystery which the Indian saw inherent in nature" (Grant 1985: 25). In the void they had helped create the Jesuits inserted a Christian worldview.

The Catholic liturgical panoply was said to draw Indians to Christian practice and identity. The Jesuits tried to appeal to the senses (and superstitions) of the natives with concrete representations of the divine and vivid displays of ritualism. Medals, rings, crucifixes, rosaries, incense, candles, communion wafers, altars, vestments, pictures, processions, bells, chants, prayers, and hymns all aimed at the Indians' imaginations, and they often hit their mark. The priests noted the "esteem" held by Indians for "the outward signs of our holy Religion. Crosses, medals, and other similar Articles are their most precious jewels. So fondly do they preserve These that they wear them around their Necks, even at preaching in New Holland, where The heretics have never been able to tear from Them a single bead of Their Rosaries" (Thwaites 1896–1901, 57:95–97). These religious charms may have struck the Indians as witchery and carriers of disease; they may have given rise to "obsessive fear" (Jaenen 1974: 276) of Christian mysteries, including the Eucharist—in which the corpse of Jesus was brought to life and eaten ritually. Yet the symbols were powerful, and the natives wished to possess them.

The Jesuits regarded their sacramentals as charmed; they could protect against weapons, and they could bring animals and fish to the flesh pot. If the Indians were to believe in the spiritual efficacy of material items, better they be Christian goods. Thus, Father Louis André replaced sacrifices to the sun with prayers to a crucifix, and when the Indians caught sturgeon shortly thereafter, he took credit for the catch and the natives were receptive to his message of Christ's salvific grace (see Jaenen 1976a: 58–61). Christian cult appealed to Indians, not necessarily as a new religion but as a novel source of effective power. Without eschewing the entirety of their own background, they accepted French Catholic religious power. "Why not? There was nothing in the principles of native religion to limit access to spiritual power to a single cult, and borrowing from religious repertoire of other tribes was a common practice" (Grant 1985: 39). To the seventeenth-century Indian convert, "Conversion itself represented not so much a rejection of the old way as a conviction that Christianity offered more powerful *mana* for a changed situation" (44). The Jesuits tried to finesse the Indian adoption of Christian cult without giving up all of the old. If one Indian claimed Jesus to be his former guardian spirit; if another converted because his dreams demanded it; if religious forms and sensibilities cojoined in the short run, they might be tolerated for the sake of strategy (see Thwaites 1896–1901, 23:29, 171). The hope was that in time, over generations, Christianity would come to replace the native religiousness thoroughly. Until then, the outward forms of Christianity would continue to entice the Native Americans to Christian worship.

If the Indians were drawn to Christianity through its efficacious ritualism, they also came to Christianity through fear of hellfire. A Jesuit remarked that Indians were desirous to die as Christians, "not, in truth, so much through love as through fear of falling into the fires with which they are threatened" (9:99). Becoming a Christian entailed at least a partial acceptance of Christian eschatology—the concepts of a heaven and a hell, and the idea that one's eternal fate is determined by one's religious orientation in this world. Through a process of "religious segmentation" (Hultkrantz 1981: 196), Indians might believe partially in two afterworlds while still clinging to the hope of a single place after death for all tribal members; but as their conversions became more intact, the Indians expressed Christian eschatological notions. Some Indians, in rejecting Christianity, told of unpleasant visits to the Christian afterworld, and they encouraged their fellows to resist baptism and Christian loyalty. Over time, Algonkian converts came to believe that the good and bad are divided at death and go to separate worlds, and that the Supreme God is involved in that decision, caring about it. In short, many converts adopted the concept of a moral universe in the way the Jesuits preached it.

Converting to Christianity meant to value the afterworld, the spiritual realm, more than the here and now. Hence, a convert reflected upon his baptized daughter's death with these words:

> It seems to me . . . that I see before me my daughter, full of joy; her death has consoled me more than her life; my mind has not been disturbed by it. Some time ago, I gave her up to GOD; he has disposed of her; she belonged to him more than to me. I do not place much value upon the life we lead here below on earth. I prize Eternity alone and the intercourse that we will have together forever. (In Thwaites 1896–1901, 23:59)

Another Indian Christian stated:

> I am more attached to [the Jesuits] than to my Country and to all my relatives, because they bring us the promise of eternal happiness. I fear not death, since GOD has enlightened my mind, and has shown me things more important than this bodily life, against which alone any design can be harbored. Let them kill my mother, my wife, my children, and my brothers; after them, the blow that is to give me happiness will fall on me! My soul is not attached to my body,—a single instant can separate them; but Faith shall never be ravished from me. (In 23:137)

It is difficult to assess the depth of conversion among seventeenth-century Indians of New France, since all of the evidence derives from the French Jesuits; however, if the Relations are to be believed at all, some Indians embraced the beliefs and cultus of Catholicism with ardor. In several communities—among the Montagnais, the Hurons, the Abenakis, and even the Iroquois—the first century of Christian contact led to strong Indian allegiance to the religion of the missioners. Amidst resistance, syncretism, and nativism, did the Jesuits make their share of Christian converts? James Axtell answers in the affirmative:

> The net result of all the Jesuits' spiritual and moral support was the formation of cadres of devout, resilient disciples who could withstand the hatred of their unregenerate kinsmen while building little Jerusalems all over New France. Recapturing much of the tenacious fervor of the original Christians, the native converts threw themselves into the life of the Church Militant with abandon. (Axtell 1986: 125)

Indians spread their new faith among their relatives, as witnessed by Father Paul Ragueneau:

> A Father will win his children to God,—a mother, her daughters; the husband will convert his wife, and the Christian wife will render her husband Christian; and frequently even children, who have first embraced the faith, sanctify their infidel parents with attractions and charms which nature, fortified by grace, and the Holy Ghost, teach them without other Master. (Thwaites 1896–1901, 29:277)

But if relatives refused to convert, the neophytes were willing to discard their loyalties of kinship. A christianized Algonkian thus addressed his pagan wife, while pinching his own arm: "Dost thou see this flesh? I do not love it; it is God whom I love, and those who believe in him. If thou art not willing to obey him, thou must go away from me; for I cannot love those who do not love God" (in 20:197). Another Algonkian Christian expressed his willingness to kill his pagan relatives, should they attack his new community of converts: "I would have obeyed our Captains, and fired right and left: I am on the side of those who believe in God" (in 21:71). Father Le Jeune was impressed by the Indian's loyalty, "so much the more as these Savages are closely bound to their relatives; but Jesus Christ came to break this bond. *Veni separare hominem adversus patrem suum*" (ibid.).

Indian converts were willing to turn their affections away from their traditional religious practices as well as from relatives. Said a shaman after his conversion:

> I have resolved to abandon forever our old customs; I no longer have any voice for the superstitious chants, my drum no longer has any sound, and my mouth no longer has any breath to deceive the sick; for all these follies cannot restore their health. I intend to obey God, and all that he forbids shall be interdicted to me forever. (In 20:289–291)

Another Indian convert at a reduction near Montreal avowed:

> I have given up pyromancy, or divination by fire; I have given up eat-all feasts; I have given up the vapor baths, or superstitious sweats, the visions of distant things, and the songs agreeable to the demon; I have given up divination by the throbbing of the breast; and, if it is necessary to abandon anything else, I am ready to do so. I love nothing,—I love not myself; I love faith and prayer. (In 29:163)

Sometimes the converts did not give up their religious capacity to dream and prophesy, only now the imagery of their visions was Christian. An Algonkian girl on the eve of the 1663 earthquake saw herself and two companions "mounting a great Stairway. At its top was seen a beautiful Church, where the Blessed Virgin appeared with her Son, predicting . . . that the earth would soon be shaken . . ." (48:53).

With the content and commitment of Christian faith in their consciousness, Indians of the Northeast appeared to the missionaries as potential models of piety. If the gentile savages exhibited nasty behaviors to the Jesuits' eyes, the neophytes seemed paradigms of goodness. Father Barthelemy Vimont wrote in 1642 of the tangible proofs of Indian conversion:

> Their frequent reception of the Sacraments, the avidity that these good Neophytes have for God's word, their observance of his commandments, their assiduity in attending Holy Mass every day, the punishments that they are beginning to inflict on delinquents, their zeal for the defense and propagation of the faith,—all these are so many proofs that Jesus Christ is taking firm hold in their hearts. . . . (22:43; see 47–91)

The missionaries described the Indian converts in their confessionals, recalling their sins with mnemonic aids—pieces of stick, drawings on bark of skin, calendric etchings, and even rosaries. The neophytes prayed many times each day, and even at night, interrupting their sleep and kneeling on both knees. Indian converts thought constantly of death and prepared their souls for the beatific vision (see 37:41–47). "It is a blessing deeply felt," wrote Father Le Jeune,

> to see them attending prayers and the instructions that we give them; present at Mass on Festivals and Sundays, and some on working days; coming to Vespers . . . ; chanting the *Pater* and the *Credo*, the Commandments of God and some Hymns composed in their Language; making their confessions with admirable candor; receiving communion with devotion and respect; reciting the Rosary every day in honor of the blessed Virgin. It is a heartfelt consolation to us to see Savages engaged in these holy exercises. (16:59–61)

Out on the hunt, away from the Jesuits' chapels, the neophytes kept up their observances. They created places of worship where they camped. They tracked the days of the Christian week and marked Sundays and Holy Days of Obligation with services, sometimes under the leadership of their prayer captains—*dogiques* who led prayers and hymns, taught from the catechisms, and enforced morality in the absence of priests. During the long winter months on their own,

> They take with them to the woods a memorandum or short Catalogue of the Festival days, which they observe with much respect, for men born and brought up in the forest like beasts. They all assemble in one Cabin, say their prayers publicly, and sing a Hymn, and sometimes one of them will give a discourse on some points of our belief. These Meetings do not prevent each one from saying his prayers again in his Cabin, . . . the bell calls them every day to Mass, and summons them at evening for prayers and instruction. This goes on regularly. (27:143)

The Jesuits were willing to excuse the Indians from strict fasting and abstinence during Lent (and it is said that French authorities declared the beaver "a fish," so it could be eaten by Indians on Fridays and other days of abstinence [Axtell 1975: 287]), because of the difficulty the converts had in obtaining foods other than meat in the late winter. However, the neophytes attempted to obey the rules of the Church. Children sometimes picked meat out of the stew and put it aside, so as to abstain from flesh. Father Le Jeune found these practices remarkable, considering the savages' previous practice of gorging themselves on meat in general, including human flesh (see Thwaites 1896–1901, 16:179–181).

As for their inner condition, the Indian converts expressed a spirituality that much pleased the Jesuits, for they seemed to accept their sinfulness and their need for redemption through Jesus Christ and His Church. They practiced penances and bloody self-flagellations in imitation of their priestly teachers—who were known to engage in extreme austerities—but also in continuity with the purifications of aboriginal religiousness. When a priest queried an Algonkian man of his faith, "What thoughts hast thou about thyself?" the Indian replied, "That I am a dog, and less than a flea before God" (37:59). Self-abnegation and orientation to the heavenly afterworld led some converts to a spirit of forgiveness toward their enemies. An Algonkian woman thus spoke of the Iroquois captives in her village:

> I love God more than I hate the Iroquois; that love alone which I bear to him prevents me from making them feel the injuries that they have done to me. I am the only one remaining of a large family; I am poor and forsaken. They have placed me in that condition, for they roasted and ate all my relatives and all my friends. In fact, my heart would hate those people . . . but it has more love for God than hatred and aversion for them. That is why I wish them no evil. (27:239)

Their zeal led the newly minted Christians to hector their pagan relatives to convert, and to enforce the rules of Christian behavior whenever they gained authority in their villages. Having come to regard their former religiousness as demonism and immorality, they insisted on similar transformations among their compatriots, and the result was severe factionalism and the breakdown of native social solidarity. When Christian converts were captured in battle by pagan enemies, the neophytes often aimed at evangelizing their captors. Among their fellows and their foes, the converts gave frequent witness to their new faith, identifying themselves as Christians and eschewing their former Indianness. Said one convert to other Indians who confronted him:

> You think that I have acted foolishly, in giving up what you consider the happiness of life; but it is you who arouse my pity. My judgment is better than yours, because I have felt in myself what you are, and you do not feel what I am. Become Christians, all of you. . . . (In 23:93)

Among the Indian Catholics there arose more than several prominent apostles, including Jean-Baptiste Negabamat, François-Xavier Nenaskoumat, Charles Meiachkawat, Estienne Totihri, Joseph Chihwatenwa, and others. These Indian Christians were said to understand Christian doctrine with subtlety; they led saintly lives. Other Indian

Catholics were willing to die for their faith, or to kill pagan Indians who refused to convert when captured by the French and their Indian allies. In becoming Christians the converts tried to become more like the French, taking on their habits and their loyalties with an imitative passion that was endearing to the Jesuits (see 29:127–129). Indeed, many became soldiers for the Church and Crown of New France: "The fiercest defenders of colonial borders were the *reserve* and 'praying' Indians, who now scalped under the sign of the Cross" (Axtell 1986: 300).

Both men and women became zealous converts, and christianization brought changes in their relations to one another. Indian women, who formerly were known for their robust sexuality, took vows of chastity, forming sodalities and calling each other "sisters" (in ibid., 125–126) in imitation of the nuns at Montreal and Quebec. If at first the girls in seminary tried to escape, some came to ask pardon for their sins, kneeling before the priests in confession, displaying angelic modesty and serving their fellows like good Christian ladies (Marie de l'Incarnation 1967: 71–74). In Christian villages Indian females were subject to public condemnation if they took suitors to their rooms, or spoke privately to pagan men, or held hands with Frenchmen in public. Girls asked to be locked up by priests, for sexual protection, and there were expressions by men and women of sexual sin and guilt.

In marriage the women were exhorted and even coerced to renounce their freedom and to vow obedience to husband as well as Church. At Sillery Marie Meiachkawat transformed her behavior in order to marry her husband Charles. The priest made her promise to conduct herself as a Christian wife, and by that he meant a docile, tractable spouse in a monogamous marriage blessed by the institutions of Jesus Christ. It is argued that Algonkian and Iroquoian women in the seventeenth century were "chained, beaten and even starved if they ran away; . . . publicly chastised if they didn't obey their husbands" (Anderson 1991: 4; cf. Devens 1992: 7–30), all in the name of christianizing the familial life of the Indians. But men as well as women were known to become obedient in their Christian marriages. Thus we read of an Indian woman who insisted that her fiancé convert before marriage. Said the Jesuits, "She has gained her husband to JESUS CHRIST. This man, who was very rough before his Baptism, has become docile and pliable as a child: the blessing of Heaven is truly upon this family" (Thwaites 1896–1901, 29:115).

In the earlier years of the Jesuit mission in New France, the authorities encouraged marriages between Frenchmen and Indian women, partially as a means of christianizing the tribes, but more importantly as a method of cementing alliances for trade. Champlain promised Indians that the French would live with them and marry their daughters, bringing with them the technological goods of France. The Montreal settlers in the 1640s expected to make such marriages, and the first sacramental union between a Frenchman and Indian woman took place in 1644, between Martin Prévost and Marie Manitouabewich, a convert. Later in the decade the Jesuits permitted marriages to Indian women who were not yet baptized but were in the process of catechetical training; the expectation was that marriage would further the cause of conversion as well as colonization. In most cases, however, the offspring of these unions were raised in Indian communities, apart from Catholic influence. In 1663 when Louis XIV made New France a crown colony, eight hundred nubile French girls were brought to Canada. The French population increased dramatically, and by the end of the century marriages between French and Indians were being discouraged, as the French closed social ranks against their former allies (see Jaenen 1976b: 28–29).

The great expectations of the early years of mission gave way by the end of the 1600s to a more sober appraisal of conversions. In the chapters to follow we shall look more closely at Algonkian and Iroquoian patterns of Catholic practice, but in general the Jesuits came to distrust the authenticity of many Indian conversions, which seemed to have had political or economic motives. Many of the baptized became apostates, having accepted christening in times of danger, disease, or death but without the intention of living a Christian life or giving up gentile ways. Others were tempted back by their pagan peers. The missionaries became more cautious in judging the genuineness of Indian expressions of faith. "The Savages very seldom contradict those who speak to them," wrote one priest in the 1670s, "and, when they are taught, they approve everything. This gives the missionaries much trouble in distinguishing those who sincerely believe" (Thwaites 1896–1901, 58:81). As a result, the Jesuits extended the period of instruction before baptism, tightening qualifications except for the children of Christians and those in immediate danger of death. Apostasy could thus be better averted, but the numbers of baptized Indians grew more slowly in the eighteenth century.

THE MONTAGNAIS

The earliest Jesuit missions in New France were among the Abenakis in Acadia. However, these were short-lived, and it was not until the 1620s that the Jesuits returned, at Recollect invitation, to evangelize the Indians. Father Paul Le Jeune devoted himself, beginning in 1632, to the Montagnais on the northern side of the St. Lawrence.

There were several thousand Montagnais in the 1630s, related by language and culture to the Algonquins to the west, the Crees to the north, and the Abenakis and other Algonkians to the east. The French encountered them regularly for trade and then for missions at Tadoussac, but their homes were in the mountains to the north, hence the French appellation of Montagnais. Their traditional way of life was based upon hunting, with family bands constituting the social and political order. Of their aboriginal religion, little is known beyond their continuities with the other Algonkian hunters of the Northeast. According to a recent Jesuit scholar, "L'adoption rapide du christianisme par les mêmes Montagnais a ensuite relégué dans l'oubli leurs traditions religiouses. Biens qu'ils aient été en contact habituel avec les Français, les Montagnais son ceux dont on connaît le moins bien la religion primitive" (Campeau 1979: 93).

Le Jeune taught these trading allies of the French the Christian creation story. He instructed them in Catholic prayer—the *Pater*, the *Ave*, the *Credo*—and he catechized them regarding doctrines such as the Holy Trinity and the Incarnation. Like other Jesuits, he tried to get the Indians to express obedience to the ecclesiastical authority of the Church, and he taught the Montagnais women to submit to their husbands and create monogamous Christian families. In general, he attempted to introduce concepts and practices of hierarchical authority, both civil and religious, with corporal punishment serving as enforcement.

Le Jeune baptized the first Montagnais in 1634—Manitougatche, Sasousmat, and other members of the same extended family, all of them either sick adults or little children in danger of death. He was not about to christen healthy adults until there were proofs of informed conversion. And so, he listened to the Montagnais as they began to see similarities between their deities and the Christian God, as they argued with him and ridiculed Christian notions, as they queried about the efficacy of Christian faith: "'If we believe in your God, will it snow?' 'It will snow,' I said to him. 'Will the snow be hard and deep?' 'It will be.' 'Shall we find Moose?' 'You will find them.' 'Shall we kill some?' 'Yes; for as God knows all things, as he can do all things, and as he is very good, he will not fail to help you, if you have recourse to him, if you receive the Faith, and if you render him obedience'" (Thwaites 1896–1901, 8:33–35). The Montagnais listened to these promises, then went off into the woods to hunt, perhaps forgetting the Jesuit's claims, perhaps impressed. The Montagnais "captains" kept their distance from Christian fealty, and those interested in Christian devotions kept their prayers secret from their fellows for fear of mockery or social ostracism. One man, whom Le Jeune termed the "Apostate," gave up his interest in Christianity, "because he could not suffer the taunts of the Savages, who jeered at him occasionally because he was Sedentary and not wandering, as they were; and now he is their butt and their laughingstock" (7:173).

During the 1630s, the first Montagnais took on a Christian identity. A girl who received instruction in France

> knew several of the lessons in her Catechism, and understood a great deal of the French language; it was through this that we had made her comprehend the three principal Articles of our belief. She could say very well that the Manitou was good for nothing; that she no longer wished to return to Canada, but that she desired to be a Christian and to be baptized, knowing well that no one could go to Heaven without that. (7:287–289)

Father Le Jeune threatened the Montagnais with the eternal punishments they would receive in hell for continuing in their traditional way of life, and he perceived some headway gained through this technique: "The dread of punishment is beginning to gain such an ascendancy over their minds that, although they do not so soon amend, yet they are, little by little, giving up their evil customs" (11:215).

By the latter part of the 1630s he had gotten some of them to pray regularly, in order to be favored in the eyes of God. Christianized Montagnais thanked God for the animals they killed, for the roots they dug up, for their very livelihood, as they had formerly evoked the powers of the spirits in successful hunting and gathering pursuits. Le Jeune quoted the prayer of the Christian Montagnais women to "our

Lord: 'Great Captain, it is you who have made heaven and earth, and these roots. You have made them for our nourishment, you have shown them to me that I might eat them. I thank you for them; if you are willing to give me more, I will take them; if not, I will not give up believing in you'" (18:149). Some of them abstained from eating meat during Lent in order to demonstrate their Catholic devotion; some agreed to live among the Jesuits to be taught catechism and hymns; some received the sacraments and appeared to the priest as transformed beings. "What a change!" remarked Le Jeune of one Montagnais man, "who has many times eaten the flesh of his enemies, now receives JESUS CHRIST with a heart full of devotion, and confesses him with a candor altogether naive! In short, he is practicing Religion, conducting himself as a true Christian" (14:147).

There were some Montagnais who were attracted to the Christian faith, listened to the Jesuits' explanations, wished for baptism, but were unable to commit themselves thoroughly to Catholic ethical standards, and thus remained unchristened. Makheabichtichiou, a Montagnais captain, was unable to contradict the priest's teachings and he desired Christian identity. "I really do wish to embrace your belief," he told the missionaries,

> but you give me two commandments which conflict with each other; on the one hand you forbid me to kill, and on the other you prohibit me from having several wives; these commandments do not agree. Of the three wives I have married I love only one, whom I wish to keep with me; I send the other two away, but they return in spite of me, so that I must either endure them or kill them. . . . (11:177)

Makheabichtichiou dreaded the fires of hell; nevertheless, he died in 1640 without receiving the salvific waters of baptism.

Father Le Jeune found the sexuality of the Montagnais women, as well as their independence of mind, to be an obstacle to christianization. The men, he said, could not imagine themselves without wives (some more than one at a time); with divorce so common among them, their need to remarry was constant. Hence, the monogamous Christian marriage seemed impossible to them. In addition, the Jesuits among the Montagnais in the 1630s were discouraged to find themselves with so little regular contact with the Indians, who traveled through the forest in search of game—at least partially because of the natives' attachment to the French fur trade. Instruction was interrupted by hunting and trapping expeditions. The Christian calendar was hard to keep. Institutions and authority could not be imbedded into Montagnais culture.

In the 1620s, the Recollects had encountered the same obstacles to their missions, and they hoped to overcome them by instructing the youths in seminaries and resettling the Indians in agricultural villages under French control. Neither experiment worked for the Franciscans. They established a short-lived seminary, but the Indian boys who attended it could not bear the dreary memorization and indoor formality of the place, and they returned to their families. As for resettlement, the French fur-trading establishment wanted little to do with taking Indian trappers out of the woods.

Father Le Jeune aimed to recreate both experiments, and he met with greater success, at least in the short run, than his Recollect predecessors. At the very start of his evangelization project, the Jesuit wrote of his plan "to build seminaries, and to take their children, who are very bright and amiable. The fathers will be taught through the children" (5:33). He feared that the "excessive love the Savages bear their children would prevent our obtaining them" (9:105); however, he still hoped to attract some youth, who would "become so accustomed to our food and our clothes, that they will have a horror of the Savages and their filth" (107). In 1636 the Jesuits established Notre-Dame-des-Anges near Quebec, a seminary of instruction for French and Indian lads. Daily prayers, mass, instruction, with some free time for hunting, fishing, and other activities were the daily routine. Each boy had agricultural duties. The Indians did not take to the seminary any more than earlier Indians had to the Recollect attempt. By 1640 it was closed.

Father Le Jeune was concerned for Indian girls as well as boys. In 1633 and again in 1634 he called upon "some brave mistress" (6:151) to found a seminary for girls in New France, and in 1635 an Ursuline nun, Marie de l'Incarnation, offered her services. With the financial backing and personal support of Marie-Madeleine de la Pelletrie, several Ursulines arrived in Quebec in 1639, inspired by their reading of the Jesuit Relations. Like the Jesuits, the Ursulines hoped to establish a new, pure Christianity among the Indians of the New World. With this goal in mind, Madame de la Pelletrie and Marie de l'Incarnation gathered Montagnais and other Indian girls to their seminary. In the same year the Hospitaliers de la Miséricorde de Jésus (the Hospital Nuns) founded the Hôtel-Dieu in Quebec, providing medical and social welfare for Indian orphans and others.

Both orders of sisters tried to inculcate Christian virtues among the Indian girls who came to them for instruction and protection. The visionary Marie and her companions coaxed the girls to emulate French dress and manner, teaching them how to play the violin, how to embroider, how to dress their hair, as well as how to pray, to read, and to care for their fellow natives. Marie mastered Montagnais language; others learned Huron, and they developed proficiency in a pidgin tongue that was common in Quebec.

The Ursulines arrived in the midst of a smallpox epidemic among the Montagnais, and there were some Indians who feared the coming of the sisters, viewing their arrival as a symbol of the diseases that were devastating the native peoples. Some natives blamed the diseases on their acceptance of Christian prayer; others interpreted the biblical story of Eve's sinfulness as the origin of sickness. "The French teach," one said, "that the first woman who ever lived brought death into the world; what they say is true,—the women of their land are capable of such wickedness, and that is why they bring them into these countries—to make us all lose our lives" (in 16:39–41). The smallpox spread among the Indian girls at Marie's birchbark seminary, and the hospital was filled with sick and dying Indians.

Some Indians may have suspected the nuns to be the source of their illness; others witnessed their selfless devotion to diseased Indian peoples and sent their daughters to receive their instruction. Within two years Marie had four dozen students at her seminary and she had received as many as eight hundred visits from Indians, curious to witness the nuns in their habits. Father Le Jeune was pleased with the progress he saw: Montagnais children, "clasping their little hands, and giving their hearts to our Lord. They attend holy Mass every day, and are so attentive—not playing and talking like the little children in France—that we are delighted. They compose their faces, and regulate their actions by ours, except that in their reverences they imitate Madame de la Pelletrie. . . . They do not fail to recite their rosary every day. If they notice some Nun going aside to say hers, they present themselves to say it with her" (19:39–41). One little Montagnais girl, Anne Marie Negabamat, said to Le Jeune following confession: "My father, I wish to be always a virgin; do not make me leave this House, I wish to live here all my life" (20:133). The priest was overjoyed at her wish, recalling how she had formerly opposed his teaching, "until he took her once and pretended to throw her in the river, seeing that she was not willing to obey her parents, who bade her remain with these good Sisters" (ibid.).

The Ursulines took in Indian orphan girls and those in need of food or protection. Honor and hunger drove these girls to the seminary; at other times their parents gave them over to the nuns for education during the period of winter hunting. Sister Marie de l'Incarnation told in 1642 of a young woman of Christian parents, sent to the seminary to keep her away from a pagan husband who would not give up his other wife. The husband came to fetch his spouse, but she found refuge in the French and Christian Indian community in Quebec City. She was forbidden from speaking to her husband, and when she met once with him, her fellow Indians sentenced her to a public whipping at the door of the church, under the watch of the local Jesuit. The Indian executioner spoke to the French as he administered the whip, "We are going to punish her as you punish your children" (in Marie de l'Incarnation 1967: 106). After three lashes the priest saved her; the next day she appeared before the Ursulines, begging for baptism, which she received under the name of Angèle. The following year she was married to a christianized Abenaki chief living in Quebec City, and so left the seminary.

The Ursulines were impressed by the devotional expressions of their seminarians. Wrote the abbess:

> I told you last year how punctual our seminarians are at making their examination of conscience and accusing one another charitably without any of them taking offense. They continue this holy practice and by its means live in a purity of heart that cannot be believed. They have also a very good inclination to be present at the sacraments of Penitence and Communion, preparing themselves with fasting and penances. Only a few days ago, on an eve of Communion, I was obliged to leave off reciting the Office to make them stop a rough chastisement that went on for so long it filled me with horror. When they are given penance of this sort, which is not as often as they would wish, they tremble with joy, believing that a singular grace has been bestowed on them. They then scourge themselves earnestly. I admire among others little Marie-Magdeleine Abatenau who, though only nine years old, is as ardent in these penitential practices as the oldest and most robust. (Ibid., 107)

These seminarians were prepared for a heroic Christian life, ready to suffer capture, torture, and even death at the hands of enemies, without ceasing to profess their faith. In 1647 a party of Christian Algonquins met their death at the hands of Iroquois while singing hymns, making the sign of the cross, and praying with rosaries, including a little girl. "Oh, how fortunate was that child to have deserved in [her] state of innocence a death like unto that of Jesus Christ!" (170), exclaimed Sister Marie de l'Incarnation.

In the 1640s several of the seminarians announced their intent to become nuns. They learned their prayers and performed their penitences with intensity. Whereas some Indian girls ran away, others viewed the lives of nuns as preferable alternatives to the existence of wives in the bush, serving as beasts of burden for the men (as Marie de l'Incarnation saw it [19]). These girls were attracted by the nuns' cloistered independence and autonomy within colonial French society and sought to emulate them. But even these zealous seminarians tended to abandon their studies and lost their fervor when they returned to their own people for visitations. The Ursulines hoped to attract novices, but they were singularly unsuccessful in the seventeenth century. In 1656 the Hospital Nuns received a young Huron girl, Geneviève-Agnes Skanudharoua, into their order; however, she died two days after pronouncing her final vows in 1657 (Jaenen 1976b: 11).

Sister Marie continued to take in Indian girls until her death in 1672. However, the Ursuline seminary became more and more a school for French girls. In her last years the nun held fewer expectations for the immediate transformation of Indian girls (including Iroquois, by then) into christianized ladies: "I do not know whether they will be . . . capable of being civilized . . . or whether they will keep the French elegance in which we are rearing them. I do not expect it of them, for they are Savages and that is sufficient reason not to hope" (ibid., 341). Despite wars, smallpox epidemics, bouts with alcohol, and social flux, some Indians continued to study at the seminaries of the Ursulines and Hospital Nuns—joined in 1677 by the sisters of the Congregation of Notre Dame who aimed to prepare native girls for "Christian motherhood" (Magnuson 1992: 57). The nuns continued their work among the Indian girls of Quebec well into the eighteenth century.

The French missioners hoped to modify the culture of the hunting Indians in the 1630s and 1640s, adapting them not only to Christianity but also to settled village life. The seminaries were one means of effecting these changes. A thoroughgoing attempt to make the Montagnais, Algonquins, and other hunting Indians more sedentary was the establishment of reductions, modeled after the famous Jesuit experiments in Paraguay. While living with Montagnais hunters in the bush during the winter of 1633–34, Father Le Jeune determined to copy the Paraguay reductions, in order to separate the Algonkian neophytes both from their Indian kinsmen and from the corrupting influence of Frenchmen.

In 1637 one of the Hundred Associates, Noël Brûlart de Sillery, granted land for an Indian reserve near Quebec, aimed especially at the Montagnais who loved the French, learned of Christianity, but who thus far had refused to become sedentary. In establishing the Sillery reduction the Jesuits had to overcome the objections of colonial leaders like Champlain, who were more interested in native fur trappers than frenchified Indian farmers. Nonetheless, the priests persevered, and attracted the Indians of the north with the promise of steady supplies of food and protection against Iroquois attack. By the summer of 1638 there were about twenty Montagnais living at Sillery.

In the 1640s it became "the Christian showplace of Laurentian Canada" (Axtell 1986: 61), a village served by Hospital Nuns and Jesuits, where hundreds of Indians were evangelized, given refuge, taught agriculture, and assimilated partially into French culture, however without daily contact with secular Frenchmen. The Indians could stay for several months, and then go off hunting, tracked by Jesuit flying missions in the bush. By 1645 there were at least one hundred sixty-seven converted Indians at Sillery, setting such an example of piety that the French referred to them as "the true believers" (in Jaenen 1976b: 27).

The missionaries saw great changes at Sillery. Sister Marie de l'Incarnation wrote in 1640: "As for the settled Savages, they dwell in the fervor of the first Christians of the Church. One could not see souls purer or more zealous in observing God's law. I am full of wondering admiration when I see them submissive as children to those that instruct them" (Marie de l'Incarnation 1967: 84). She told of Algonkians, returning from the winter hunt, calling out as they arrived in the village, "'Tell us if today is Easter Day when Jesus is restored to life. . . .' They were thirsty as deer with the desire to hear Mass and to receive the Blessed Sacrament, having been deprived of them for almost four months" (103). A Jesuit remarked of the Sillery neophytes, that "their first and last action every day is to kneel before a Crucifix or a Picture which they fasten to a piece of bark, and there say their prayers. They observe Sundays and Festival days by abstaining from hunting, and by saying longer prayers" (Thwaites 1896–1901, 25:163). They performed the stations of the cross, made processions, and said their rosaries with visible attention. Many of them were reputed to carry their newfound zeal back to their native communities.

Perhaps no Sillery inhabitant was more famed in his devotion than the Montagnais Charles Meiachkawat. In 1638 he received a vision in the woods which determined him to quit the ways of his ancestors. In 1640 he moved to Sillery, where he received baptism and became a pillar of the community. With his help a permanent mission was established among the Montagnais at Tadoussac in 1641, and he served as an evangelist to the Abenakis between 1643 and 1645, trying to draw them away from the English orbit. This "nouveau saint Paul" (Campeau 1979: 121) was killed while serving on this Abenaki mission, and his holy reputation was used as an example for other christianized Indians in New France.

Throughout the 1640s Algonkian gentiles lived at Sillery alongside their neophyte relatives, and it was necessary for the authorities to assert Christian hegemony. When sickness came, there were traditional healers ready to employ their pagan spirituality to effect cures, and the Christian Indians needed to resist their overtures. The Jesuits and the Indian Christians themselves were loathe to witness any sign of an aboriginal custom within the confines of Sillery reserve, and they worked to convert the pagan Indians or at least to shame them publicly from their aboriginal religious praxis. When an Indian named Estienne Pigarouich abandoned his Catholic faith temporarily, the Jesuits demanded open penance:

> In the first place, thou shalt announce aloud, outside of the cabins, according to the custom, that thou hast behaved very badly, and that thou dost condemn all that thou hast said and done to the scandal of prayer and of the Christians. Secondly, thou shalt state, aloud and publicly, that thou abandonest the company of those who do not pray, and, in fact, that thou dost abandon them, and dost range thyself with those of Sillery who make a practice of praying to God. Thirdly, thou shalt in the Chapel and on thy knees ask pardon of all those who are baptized, and beg them to pray to God for thee, and to pardon thee. Before doing the latter, thou must prepare thyself for confession; and, after having made it, and having asked pardon of the Christians, thou shalt, in the fourth place, take the discipline publicly as an atonement for thy faults, to punish thy flesh, and thereby to show the hatred that thou hast for thy sin. (Thwaites 1896-1901, 25:277)

At Sillery there were struggles between pagans and Christians, priests and natives, men and women. One woman was chained up for not accepting her subservient role as a wife, and young women were imprisoned for their courting practices. Public floggings were commonplace, and Indian youths fought with one another over their religious beliefs (see Ronda 1979: 6–13).

When the Iroquois destroyed the Huron missions in 1649, Sillery and other reserves became asylums for the fleeing Christians. Some of the reductions proved partially successful as forts against Iroquois invasion; others became magnets for Iroquois attacks, and French troops were helpless to defend the Christians under their protection. Under siege Sillery took on the complexion of a military base, and the neophytes were sometimes prevented from coming and going as they pleased. Algonkians entered Sillery to seek refuge from the Iroquois, as well as to find God, and pagan-Christian factionalism flared within the reduction. There were devout Christian Algonkians at Sillery, but some said that the majority of Indians living there continued in their aboriginal religiousness, largely in their own cabins, away from the sight of Jesuits. The Christian Algonkians let it be known that their relatives continued to traffic in old practices and were, as one Indian put it, "persistent in their slavery to Satan" (in Ronda 1979: 14). A liquor traffic further demoralized the Sillery inhabitants, even when the perpetrators were excommunicated (Marie de l'Incarnation 1967: 273–275, 355), and smallpox ravaged the community in 1669–70. As Montagnais and Algonquins abandoned the reserve, Abenaki Christians took refuge there; however, by the middle of the 1670s Sillery was deserted and the first reduction experiment came to an end.

When New France became a royal province in 1663, frenchification once again became a colonial goal and the Jesuits were scolded for keeping Indians separate from the French. Nonetheless, the priests continued to establish and maintain reserves for Christian Indians. Sillery was the first reduction in Canada, but others followed: St. Francis (Onondak), Bécancourt, Lorette, Sault St. Louis (Kahnawake, Caughnawaga), Lac-des-Deux-Montagnes (Oka), St. Regis (Akwesasne), La Présentation, and more (see Axtell 1986: opposite 62). In the eighteenth century, however, as missionary endeavors waned, French policy gave little support to reserves.

Outside the Sillery enclave the Jesuits earned some success among the Montagnais at Tadoussac, beginning in 1640. With the help of

Charles Meiachkawat, the priests established a station that overcame local native opposition and spread the Christian faith to the north and east, for example to Betsiamites, where the faith has persisted among the Montagnais for three centuries and more (Betsiamites, July 27–28, 1990). In 1641 Sister Marie de l'Incarnation praised the evangelical efforts of the Montagnais Charles Kariskatisitch, baptized at Tadoussac only six months previous, who "has accomplished more by his sermons than a hundred preachers could have done in several years" (Marie de l'Incarnation 1967: 86). He built a chapel and house for Father Le Jeune at Tadoussac and protected him from enemies of the faith with his pistol. He and his fellow Montagnais engaged in Catholic devotions, including public prayers and hymns, and they were reported to listen attentively to catechetical instruction, coming to comprehend "very well" the exercises of "inner recollection" (87). Kariskatisitch had a pagan wife "of the most wicked and intolerable sort" (ibid.), whom he attempted to convert, and he applied the same efforts toward his other Montagnais tribesmen.

Scholars have doubted the thoroughness of Montagnais conversions to Christianity in the first decades of evangelization and even beyond. The spread of Catholic faith was "more apparent than real" (Bailey 1969: 131), one remarks, with the Jesuits incapable of expressing in Montagnais language the "arrière-pensées of the Christian concepts" (ibid.). Deep-seated native beliefs and practices did not disappear, especially since the Indians spent a substantial portion of every year apart from the priests. The Indians employed traditional methods of religious communication, dreams in particular, as part of their Christian practice; Jesus became associated with the sun and his grandmother, Ste. Anne, with the earth. Her feast day became a vehicle for old-time dances, and Christian sacramentals like rosaries and crosses took the place of good-luck stones and other aboriginal amulets. Saints and guardian spirits were combined in the Montagnais pantheon and God took on some of the aspects of their mythological culture heroes. At the same time, almost all the Montagnais were baptized by the 1670s and many had given up polygamy and other aspects of aboriginal culture.

In the years that followed, the Montagnais persisted in Catholic catechism and devotions, even though they spent most of the year separated from Church personnel. The English Hudson's Bay Company controlled the northern trapping areas of the Montagnais from 1670, and the Jesuits did not keep up with the dwindling numbers of these northern Algonkians in the late seventeenth and early eighteenth centuries, as disease and warfare took their toll in the forested regions. There were intermittent Jesuit efforts in the mid-1700s, but English victory over New France in 1760 spelled the decline of these missions. From 1782 until 1845, when the first Oblates arrived, the Montagnais were largely separated from clerical contact.

It is not our object here to follow the history of these Canadian Indian Catholics, but rather to establish the baseline of Catholic evangelization in the early decades of New France. The Montagnais mission of the seventeenth century was not without its successes, and in the present day the descendants of the first neophytes hold to their Catholic (and Indian) identity in Quebec. To the contemporary Montagnais the Catholic religion is a "spiritual reality" in their lives: "They now live in well-organized Christian communities with their own pastoral workers" (Peelman 1995: 100). Nevertheless, the Jesuits were impatient with their progress among these Algonkian hunters, whose winters were spent apart from the mission stations at Sillery and Tadoussac and whose small numbers constituted a meager accomplishment, especially when there were larger, more sedentary groups of Indians to be approached and won to Catholicism.

The Hurons were the most promising candidates for conversion in the first half of the seventeenth century in New France. The Recollects had regarded them as such from 1616, and in 1623 three priests attempted a mission among them. In two years of work, however, only three Hurons received baptism. Most of the Indians regarded the Recollects as witches: anti-social, dangerous, and rude. When the English took over Quebec in 1625, the Recollect effort ended.

The only palpable result of the Recollect mission concerned a Huron youth, Amantacha, who traveled with the French to Rouen, where he was baptized in an elaborate public ceremony in the cathedral in 1627. Christened Louis de Sainte-Foi, the Huron convert returned to his people the following year amidst the English regime. In 1634 the Iroquois captured him and cut off several of his fingers before he was able to escape. The Jesuits were just then establishing a new mission among the Hurons, and Father Brébeuf met with Amantacha, finding him less a Christian than he had hoped. During the next year, however, the native served as a link between the Jesuits and the Hurons, translating catechisms and dwelling with the priests. The Iroquois captured him again in 1635, and this time he was killed.

Amantacha and his father were both interested in cementing economic alliances with the French; some Jesuits regarded them as "crafty spirits" (Trigger 1976: 547), eager to put on Catholicism for the sake of the fur trade. The father died unbaptized in 1636, as the priests were constructing their Huron mission.

Father Paul Le Jeune predicted in 1633 that the Hurons of Georgian Bay would be "easily converted" (in Axtell 1986: 46), because they lived in sedentary villages, had a substantial population (estimated between eighteen and forty thousand [Trigger 1976: 31–32]), and had chieftaincies, all of which made suitable mechanisms for evangelization. From 1634 until the 1650s and beyond, the Jesuits toiled to realize this prediction, but the missionization process was far more complex than anticipated, and even tragic (see Campeau 1987b; Donnelly 1975; Trigger 1976). Jean de Brébeuf, François Le Mercier, Paul Ragueneau, Charles Garnier, and other Jesuits initiated a mission that the Iroquois undid in 1649; however, the converted survivors of the devastated Huron villages spread their newfound faith among their Iroquois captors.

The Jesuits were convinced that the Hurons wanted a mission. In 1633 Father Le Jeune put the words of the Macedonian to Saint Paul into the mouths of the Indians: "Come, help us, bring into our country the torch which has not yet illuminated it" (in Thwaites 1896–1901, 6:25). For all their physicality, superstitions, and polygamy, the Hurons appeared "docile and flexible" (8:151). The Jesuits told the Hurons in 1635 that the priests wished to preserve and strengthen friendship with them, which would profit, bless, and protect the Indians; and they wished to promote French intermarriage with the Indian daughters, "when they become Christians" (ibid., 49). They tried to impress French superiority upon the Hurons, presenting God as the source of all foods and goods as well as spiritual nourishment. "The more imposing the power of our French people is made in these countries," wrote one Jesuit, "the more easily they can make their belief received by those Barbarians, who are influenced even more through the senses than through reason" (15). In the first year of the Huron mission the Indians—according to the priests—turned "willingly to God in their necessities; they come to get their crops blessed, before sowing them; and ask us what we desire of them" (153).

The Jesuits sought to find in Huron culture the bases for a future Christian spirituality. There was aboriginal belief in a god above, in spirits like angels, in good and evil, in vision quests that resembled Catholic fasts. A transformation would have to take place—away from blood feuds, polytheism, and reverence for nature—but the priests thought that they saw the makings of ideal Christians in the Hurons they encountered in the 1630s. In their catechisms (see Steckley 1992) the Jesuits expounded upon the spiritual dimension of life, and the differences between human body and soul as well as between God and all creatures. They spoke of the destiny of heaven or hell for all individuals and emphasized the role of baptism in deciding eternal destiny. Le Jeune's dictum that "fear is the forerunner of faith" (Thwaites 1896–1901, 11:89) found its expression in the instruction given by the Jesuits among the Hurons. The priests tried to scare the Indians into baptism with terrifying portraits of damned souls in hell. God and the Devil were warriors in the Jesuit teachings, waging attacks upon one another, and humans must choose which standard to follow. Just as the Hurons feared capture and torture by their enemies, the Jesuits pictured salvation as a battle. Jesus was a war chief, carrying the war bundle, overcoming enemies, protecting His allies. No wonder that the Hurons regarded conversion to Christianity as a protection in warfare, a medicine for military power. Hope for protection and terror of the eternally consuming fires of hell drew some Hurons to accept baptism.

Father Brébeuf recorded the baptism in 1635 of an aged Huron named Martin Tsicok:

> This good man did not cease to invoke Jesus and Mary from his baptism until the 15th of December, when he died. I began to instruct him with this truth, that our souls after death all go to Hell or to Paradise; that Paradise is a place full of delights and contentment, and on the contrary that Hell is a place of fires, of pains, and eternal torments; that, besides, he should think, while he was yet in life, to which of these places he desired to go and dwell forever. Then this good old man, turning to his wife, said to her, "My wife, is it not indeed better to go to Heaven? I am afraid of those horrible fires of hell." His wife was of the same opinion, and thus he willingly listened to the instructions we gave him. (8:139)

The Jesuits also emphasized the role of baptism in cementing trade alliances between the French and the Hurons. To be christened, the catechisms said, was to ally oneself to God, to become a member of His lineage, with the Virgin Mary as a kind of clan mother. Baptism was thereby a ritual of adoption. The Eucharist was a common meal, a reminder of shared fealty, a memorial of alliance in the name of Jesus. The Jesuits downplayed the transubstantiational aspects of the Eucharist, so as not to reinforce Iroquoian ritual cannibalism (Bowden 1981: 86–87). Instead, the sacraments were depicted as means by which the Hurons could bind themselves to French power and wealth. The Hurons permitted the Jesuits among them because the Indians wanted French trade, French spiritual power to defeat enemies, French goods, and French alliance.

In the first two years of their Huron mission the Jesuits got the Indians to recite catechetical responses, rewarding youths with beads for correct answers. The Hurons memorized well, although from the priests' reports it appears that the natives were repelled by Jesuit obsession with death and shocked at the brazen character of evangelical preaching. Brébeuf, for example, called Huron myths "unbelievably stupid" (Thwaites 1896–1901, 10:149). To ridicule Indian beliefs was rudeness bordering on witchcraft. On the other hand, the priests seemed to have power, perhaps over drought and disease. Twice in 1635 the Jesuits performed novenas and processions that seemed to bring rain, after the failure of traditional religious practitioners (Trigger 1976: 510). When some sick girls recovered their health following baptism, the ritual became popular as a cure-all. Brébeuf remarked in 1636 that the Hurons "seek Baptism almost entirely as an aid to health." The Jesuits tried to dissuade them of this view and "teach them that the life-giving waters of Holy Baptism principally impart life to the soul, and not to the body. However, they have the opinion so deeply rooted that the baptized, especially the children, are no longer sickly, that soon they will have spread it abroad and published it everywhere. The result is that they are now bringing us children to baptize from two, three, yes, even seven leagues away" (Thwaites 1896–1901, 10:13).

Some Hurons believed that the power of Christians protected them against fires in their villages; others looked to the sacraments of the Jesuits to keep them from the "fiery furnaces of hell" (10:29). To learn the secrets of Christian potency and to bind themselves to the French, the Hurons sent some of their youths to Quebec for schooling. These seminarians said their prayers, especially in times of illness, like the Huron boy Satouta: "Jesus, my Captain, since you have suffered so much to open Heaven to men, do not let me fall down into the fire; but, on the contrary, grant that I may see you as soon as possible in Heaven" (in 12:55). One of them preached among the Algonkians, and another among his own people. On the whole, however, the Jesuits decided that it was not such an effective plan to convert Huron children in Quebec, away from their communities, and they focused their attention on the Huron towns.

Diseases ravaged those communities, particularly in 1636 and 1637. Influenza, measles, and smallpox spread from the French to the Indians, so that within six years of the Jesuit arrival in 1634 half of the Hurons had died of epidemics (Trigger 1976: 499–501). This first major epidemic in eastern Canada convinced the Hurons of Jesuit power; however, it was a potency of evil, according to some of the Indians. Noted Father Le Jeune:

> These tribes believe that we poison and bewitch them, carrying this so far that some of them no longer use the kettles of the French. They say that we have infected the waters, and that the mists which issue thence kill them; that our houses are fatal to them; that we have with us a dead

body, which serves us as black magic; that, to kill their children, some
Frenchmen penetrated the horrid depths of the woods, taking with
them the picture of a little child which we had pricked with the points
of awls, and that therein lay the exact cause of their death. They go even
farther—they attack our Savior, Jesus Christ; for they publish that there
is something, I know not what, in the little Tabernacle of our Chapel,
which causes them to die miserably. (Thwaites 1896–1901, 12:237–239)

All the things that amazed the Hurons about the priests—their writing, their striking clock, their weather vane, crosses, chants, and incense—became ominously evil in 1637, and the priests fully expected to
be murdered as sorcerers, even writing out their last will in October of
that year (Donnelly 1975: 127–136).

If some Hurons accused the priests of deadly sorcery and threatened them with death, others reasoned that their own deaths would be
forestalled if they received baptism. Deep divisions formed among the
Hurons, between those who regarded the Jesuits as the source of all
afflictions and those who looked to them for cures. If one woman said
that she preferred "going to hell and being burned there forever"
(Thwaites 1896–1901, 13:153), rather than receiving the dreaded sacrament, another (named Arendaonatia) spread the good news of her
christening: "God, having . . . restored her health, she has conceived a
very high opinion of holy baptism, and has evinced much good will in
keeping the commandments of God and even in aiding to instruct
some of the other Savages" (14:13). As their numbers fell to the
scourges, some Hurons chose baptism so as to be reunited in heaven
with christened relatives who had recently died.

Rather than killing the Jesuits, the Hurons underwent their first
mass christenings in 1637. Although many who received the sacrament
died, and others had little to do with the priests once they recovered
and were regarded as "apostates" (Trigger 1976: 546), the Jesuits reported as many as a hundred practicing Christians among the Hurons
by 1639 (Thwaites 1896–1901, 15:187). Among these were Tsiouendaen-
taha, the first adult Huron in good health to receive baptism, who
served as a catechist and translator for the Jesuits. "Having been very
carefully instructed," this Huron "earnestly requested baptism . . . and,
on the day of the most holy Trinity, he was baptized publicly, and with
the ceremonies of the Church, in the presence of the chief persons of
this village, some of whom regarded this act with astonishment, and
others with a desire to imitate it" (14:77).

Even more famous among the converts was Joseph Chihwatenwa, christened in 1637 during the Huron epidemic. The Jesuits lionized him for his morality and industriousness. He had but one wife; he worked his garden; he forewent the usual charms of his people and "never indulged in the diabolical feasts. Add to all this," the priests wrote, "a fine disposition, wonderfully docile, and, contrary to the humor of the country, anxious to learn" (15:79). One might doubt that many Hurons became thorough Christians in the first years of the Jesuit mission, since they remained Huron in culture. And yet, one is struck (see Campeau 1987b: 355–359) by the constant devotions of Chihwatenwa —his "many acts of Adoration, which he finishes by an act of contrition" (Thwaites 1896–1901, 15:87) —even in the face of derision by his relatives. "It is wonderful how much strength God gives him," commented one priest, "to combat at every turn the great difficulties that the Devil continues to raise for him through the people of his nation—some by inviting him to their infamous and superstitious feasts, others by openly ridiculing him" (97). In the Jesuits' eyes he held steadfast for his newfound faith, serving as a lay native preacher among the Hurons. Chihwatenwa led devotions, healed the sick, fought evil with the rosary, and sang to God in the sweat lodge. He proclaimed God's sovereignty as the ground of his being and strived to do good according to Christian values. His theological sophistication was impressive to the Jesuits (see 19:137–149, 245–257), and when met with opposition from his people, he "publicly reproves the diabolical superstitions and the folly of his fellow countrymen" (245).

Chihwatenwa dreamed of being killed by Iroquois and felt that he could avert this fate by offering a sacrificial feast of dogs to the spirit of his dream. The Jesuits interpreted this vision as a temptation sent by the devil to return the Huron convert to his aboriginal cult (see 21:161–163). He refused to make the sacrifice and thus resisted the devil's overture. Soon after, in 1640, he died in precisely the way he had dreamed at the hands of Iroquois or Hurons, and the Jesuits memorialized his martyrdom. During the smallpox epidemic of 1639, Chihwatenwa persistently identified with the Jesuits and their Catholic faith, while his fellow converts abandoned their vows and vilified the priests as the causes of their illness.

The Hurons wavered in their commitment to Catholic identity even when not ravaged by disease. Father Jerome Lalemant witnessed "the spirit of God and of the devil struggling in their minds and hearts.

One day, you see them all killing themselves to say that they believe, and that they wish to be baptized; another day, everything is overthrown and hopeless. This contrast is a manifest sign of combat . . ." (17:125). When a smallpox epidemic struck in 1639, making the Hurons "a declining people" (Donnelly 1975: 172), Christian loyalty offered no solace and appeared as the root of evil. Almost all of the Hurons renounced their Christian attachment, in spite of the founding of Sainte-Marie, a Huron mission center. A thousand had received baptism, but only three or four heads of families and a few old women continued to profess their faith by the time Chihwatenwa was killed (Thwaites 1896–1901, 17:229; Trigger 1976: 701).

In 1640 Christianity was "in disgrace" in the christianized Huron towns, "but also in the neighboring hamlets which, seeing themselves less attacked with the trouble, rejoice to have continued obstinate in infidelity . . ." (Thwaites 1896–1901, 19:213). Over the next several years, however, the inducements of the French fur trade drew the Hurons back to baptism and catechism. Christened Indian traders were given lower prices for French goods and only they, not their pagan kinsmen, were allowed to buy guns and ammunition (Trigger 1976: 702). As a result the Hurons expressed such an interest in baptism that the Jesuits had to slow down the process of instruction in order to test the natives in their faith.

These new Huron converts were motivated by economic interests; however, they were also moved by fear of hell and the value of an eternal soul. They expressed their desire to attain heaven and they identified themselves as comrades only to other Christians. As one Huron Christian told another candidate for baptism, "We shall be very soon relatives indeed; my true relatives are those who believe in God, and who are baptized, for I shall be eternally with them. We have only one Father, who is God; since thou desirest to know him, thou wilt very soon be among my relatives. The kinship that we have according to the flesh, is a trifling matter; thou must be baptized, to be my true relative" (in Thwaites 1896–1901, 20:279). When nuns asked a Huron girl at a Quebec seminary if she missed her mother at home, the girl replied, "She whom I have in my country is no longer my dear mother because she does not believe in God; it is you who are my true mothers since you instruct me" (in 20:37). In their zeal the Huron Christians put pressure on their fellows to live according to Christian rules, observing the sabbath, practicing monogamy, and refusing to engage in feasts and orgies. When the gentiles resisted, factions arose in most of the Huron towns. By the mid-1640s there were about five hundred professing Christian Hurons, a vocal minority more attached to the French priests than to their kinsmen. Said a council of Christian Hurons, "The Name of Christian is a tie more binding than Nature's bonds. Let us inform our Relatives who are not of the same Faith as we, even if they be our fathers and our children, that we do not wish our bones to be mingled together after our death, since our Souls will be eternally separated, and our affection will not continue beyond this life" (in 23:31). When the Christian Huron Joseph Teondechoren lost his daughter to death, he seemed well reconciled:

> I see before me my daughter, full of joy; her death has consoled me more than her life; my mind has not been disturbed by it. Some time ago, I gave her up to GOD; he has disposed of her; she belonged to him more than to me. I do not place much value upon the life we lead here below on earth. I prize Eternity alone, and the intercourse that we will have together forever. (In 23:59)

Estienne Totihri confronted violent opposition to his faith with these words, recorded by the Jesuit Father Jerome Lalemant: "I fear not death, since GOD has enlightened my mind, and has shown me things more important than this bodily life. . . . Let them kill my mother, my wife, my children, and my brothers; after them, the blow that is to give me happiness will fall on me! My Soul is not attached to my body" (in 23:135–137).

By the early 1640s the Iroquois tribes of the Confederacy were already striking terror among the Hurons as the two groups competed for furs. In their trade with the Dutch and French, respectively, the Iroquois and Hurons tied their futures to European colonial powers. The lure of trade goods motivated the Indians to harvest the forests for beaver and other furbearers; where trapping and trading areas overlapped, the competition proved fierce. The Hurons established themselves, at least partially through their association with the Jesuits, as key members of the French trade, serving as middlemen between the Algonkian trappers—Ottawas and Ojibways, for example—and the Frenchmen. Huron allies like the Eries and Neutrals solidified the economic network. For their part the Iroquois wished to seize the regional advantage of the Hurons in order to trade both with the Dutch and French. As the Iroquois began to deplete their own resources, they eyed Huron stores with desire.

The hotblooded beaver wars that ensued proved a deadly context for Catholic missions in the Northeast, both for Hurons and Iroquois, and also for the Jesuits. The priests protested that their missions were meant not as commercial outposts for "the traffic of skins and dead beasts" (25:75) but merely as a place for spiritual harvest. On the other hand, the Hurons hoped their alliance with the missioners would gain them French goods and French protection. They hoped for French arms and they prayed to the God of the Frenchmen to guard them from Iroquois attack. As one Christian Huron prayed, "Thou who hast made everything, help our young men, and defend them against our enemies. Thou canst do everything; give them courage to overcome them" (in 24:245).

Supernatural aid did not prevent the capture and torture of Father Isaac Jogues in 1642, or the killing of many Hurons and Frenchmen by the Iroquois. If God could not defeat the Iroquois, at least the Christian Indians could turn to Him for fortitude. In the words of the Montagnais Charles Meiachkawat: "I do not fear the Iroquois; I fear God alone. If he choose, he will preserve me; if not, he knows why. I do not mind being captured, burned, and eaten for such a cause" (in 25:179).

What was the cause of which Meiachkawat spoke? One is tempted to say that the colonial trade transcended all spiritual issues, that the Hurons put up with the Jesuits in order to win metals, cloth, firearms, and alcohol; and that the Iroquois waged wars for the same. In such a view a Christian Huron was little more than a French ally, prepared to fight and die for colonial profits in the name of God.

The testimony of the Jesuits suggests more religious dimensions, without denying the presence of the fur trade as a powerful motivating force. In the 1640s thousands of Hurons sought baptism—seventeen hundred in 1648 alone (33:257)—and they did so because they feared hell as much as they feared their enemies and they professed love for God as firmly as they desired French wealth. At the time of her baptism one Huron woman stated, "I renounce all my wickedness. I do not wish to go into the flames; I wish to be blessed, and a friend of God" (in 26:97). When the Jesuits saw how zealous the converted Hurons could be, they commented that "The souls of the savages are as capable of perfection as those of Europeans" (119). One christened Huron "had his head shaved like ours, and, taking a whip of rope, he went through the cabins calling the others to prayers and striking those who did not promptly obey. 'I am doing the Fathers' office,' he cried"

(117). Some Huron converts sought penance, saying "that it was necessary that they . . . appease God. . . . some chose fasting; others chastised themselves, and beat themselves with thorns" (147). Some Huron converts traveled to mass daily, no matter the distance or the weather. They confessed weekly and prayed constantly with their rosaries. They engaged in theological discussion and believed fervently in the efficacy of Catholic ritualism. There are many devout Huron Christians depicted in the Jesuit Relations, with enough known of them and their faith that a Jesuit compiled fifty-two of their biographies in a Montreal archive (Pouliot 1940: 91).

Huron Christians tried to adopt the mores of the Jesuits, and some even became evangelicals, not only among their family members but also among those in neighboring towns. A few were so fervent in their faith that they sought converts among their allies and even among their enemies, the Iroquois. The intensity of their religious convictions led the neophytes, under Jesuit direction, to attempt imposing their codes of behavior on their fellow Hurons. When their gentile relatives resisted, internecine struggle ensued, and in some cases Christians had to separate themselves from the pagans, setting up separate villages. The Jesuits tried to attract the Christians to the several mission centers such as Sainte-Marie for festivals and other religious observances. With the converts, they planned the overcoming of paganism and they tried to establish a Christian Huron identity apart from the ritual alliances of traditional Huron polity. There was to be no more dream-guessing, no more participation in the feasts of the dead. Burials would take place in Christian graveyards, and Christian Hurons even resisted fighting alongside their pagan relatives who continued to seek omens in dreams.

The result was a dissolution of Huron society. Christian Hurons could no longer be headmen in traditional villages, since to do so was to observe dances, festivals, feasts, and ritual lewdness. The Jesuits tried to get Huron converts to eschew extramarital sex, and then to resist the advances of pagan men and women. The converts tried to make themselves unattractive (for instance, girls appeared with melancholy countenance), and they rolled in the snow to subdue their own sexuality. The bonds that used to hold together a people—the political authority, the ritual communion, the sexual unions—were broken by Catholic identity, as the Jesuits tried to establish a new society among the Huron converts.

Huron gentiles were infuriated by the Christian faction of the 1640s. They blamed the Jesuits for all natural and political misfortunes. They accused the Christian Hurons of witchcraft, since the latter would not engage in social rites for the commonweal. Families were in disarray; tempers were lost; marriages came apart. Traditionalists threatened, mocked, cajoled, and seduced the converts to engage in rituals and abjure their newly acquired faith. Pagan seductors told the Christians how foolish it was to deny themselves sexual pleasure for some imaginary heaven. Anti-Christian stories spread among the Hurons, telling how a christianized Huron died and went to the French afterworld, only to be tortured as a prisoner of war. These visionary accounts denied the validity of Jesuit teachings regarding heaven and warned against conversion, thus serving nativist purpose (Trigger 1976: 722–723; see 710–723). When these rumors failed to turn the tide of Huron conversions—one convert attested, "I am more attached to the church than to my country or relatives" (in Jaenen 1976b: 30)—the pagans threatened the priests and their allies with violence. In 1648 the pagan party killed one of the Jesuit domestics and demanded that all Christians be thrown out of Huronia.

By this time it was too late for the pagan party to oust the converts, because their numbers and influence were increasing markedly. By the middle of 1649 another two thousand Hurons had received baptism (Thwaites 1896–1901, vol. 34; Trigger 1976: 739), so that approximately half of Huronia was at least nominally Christian. Huron converts attended mass in large numbers and flocked to the Jesuits for instruction and blessing. The Christian party controlled daily life in several towns, leading the gentiles to withdraw and in some cases to ally themselves with the Iroquois, who were already attacking Huronia.

The Iroquois plunder of the Hurons and their allies began frontally in 1648, as a culmination of the beaver wars, and it was probably protection that the thousands of Huron converts sought from the missions in the last year of Huronia, 1648–49. The twenty-two Jesuits were helpless, however, when the Iroquois invaded Huronia. Fathers Jean de Brébeuf and Gabriel Lalemant were tortured and murdered along with hundreds of Hurons as the Iroquois devastated one Huron town after another and dispersed the population. The Iroquois were fighting to gain trapping territory from the Hurons, but they were also waging war against the allies of Christian New France. In such a battle, there were some pagan Hurons who became Iroquois adoptees and played an "active and willing role in killing these two Jesuits" (Trigger 1976: 765) and their Christian converts. Huron factionalism, created by Christian conversions, made defense of Huronia nigh impossible, and the Hurons fell easily to their powerful foes.

In the midst of the horrific events of 1649, many gentile Hurons sought to join the Iroquois; thousands of others turned to the Jesuits for aid. The calamities of famine and plague killed many Hurons; however, the priests found the events "salutary to their souls,—for, up to this time, our labors have not yielded greater fruits; never before has faith gone more deeply into hearts, or the name of Christian been more glorious, than in the midst of the disasters to a stricken people" (Thwaites 1896–1901, 35:23). Some Hurons blamed the Jesuits for the Iroquois invasion, and there was a "mutinous rebellion" against them at one mission station. At other locations the priests perceived that "the common misery was bringing down the arrogance of those who, at first, refused to listen. . . . Now they flocked . . . like sheep, and entreated for holy Baptism" (177). Some hoped to be saved from annihilation; others sought succor in a time of certain destruction. Father Paul Ragueneau recorded the testimony of one such convert, Michel Ekouaendae, who said "with a joyful countenance" that he did not fear death. Rather, he stated, "I desire it with love, for I am anxious to be in Heaven where my heart assures me that God will reward me for my faith, and for the confidence that I have in him. What I dread is sin; but I would rather be burned by the Iroquois, than offend so good a God" (in 36:205).

Georgian Bay could no longer house the Hurons after 1650. Their towns were destroyed, and it became impossible for them to farm in the midst of attacks. Iroquois continued to raid the area for several years, seeking further victims in their intent to keep the Huron confederacy from ever reconstituting. Neutrals and Eries fell to the Iroquois by 1654, and with them all hope of Huron resurgence. The Iroquois incorporated several thousand Hurons into their societies as adoptees and servants. Other Hurons escaped to the west to live among the Ottawas and Ojibways, where they received Catholic missions in the 1660s. Some of these settled eventually in the vicinity of Detroit at Sandusky. These Hurons (called Wyandots) maintained contact with French Catholicism until the late 1700s; however, they became Protestants in the nineteenth century before their removal to Indian Territory. The remaining Christian Hurons sought asylum with the Jesuits in Quebec City and its environs. Father Ragueneau brought several hundred Hurons to Quebec in 1650, where the nuns cared for them until they could establish a community. One of these refugee Hurons, Geneviève-Agnes Skanudharoua, stayed with the Ursulines and took her final vows as a nun before her death in 1657. With Huron society in shambles, other converts sought thorough identification with their protectors. As one Huron convert said in 1652, "I am almost wholly French" (in 38:65).

As many as a thousand baptized Hurons were living in Iroquoia in the early 1650s, many of whom remained faithful to their Catholic identity and wished their children to be baptized and instructed in Christian doctrine. Some of the baptized Hurons became apostates, but others held firm in their Catholic allegiance. François Le Mercier, S.J., noted in 1654: "Some come and confess, while others give me an account of all their sufferings, and, at the same time, of the blessing that remains to them that their Faith is not held captive in their captivity" (41:105). At the same time there were perhaps twice those numbers of captured and adopted Hurons who were vociferously anti-Jesuit. Thus the factionalism fostered by the missions persisted among the Hurons of Iroquoia in 1654. The Jesuits who sought out the captive Hurons met spirited resistance along with evidence of continued faith. The Huron traditionalists reminded their fellows that "the moment the Hurons received the Faith and abandoned their dreams, their ruin began, and their whole Country has ever since been declining to its final total destruction" (42:135). These gentiles warned the Hurons and Iroquois that the same would be their fate if they accepted the Jesuits among them.

For the next generation the Huron Christians among the Iroquois attempted to practice their faith, as Jesuits continued to visit their villages. Their captors wavered in attitude toward the Huron Christians in their midst, sometimes permitting them sacraments and congregations and other times killing them when they professed their faith. As the vagaries of French policy led to alternating alliance and warfare, the Huron Christians were accordingly either secure or endangered. The Jesuits recorded the continuing faith and heroic deaths of these Indians, including, e.g., one Dorothee, who saw her daughter weeping over the mother's torture: "My daughter, weep not for my death, or for thy own; we shall . . . go to Heaven together, where God will have pity on us for all eternity. The Iroquois cannot rob us of this great blessing" (in 44:169). Mother and daughter died together. Some captive Huron girls wished in vain to take vows as nuns. Others refused to marry gentile Iroquois or Hurons. Still other men and women looked forward to escape or hoped for death, so that they could be united with God in heaven.

Around Quebec City the refugee Hurons established a series of villages from 1651 under Jesuit direction—at Orleans, Beauport, Sainte-Foy, and Ancienne-Lorette. Some lived for a while at the reduction at Sillery. These Christians lived in fear of Iroquois raids, while at the same time hoping to renew contact with their captive Christian relatives. In the early 1670s an old Huron man still prayed for the future of his people: "Courage, little remnant of the Huron Nation! Your stock is not yet withered; it will send forth fresh branches; Jesus, risen again, will make it revive and bloom anew" (in 55:275). With this faith the Christian Hurons lived more and more like Frenchmen, while paying lip service to traditional Huron customs. Christianity was their consolation in dispersal; their men fought in the armies of New France; their architecture, clothing, language, values, and village polity became increasingly frenchified, so that by the time they settled their present reserve in Jeune-Lorette in 1697 under Jesuit direction, they were firmly part of French culture.

Our concern here is with the Catholic identity of the Hurons in the seventeenth century. It survived in the reserves around Quebec City and for a while in Iroquois captivity. It has continued to the present day among the thousand or so Lorette Hurons, who have intermarried with their Quebec neighbors for centuries now. French replaced Huron as the language of the Lorette reserve by the early twentieth century, and their community has been "exclusively Roman Catholic" (Morissonneau 1978: 390) since its inception. In 1984 a delegation of these Hurons met Pope John Paul II when he visited Sainte-Marie, the ancient mission site among the Hurons on Georgian Bay, where their forebears' Catholic faith commenced in the 1630s. Together with other Canadian Catholic Indians, they celebrated their long association with the Catholic Church.

By 1800 the first wave of French Jesuit missions in North America had come to an end. The task of christianizing the Indian cultures of the Northeast was far from complete. Perhaps the Catholics were only marginally more successful than the English Protestants on the eastern seaboard (see Axtell 1975: 277–288). Montagnais identified themselves as Catholics, although they lacked regular sacramental contact with the Church. The Hurons were in disarray; some were organized as Catholics, while others blamed their societal demise on the missions among them. In the chapters which follow we shall examine the isolated conversions of Iroquois along the valley of the St. Lawrence River and the loyalty of the Eastern Algonkians to their newfound faith. By the turn of the nineteenth century the Central Algonkians of the Great Lakes had received the words and gestures of French Christianity, but with little permanent effect.

The first two centuries of missions in New France demonstrated that Indians could be fervent Christians without necessarily giving up their Indian cultural spirituality. Many of the Indian Catholics "gradually evolved a distinctive style of Catholicism that combined their own traditional sensitivity to the spirit world with the rich visual and audial imagery of the baroque" (Grant 1985: 69). One of the locales at which Indian Catholicism flourished was a sacred site dedicated to Jesus' grandmother, Ste. Anne, on the Saint Lawrence River, north of Quebec City.

For many of the Catholic Indians of the former New France, Sainte-Anne-de-Beaupré still serves as an annual pilgrimage site, one that has functioned for over three hundred years. Montagnais and Hurons from Quebec, Penobscots and Passamaquoddies from Maine, Micmacs from New Brunswick, Mohawks from New York, as well as Indians from further afield, including Ojibways from west of the Great Lakes, travel today to a modern basilica constructed in 1923, following the paths of their ancestors who were drawn to the location by its miraculous repute.

Faith in Ste. Anne, mother of the Virgin Mary, came to New France with the Norman and Breton emigrés who entrusted their safety to her in their ocean crossings. Because of her reported intercession during violent storms, the Frenchmen established a shrine for her in 1658. One of the workmen at the locale was said to be cured of rheumatism. Within a decade the Jesuits had spread the word of Ste. Anne's powers and favors. Their Relations trumpeted the divine workings in New France through her agency; by her cult the Canadian land received its Christian sanctification (see Pouliot 1940: 90–91). Marie de l'Incarnation wrote of miracles at Ste. Anne's church: the paralyzed walked; the sick recovered; the blind came to see (Marie de l'Incarnation 1967: 312–313).

Before long the Indians of New France joined the pilgrims who adopted Ste. Anne as their special patron. A Huron named Marie Oendraka organized a pilgrimage to Sainte-Anne-de-Beaupré in 1671 from the Christian enclave of Sainte-Foy; the Jesuit who accompanied them described them in their line of canoes, chanting and praying in their native tongue in honor of the beneficent saint (see Thwaites 1896–1901, 54:298–300, 236–237). For many years they brought the remains of their deceased to be buried at the shrine. There are seventy-four Indian bodies in the cemetery, dating back to the 1670s, including one Larry Sock who died while participating in an "Indian Pilgrimage" in 1977 (Ste.-Anne-de-Beaupré, July 26, 1990). They named their local parishes after her and set up local shrines to her; however, on her feast day each year (July 26) and on their special pilgrimage day in late June, they have journeyed in large numbers to be with their preeminent Canadian saint. Along the way many of them (particularly Mohawks) stop at Cap-de-la-Madeleine, a sanctuary on the St. Lawrence north of Trois Rivières, dedicated to the Madonna.

Both shrines are major pilgrimage sites for Canadian Catholics, particularly for the Québecois. The Catholic Indians have thus come to share in the spiritual culture of New France. Annually they join a million pilgrims from across Canada and the United States—an estimated sixty million have visited the shrine over the centuries—to the grand basilica of silver granite. In their family units they park their campers and pitch their tents on the bank of the St. Lawrence. They light candles and kneel at the miraculous statue of Ste. Anne holding the Virgin Mary. They place photos of their loved ones to be blessed and healed. They make the stations of the cross and climb the twenty-eight holy stairs on their knees, along with other pilgrims. They bow before a relic of Ste. Anne—a portion of her forearm, and they join in the candlelight procession, walking beneath the hundreds of crutches and other symbols of miraculously cured maladies that hang from the pillars and arches. Like other pilgrims, some Indians come in hope of miraculous healing.

In 1990, amidst the acrimony of a standoff between Mohawks and Canadian military over the issue of land rights at Oka Reserve—a summer in which a Quebec policeman was killed in the fracas and Indian communities across Canada blockaded the roads crossing their territories in solidarity with their fellow First Peoples—Indians and other Catholics prayed in unison for the blessings of Ste. Anne. While commuters called Caughnawaga Mohawks "savages" for having disrupted their travel to work in Montreal, hundreds of pilgrims from many nations attended a "Messe en Montagnais" in the basilica. Elderly Montagnais women wearing *chapeaux* in the old style of New France sang and prayed in their native tongue, kneeling to tell their rosaries amidst their families. Some wore large crosses around their neck. A Montagnais deacon named Moises Bacon gave the sermon, which was translated into French for those pilgrims who did not speak Montagnais. Later in the afternoon, the Archbishop of Quebec, Maurice Couture, blessed Indians along with Blacks and Whites, with the unction of health, in order to cure their maladies. For all their differences of politics and culture, the Indians shared with other Canadians in the ritualism of the shrine to Ste. Anne.

The early Indian converts to Christianity in New France may have been attracted to Ste. Anne because their own mythologies often emphasized the closeness of their culture hero to his grandmother. Perhaps the story of Ste. Anne's miraculous fertility after many years of childlessness appealed to people among whom progeny were highly valued. Her healings were enough to draw Indians into the cultus in the seventeenth century, even without these adaptations of indigenous worldview. Over the centuries they have traveled to Sainte-Anne-de-Beaupré because she has become their beloved Catholic saint, whatever traditional attributes she may convey. It is her relation to the Virgin Mary and to Jesus that marks her as special, and her ability to cure that makes her so enduring over the years. Indians healed at Sainte-Anne-de-Beaupré tend to return annually (Bigtree, July 9, 1989).

One might say that the pilgrimage is primarily a social event to the Indians, born of a love of traveling and visiting. It is also true, however, that the Indians have designated *this Catholic shrine* as a place to journey to, a place for camping, a place for visiting, and a place to receive blessings for life. Their children learn about the shrine through yearly visits, and it becomes a familiar and special spot in their sacred geography. It is a place at which to conduct oneself with decorum. It is a location at which to pray. It fosters religiousness in a Catholic context and nurtures Catholic identity. Watching the Indian men and women saying their rosaries in the quiet corners of the basilica, one cannot doubt that they identify with the tradition of the place, and that Catholicism excites and inspires their acts of devotion.

✳ II ✳

Eastern Iroquoians,
Algonkians, and Muskogeans

The Iroquois, 17th - 20th Centuries

PEOPLES
○ Cities and towns
● Indian communities

QUEBEC

St. Lawrence River

Montreal

Caughnawaga (Kahnawake)

Oka (Lac-des-Deux-Montagnes)

St. Regis (Akwesasne)

Hogansburg

Ogdensburg (La Présentation)

Cornwall Island

ONTARIO

Bay of Quinté

Lake Ontario

Oswego

Syracuse

Onondaga

Rochester

Niagara Falls

Buffalo

NEW YORK

MOHAWK

Fonda (Ganadawage)

Auriesville (Ossernenon)

Albany

Mohawk River

Utica

ONEIDA

ONONDAGA

CAYUGA

SENECA

THE IROQUOIS AND THE JESUITS

The five nations of Iroquois who comprised the People of the Long-house (the *Hodenosaunee*), were the Mohawks, Oneidas, Onondagas, Cayugas, and Senecas. In the early seventeenth century, when they first encountered the French and Dutch in what is now New York State, they numbered over twenty thousand and were organized in a ritual and political confederacy. The League of the Iroquois provided these people with the potency to conduct effective economic and military strategies throughout the seventeenth century, and over the centuries they have displayed a reputation for persistent autonomy.

The national identities of the tribes in the League were based upon language, cross-binding lineage systems headed by clan mothers, chieftaincies representing both nations and clans in a centralized government, a system of condolences for mourning deceased leaders and selecting new ones, a cycle of seasonal ceremonies with a goal of uniting the earthly and celestial realms, mechanisms for adopting foreigners into the families of the League, and a powerful military tradition. The continuity of their institutions made the Iroquois formidable players in the colonial struggles of the 1600s and 1700s. Over the past two centuries several Iroquois communities have maintained a degree of independence within the United States and Canada, thanks to the persistence of these institutions.

In this context of stalwart persistence, many of the fifty thousand extant Iroquois have resisted the overtures of Christendom. From the viewpoint of the seventeenth-century French, the Iroquois constituted "the tyrants and persecutors" (Thwaites 1896–1901, 25:193) of the Church in the New World, and attempts to convert these natives were fraught with combat. Perhaps the first Iroquois instructed in Christian doctrine were two prisoners near Quebec in 1621. For decades to come, only the occasional Iroquois fell into the realms of the Jesuits, as the League (particularly the Mohawk nation) allied itself with the Dutch and against the French. By the early 1640s the Jesuits lamented that if the Iroquois were not defeated, the "country is always in danger of being ruined, the mission of being broken . . . ; the door of the gospel is closed to very many populous nations" (21:271). French policy vacillated between winning the Iroquois to friendship and trade, and decimating them in battle. Jesuits served both aspects of these colonial goals; hence, they wrote of the need to "vanquish the fury" of the Iroquois or to "succeed in means of winning them" to peace (125).

When Mohawk soldiers captured Father Isaac Jogues (along with Huron neophytes) in 1642, he tried to win his captors to his faith, and he was reported to have baptized several dozen Iroquois during a year of imprisonment before escaping (Donohoe 1895: 36–39). Having learned some of the Mohawk language, he returned to renew the evangelism of these foes of New France. Although he earned Iroquois respect for his bravery in the jaws of torture, he represented the enemies of Iroquois-Dutch trade and he was killed at Ossernonon (Auriesville, New York) in 1646. His Mohawk assailant was caught and killed by christianized Algonkians of the Sillery reserve in the following year, but not before he was baptized and given the slain priest's name. The Jesuits said that the slayer died with "the holy name of Jesus on his lips" (48). Jogues' death served as a paradigm for missionary martyrdom among the Iroquois and earned for them a fierce repute. Regarding the "blood of martyrs" as the "semen of Christianity" (as proclaimed in Latin on an interior wall of the church of Sainte-Anne-de-Beaupré), the Church of New France glorified Jogues and his fellow American martyrs as the sacrificial patriarchs of New World Catholicism. The Iroquois became the archetypal nemesis of noble Christians whose deaths would eventually nourish the faith of converts.

Even in the present day one can find expressions of this longstanding image within Catholic circles, for instance in a newsletter of the Catholic Worker movement in Syracuse, New York: "When the Jesuits arrived here in the 17th century, they faced not only the religion of the Iroquois which was a mixture of Manicheanism and cosmology dominated by dreams and spirits; but also, they confronted the Iroquois culture of war-making, torture and killing of their enemies" (*The Unity Grapevine,* March–April 1995: 4). The Iroquois have served as the bogeymen of missionary Catholicism in North America for several hundred years, wicked foils to the heroic Jesuits in books, plays, sermons, and pamphlets—much to the aggravated resentment of the Hodenosaunee and their defenders (see Lunstrom 1973). A contemporary Mohawk who grew up "in the shadows of the Church," but who identifies himself today as a "traditionalist," acknowledges that his people "actively persecuted" the priests and the Iroquois they converted in the seventeenth century. "We saw them as agents of radical change, military agents of the French during times of warfare." Iroquois violence against colonial Catholicism "gave us a colorful label in Jesuit history," he states—an image which has been "devastating" to Indian children who encountered it in parochial schools (George, November 19, 1996).

During the horrific beaver wars against the Hurons and their allies, particularly in 1648 and 1649, the Iroquois merited their renown, torturing, killing, and devouring a handful of Jesuit missionaries along with hundreds of Christian (and non-Christian) Hurons. The surviving Hurons dispersed and the remaining Jesuits retreated to the St. Lawrence strongholds of Quebec and Montreal. No sooner had the Iroquois demolished their Indian adversaries than, in 1653, they sent a delegation to Montreal, asking for a priest to live among them. It is not easy to understand the motivation of the Iroquois in making such a request. It would appear that the particular Iroquois in question were Onondagas, embroiled in an intra-league rivalry with the Mohawks. The former perhaps sought leverage by securing a fresh affiliation with the French.

When Simon Le Moyne, S.J., visited Onondaga in 1654 to test the sincerity of the Iroquois request, he found living among them and their fellow Iroquois many Huron adoptees, captives, and slaves, including what the Jesuits called a "Captive Church, embracing more than a thousand Christians" (Thwaites 1896–1901, 41:133). Without the benefit of sacraments or clerical contacts, these scattered Huron Christians were practicing aspects of Catholic worship. As Le Moyne passed through Iroquois villages, many Christian Hurons expressed a desire to receive his blessings and christenings for their children born since the time of their captivity.

There were also many Hurons among the Iroquois with strong dispositions against the Jesuits, having experienced the diseases, arguments, and dissolution of the Huron society under the priestly aegis in the 1640s. These Hurons warned the Iroquois against purported Jesuit witchery. They said that the priests forbade native rituals, brought scourges with them, and that the rite of baptism caused death among the Indians (Richter 1985: 2).

Hurons of the Christian party spoke favorably of their religion and its sacerdotal practitioners, thus making some Iroquois receptive to a Jesuit mission. The Onondaga ambassadors who came to Quebec were favorably impressed by the Ursuline seminary. An Onondaga spokesman thus welcomed Le Moyne in council, pledging to send his young girls "as hostages to the sisters in Quebec" (Donohoe 1895: 67; cf. Marie de l'Incarnation 1967: 213–214), if the priests would establish a permanent presence among the Iroquois. At Onondaga Father Le Moyne made his first Iroquois conversion, that of John Baptist Achiongeras.

The Iroquois wished to swell their forces by making their Huron captives a loyal population. The captors therefore permitted them their religious practice and invited the Jesuits to enhance it with their presence. Indeed, it would appear that the Onondagas hoped to import refugee Hurons from Quebec to Iroquoia through the strategy of establishing Jesuit missions. The Onondagas invited the Hurons to come live with them—and not with the Mohawks—now that they were defeated. Together, the Iroquois and Hurons (for the Onondagas claimed to represent Oneidas, Cayugas, and Senecas, too) would make a populous people, cemented through profitable trade with the French. After all, it was for the trade that the Iroquois had waged war so recently. The Hurons feared a deadly ruse, and yet they hesitated to refuse such an invitation from so strong a foe. When they consulted with their French hosts, the Jesuits offered to plant themselves among the Iroquois. After the priests were settled, it would be safe for the Hurons to accept the offer. For their part, the Jesuits hoped to effect the conversion and pacification of the Iroquois by living among them and by bringing a substantial number of Huron Christians to set an example of French Catholic culture.

Father Le Moyne was startled to find so many Christian Hurons, particularly women, already present in Iroquoia. He wrote, "One calls me a brother, another an uncle, another a cousin; never have I had so many kinsfolk" (Thwaites 1896–1901, 41:99). Perhaps, then, the defeat of the Hurons would prove to be a blessing in disguise, because it would lead to Iroquois conversions under the influence of the Huron neophytes. Father Le Moyne agreed to send his fellow Jesuits to the Iroquois, and from 1656 to 1658 they labored in this new field. Fathers Joseph Chaumonot and Claude Dablon said what was probably the first mass in what would become New York State. The priests offered catechetical instruction, preaching the doctrines of sin, guilt, heaven, and hell. One Jesuit wrote that among the Iroquois, "We hardly ever ceased from morning to night to Preach, to Catechize, to Baptize, to teach the Prayers, and to answer the questions put to us on all sides, so great was the inclination manifested by those good people toward the Faith" (43:181). The Iroquois "nature is not so barbarous," commented another priest, "that it cannot be tamed, and made to take pleasure in our ingenious devices for making them enjoy our Mysteries" (42:131).

The priests asked the Iroquois to alter their cultural patterns, doing away with pagan feasts, dances, polygamy, dream-guessing, and healing rituals. The Onondagas, Oneidas, Cayugas, and Senecas greeted the priests generously in 1656 and 1657, asking for French traders to live among them; however, they balked at the changes. "The Jesuits, for all their tolerance and cultural relativism when compared to other seventeenth-century missionaries," notes a modern scholar, "required of their converts massive reorientations of behavior and belief" (Richter 1983: 11). The Iroquois as a people were not prepared to alter their lives so radically or to accept Christian theology so thoroughly.

Nonetheless, baptisms did take place, and in substantial numbers. "The women especially listened to the words of truth" (Shea 1855: 235) orated by the Jesuits. The first female Onondaga to be christened was Madeleine Totonharason, who resisted the gentile ministrations of her fellows on her deathbed. After her passing her relatives begged for baptism because they wanted to emulate the peace of her death, secure in knowing where they would spend the eternity of afterlife (Thwaites 1896–1901, 44:37–39). By the late 1650s there were as many as sixteen hundred Iroquois converts, according to the Jesuits. Their Christian community consisted primarily of Onondagas, Hurons, and Neutrals, "all bound together by the common tie of faith, which made master and slave kneel down side by side" (Shea 1855: 235).

If the Onondaga plan was to gain preeminence in the League of the Iroquois by securing French priests and trade along with Huron adoptees, their rivals, the Mohawks, were intent upon obstructing them. In 1656 they attacked Hurons near Quebec, threatening to annihilate them if they did not come to live with *them*, the Mohawks. Over the next two years they killed dozens of Huron Christians, apparently focusing upon the most fervent believers, such as Jacques Oachonk, whom they tortured mercilessly. The Mohawks hoped to terrorize the Hurons into their own villages; the effect was to scare off the Jesuits, who abandoned the Iroquois missions in 1658 under threat of Mohawk attack.

From the relative security of Quebec City, the first Bishop of Canada, Francis de Laval, encouraged the defeat of the Iroquois in 1659 for being "a scourge" (in Jaenen 1986b: 31) upon New France. A Jesuit stated at the same time that the use of military force would perhaps be the best plan to promote Christianity among these peoples:

> [T]he destruction of the enemy would give new life to this whole coun-
> try and cause here a reign of peace, the sweets of which France is now
> tasting, and can share with us if she will. Let her only say, "I will;" and
> with the word she opens Heaven to a host of Savages, gives life to this
> colony, preserves her new France, and acquires a glory worthy of a most
> Christian Kingdom. (Thwaites 1896–1901, 45:199–201)

Throughout the 1660s hostilities alternated with peace overtures. At one point a delegation of Onondagas and Cayugas came to Montreal asking for priests and sisters. They claimed that there were more Chris-tians than pagans at Onondaga, and one of their members led the faithful in prayer each morning (Donohoe 1895: 95–97). At other times the French and Iroquois warred upon each other, setting back any hope of constructing permanent missions.

In 1666 the Marquis de Tracy led thirteen hundred soldiers, includ-ing christianized Indians, into Mohawk country, singing hymns and erecting a cross on the site of a subdued principal village "as a re-minder of the power of the French and the importance of Christianity" (ibid., 101). With this victory the French hoped to end the years of in-termittent missionary efforts with a decisive thrust. They established a peace with the Iroquois and the Jesuits once again entered Iroquoia.

As in the 1650s, the Jesuits were amazed to find so many devout Christian Hurons in the Iroquois villages, including those of the Mo-hawks. The Huron devotionalism drew the interest of Mohawk gen-tiles; in the other Iroquois cantons there were Iroquois neophytes eager to greet the priests once again. "The mothers bring us their little children," reported Father François Le Mercier, "that we may make the sign of the Cross on their foreheads; and they themselves are accus-tomed to do the same before putting them to bed. Their ordinary con-versation in the Cabins is about Hell and Paradise, of which we often speak to them" (Thwaites 1896–1901, 51:209–211). The Jesuits built chapels, ministered to the sick and dying (including captives about to be tortured and killed), and led the interested Indians in hymns and catechism.

There was also great opposition to the priests. The Iroquois resorted to their dreams to counter the claims of the missionaries regarding heaven. For example, at Onondaga an Indian envisioned men falling from heaven with wounds given them by their enemies. Father John Pierron found the Mohawks in the same year clogging their ears so they would not have to hear his sermons. To overcome their resistance he drew an illustration of hell.

> full of demons so terrible (both in their faces and in the chastisements they are inflicting upon damned Savages) that it is impossible to look upon it without trembling. In it is depicted an old Iroquois woman, who is stopping up her ears so as not to hear a Jesuit that desires to instruct her. She is surrounded by devils, who are hurling fire in her ears and tormenting her on other parts of her body. (Marie de l'Incarnation 1967: 352)

He also painted a portrait of paradise to demonstrate the benefit of a Catholic baptism.

With so much emphasis placed upon the afterlife, some Iroquois began to dream of heaven and hell, desiring the former and dreading the latter, and once again they asked to be baptized. Their relatives argued against them, and as among the Hurons in the previous generation, factions started to form over the issue of Christian association. By 1670 there were at least ten Jesuits among all five nations of Iroquois; in each there were Hurons—including professing Christians, gentiles, and apostates—and there were Iroquois both for and against the missionary enterprise. Some built crosses in their towns. Others warned that Christianity was the root of new diseases. Still others sought baptism, but when illness struck they turned to their native religious practitioners for cures.

The Christian Hurons constituted the bulwark of the missionized community, some serving as hosts for the priests, others leading prayers and instructions. They defended the Catholic faith against the Protestant critique of Dutchmen, explaining their devotion to Mary, the use of rosaries, the cross, and telling in theological terms why their carrying these holy items should not be construed as idolatry. We do not pray to a cross or a rosary bead, they explained; these things remind us of God, a pure spirit who cannot be seen (Donohoe 1895: 130–131). These Hurons were joined by new Iroquois converts like the Onondaga Garakontie, who protected Jesuits and native Christians in the 1660s and 1670s. He allied himself with French power, both military and spiritual, serving as a negotiator between his people and the French, and in the process gained a reputation as a "chief" (Richter 1984: 154–156). He renounced his traditional use of dreams for spiritual enlightenment, gave up polygamy, and turned his back on the cycle of Iroquois ceremonialism, receiving the name Daniel through baptism in Quebec in 1670. "I cannot deny that I have been sinful," he proclaimed openly; "my conduct, in the license that I have allowed myself in the misuse of the marriage relation, is only too well known. I have blushed for it before God. . . . But you will bear me witness to the vow which I have taken, and which I now once more renew, to change my manner of life. . . . Cease to expect me," he declared to his fellow Iroquois, "to lend my support and countenance to your dreams, or to uphold and sanction the superstitious practices of our ancestors. All this is forbidden to me, as contrary to God's Laws" (in Thwaites 1896–1901, 55:57). For the Jesuits he became the leading Iroquois, the model of Christian piety, the ally they could rely on until his death in the winter of 1677–78 (see Shea 1855: 242–286).

By the time of his death the Jesuits believed that they were making some headway among the Iroquois. In each Iroquois canton there were Indians who had eschewed the ceremonial solidarity of aboriginal life. There were frequent acts of devotionalism. A woman refused sin with a medicine man. A man prepared for his death with prayer. Another counted his sins with piles of corn kernels, each heap representing a type of offense to God. Some seemed willing to lose status or ceremonial authority among their tribe in order to take baptism; others turned to Christian rituals after defeat in combat or illness. In 1673 the Jesuits established the Confraternity of the Holy Family at all their Iroquois missions, in order to teach the catechumens "how to form the family life according to the model Christian home" (Donohoe 1895: 168). Despite the opposition of the Protestant Dutch and English (themselves battling over control of New World trade), the French missioners held firm in their purpose for a decade.

From 1668 to 1678 they baptized over two thousand (ibid.), making perhaps four thousand Iroquois conversions from the 1650s to the 1670s (Richter 1985: 8); however, most of these were among the sick and dying, and so there was still much to accomplish. In 1679 perhaps eighteen hundred of the nine thousand living Iroquois regarded themselves as Christians, including children (ibid.). These converts may have been drawn to baptism by political or economic motives—the hopes for French alliance or trade—or by the desire to attract supernatural power in earthly enterprises such as healing and fighting. They may have been guided to christening by traditional patterns of dreams or by an awe for the Jesuits' spiritual prowess. Nonetheless, more than one Iroquois followed the pattern of Garakontie and remained a "committed Christian" (7), passing on aspects of the faith to their children. Some of these Christians faced persecution in their villages; many left their own people to live among fellow Christians in the reserves established by the Jesuits along the St. Lawrence River. Still others were "killed witnessing to Jesus and the Church" (*The Unity Grapevine,* March–April 1995: 4) as pagan Iroquois attempted to force Christian escapees to return to their homes and aboriginal ways of life. Catholic hagiographers still regard them as "martyrs" (April–May 1994: 2) who suffered and died under "demonic attacks against the nascent Church and its early disciples of Jesus" (March–April 1995: 4). The names of Etienne Teganauokoa, Françoise Gonannhatenha, and Marguerite Garongouas, stand among the lists of U.S. Catholic martyrs (see Béchard 1976: 203–223).

There were enough christened Iroquois in the 1670s that the social fabric of the villages was ripped along its seams. When leaders like Garakontie became sincere Christians and refused to participate in traditional ceremonies; when they refused to recite legends of the origin of the League, calling them false stories (Thwaites 1896–1901, 58:211); when they eschewed kinship with their pagan relatives and faced ostracism with a bold calm or by withdrawal to afar; the Iroquois faced the same kind of dissolution experienced by the Hurons before them. If the Christians remained, factionalism was inevitable, since one part of the community boycotted the religious events of the other and this "opposition was mandatory" (Richter 1983: 15). If the Christians fled, and as many as fifteen hundred did so in the 1670s and 1680s (Donohoe 1895: 200–202), the Iroquois home communities suffered from a significant loss of population. Whether they stayed or left, the Christians brought about internecine violence, as fights broke out in the cantons, or as the home communities raided the Christian reserves to regain their kinsmen.

In the 1680s the ascendant English in New York encouraged the Iroquois to expel the Jesuits from their midst, in order to solidify the "Covenant Chain" (the system of alliance between the British and their Indian partners) against New France. With most Christian Iroquois having abandoned their homes, the gentile parties held power and were only too glad to rid themselves of Catholic influence. By 1687 only two Jesuits inhabited Iroquoia, and they fled in that year before the French attack on the Senecas launched by the Marquis Denonville. Catholic missions resurfaced in the 1690s, but in the first decade of the eighteenth century the English authorities of New York outlawed Catholic priests from their territories, and by 1709 no priests remained in the English portions of Iroquoia.

As long as the French remained a colonial power, some Iroquois in the English realm were willing to entertain the claims of the French faith and receive Catholic baptism in Montreal and other French strongholds. As late as the mid-1700s there were still Iroquois with Catholic leanings. For example, at Onandaga in 1750, a Catholic chief was observed (Wallace 1945: 311–313) in friendly debate with a Protestant compatriot regarding the relative merits of their respective sects. The Catholic, named Tahashwuchdioony, related the assertions of the French fathers to Catholic biblical primacy and spiritual authority. Moreover, the priests were reported to have the power to determine the eternal resting-place of baptized Indians' souls. The priests assured Tahashwuchdioony that with their help, he could decide whether to enjoy his afterlife in the paradise of the good Frenchmen, or—if he so desired—in "the place where the forefathers of the Indians go" (312). For all his faith in the priests' prowess, Tahashwuchdioony had caught the clerics in "Lies" (312) about their ability to visit heaven and hell, and he was determined never to enter the French afterworld. "We are cheated by the white people in this World," he concluded. "If we don't stand clear of them, the[y] will cheat us in the other and make Slaves of us" (313).

A Catholic commentator has stated that "Apparently, the Iroquois was the greatest failure of the Jesuit missions" (Mulvey 1936: 120). To agree, however, is to ignore the history of Iroquois Catholicism in the reserves established by the French in the St. Lawrence River valley. The Jesuits exhorted Christian Hurons and Iroquois to emigrate from Iroquoia to the reductions around Quebec City and Montreal, to Lorette, the Bay of Quinté (where Sulpicians served them from 1668), and most prominently to a site within the seigniory of LaPrairie named for St. Francis Xavier.

Father Pierre Raffeix initiated a colony of Frenchmen at LaPrairie in 1667, constructing a chapel, and in the following year a dozen Indians spent their winter there, receiving religious instruction. Among these were an old Huron, Francis Xavier Tonsahoten, whom the Jesuits had found living his Christian faith among the Oneidas, and his wife, a former Erie slave, Ganneaktena, now adopted by the Oneidas. She took the baptismal name of Catherine in 1668. These became the first leaders of the Christian Indian enclave at LaPrairie (Kentaké) and received sacramental blessing for their marriage by Bishop Laval. Tonsahoten built a cabin for the neophytes, and in 1669 Catherine and other women sowed the first plots of corn. In 1670 as many as twenty families of Indians traveled to LaPrairie to investigate the conditions of the fledgling colony, and many of them decided to stay. The next year the community elected Tonsahoten as war chief and another Huron, Paul Honoguenhag, as *dogique*. Father Jacques Fremin became the religious superior at LaPrairie. He found the Indians devout in their reception of Holy Communion and in the singing of hymns, exceeding, he said, the spiritual practices of the French. The catechumens had decided that anyone who wanted to live in the reduction would have to give up "dream superstition, polygamy, and drink" (Béchard 1976: 30). When French traders opened a liquor shop at LaPrairie in 1672, the Indians refused to have any of it. With the help of Ganneaktena, Father Fremin formed the Confraternity of the Holy Family to foster Catholic solidarity, particularly among the women.

By 1673 LaPrairie had gained the attention of eight hundred Indian visitors, two hundred of whom had decided to make the reserve their home. There were as many as twenty-two different Indian nations represented at St. Francis Xavier, including Montagnais and other Algonkians as well as the Iroquoians (ibid., 38–39). The largest number came from the Mohawk country, where the sizable number of converts felt the blow of recrimination from their gentile relatives. Some of these settlers at the reduction were refugees, their peoples having been scattered by colonial wars. Others chose to leave their home villages in order to dedicate themselves to a new, Christian way of life. "It is no slight proof of faith of These good savages," wrote Father Jean de Lamberville in 1673,

> that they have abandoned Their Native country, Their petty household effects, and Their fields abounding in corn; and have sought a foreign land, to live there,—in poverty and want, it is true; but also that they may be able publicly to profess Christianity there, which they could not do at home on account of the great disorders caused by intemperance. (Thwaites 1896–1901, 57:109)

Not every emigrant was a Christian, although almost all became so under the strict rule of Fremin and the Indian *dogiques*. Hospitality prevailed at LaPrairie, and the newcomers found themselves enveloped by a peacefulness not unlike that idealized by their native culture. Perhaps the greatest attraction of the reserves like St. Francis Xavier and Lorette "was the way in which the Christian villages paradoxically provided a social environment in keeping with the traditional values that now seemed seldom to exist in the faction-ridden villages of Iroquoia" (Richter 1984: 196). In a fifteen-month period in 1673–74 almost two hundred Iroquois moved to LaPrairie, and by 1682 the village housed six hundred people, in more than a hundred families (179–184). These included assorted Algonkians and Iroquoians.

"As their numbers increased daily," the Jesuits recorded, "it was soon found necessary to appoint captains to govern the village, and especially for the preservation of the Faith. . . . no one would be admitted into the village who was not resolved to abstain from three things, namely: the idolatry of dreams, the changing of wives, and drunkenness" (Thwaites 1896–1901, 58:77). The *dogiques* made everyone swear publicly to live according to these strictures, and "if any one relapsed . . . he should be shamefully expelled" (ibid.). Under this regimen the Indians attained a standard of devotionalism that impressed the missionaries mightily. On Sundays and feastdays the catechumens attended mass faithfully:

> After the sermon, the Dogique Intones the *Credo* in Their language, in The Church plain-song, and they thus continue Their Chanting Until the end of the mass. About 10 o'clock the bell rings once more, to call them to the Chapel; and then, instead of the 2nd mass that they were in the habit Of hearing, they recite The Entire Rosary of the blessed Virgin. (60:281)

In private the Indians said acts of contrition and other prayers and began to engage in various penitential practices: "The humble and cheerful acceptance of the trials of everyday existence, the voluntary deprivation of the comforts of life in order to reestablish the order disrupted by sin and, finally, voluntary, self-inflicted suffering justifiable only in relation to the Transcendent Being" (Béchard 1976: vii–ix). In particular some women "performed incredible mortifications" (ix) which matched the Counter-Reformation asceticism of the priests and nuns of New France.

The *dogiques* like Paul Honoguenhag and the Oneida Garonhiagué proved to be vigorous exhorters of the faith, delivering sermons, leading prayers and hymns, administering baptism, and supervising moral life both in the village and on hunting parties, away from the priests. These catechists explicated "the mysteries of the faith, the Incarnation, Redemption, the Last Judgment, the pains of hell, the joys of heaven" (Shea 1855: 300). Father Fremin "unhesitatingly admitted that these laymen were a hundred times more effective than he" (Béchard 1976: 129) in spreading the faith. Other Christians—including those who were converted at LaPrairie, like Joseph Togouiroui the Mohawk—returned to their native cantons to recruit for the reduction, or wrote letters to their people, encouraging emigration to the Christian community. And so the numbers continued to swell. In 1675 Bishop Laval confirmed eighty LaPrairie natives, and "the mission now rivalled that of Paraguay" (Shea 1855: 300) in Christian holiness.

The Jesuits fought against the French traffic in alcohol among Indians, seeing as they did its baneful effects. The priests tried to have laws passed against the trade, but the French authorities wanted to profit from it, arguing that the Dutch or English would provide liquor if the French did not. In the mid-1670s LaPrairie's vows against alcohol were tested because the Frenchmen among them, both within LaPrairie and at nearby Montreal, undermined sobriety. Father Fremin realized that he would have to move his Indian colony, making it more isolated from demoralizing influences. At the same time the soil at LaPrairie was becoming depleted, as a result of continuous corn horticulture, and so in 1676 the reduction moved to Sault St. Louis (Kahnawake), two miles up river from the prairie to the rapid, and changed its name to St. Peter's. Here the Indians left the Frenchmen behind to form an all-Indian village under Jesuit direction.

At Kahnawake their devotional life continued to flourish. They learned their chants—more than thirty of them, according to their chronicler, Father Claude Chauchetière. They marked Ash Wednesday, Palm Sunday, Good Friday, and the feast of the Assumption with pious ritualism. Boys served at mass as acolytes. Women engaged in private acts of self-abnegation, led by the new Mohawk arrival of 1677, Kateri Tekakwitha, and others. When a smallpox epidemic in 1678 struck the village with less severity than the pagan Iroquois cantons, the Christians thanked God and reaffirmed their faith.

François Tsonnatoüan and Marguerite, newlyweds in their early twenties, came to Kahnawake in 1670. So struck was he by the Christian value of virginity and by his sinfulness before marriage, that he wanted to live with his wife as brother and sister. The Jesuits recommended against this asceticism but encouraged him in other devotions. The Iroquois man always wore a rosary, by which he prayed the Apostles' Creed, Our Fathers, Hail Marys, and Glorias. He carried with him a picture book (developed by Chauchetière, following the technique of a fifteenth-century Breten missioner) illustrating scenes from the Old and New Testament as well as commandments, vices, and virtues. He was a member of the Confraternity of the Holy Family, and until his death in 1695 he maintained a pious Christian life, according to the Jesuits (see Béchard 1976: 145–149).

A circle of women at Kahnawake, including Jeanne Gouastraha (Oneida), Marie-Thérèse Tegaiaguenta (Oneida), Marie Skarichions (Huron), Marguerite Gagoüithon (Onondaga), and Kateri Tekakwitha (Mohawk) flogged each other with willow shoots, stuck themselves with thorns, and wore iron belts as implements of chastisement (see ibid., 159–198). We shall examine Tekakwitha's life and cult more closely; however, all of these women were renowned for their ascetic practices at Kahnawake in the late 1670s and 1680s.

These practices combined the intensity of Iroquois and Catholic traditions, as the Indians attempted to create a religiousness that would inspire the community to unity. Traditional Iroquois religion's focus had been to gain contact between the humans of the earth and the first people of the sky world; this they attempted through rituals of thanksgiving and acts of self-transcending ecstasy. At Kahnawake the priests permitted the major Iroquois festivals of the year, even syncretizing them with the Catholic liturgical calendar. Harvest coincided with All Souls' Day, Green Corn with Corpus Christi, Midwinter with the Circumcision of Jesus, and so forth. Dream divination was strictly prohibited at St. Peter's, however, and so (at least according to one modern theorist) the Christian Indians turned to public penance in order to achieve personal ecstasy. In their encouragement of intense asceticism at Kahnawake, "the Jesuits unwittingly contributed to the creation of a ritual system for allowing Iroquois to travel again, to the other side of the sky" (Blanchard 1982: 97).

If Kahnawake became famous for its praxis of self-torture, it was also known as a bastion of French loyalism among the Iroquoians. The Indians of the reserve served as eyes and ears for the leaders of New France against possible Iroquois attack, and over the years the Christians joined military campaigns against their pagan relatives. On occasion pagan and Christian Iroquois killed one another in these battles; however, they often let it be known that their fight was not with each other (see Devine 1922: 100–104), even though some Iroquois, especially at Onondaga, came to despise the Jesuits and other Christian evangelizers. They continued to communicate and trade with one another across the religious divide and to regard each other as relatives, albeit removed by differences of faith. As the Jesuits abandoned the Iroquois cantons after Denonville's expedition of 1687, the stream of converts emigrating to Kahnawake dwindled to a trickle; gentile Iroquois called then for their christianized relatives to return home to Iroquoia. But even when the Protestant English at Albany tried to woo the Kahnawake inhabitants with promises of profitable trade, they would not leave their reduction. A Kahnawake chief stated in 1700, "I am wholly beholden to the French in Canada for the light I have received, to know that there was a Saviour born for mankind" (in ibid., 140). By that year nearly two-thirds of the Mohawks were already living in Canada, clothed and protected by the French, and providing warriors for the French fight against the English. Onondaga and Mohawk pagans might tempt their Christian relatives to return, but the converts would not live apart from what they viewed as the essentials of their new religion: "1. forgiving of sins By the preist [*sic*]. 2. prayers for the dead. 3. That the mother of Christ must be worshipped. 4. That the signe of the Crosse must be Used. 5. That the pope alone is ord[a]ined to speak with god. 6. That prayers must be used before the Images" (in Axtell 1986: 256).

There were several other moves before the reduction finally became established at its present location at Caughnawaga in 1716. By this time the community had almost two generations of Christian tradition. Most inhabitants had been born in the reduction and baptized in infancy; these had little or no contact with any religious life other than that of Christianity, however influenced it might be by Iroquois ritualism. They spoke Iroquois language (Mohawk predominated) as their primary language, but the priests who served them saw little else to distinguish them from the Frenchmen of surrounding parishes (Devine 1922: 183–184). Among the denizens of Caughnawaga, however, were captives gained in forays against the English in the eighteenth century, including the 1704 raid on Deerfield, Massachusetts. Many of the family names at Caughnawaga—Rice, Tarbell, Hill, Williams, Jacobs, and others—came from these captives, who, along with their descendants, became over time "both Catholic and Iroquois" (153).

Throughout the 1700s the Caughnawaga Catholics proselytized the Mohawk Valley Mohawks with some success. They also kept contact with other Catholic Indian communities, including the mixed Algonkian and Iroquoian reserve at Oka (Mission du Lac-des-Deux-Montagnes), ministered by Sulpician priests, the Hurons at Lorette, the Abenakis of St. Francis, and the christianized Onondagas and Cayugas on the St. Lawrence River at a reserve called La Présentation. These Indians formed a "partly religious, partly political confederation known as the Seven Indian Nations of Canada, . . . united mainly by their Catholicism" as well as "their loyalty to French interests" against the British (Snow 1994: 140). By midcentury, however, the Caughnawaga community was feeling the pinch of population, both within its own ranks and from the expanding city of Montreal. There was not enough arable land for the Indians to maintain subsistence, and the brandy traffic periodically debauched the Christian band. As a result, Father Antoine Gordon, S.J., persuaded some Caughnawaga families to remove themselves in 1755 to a new upriver site, St. Regis, the last mission founded by the Jesuits of New France. This new community, was joined in the late 1750s by various Catholic Iroquois from other Jesuit missions in Quebec; Onondagas and Cayugas who had been living for a short time at the mission of La Présentation; and some Mohawk refugees from the Mohawk River valley. Some Abenakis and Senecas were incorporated into the village in the early 1760s.

Many of these refugees were escaping from the violence of the French and Indian War, in which they were French allies. The Iroquois at La Présentation, for example, had been active combatants against the British at Oswego; when the English gained the upper hand in the area surrounding Lake Ontario, the Catholic Indians were forced to seek refuge at the new mission at St. Regis, halfway between the Great Lake and Montreal. St. Regis thus served the French as a buffer against English inroads, whereas for the Caughnawaga emigrants it posed a solution to the "continual drunkenness" (St. Louis 1951b) they witnessed in their old reserve. Some historians suggest that St. Regis also attracted a number of gentile Mohawks, eager for trade with the French but unwilling to live in close proximity to Montreal (see Devine 1922: 253–255), and others say that Caughnawaga Iroquois of white heritage preferred the new mission to the squabbling confines of the old reduction (see Donohoe 1895: 254–255). St. Regis therefore came into existence as a settlement of diverse ethnicities and interests. Welcoming the refugees to St. Regis was Chief Pierre Karekohe Tarbell, son of a captured and adopted Englishman and a Caughnawaga Mohawk mother.

When France capitulated to Britain at the close of the French and Indian War, the Jesuits were curtailed in their missionizing; however, they were not immediately banned, and they continued to minister at Caughnawaga at least until 1783. Concurrently, the British made allies among the Mohawk Valley Mohawks and other Iroquois within New York State, and this "Covenant Chain" stretched its loyalties to the Catholic Indians. During the American Revolution the Caughnawaga Indians maintained their neutrality, and in the years following the death of their last Jesuit missioner, they kept their distance from the institutional Church. They expected to gain ownership of their land once the Jesuits retired, but the Diocese of Quebec claimed the property for its own. This led to a cooling of relations between Church and Caughnawaga. The Indians refused to support a diocesan priest and form a parish; the diocese was reluctant to take on all the costs of maintaining a mission. The pastor in charge of Caughnawaga at the turn of the nineteenth century found the Indians were ungovernable and called upon the bishop of Quebec to admonish them. In 1802 the prelate wrote to Caughnawaga, exhorting its parishioners to live up to the spiritual example of their forebears. Their ancestors, he said, had been tractable, sober, pious Catholics, whereas they were insolent to the priest, frequently drunk, and concerned only with idleness and worldly things (Devine 1922: 315–316).

Other diocesan priests throughout the nineteenth century struggled against the independence of the Caughnawaga Catholics, as well as against the periodic inroads of Protestantism and alcohol abuse. In 1836 the bishop deprived the Indians of Corpus Christi and Assumption processions, a bonfire on the eve of the feast of St. John the Baptist, and midnight mass at Christmas, as punishment for their "harshly treating" (ibid., 406) Rev. Joseph Marcoux, who served there for thirty-six years and who supervised the construction of the present church, St. Francis Xavier, in 1845. The priest said that the Indians' morals were good and that they were loyal Catholics, but the bishop further threatened to deprive them of high mass on Sundays if they were not more obedient to their pastor.

In the early part of the nineteenth century, many male Caughnawagans traveled to the western parts of North America as furtrappers in the employ of the North West Company. Especially between 1800 and 1820, but even in later decades, their long absences were blamed for the dwindling population and familial instability at the reserve. In the West, however, they acted as missionaries for their Christian faith. Among the Flatheads they found especial welcome, and they brought to these Indians the religious observances of Christian Caughnawaga. Ignace Lamoose was the leader of a band of Caughnawagans who intermarried with the Flatheads, and he became a veritable apostle among them, serving as catechist and prayer leader. He introduced a seven-day Christian calendar and instituted formal Sunday devotions. His praise of the virtues of Christendom led to a Flathead search for a permanent Catholic mission, a subject of a chapter to come in this volume.

At home in Caughnawaga, Catholicism was a family tradition throughout the nineteenth century. For instance, Joseph Delisle and Anne Katsitsiaroroks, both from the reserve, married in 1846, and by the early twentieth century they had 122 living descendants, all baptized Catholics. Delisle was master of the children's choir at Caughnawaga, and in 1910 he participated in a Eucharistic Congress in

Montreal, parading with other Caughnawagans past the church of Notre Dame and fasting to mark the special event in the Catholic calendar. He and his family were prominent representatives of the three thousand Catholic Iroquois in Lower Canada—Caughnawaga, St. Regis, and elsewhere—in the early 1900s (see *The Indian Sentinel* 1912: 5–14). Catholic spokesmen might complain that these Indian Catholics preferred to fish, hunt, or "lazily till the soil" (Donohoe 1895: 205), rather than pursue formal education; however, in the eyes of Church authorities Catholic faith had taken firm root among the Iroquois of the St. Lawrence reductions, particularly Caughnawaga, Oka, and St. Regis.

KATERI TEKAKWITHA

The Jesuits entered the Iroquois heartland in the 1650s in order to minister to the Christian Hurons captured and adopted by the Iroquois between 1649 and 1654. The priests also hoped to subdue the Iroquois through diplomatic and spiritual ministrations. Some of the Iroquois nations permitted the Jesuits' incursion; however, the Mohawks resisted until a French army invaded their territory in 1666. The following year, three Jesuits came to their first Mohawk village in the Mohawk River valley, Ganadawage. Among the Mohawks in this village was a young girl born in 1656 at another Mohawk village, Ossernenon (now Auriesville, New York, where Father Jogues was killed in 1646). She was the daughter of an Algonkian mother and an Iroquois father, both of whom had died in a smallpox epidemic when she was four. The girl was left pockmarked, partially crippled, and nearly blind by the disease. In 1667 she was living with the family of her uncle, Iowerano, a longtime trading ally of the Dutch and an opponent of French Catholic inroads. The girl's name was Tekakwitha, which has been interpreted in various ways: "she-pushes-with-her-hands" or "who walks groping for her way" (because of her faulty eyesight), "hard-working-woman," or "gathering-things-in-order" (Béchard 1994: n.p.; Weiser 1972: 36–37; Mitchell, August 7, 1986).

At Ganadawage the Jesuits built a chapel resembling a longhouse. A painting of crucified Christ hung over the altar, with images of Mary and Joseph to either side. The priests performed mass daily for the baptized Huron captives, and some Mohawks took an interest in the proceedings. Several of these learned lessons from a catechism and became attached to the Jesuits. At this and other Mohawk towns there were baptisms of youths and even adults.

In 1675 Father James de Lamberville, S.J., came to Ganadawage; within a year he had interested Tekakwitha in receiving baptism, along with two other girls. These joined the twenty-odd Christians in the town, not counting those who had already migrated with Joseph Togouiroui the catechist and others to the Jesuit reduction along the St. Lawrence River at LaPrairie. Having received her christening, the newly named Kateri (Catherine) tried to observe the Christian calendar, keeping Sundays free of work and attending mass regularly. Her conversion aroused opposition within her extended family, and before long, encouraged by Lamberville, she decided to flee to the St. Lawrence reduction. She arrived at St. Peter's Mission (Kahnawake) in 1677 with a letter of introduction for Father Pierre Cholenec, and she immediately joined the rounds of piety that ruled there.

At St. Peter's the bell rang every morning at 4:30 to wake the inhabitants for 5:00 A.M. mass. A second mass followed, which most adults attended, and a third mass at 8:00 A.M. drew the children, who then took their catechism. The Mohawks and other Iroquoians (including some Hurons) who dwelled in the reduction were isolated from non-Indians, who were permitted to visit the village but not to live there. The natives attended religious services freely and frequently, and sang hymns in their own language. They sang the ten commandments, the rosary, the creed, and the stations of the cross. They sang in their fields as well as in church. Like traditional Iroquois, they blessed their seasonal activities—their harvesting of corn, their fishing and hunting—with songs of thanksgiving, only now the words and melodies were derived from French Catholicism.

Kateri Tekakwitha entered these patterns and added to them, becoming, according to Father James Fremin, an "angel of charity" (in Weiser 1972: 149), looking after the old and infirm, delivering firewood to the needy, speaking words of kindness to everyone she encountered. At Christmas 1677, only a year after her baptism, Father Cholenec heard her first confession and she received her first communion. Usually the Jesuits were reluctant to let Indian converts receive the body of Christ until they completed several years of religious instruction. In Kateri's case, her intense devotional demeanor convinced the priest to avoid further delay. Her second Eucharist did not come until Easter 1678, since she spent the winter months hunting with her fellow Indians. All the while, she yearned for the reception of the blessed sacrament. Like the other Christian Iroquois, Kateri kept track of the passing days, observing Sundays with special prayers. On this hunting trip Kateri was humiliated by an accusation made against her—apparently unfounded—of sexual impropriety. She was determined to demonstrate her state of innocence when she returned to St. Peter's.

The Christian Indians at Kahnawake engaged in numerous sacrifices and penances to expiate their "sins." They wore hairshirts, kept fasts, exposed themselves to the cold, and performed other acts of self-abnegation. They did these things as good Iroquois would, hardening themselves against pain, torture, and starvation. Now they engaged in such asceticism as Christians, combining the native and Christian ethos of self-sacrifice.

Kateri struck up a friendship with an Oneida widow, Marie-Thérèse Tegaiaguenta; together they performed acts of penance, emulating the model set them by the Hospitalier nuns at the Hôtel-Dieu in Montreal. A third Indian woman, Marie Skarichions, joined them in their fasts and sacrifices, and they began to consult with Father Cholenec regarding their intensive devotionalism. More women joined this ascetic group, which they referred to as the "Slavery of the Blessed Virgin" (Béchard 1994: 104). Convinced of their innate sinfulness, "they scourged each other, 'intermingling prayer and penance,' after which they ran to the church, their hearts overflowing with joy. . . . They had never felt happier in their lives," it is said (108).

Soon Kateri outstripped the others in her imitation of Christ. She ceased to take part in amusements. She said the rosary in scant garments in the snow. She refused to wear moccasins and froze her feet, walking barefoot on the ice of winter. She ate sand and glass and scourged herself with branches until she bled. She continued to engage in charitable acts; however, she dedicated herself to the mortification of her flesh. She became a "great penitent" (109).

Taking a vow of perpetual sexual abstinence, she and her cohorts sought even greater identification with the Blessed Virgin and the nuns of their ideals. Kateri's little band of ascetic women, primarily virgins, possibly derived from the traditional Iroquois practice of secluding maidens in order to garner the spiritual power of their virginity for the benefit of the community. These virginal sodalities (*Ieouinnon*, in Blanchard 1982: 94) had fallen into decay during Kateri's lifetime, as European alcohol converted Iroquois maidens into foolish virgins, who would get drunk and perform extravagant acts. At Kahnawake it was possible for Kateri and her associates to reestablish the ideals of the traditional virgins, free of alcohol. Hence, according to some modern theorists, Kateri was resurrecting an Iroquois custom even as she imitated the Christian asceticism of the Hospital nuns and Jesuits. She was "no mere passive spectator in this unfolding of her life story: she embraced what the missionaries and other converts held out to her" and she engaged in a "revitalization" of Iroquois culture through her conversion and asceticism (Koppedrayer 1993: 294–295).

By 1679 Kateri's privations began to weaken her. The Jesuits tried to moderate her practices, yet in spring 1680 she increased her mortifications, and in April of that year, during Holy Week, she died, at age twenty-four, having received last rites.

Kateri Tekakwitha's life and death became central icons of the Jesuit missiology in North America. Father Cholenec penned a memoir of her saintliness within two weeks of her death and wrote several biographies of her over the decades, attributing miracles to her. Claude Chauchetière, S.J., memorialized her hejira to Kahnawake—escaping her pagan Mohawk relations—and her ascetic excesses unto death, thus fabricating a cult that developed around her at St. Peter's and its environs and especially among the Jesuits. She appeared to Chauchetière in his visions. He purportedly painted her portrait, which hangs at Caughnawaga where her bones were brought in 1720 from an earlier resting place. The record of her spiritual practices "deepened the piety of the French Jesuit community" (Grim 1991a: 15) in the late seventeenth and early eighteenth century, and in other realms worked by the Jesuits her name came to symbolize the miraculous transformational efficacy of Catholicism among Indian peoples—even though her asceticism combined Iroquois and Catholic ideals. She embodied the ideals of late medieval hagiography and proved the success of Jesuit efforts. A German Jesuit laboring among the Spaniards of Baja California in 1771 contrasted his lack of missionizing success to the glorious conversion of the Mohawk maiden, "whose grave with its many miracles shines brightly in Canada, and likewise the fortitude of so many others, women among them, who faced the cruel torture of fire among the inhuman Iroquois Indians" (Baegert 1979: 86). Thus her story grew. The suppression of the Jesuits worldwide in 1773 submerged the attention paid her, but in the nineteenth century the Jesuit revival resurrected the legendary Kateri.

Among the Catholic Iroquois, devotion to Tekakwitha never ceased in the eighteenth and nineteenth centuries. St. Peter's reduction burned down in 1690, and when the new Caughnawaga—now named for St. Francis Xavier—was founded in 1716, her body was transferred to the site. Over the centuries many thousands of Indians and non-Indians have journeyed to Caughuawaga to pay respects to the perpetual native virgin enshrined there. Jesuits have cared for the shrine since the early 1700s, and in 1972 her remains were placed in a marble tomb in the right transept of the church.

When a contingent of Caughnawaga families established the new Catholic community at St. Regis in 1755, they took with them half of her body for devotional purposes. A fire in 1762 destroyed that relic, and the cult of Kateri did not become palpable again at St. Regis until the Caughnawaga Mohawk priest, Michael Jacobs, S.J., initiated prayers regarding her in the mid-twentieth century. At Caughnawaga, however, the cult was continuous, fueled by Jesuits and by native oral tradition.

The Society of Jesus forwarded a petition in 1884 to the Third Plenary Council of Bishops in Baltimore for her canonization, and Indian communities administered by Jesuits—e.g., the Flatheads in Montana—reportedly called for Kateri to become "an object of . . . veneration in the church" (in *The Indian Sentinel* 1908: 5), along with the Jesuit martyrs such as Father Isaac Jogues. The Jesuits hoped that such veneration would bring more Indians into the Church, in addition to inspiring piety among all Catholic faithful. Beginning in 1885 pilgrims began to arrive at Kateri's birthplace in Auriesville, New York, to honor her and the French Jesuit martyrs who brought Catholicism to the Indians of the Northeast.

In 1932 Kateri was presented formally to the Vatican for consideration of sainthood, and in 1943 Pope Pius XII declared her venerable at the recommendation of his curial Congregation of Rites. As the Jesuit martyrs received their canonization, Kateri's shrine was established separately from theirs, in nearby Fonda, New York (where she had lived at Ganadawage), and the Conventual Franciscan Friars became custodians of the National Kateri Tekakwitha Shrine, replete with gift shop, museum, and an outdoor prayer pavilion, as well as a pilgrimage hill of the saints. The National Shrine also contains a Native American Peace Grove, featuring a quotation from Handsome Lake, the "Iroquois Prophet" who formulated the Longhouse Religion enjoined by traditionalist Iroquois in the United States and Canada. Nearby there is an archaeological investigation of Kateri's village.

From the 1930s the devotion to Kateri Tekakwitha grew beyond Iroquois circles. A Jesuit from Oregon wrote, "We lean on Catherine Tekakwitha's aid to provide us with needed funds to pay our bills and carry on" (*Our Negro and Indian Missions* 1933: 41). Another priest in Minnesota erected a local shrine to the Lily of the Mohawks, "for whose beatification the Indians are eager, having formed a Tekakwitha League" (ibid. 1939: 42), where they read Catholic devotional literature and recited prayers and hymns. Catholic clergy put on plays at Indian missions, celebrating Kateri's conversion, persecution, and death, and local Indian artists—e.g., the Coeur d'Alene Robert Campbell—recreated her imagined likeness in statuary, around which their people prayed (*The Indian Sentinel* 22, no. 7, September 1942: 99–100). In 1939 the Bishop of Fargo, North Dakota organized a support group for missionary priests and brothers in the central plains and northwest United States; he named it the Tekakwitha Conference. For four decades several dozen missioners attended annual meetings under Kateri's name, praying and planning strategy for the conversion of American Indians to full Catholic participation.

In the late 1970s devotions to Kateri Tekakwitha intensified, more than partially through the efforts of the reinvigorated and transformed Tekakwitha Conference. In 1976 the conference focused attention on the relationship between "native symbolism and Christian spirituality" (Starkloff 1982: n.p.)—a topic fitting to post–Vatican II experimentation, but also suitable to Kateri's syncretistic spirituality. There were only two Indians in attendance, however, among the three dozen conferees, and the following year the annual meeting determined to take a more critical examination of the Church's relation to native peoples. Father Gilbert Hemauer, O.F.M. Cap., was elected president of the Tekakwitha Conference that year, with Sr. Genevieve Cuny, O.S.F., a Pine Ridge Lakota, as secretary. Under their leadership the conference rapidly expanded its mission and appeal. The 1978 meeting in Rapid City included provocative speeches by Cahuilla Indian historian and activist Rupert Costo, Protestant missiologist R. Pierce Beaver, and Seneca sister Jose Hobday, all of whom criticized the role of the Church in evangelizing Indians. Father Paul Lenz, the new director of the Bureau of Catholic Indian Missions, provided funding for this and future conferences, which drew increasing numbers of Native Americans.

In 1978 fifty Indians joined three times that number of non-natives. The following year in Yankton the Indians took over the meeting, evicting all but a few white priests, including Father Lenz. The Indians demanded increased native participation in the conference and in the Church at large. They wanted to enact Vatican II theological impulses in explicit ways, cojoining Indian cultural expressions in Catholic liturgy. In short, they called for an "encounter of accommodation" (Grim 1991a: 13) between Indian and Catholic paths. The response of the Catholic authorities was to create a national organization, amply financed, whose purpose was to foster the spirit of Kateri Tekakwitha, first, by promoting the cause of her canonization, and secondly, by engaging in the project of liturgical, theological, and ecclesiological inculturation among the American Indian Catholics.

The National Tekakwitha Conference became a force in native Catholic communities nationwide, through the formation of local Kateri Circles. These prayer groups aimed for Indian spiritual growth through the explicit intercession of Kateri. They also raised funds for Indians to attend the annual Tekakwitha conferences, where they could gather in pan-Indian unity under Kateri's name and banner. Under the auspices of the National Conference, these Kateri Circles encouraged native leadership in various Catholic ministries, following Kateri's model in order to develop a "Native Catholic Church, not in traditional Roman Catholic ways but in Native ways" (*Tekakwitha Conference Newsletter* 9, no. 2, June 1990: 22). By 1992 these Kateri Circles numbered eighty-three across the United States and Canada, on and off reservations, in rural and urban Indian communities, and even among some non-Indians. Thus Kateri Tekakwitha became a kinswoman to Native American Catholics throughout North America.

In 1980 two events propelled the Lily of the Mohawks to greater prominence. First, the Vatican beatified her, declaring her blessed feast day on July 14th. Pope John Paul II presented her as a model for Native American Catholic spirituality, and he addressed a delegation of 450 Indians on hand for the celebration: "Tell your People I love them" (in Marquette. DCRAA. 1980).

Later in the same year, close to a thousand Catholics—half of them American Indians—attended the Tekakwitha conference in Denver, including a large contingent of bishops. There was a feeling of unity and purpose at the meeting, as the delegations celebrated Kateri's beatification and prayed for the last miracle that would bring her to canonization. Indians combined native and Catholic liturgical forms, smoking their pipes and blessing one another with sage. At workshops they discussed native vocations to the ministry and other means of accomplishing "the inculturation of the gospel in native life" (Starkloff 1982: n.p.). Here were hundreds of Catholic Indians in conversation with Church hierarchy, planning a future in which Indians might feel themselves integral to Catholicism. There were more than a few who felt Kateri's spirit at this conference, and who have felt it in the years following 1980, as devotion to Kateri has spread as a movement among Native Americans in the United States and Canada.

Only two Indians of North America have been brought to Rome for consideration as saints: the legendary Juan Diego, to whom the Virgin of Guadalupe was said to appear in 1531 outside of Mexico City, and Kateri Tekakwitha. Neither has received canonization yet, which is a disappointment for some who would like to witness the concrete sign that Catholicism can take on sanctification in an Indian body and face. Others are more patient, realizing that the extended period of promoting her cause publicly has fostered Indian devotion to her. Church authorities hope that a cult of Kateri, sponsored tirelessly by the National Tekakwitha Conference, will have the effect of binding Indian Catholics to the Church. Before her beatification in 1980, Kateri was known primarily where Jesuits or Mohawks had spread her news. Now she is an American Indian saint-in-the-making, a symbol of Native American Catholic ideals and practice.

James Preston, a scholar who has analyzed the devotions and controversies surrounding Kateri, both in non-Indian and Indian populations, states that the Roman Catholic Church has an opportunity to embrace Native American Catholics by canonizing the Lily of the Mohawks. Indian Catholics feel persistent disaffection from Church institutions, and the making of saints in various ethnic communities is a strategy often used to overcome local alienation. The Church makes saints with clear political objectives, to make a people identify themselves, through their saint, with the universal Church. The time seems right to elevate an American Indian to sainthood (Preston 1991). At the same time, he and others worry what might happen if Kateri's canonization is accomplished. Perhaps the sense of purpose will be drained from the Tekakwitha Conference and its momentum will be lost (Fonda, July 15, 1989).

It is apparent to many in the Church hierarchy that since 1980, Kateri Tekakwitha "has virtually been adopted by all Native Americans throughout the country. There are very few reservations where they don't have her picture" (in McDonnell 1987: 19), according to part-Abenaki Bishop Donald E. Pelotte. Msgr. Lenz of the Bureau of Catholic Indian Missions opines that the last miracle needed for Kateri's canonization " 'has already occurred: It is the spirit of unification that has been growing among the various Native American nations since Kateri's beatification. There has been 'a healing effect,' he says, that has brought many tribes to work and pray together, despite past problems" (22). Lenz is referring to the National Tekakwitha Conference as the miraculous agent of Kateri's presence among American Indian Catholics.

At Tekakwitha conferences it is common to meet Mohawk women who openly express their devotion to Kateri. Josephine Angus and Cecilia Cree (Angus and Cree, September 13, 1987), both of St. Regis, met the pope at the 1980 beatification, and they journeyed to Phoenix in 1987, hoping that John Paul would announce her canonization there. They were disappointed when he did not, but they continue to pray for her elevation.

Devotion to Kateri is no more palpable than in Sarah Monroe Hassenplug, a Mohawk woman who has portrayed Tekakwitha in pageants for two decades. Raised at St. Regis Mohawk Reservation, she has lived for many years near Syracuse, but she travels often to the National Kateri Tekakwitha Shrine in Fonda, where she says, "I feel Tekakwitha's presence here always" (in Bandy 1974: 4). She attended the beatification ceremonies in 1980: "To hear the Mohawk language spoken at St. Peter's was one of the . . . highlights of my life" (Fargo, August 5, 1989). Her likeness appears as the image of Kateri in devotional literature distributed by the custodians of Kateri's National Shrine, and she is always revising the text of her performance to make it more authentic and accessible to performers from other tribes who wish to memorialize the Lily of the Mohawks in plays. When she and other Mohawk women have performed their monologues of Kateri's life (e.g., Phoenix, September 13, 1987; Fonda, July 15, 1989), Indians weep, and give the pageant a standing ovation. Hassenplug says (Fargo, August 6, 1989) that she gets "goosebumps of excitement" planning the performances, as she meditates upon "kind, sweet, gentle" Kateri Tekakwitha. As she has become too old to impersonate the saintly maiden, she is always on the lookout for young Indian women whose appearance and character are fitted to the task.

Sister Kateri Mitchell—a Mohawk sister named for her famed spiritual forebear—often sings a hymn about the saint-to-be at Tekakwitha conferences and retreats: "Kateri Tekakwitha, Noble Mother, Turtle Earth Gathers her people, East, South, West and North" (Phoenix, September 13, 1987). She says that the Lily of the Mohawks is gathering diverse Catholic Indian peoples together by focusing their devotion upon herself. It is Kateri's power, she avows, to "inspire Indian Catholicism" (Mitchell, August 7, 1987).

Indians other than Mohawks attest to Kateri's symbolic power. Ron Boyer, a Canadian Ojibway deacon, claims that the Kateri Movement has strengthened Catholic practice in his home village since 1980 (Boyer, August 11, 1986). Papagos in Arizona have prayed the rosary, attended mass, and held communal feasts in the presence of a Kateri shrine donated to their tribe in 1990 by a Yaqui woman. They have accepted her as an expression of Christ, a new saint in their pantheon of divinities, a symbol of Indian spiritual potential (Kozak 1991: 2–4, 35–36). At annual Tekakwitha conferences one can witness the devotion of Papago women praying profoundly with their rosaries before statues of Kateri (Fargo, August 6, 1989). Other Indian women, too, pour out their devotion to Kateri's image. At a recent Tekakwitha conference (Potsdam, August 3, 1995) a woman stood before a banner of Kateri, touching the picture's face tenderly and repeatedly with her hand, and then applying the same hand to her own facial features, thus identifying herself with the Mohawk maiden's characteristics.

Terry Steele, an Algonquin from Canada who has lived in Syracuse for four decades, notes, "Growing up, Kateri was always our saint. We didn't even know that she *wasn't* a saint yet" (Fonda, July 15, 1989). She reminds her Iroquois friends that Kateri was of Algonkian as well as Iroquoian heritage, and therefore was an *Indian* rather than merely a Mohawk. "The Mohawks forget this sometimes. I remind them of it," she adds. Steele cares deeply about the cause of Kateri's canonization, and she gets a little discouraged on occasion that sainthood is not "just around the corner." Yet she is confident that with the "years of prayer" that have supported Kateri's case, canonization will occur, "in God's time, not our time." In the meantime, the cause continues to bring together various Indians—as well as non-Indians.

Many non-Indian Catholics are drawn to Kateri because she is an Indian. They view her as a member of an oppressed people, and they place upon her all sorts of romantic notions; for instance, she is sometimes regarded as a paragon of ecological values (see Preston 1991). Her conversion to Catholic faith, her intense asceticism, and her sexual purity make her an ideal to many conservative, devotional Catholics in America. Father Bernard Fagan, S.J., a longtime missionary to the Lakotas, carries a relic of Kateri's bones wherever he goes. He says that he has used it in hope of curing people; indeed, he attests to its miraculous properties, not only in healing physical ailments but also in comforting the hearts of the afflicted (Fagan, August 4, 1995).

For many American Indian Catholics, the identification with Kateri is more intense. Sister Marie-Therese Archambault, O.S.F., a Hunk-papa Lakota Sioux, finds Kateri the perfect symbol of Indian peoples who experience hurt in their own lives (Archambault, August 5, 1989). She was orphaned, persecuted, made a refugee, and damaged by disease. She wore her suffering on her face in her pockmarkings; she died an early death. Sister Archambault says that her Indian people are scarred, too, so they identify with the Lily of the Mohawks. They suffer from alcoholism; they get into fights, and their faces are scarred from these episodes. They wear broken noses, cut lips, and deep scars of pain. So, when they hear in litanies that Kateri is "scarred but beautiful," they feel themselves akin to her. She is a human symbol of their hurt humanity. Thus, the sister finds the devotion Indians pay to Kateri a first step to their healing, the raising of their self-esteem.

She has this power, according to Archambault, because Kateri is also an expression of divinity, a symbol of divine love, a self-offering like Christ Himself. Especially because she was an Indian, she can serve as meditational device for Native Americans. Indians can think of her to reflect upon their condition, but also to reflect upon sanctifying grace. When Indians pray for more miracles from her, when they pray for her canonization, they are meditating on her sanctified nature—which is the role of saints in the cultic life of Christians. That is, she already functions as a saint in the minds of many Indians.

Sister Archambault also suggests that Kateri's "relational, feminine" (Archambault 1991: 6) qualities are appealing to Indians for whom the earth, the circle, and the giveaway are expressions not only of native holism, but also of the Mystical Body of Christ. But these values seem secondary to the Indian identification with a saintly woman who lived an existence of illness, exile, self-mortification, and early death. When Indians speak in public of their alcohol or drug addition (Fonda, July 14, 1989), they refer explicitly and emphatically to their "pain," and they look to Kateri Tekakwitha as a Native American who accepted, embraced, and overcame pain, and in so doing became a symbol of godliness on earth. Furthermore, according to Bishop Pelotte, the Church's honor for Kateri is an honor for all Indians, a "marginalized and battered" (in McDonnell 1987: 19) people, who feel loved and respected by the Church through the Church's recognition of Kateri as a saintly Indian. Through her, they affirm themselves as participants in the Church.

Like any people, American Indian Catholics turn to their ancestors as a means of asserting their continuing peoplehood. By idealizing their dead, by telling their heroic legends, and by visiting the sites of their birth or burial, a people can express its own values and identity. Kateri Tekakwitha has long functioned within the non-Indian Church as an ideal convert who purportedly left behind her native culture to participate in Catholic behavior. The Tekakwitha Conference has promoted her cause and that of Juan Diego—as ideal converts—in order to channel American Indian spirituality into forms that support the Church and its history. Church authorities want Indian Catholics to emulate Kateri by converting wholeheartedly to Catholic identity. It is for this reason, one observer proposes, that "Indian Catholics are being directed by the Church hierarchy to accept and work toward the canonization of their own saint" (Kozak 1991: 4). For many American Indian Catholics, however, it is her identity as an *Indian*, not necessarily as a *Catholic*, that they find so appealing. The Church wishes Kateri to be a means for them to enunciate their Catholicism; many Indians find her a means of asserting their Indianness. They call her "Saint Kateri" (Orono, August 8, 1992), even without approval from the Church, because she epitomizes ideals "the people" have canonized for themselves. One Mohawk woman told an observer that she did not believe in the Christian God, but she did have faith in Kateri (Preston, August 4, 1995).

At the same time, there are some Indians, particularly among the younger generation of Mohawks, who reject veneration for Kateri Tekakwitha. They suspect that the Church is using her—her virginity, her conversion, her close association with the Jesuits—to acculturate Indians even further than the missionary process has done thus far. They resent her as a "traitor" (see Preston 1991, 1993) to her own people, a "prostitute" (in Koppedrayer 1993: 277) to missionary domination, a "minor figure" (Shillinger, August 5, 1993) who was perhaps even a mythological concoction of Jesuit self-promotion. "I suppose I shouldn't be saying these things at a Tekakwitha conference," says a young Iroquois scholar, herself a convert to Catholicism, "but Kateri was possibly a composite of various Indian converts" (ibid.). Mohawk traditionalists, long embattled against the Church, are "driven wild"

(Fonda, July 14, 1989) by the cult to Kateri. They have even threatened to burn down her shrine at Caughnawaga, causing the parish priests at times to sleep in the church to protect it against arson. For these critics, the Jesuit "martyrs" comprise a myth that explicitly condemns the aboriginal Iroquois for resisting Catholicism. In this myth, Kateri Tekakwitha functions to highlight the paganism of her people, from whom she defects to join the Christians. For these Iroquois, Kateri is a symbol of the revulsion long felt by Jesuits and Jesuit hagiographers for Iroquois culture, past and present (Lunstrom 1973: 1–4).

For other Mohawks, however, particularly the elderly Catholic women, those who attend mass at St. Regis or St. Lucy's Church in Syracuse, who organize and attend Tekakwitha meetings locally and nationally, Kateri was a "traditional" Indian whose Catholic saintliness grew out of her "native spirituality" (Fonda, July 15, 1989) as well as her Christianity. They see in her the potential for bringing together not only Mohawk factions but all Indian peoples through the grace of God. For them, her syncretistic spirituality "does not diminish either tradition but it moves toward accommodation of both" (Grim 1991a: 15) native and Christian expression.

More skeptical observers suggest that her cult makes obvious the divisions between traditionalist and Catholic Indians, since different factions regard her from radically different angles (Preston 1991: 16–22). Furthermore, alienation is apparent between those non-Indians sponsoring the veneration of the Jesuit martyrs at Auriesville and the Indian cult of Kateri at nearby Fonda. James Preston states frankly, "The Indians hate the martyrs" (Fonda, July 15, 1989). On Kateri's feast day the schedules at Auriesville and Fonda have to be arranged with diplomatic finesse, so as not to offend either the non-Indians who venerate her at the Shrine of the American Martyrs in Auriesville, or the Indians at Kateri's shrine in Fonda.

ST. REGIS, AKWESASNE

By the early 1900s the St. Regis reserve had a century and a half of history and its stone church was over a hundred years old. When the Indians who settled St. Regis left Caughnawaga in 1755, the Caughnawagans gave their departing kinsmen "a gift of some precious relics, namely, the skull and a few of the bones of their saintly sister, Kateri Tekakwitha" (in St. Louis 1952: n.p.). The two villages maintained relations with one another over the years, even after the Treaty of Paris in 1783 divided St. Regis into Canadian and American jurisdictions. With portions of the reserve within New York State, Lower Canada (Quebec), and Upper Canada (Ontario), straddling the St. Lawrence River, the opportunities for bureaucratic confusion were many. Nonetheless, the bishops of Quebec and Baltimore in the 1790s cooperated to maintain the mission, and to this day three dioceses in Canada and the United States—Valleyfield, Alexandria-Cornwall, and Ogdensburg—share the spiritual responsibilities for St. Regis Catholics (Jacobs and Egan 1973, 1989). In 1801 the Bishop of Quebec reported a St. Regis population of six hundred of whom 270 were full communicants. A century later the population of St. Regis was twenty-five hundred, consisting of two thousand Catholics and five hundred Protestants. The pastor at the time, however, stated that there were only five hundred actively practicing Catholics at St. Regis in 1902 (ibid.). St. Regis Catholics had their children baptized and at time of death the priest "endeared himself" (Egan, July 10, 1989) to the Indians with a church burial. There were Catholic schools on the reserve by the 1900s. Most of the population resisted Protestant overtures. In 1835 the part-Mohawk Anglican minister, Eleazar Williams, had said that he was quitting St. Regis because the Mohawks there would not give up their fidelity to Roman Catholicism; he could not sit by and watch a "Popish Priest" instilling "degraded and misguided" devotion to the "miserable System of the dark Ages" (St. Louis 1951b: n.p.). The Indians engaged the sacramental Church at birth, marriage, and death (there were 1,481 baptisms, 316 marriages, and 861 funerals recorded, e.g., in the period between 1881 and 1897 [Jacobs and Egan 1973,

1989]); however, their pastors sometimes found the daily participation in Catholic life to be standoffish and theologically inadequate.

Perhaps the St. Regis Catholics did not provide sufficient funds for the support of the diocesan priests; perhaps they represented an ethnic enclave which would not be assimilated into the surrounding culture and body politic. The Mohawks who predominated at the reserve were intent upon maintaining aspects of Iroquois culture, and the entire community made certain that its land rights were secured against the desires of white Americans and Canadians. In the 1930s, when the Caughnawaga Mohawk Jesuit, Father Michael Karhienton Jacobs (whose biography appears in volume 3 of *American Indian Catholics*), attempted a census at St. Regis, he found that "The Indians are very suspicious, particularly when it comes to taking down their names, their age, social conditions and their religious life" (Ogdensburg. June 8, 1936). Of the twenty-five hundred Indians (Jacobs surveyed only fifteen hundred), over 90 percent were baptized Catholic, but their loyalties were often hard to fathom for the mainstream Church authorities.

The pastors lived at St. Regis and visited each Indian family at least once a year, recording births and deaths. The priests attempted to reach their flock at times of emergency. Sisters conducted schools for the young children, some of whom continued in public high schools at nearby towns. But through most of the year, the majority of St. Regis Indians conducted their lives apart from Church institutions. Partially this was the result of their isolated rural existence on the reserve, where they farmed and fished for their subsistence, and partially because many of the men were often away from the reserve, involved in the construction of steel span bridges and skyscrapers throughout the Northeast. Attendance at Sunday mass was difficult and infrequent.

The Indians' adherence to their own culture, including the Mohawk language, presented obstacles to some priests. An English-speaking American cleric wrote that 70 percent of the Indian Catholics at St. Regis "could not sufficiently grasp the truths of our religion in a foreign tongue. . . . They are Catholic. They are attentive in their own way but it will take a long time even beyond your days and mine to make them what we all would wish them to be" (ibid., March 16, 1934). He and his bishop from Ogdensburg were impatient with the continuing use of Mohawk in Catholic liturgy, but as far as the Mohawks were concerned the Catholic faith was an expression of their native tongue, even as more and more of them learned English as well as French. From the earliest days of the reserve, services had been conducted in Mohawk with papal permission, including prayers, hymns, and sermons (the priests used Latin, too), and the Indians aimed to continue that tradition. The bishop of Valleyfield was sympathetic to that heritage: "je reste convaincu que le jour où les Iroquois auront perdu leur langue maternelle ils seront eux-mêmes définitivement perdus pour la foi" (October 29, 1934). He argued that the Indians understood the Catholic faith in Mohawk, and to translate that faith into English or French would require a great changeover in their spiritual comprehension and their concrete grasp of dogma would weaken. He also recognized that speaking Mohawk was a matter of ethnic pride and social cohesion, setting them apart from their snobbish white American neighbors and serving as a hedge against white encroachment. The bishop of Ogdensburg saw the matter differently. In 1934, as the Indian New Deal was encouraging the expression of traditional culture among Native Americans throughout the United States, a policy most unpopular with the U.S. Catholic hierarchy, he wanted to guide the St. Regis Indians toward greater conformity with the culture of their white neighbors, "instructing the Indians in the fear and love of God which would mean that they would be true and loyal Americans" (May 22, 1935). He remarked that many St. Regis Mohawks "have become indifferent to religion and are threatening to go back to the 'long-house'—which means reversion to paganism" (ibid.).

Church authorities in Canada and the U.S. saw a danger to Mohawk morals posed by the bootlegging of alcohol across the border in the 1920s and 1930s, and they warned that the "young girls are being inveigled from the reservation and placed in houses of ill fame" (ibid.). Measures were needed, they said, "to instill proper moral and social values" (January 3, 1934) on the reserve against the corruption brought by the surrounding white culture. The Great Depression made the continued funding of parish priests a difficulty, and when the cleric in nearby Hogansburg (on the American side) tried to conduct catechism for the Indians, "his white people" were said "bitterly" to "resent any attempt to bring the Indians into their church, or to countenance any mingling of white and red children" (March 24, 1936).

The solution, then, to an Indian ministry at St. Regis was to ask the Society of Jesus to take up once again the mission it had begun in the 1600s and brought to St. Regis in the 1750s. Father Jacobs, the

Mohawk Jesuit, began his ministry there in 1936. He found among the Cooks, the Jacobs, the Lazores, the Tarbells, the Whites, the Terrences, the Abrams, the Benedicts, the Bigtrees, the Crees, and the other extended families at St. Regis, an eagerness to welcome a priest of their own who spoke their language and was committed to their persistence as a people.

Father Jacobs and other Jesuits worked to instill normative Catholicism among the people while fostering Mohawk language on the reserve. They soon came into fierce competition, however, with the growing Longhouse religious movement among the Iroquois, and for decades to come—even to the present day—Catholic practice at St. Regis took shape amidst the forces of Iroquois nationalism. Even as early as 1939 Jacobs identified eighty "Neo-pagans" (July 13, 1939) at St. Regis. Catholic devotionalism flourished in the 1940s and 1950s but it was colored by an awareness of a growing "traditionalist" movement, which accused the Catholic Church of collusion with the forces of Western colonialism. There were more than two thousand Catholic Indians in 1958, augmented by a hundred or so infant baptisms each year (August 18, 1959); however, there was a growing undercurrent of discontent with the Church. At Caughnawaga and Oka as well as at St. Regis (which was coming to be known by the aboriginal Mohawk name of Akwesasne) many Indians "*apostatized*" (February 14, 1961, emphasis in source) as they ceased to see the Church as their own. The Jesuits could preach hellfire and damnation—and Jacobs did until his retirement in 1965—but the disenchantment with Catholic institutions continued to grow. The fact that so many Mohawks traveled from the reserve for employment in New York City, Syracuse, Buffalo, Niagara Falls, and Rochester meant that the local priests could not keep their hold on the Indians' loyalty. Iroquois nationalism, evangelized most effectively from Onondaga, where Catholicism was anathema, undercut whatever hegemony the Church once had at St. Regis. By the 1970s the local priests had to admit that the Longhouse resurgence was "an ever increasing threat to the continued Catholicism of the Indians, especially the younger generation" (December 4, 1976).

The Second Vatican Council changed the practice of Catholicism among the Indians at St. Regis. The Mohawks had been singing hymns in Mohawk for centuries, but their liturgy was otherwise strictly Latin rite. Vatican II encouraged the use of the vernacular at Mass, and in spite of all the emphasis on Iroquois nationalism of the 1960s, the first language on the reserve was now English. However, priests who introduced the English rite encountered resistance among older Mohawks who identified "traditional Catholicism" (Mitchell, August 7, 1986) with Mohawk and Latin. Yet there were not enough native speakers of Mohawk to conduct services in Mohawk—what priest beyond the aging Father Jacobs could accomplish that feat?—and English struck a raw nerve in those Mohawks still loyal to Catholicism.

As new priests arrived, they attempted to enforce Catholic Church authority at St. Regis, where, according to Bishop Stanislaus J. Brzana of Ogdensburg, "A superstitious heritage has its influence even on Christian groups, especially on the youth" (Marquette. DCRAA. 1976). Father Gordon Bazinet, S.J., took charge in 1977 and insisted that if Catholics could not attend weekly mass and support their priest, they could not expect baptisms and marriages in the Church. His sermons and bulletins charged the Mohawks with laxity in the practice of their faith. He announced the "No Cop-Out Sunday" (Ogdensburg. January 8, 1978) to his parishioners. If you think Sunday is for sleeping, he said, we shall hand out cots. If you complain that the church is too cold, we'll hand out blankets. Too hot? We'll distribute fans. We'll give calculators "to count the hypocrites whom they say are in church," and hearing aids for those who cannot hear the priest. For those who say that the priest speaks too loud, we'll give cotton for their ears. We'll put out Easter lilies and poinsettias for those who come to Mass only on Easter and Christmas.

A Mohawk woman who had cleaned the church for thirty-five years found Bazinet's sarcasm insufferable: "He preaches like we don't know our religion[,] treats us like pagans, even the choir is complaining" (ibid., March 11, 1978). A member of the parish council complained to the bishop of Ogdensburg: "Never in my fifty years as a member of this mission have I heard so much dissen[s]ion . . . some prefer to stay home and pray. Others are attending some other churches nearby. . . . He says we are a strange people when he is really a stranger to us" (March 12, 1978). When Father Bazinet was present, the parish council would speak in Mohawk. "What are they saying?" (Bigtree, July 9, 1989), he asked one member. "They're talking about how to get rid of you," came the reply.

Father Bazinet organized the St. Regis Parish Council at the request of the Bishop of Valleyfield, in order to comply with Vatican II fostering of local lay leadership. It was a way for parishioners to share with the priest in the operation of their church. The men and women in the council, representing sodalities such as the Altar and Rosary Society, St. John the Baptist Society, and Knights of Columbus from both American and Canadian sides, fell immediately and irrevocably into dispute with their pastor. Nine members wrote to Bazinet's Jesuit provincial in Montreal to "demand the immediate removal of one Gordon Bazinet from the St. Regis Mission. . . ." They contended, "He is a liar. . . . he is a hypocrite. He administers the mission like Fidel Castro governs Cuba." They resented particularly his purported hostility to Mohawk culture and they sought to control their own liturgical and ecclesiastical affairs: "we want the right to reject this priest and any other priest" (St. Regis Parish Council, November 11, 1978). The provincial met with the council members in 1979 and admitted Bazinet's faults of diplomacy, but he asked the Mohawks for patience. Ruth Papineau's minutes of the parish council's 1979 meetings bore the guiding invocation: "We must never go off the deep end. We must gather wisdom always and conduct ourselves accordingly. Don't fly off the handle. Don't jump to conclusions. Ask for time to weigh the matter. Then pray that you conclude with the correct opinion" (n.d., 1979). Nonetheless, they found their pastor unbearable.

Bazinet lasted two years, by which time few Indians were attending mass at St. Regis. There were threats upon his life and destruction of rectory property, and it might be said that his unbending personality was a cause of the brouhaha. Certainly his attitude toward his parishioners was unsympathetic, speaking as he did about the "mentality . . . [of] these people" (Ogdensburg. n.d., 1979). Yet, he saw himself as the upholder of Catholic sacramental, ethical, and ecclesial standards— refusing to bless the marriage of a thirteen-year-old pregnant girl to a man older than her parents, speaking publicly against the beatings of women and children in the Mohawk homes, protecting the church graveyard against desecration, and combating the traditionalists in their effort to alienate the Mohawks from Catholic identity. The fact that he was more comfortable in French than in English made him ineffective in a community where virtually no one spoke the Gallic tongue anymore. One of the Mohawk trustees reminded his fellows that "In my fifty some years of membership in this parish there have been people that were never happy with any new priest" (September 13, 1979), so jealous were the Mohawks of their own autonomy in the parish. Even Father Jacobs became a pariah to many of his fellow Iroquois in his strict enforcement of Church rules, although in his dotage he became a beloved symbol to some of a golden age now passing. An anonymous Mohawk penned a note in 1978 regarding Father Jacobs: "I think he deserve to stay as long as he want[,] when he be gone we will loose [sic] our Indian language and that will be the end of us" (n.d., 1978).

By the end of the 1970s, Catholicism at St. Regis was in disarray. There were over six thousand Catholic Indians according to the baptismal records, but they were divided into various parties. The Indians on the American and Canadian sides of the reserve were divided by school and governmental office. Class lines had formed during the middle part of the century, and the educated differed in their orientation from the illiterate. Some Mohawks were sympathetic to the Longhouse movement, even while maintaining their Catholic identity; other Catholics despised the traditionalists for their attacks on Catholicism and itched to compete with the Longhouse for the loyalty of their kinsmen. The reforms of the Second Vatican Council had attracted some, particularly those who did not speak Mohawk, whereas the older Indians wanted to maintain the Mohawk-Latin rite. Father Bazinet's zeal had impressed a minority of the Catholics at St. Regis, while repelling most. In keeping with Vatican II directives, Bazinet had insisted upon six months of catechetical training before marriages, and he wanted the parents of children to be baptized to attend mass regularly. Father Jacobs, for all his condemnation of devotional laxity and the inroads of the traditionalists, delivered sacramental services immediately upon demand. Bazinet felt the Mohawks to be "lacking in knowledge of their faith" (September 1979) and insisted upon lengthy instruction, much to community resentment.

An observer wrote in 1979 that, "the Mohawk people cling to tradition, symbol, ancestral respect and view the changes in devotional practices as undermining the Catholic faith among them" (ibid.). In short, confusion and disunity were widespread within the Catholic community. Some Catholics at St. Regis wanted to attend church outside their own parish, but they were treated with disdain by the "segregated church" (ibid.) in the surrounding white communities both in Canada and the United States. Others moved to the cities of New York and found parishes that had more "vitality" for them than the one at home.

Sister Kateri Mitchell, S.S.A., a Mohawk with deep roots in the community, tried to engender a dialogue between Longhouse and Catholic adherents. As principal of the Cornwall Island School on the reserve, she wanted the children to unite: "Through contact with each other, traditional and progressive children will gain a greater understanding of their different ways" (Lalonde, June 21, 1978). While she worked on her fellow Mohawks, others in the Church sought more Catholic outreach. Sister Mary Christine Taylor, S.S.J., a non-Indian historian and catechist on the reserve, urged more coordination among the three dioceses serving St. Regis, not only in delivering sacraments to the outlying regions of the reserve (particularly to the sick and elderly) but also in welcoming Mohawk Catholics to neighboring Catholic churches. She encouraged greater religious education (both in English and Mohawk) and the expansion of social services on the reserve, and she called upon offices such as Catholic Charities, Catholic Youth Organization, and Summer Missionary to address the various needs of St. Regis inhabitants. Even after the summer of 1979, when entrenched Longhouse and Progressive political factions had eyeballed each other through gunsights, she saw hope for the future of a Catholic community at St. Regis. Indeed, she and others demanded hope because of the dire condition of the reserve. She wrote to her superiors that the St. Regis parish council had "deep faith. . . . Their primary concern now is that a whole generation has been lost to the Church" (Ogdensburg. January 27, 1980).

Rev. Gerald Lavigne, S.J., Father Bazinet's successor, expressed the need for renewal: "Since coming to St. Regis Mission, I have found a serious need of Religious Instruction for all my parishioners. While there is a population of 6,200 Catholic Mohawk Indians, only about 350 attend Sunday Mass" (ibid., January 19, 1980). There was disinterest in Catholic sacraments, particularly matrimony. Taylor and Lavigne determined to build a new Catholic infrastructure on the reserve, with bible courses, Pre-Cana Conferences, a Kateri Hall for parish meetings, religious instruction for youths, training of family catechists, sacramental visitations, and social services, including a halfway rehabilitation home for alcoholics. "There is great potential here for evangelization" (January 9, 1982), Taylor wrote. Sister Kathleen Navarra, S.S.J., joined the catechetical effort in 1980 at the request of Bishop Brzana, who wrote: "Hundreds of Indian children who are baptized Catholic never receive any formal religious instruction" (February 18, 1980). He added that the Indians should be the diocese's "highest priority"; through his chancellor he forced the local priest in Hogansburg to accept responsibility for the Indians in his parish.

While the diocesan offices tried to vitalize Church attitudes toward the Mohawk Catholics, members of the Catholic community wanted to reformulate the relations between Catholics and non-Catholics on the reserve. Brenda LaFrance called upon Bishop Brzana to help calm the bickering at St. Regis, asking him to speak with members of the Knights of Columbus, the Altar and Rosary Society, and the St. John the Baptist Society—the hard core of Catholicism (June 17, 1980). Her goal was to cool the tensions between the Church and the Longhouse, and her efforts had an effect. After several decades of hostility between the Mohawk traditionalists and the Catholics at St. Regis, the Church authorities—including the bishops of Valleyfield, Alexandria-Cornwall, and Ogdensburg, in consultation with Catholic representatives from the reserve—determined to treat their rivals with an ecumenical spirit. They agreed that

> the policy towards the Traditionalists should not be opposition but friendly interest. The Traditionalists contend that they worship the one true God and many elements in their belief are not opposed to Christianity and could be "baptized." It is important to slowly work for a reconciliation of the Catholics and the Traditionalists. (February 4, 1981)

Although Father Jacobs still opposed any such rapprochement, after a generation of mutual recriminations the bishops declared: "There should be no specific opposition to the Traditionalists" (ibid.).

When Father Thomas F. Egan, S.J., took over as pastor at St. Regis in 1982, he and his assistants "tried to establish good relations with all parties. We have had to move slowly," Father Egan said, "to avoid offending our own ultra-conservative parishioners who are still quite reserved toward the longhouse people, even to their own relatives who have become traditional" (June 14, 1983). At the same time, he met with Longhouse leaders and attended some of their services, making the first steps toward overcoming their hostility toward him. With Father Jacobs retired to a Jesuit home and the Father Bazinet debacle fading in memory, Egan and the various Church personnel at St. Regis began slowly to carry out the rebuilding begun by Sister Taylor and Father Lavigne, ministering to the fifty-three hundred Catholic Indians within the Diocese of Ogdensburg (Marquette. DCRAA. 1983). "Our Mohawk parishioners," stated Father Egan, "always show themselves

generous and eager to cooperate with their contributions when a concrete need for the upkeep of the church is presented to them" (Ogdensburg. September 21, 1983), and he found in the various Catholic
Mohawk sodalities—the Mohawk Choir, the Parish Council, the
charismatic Prayer Group, the Homemakers, as well as the Altar and
Rosary Society and the St. John the Baptist Society—an active participation in liturgical and ecclesiastical work. Sister Taylor had a communion list of 150 shut-ins, whom she visited regularly. A priest said
weekly mass at the Akwesasne Nursing Home in St. Regis Village, and
the Mohawks were receiving other sacraments more regularly than in
the previous decade.

In June 1982 the Mohawks of St. Regis and those who were establishing themselves as a community in St. Lucy's parish in Syracuse
sponsored jointly a regional Tekakwitha conference at Le Moyne College in Syracuse. The next year it was held at Kateri Hall on the reservation. At the urging of Sister Mitchell, who left St. Regis in 1982,
a few dozen Mohawk Catholics began to participate in the annual
Tekakwitha gatherings around the United States. Several years before,
the Church authorities in Ogdensburg had demurred at an invitation
to attend the national Tekakwitha conference—"At present there is a
serious controversy on our reservation between the Traditionalists and
other Mohawk Indians," an assistant chancellor had written (Ogdensburg. June 17, 1980)—but now the situation seemed secure enough to
encourage connections to other Indian Catholics without arousing the
suspicion of Longhouse proponents.

The greatest problem at St. Regis, according to Father Egan, was
not traditionalist-Catholic hostility, although it still existed in the early
1980s, but rather the lack of Catholic connectedness to the serious life
problems of Mohawks. Teenage pregnancy, lack of spiritual direction
and parental guidance, drugs, alcohol—these were "giant-sized problems" (September 21, 1983) on the reservation, and he hoped the
Church would face them rather than blame the Longhouse, which was
a grass-roots movement meant to address the many dysfunctions of
modern Indian existence.

Father Egan continued to regard the Longhouse as an innovation,
rather than an expression of traditional Mohawk religion. "Our Catholic people here," he stated, "have hardly any recollection of their pre-
Christian past" (Marquette. JINNAM. June 29, 1984). Nonetheless,
he wanted the Mohawks to retain any aspect of their culture that had

survived the centuries and that played a role in maintaining their stability as a people. The seasonal cycle of rituals, the old-time chieftaincies, these were to be encouraged. The Church, too, was part of their
traditional culture, and he saw it as a positive force in holding the
St. Regis community together. "The Mohawks are presently in grave
danger of losing their language," he declared. "Its use in the liturgy,
a much appreciated privilege for nearly three centuries, has long contributed to its preservation. But television has had a devastating effect
in the past three decades" (ibid.). Not only had traditionalists emphasized the modern use of Mohawk language, but also Catholic litur-
gists like Sister Kateri Mitchell were furthering the use of their native
tongue.

If the Mohawks had their own cultural emphases within their practice of Catholicism, the Church authorities of the 1980s were willing
to accommodate them. Father Egan remarked upon the Mohawks'
"great reverence for the dead" (Ogdensburg. September 21, 1983) at St.
Regis. They held a two-night wake, a funeral mass, a journey to the
cemetery, dinner with family and fellows, and prayers in the home up
to nine evenings after the funeral. The wake was at home, lasting all
night, with prayers and hymns offered by the Catholic Mohawk choir
as well as several rounds of rosaries All these services for the deceased
were conducted with "solemnity," Egan noted. He said that deaths
brought on "long confession lines," with many questions about marriage requirements. Sunday mass attendance usually increased for the
family of the dead, at least for a short time, and they appeared regularly for weekday masses offered for the deceased. Egan commented
that duty for the dead was for them an obligation more serious than
the Sunday mass, and he did not criticize them for it. As in other
Catholic Indian communities, religious identity was satisfied through
reverence to dead kinsmen. In the ethnic enclave at St. Regis the passing of tribal members was more important than the marking of weekly
services in the Roman Catholic calendar. The parish priest was willing
to let this pattern stand.

If the Church was more flexible in assessing the patterns of St.
Regis Catholicism, the Indians were more appreciative of the catechet-
ical and sacramental efforts among them. When the Catholic Church
Extension Society gave its Lumen Christi award in 1984 to Sister Mary
Christine Taylor for her work at St. Regis, one hundred and thirty
Indians came to honor her. They recalled not only her teaching and

social work, but also her service as a go-between when violence erupted between Christians and traditionalists (Marquette. DCRAA. June 26, 1984). The number of Mohawks attending Sunday mass increased to about six hundred, with sixteen hundred at Easter services (Ogdensburg. September 26, 1984). Bishop Brzana saw reason to hope: "I do feel that great progress has been made at St. Regis and that the Church is much better accepted by the Native Americans now than it has been in many years and that the time is ripe for us to make steady but slow progress in our evangelization efforts" (Marquette. DCRAA. June 26, 1984).

For all the "progress," the priests at St. Regis were still concerned about "Sacramental Preparation" (Ogdensburg. September 26, 1984). "How strict should we be?" they asked, when over half of the babies brought for baptism came from unmarried parents, often with no father in sight. To what degree could it be said that these children were being inducted into Catholic families? When they received first communion, most of their families did not even attend mass, and the Indians did not see the need for religious instruction before receiving confirmation. Their elders never received catechetical help; why should they? When the Indians desired a church wedding, it was difficult to make them attend more than an "afternoon" of Pre-Cana instruction. The result was a family tradition without knowledgeable engagement in Catholicism. If the priests were to withhold the sacraments, the Indians would resent it mightily; if the priests were to overlook the deficiencies, they felt in danger of not performing their sacerdotal duties. In the 1980s there were around a hundred baptisms, seventy first communions and confirmations, twenty marriages, and forty funerals each year. Sacramental life was taking place. Sacramental participation held steady, in fact, over a whole century from 1898 to 1988, with 8,575 baptisms, 2,015 weddings, and 4,141 funerals in a growing population (Jacobs and Egan 1973, 1989). But there was not sufficient instruction even in the 1980s, despite the efforts of Sister Taylor and other teachers (Marquette. JINNAM. April 1986; Ogdensburg. October 19, 1989).

When St. Regis Catholics attended the national Tekakwitha conferences, they saw other Indians performing "Indian" liturgies and they asked permission to incorporate traditional Iroquois devotionals into their contemporary Catholic worship. "Yet anything that is tried," said the priests, "is immediately criticized by those who want nothing In-

dian in the mass" (Ogdensburg. September 26, 1984). The conservative Catholics wanted nothing of Iroquois tradition in their worship,
except for the use of Mohawk language. Nor were they happy when
Pope John Paul II visited the site of the seventeenth-century Huron
missions in 1984 and was greeted by the Mohawk traditionalist leader,
Ernie Benedict, who presented an eagle feather to the pontiff. Michael
Mitchell, a baptized Catholic involved in the traditionalist North
American Indian Traveling College at Akwesasne, put on a sweetgrass
ceremony for the pope, much to the ire of some "entrenched" Catholic
Mohawks who thought that St. Regis should have turned its back on
such ritualism centuries ago. The Catholic priests at St. Regis were far
from hostile to expressions of native spirituality, either at mass or in
the presence of the bishop of Rome. They stated, "We certainly should
do our best to promote such an era of inculturation" (ibid.). With a
thousand (or even two thousand) Longhouse adherents at St. Regis in
the mid-1980s—including some of the five thousand baptized Catholics—and with hundreds of Methodists, Mormons, and members of
the pentecostal Assembly of God (Marquette. JINNAM. April 1986),
ecumenism was the most prudent policy for the priests.

As Father Egan surveyed his parish at the end of the 1980s, he saw
a viable Catholic community at St. Regis. Sunday collections paid for
a third of the church expenses, with additional monetary help coming
from the Bureau of Catholic Indian Missions and the three dioceses in
charge of the area (Ogdensburg. 1988). The Altar and Rosary Society
and the St. John the Baptist Society continued to function for women
and men, respectively, although their numbers declined, particularly
the men. The Knights of Columbus was less active than in previous
years; however, fifty men belonged to a nearby chapter. The Mohawk
Choir still sang in the native language and a prayer group attended funeral services and wakes. There was a pastoral outreach team, with a
dozen members, visiting shut-ins and mourners, and a Kateri Circle
gained several dozen members under the influence of the National
Tekakwitha Conference. The Akwesasne Dancers, organized initially
by Sister Kateri Mitchell a decade earlier, continued to perform at
home and in other churches. Attendance at mass decreased markedly
in the late 1980s, "due in large part to the multiplication of bingo par-
lors and casinos," according to Egan. "Many who used to be regular
in attendance at church are now working the entire weekend" (October 19, 1989). Seventy-five percent of the eight thousand inhabitants of

St. Regis "still think of themselves as Catholics" (Jacobs and Egan 1973, 1989), said Egan, but only 80 percent of the Mohawks who received baptism went on to receive first communion, and only half received confirmation. Only a few hundred Indians attended Sunday mass each week.

If anything, the Longhouse had increased in importance by the end of the 1980s. Its Great Law was read ceremonially throughout the year and the thanksgiving prayers were heard regularly. The Mohawks perceived the Longhouse as an institution of their own, addressing many of the aspects of Mohawk life that were of immediate and ultimate concern, including the environmental deterioration caused by non-Indian pollutors and, more generally, the political autonomy of the reservation. Catholicism was not viewed as relevant to these issues, and so Father Egan was left with an elderly, marginal remnant of his flock. Father Jacobs had once claimed that the church at St. Regis was like the Temple of the Jews in Jesus' time: "the most sacred spot on the face of the earth . . . a sign for them of God's special presence among them" (Jacobs and Egan 1983, 1989). In well over two centuries the community at St. Regis had grown from two hundred to nearly eight thousand people. Originally almost all were Catholic and Catholicism had played a central role in the life of the reserve. No longer could this be said (Lickers, May 4, 1989). Christened Catholics still composed the greater majority of Mohawks, and fewer than two thousand Mohawks were Longhouse participants. However, the traditionalists were more politically outspoken than the Catholics. They identified themselves on public issues as Mohawks, standing for Akwesasne nationalism. Making more noise, they carried more weight on the reservation. Combining their spirituality and their social consciousness, they constituted something closer to a "base community" than the Catholics (Egan, July 8, 1989).

Part of the Longhouse appeal was its defense of traditional Mohawk culture. It was a religion of Iroquois for Iroquois. The Catholic Church was seen as a foreign intrusion, even after centuries of Catholic Mohawk tradition. Whereas some Catholic hymns at St. Regis dwelled upon the supposed "dark vices" of aboriginal Mohawks, and Catholic hagiography extolled the virtues of the seventeenth-century missionaries like the martyr Father Isaac Jogues, S.J., the Longhouse members voiced solidarity with their aboriginal past. For centuries Mohawk Catholics had been expected to take the side of the Jesuits against their own ancestors. Now the traditionalists called their fellow Mohawks to stand up for their own people against what they saw as missionary propaganda. Their newspaper, *Akwesasne Notes*, criticized the continuing Catholic demonizing of the aboriginal Mohawks and won influence on the reservation. Even Catholic Mohawks did not want to be reminded that they were the object of missions and that their ancestors had once resisted the Catholic faith. In a struggle for the loyalties of the Mohawks, Father Egan admitted, the Catholic Church did not have an easy time of it. He acknowledged that the Church had not always been good to Indians, even with the best of intentions, and so he understood the political causes for falling away from Catholicism. "It's a wonder so many Indians are still Catholic" (ibid.), he remarked.

The tensions between the Mohawk community and the Church at St. Regis have been palpable for years. At times the priests seem to be under siege in their rectory. When a "drugged up . . . wild man" broke into the shrine for Kateri Tekakwitha in 1988 and wrecked it, no one would testify against him. Men who wanted to drink behind the rectory yelled at an old priest, thinking that the clerics had closed off the area to the Indians. In his sermons Father Egan (now deceased) had to counter such rumors. In fact, the Band Council had closed the spot because people were dumping garbage there—"a very un-Mohawk thing to do," Egan added (Egan, July 9, 1989).

At Sunday Mass Egan called upon his parishioners to consider their duty to help other Indians less fortunate than themselves. The Mohawks at St. Regis are far wealthier than other Native Americans, he said. They should also think about religious vocations. Even if they are too old themselves to become priests and sisters, at least they should pray for vocations among their children. Egan chided them for their "bourgeois" displays at weddings—the tuxedos and chiffon gowns witnessed the previous day (July 8, 1989). At the same time he appreciated their Mohawk hymns for the dead, their animation in prayer, and their decorum at Sunday mass. The five to six hundred Indians who attended mass each Sunday constituted the core of the Catholic community, only one-tenth of the christened Mohawks enrolled on the reservation.

One Sunday afternoon Egan performed a baptism for an infant, born May 23, 1989. The mother was a practicing Catholic but the father was a Longhouse member, baptized a Catholic himself as an infant at St. Regis. This was their fourth child but they were not married. The woman wanted a Catholic wedding but the man refused. The godparents vowed to help the child in the Catholic faith, but the father stayed aloof throughout the service, refusing to participate in any of the prayers. Even the godfather appeared tepid at best in his duty. Father Egan called it "the coldest baptism I've had in a long time" (July 9, 1989), and yet he noted that the couple's eldest daughter had just received her first communion and he had every reason to think that the youths would continue to hold a Catholic identity as they grew up, despite the alienation of their father from the Church. In church the priest "claims" the infant for Christ and the Church. He asks that everyone say the Apostles' Creed. He closes the service by noting how "my people, the Irish," had once been pagans but had received Christianity, just as the Mohawks had received the Christian faith through the baptisms delivered by missionaries. He attempts to establish a continuity between himself and his parishioners—both coming from tribes christened by the sacraments—but for most of those present, particularly the men, the sermon falls unreceived.

After the baptism Father Egan was discouraged. "I think we've lost the father for good." The Longhouse has claimed the man's loyalty and the Church seems powerless to win him back. Egan even wondered if he should be performing such a baptism under the circumstances; however, he checked with his superiors and they all agreed that he should "go easy, err on the side of leniency" in such matters at St. Regis. And so he performed a baptism, even though he perceived an obvious lack of sincerity, at least on the part of the father and god-father. Egan said that this is no new pattern. The old St. Regis records from the turn of the twentieth century reveal the same pattern of men removed from the Church and uncommitted to the faith. He thought that the percentage of uncommitted had been rising, however, in recent decades. He told of a Mohawk teenager who was always "with the Church," but who now sees that his father never attends mass and he thinks, why must I? Father Egan told of a St. Regis girl who took up with an Onondaga man, had a child, and wanted it to be baptized. Egan asked her who performed the marriage and she replied, "a woman Catholic priest." Egan retorted that she could not receive the sacraments, nor could her child be baptized at St. Regis. She left the rectory in anger and her father called later on the telephone. "It's 4:45, and as of this minute we are no longer Catholic," the man said. Later, when he saw Egan, he said, "'If I had seen you that day, I would have knocked your block off'" (July 9, 1989).

Father Egan got along with the Longhouse leaders at Akwesasne. He won the trust and affection of the Catholic core. He worked with the parish council and provided the services expected of him, not only delivering the sacraments but also keeping vital records regarding births and deaths. When little boys came by for candy or rhubarb—the latter was grown in the garden next to the rectory—the priest

dispensed favors. And yet he continued to feel himself an outsider, regarded not only with diffidence but with some hostility. Parishioners
questioned his sources of funding. Is he taking money from the Mohawk people to pay for his automobile? Who pays for the rectory rent?
He was devoted to "his people," as he called them (July 10, 1989), but
his real society was the Society of Jesus, not the St. Regis Mohawk
people. He may have known everyone's name and everyone's relations,
but he was not a kinsman, not even when he died of cancer in 1994.
When they needed something of him, they could be demanding.
"Priest! Write this down!" (July 9, 1989), they barked, when they
wanted him to fabricate records to suit one bureaucracy or other. At
times the parish council told Egan to "butt out" of their economic
business (Bigtree, July 9, 1989), and after a new priest succeeded Egan,
the Mohawk Catholics have tried to keep his authority at bay as well.

On the other hand, the heart of the Catholic community at St.
Regis is made up of theological conservatives, "papists" like Father
Egan. He found that many issues important to mainstream American
Catholics, such as the ordination of women and birth control, are ir-
relevant to the Mohawk Catholics. They are against abortion. They be-
lieve in the efficacy of prayer and the mediation of the saints. They
seem to be made in an older mold than mainstream Catholics in the
United States.

They are most like their relatives at Caughnawaga in Canada, the
community from which they sprang in the mid-1700s. Although there
is not a great deal of communication between the two reserves, they
have maintained similar religious profiles. The greater majority at
Caughnawaga (five thousand out of approximately six thousand) have
received baptism (*Tekakwitha Conference Newsletter* 11, no. 2, July–
August 1992: 3). Both reserves have kept up the use of Mohawk in
Catholic liturgy; both have been weakened by the Longhouse tradition which has taken root during this century. As many as 20 percent
of the Caughnawaga Mohawks regard themselves as traditionalists;
another 5 to 10 percent are Protestants (Preston 1991: 15–16). In the
past decade the tensions between the three camps—Catholic, Longhouse, Protestant—have lessened, and dual participation in religious
traditions takes place among some of the populace. At both reserves
the Catholic priests no longer have the authority they once held, as the
Longhouse has competed for loyalty. In addition, the widespread existence of television, automobiles, outward migration for employment,

as well as drugs, drinking, gambling, and the culture of youthful excitement have all taken their toll on Catholicism as well as the Protestant faiths at both Caughnawaga and St. Regis. Some say that St. Regis has a stronger Catholic tradition (Boyer, August 11, 1986, October 14, 1990) than Caughnawaga. There have been attempts in recent years to bring "fallen away" Mohawks from Caughnawaga back to church. Some of these were "afraid to come back," according to a Caughnawaga Mohawk Catholic (Fargo, August 3, 1989), despite invitations from the priests to validate their common-law marriages and receive general absolution for their sins. It is possible that the more energetic Catholics at St. Regis may play a hand in strengthening the Catholic tradition at Caughnawaga in the years ahead.

*   *   *

At the Northeast Tekakwitha Conference in Fonda (Fonda, July 14–16, 1989), Mohawks from St. Regis Reservation and St. Lucy's Church in Syracuse join together to honor their beloved forebear, the Lily of the Mohawks. The matrons hold the central tables in the eating hall, smoking cigarettes, praying, and discussing the lineages of the assembled clans. Younger Indians purchase books published by the North American Indian Traveling College at Akwesasne, savoring the traditionalist teaching by authors such as the late Michael Mitchell, Catholic Longhouse participant. Some of these Indian Catholics want to know more about their people's ancient myths, and so at Kateri's shrine they buy literature in order to learn. Together they pray the rosary, including a Hail Mary or two in Mohawk language, intoned by Anna Dyer and others. Some of these Catholics laugh nervously in fear of forgetting the words to the prayers in English, indicating that they are not regular church-goers. Others pour forth their painful personal histories, breaking down in sobs when discussing drugs and alcohol or their recently deceased relatives. They look to Kateri for strength and guidance and they look to each other for community.

Nancy Kilcoyne, born a Mohawk, raised outside her community, and married to a non-Indian, has come to reclaim her Indian identity under the tutelage of Catholic matrons such as Anna Dyer. For these women, Catholicism is part (but not the entirety) of their Mohawk tradition, and at the Tekakwitha conference they conflate the two identities. Kilcoyne spent two weeks making a fabric wall-hanging for the

altar in a pavilion at the shrine. It illustrates the theme of the conference, "A Spiritual Journey Home with Tekakwitha," by depicting a
Mohawk man and woman walking up a road toward a cross-shaped
star. Along the path are the white pine, tree of peace in the Iroquois
Confederacy, and strawberries, Iroquois symbols of the afterworld.
There are turtles on the man's breechcloth, representing the community of clans, and crosses on the moccasins, indicating Christian guidance. Kilcoyne has not shown the faces of the humans, so that they can
represent anyone—in the manner of traditional cornhusk dolls. Thus
the artist has tried to combine Mohawk and Christian symbols. Before
she started her project, she prayed, "Listen, God. If you want to frus-
trate me, prevent me from this task, then get in my way, stop me."
Then she took a thread and needle and began her work, knowing that
God would aid her. She also got help from an Onondaga artist—the
son of the spiritual chief of the Iroquois Confederacy, the late Leon
Shenandoah—in composing the figures. Kilcoyne laughed to think
that an offspring of the Longhouse leader would lend such a hand to
the Kateri movement.

* * *

Leaders of the Catholic community at St. Regis say that the middle-
aged Mohawks are coming back to church after many years of disaffection (Fonda, July 14–16, 1989). A "unity group" on the reservation
fosters ecumenical relations with traditionalists and Protestants, bringing Mohawks of various denominations together for the commonweal. A sizable contingent of Mohawks attends the annual Tekakwitha
conferences, traveling by cruiser bus and singing hymns along the way
in Mohawk and English. In modern Mohawk style, they also run their
private bingo operation from behind the driver's seat. Ms. Elaine
Cook, long a pillar of the St. Regis Catholic community, has organized
an Easter Sunrise service at the reserve, one she learned from Indians
in Minnesota. At first some of the Mohawks were "leery of putting Indians things into church," she says (ibid.), but each year more people
have attended. Some older Mohawks like Cecilia Cree still eschew "Indian" expressions in Catholic liturgy, except for Mohawk hymns and
prayers, but others are now eager to mix Longhouse and Catholic rituals and even beliefs (Cook, August 7, 1993). Peg Bova sees no reason
that the two groups should remain apart in certain liturgies, especially

since most of the Longhouse people are baptized Catholics (St. Lucy's Church, November 6, 1993). While Church representatives say that "The Longhouse has been totally against the Catholic Church" for years at St. Regis (Lenz, November 19, 1993), the Catholic and traditionalist Mohawks themselves seem to be overcoming their hostilities toward one another, despite lingering bitterness. There have been some "rough years" at St. Regis, when people would "take it out on God" as well as their factional enemies (Egan, June 5, 1991), but Father Egan, then in failing health, saw the hand of Kateri Tekakwitha in preserving the Mohawk community and leading it toward a time of relative peace (Seattle, Swinomish, Lummi, August 5, 1993).

In recent years Mohawks have performed their native Catholic liturgy in St. Patrick's Cathedral in New York City and in the National Cathedral in Washington, D.C. They have formed their own Knights of Columbus chapter at St. Regis, the first such Native American charter in the United States, named after Father Michael Jacobs, S.J., the late Mohawk Jesuit. (In 1916 the first Knights of Columbus from Caughnawaga were inducted into an integrated local chapter; in 1959 they became a separate section, and in 1966 the first Indian Daughters of Isabella chapter was formed at Caughnawaga.)

* * *

In the late 1970s there were enough Catholic Iroquois living in Syracuse—mostly Mohawks from St. Regis—that the Diocese of Syracuse organized an Indian parish group at St. Lucy's Church. Sister Mary Elizabeth Lagoy, who is partially of Algonquin heritage, created a steering committee for the devotees of Kateri Tekakwitha within the parish. When Kateri's beatification was announced in 1980, the parish became a center for celebration. The Bishop of Syracuse, Frank J. Harrison, wanted the Catholic Iroquois to become missioners to their relatives in the area, to become "the channel that the Spirit will use to touch and heal their people. . . . They are the small community in solidarity with the Church becoming proclaimers of the Gospel themselves" (Marquette. DCRAA. 1980). By encouraging Mohawk dancers and singers, by carving Mohawk prayers into the Stations of the Cross, by incorporating Iroquois myths into the readings at mass, by staging a powwow and other "para-liturgical celebrations," Harrison and Lagoy

sought to show the Iroquois of central New York "that they can be Indians and Christians at the same time" (ibid.).

Harrison estimated in 1980 that there were thirty-five hundred baptized Catholics among the five thousand Indians in his diocese, and he
designed to draw as many as he could to St. Lucy's. He constructed a
social mission to the financially disadvantaged Indians, offering
Church help in finding jobs and housing. "Liturgically," Harrison said,
"we will continue to celebrate and affirm the culture and spiritual heritage of the Iroquois Nation by prayer, dance, hymns, art and symbols" (ibid.). Sister Lagoy set up an Indian chapel within the parish
church, decorated with birch logs and deerskin. The stained glass windows portrayed the Iroquois clans, the tree of peace, and the four sea-
sons springing from a longhouse. A large mural of Kateri balanced the
traditionalist emphasis with the image of the Catholic convert. On
some days there were tellings of the Iroquois narrative of creation, followed by a discussion of parallels to the Christian story. At other times
there were hymns and prayers in Mohawk, to the accompaniment of
drums and rattles.

Some of the Indians at St. Lucy's were not ready to give the Iroquois creation story equal value to that of the Bible; nor did they
want to join Catholic worship to archaic Iroquois forms. "I can't relate
to the Turtle," said one Indian woman. "I relate to Genesis. That's
what I grew up with." Others enjoyed the "nice myth" but they wanted
to focus on Christ the redeemer rather than the legendary Iroquois
creator. These Mohawks had viewed traditionalist dances as "mortal
sins" only a decade before, and they were uncomfortable about viewing them at mass, much less taking part in them (in Marquette.
DCRAA. 1982).

At the same time, the non-Indians of St. Lucy's, including the
parish priests, took to the Indian liturgies. The mainstream parishioners found their Catholic faith renewed by the Indian liturgies and
the celebrations of Kateri Tekakwitha's saintliness. When the Kateri
Committee put on dramatizations of Kateri's life, the community was
spiritually moved. Rev. Frank Haig, president of LeMoyne College in
the 1980s, supported the Indian community at St. Lucy's and accompanied them to national Tekakwitha conferences along with a contingent of non-Indian parishioners.

Throughout the 1980s the Kateri Committee officers—most prominently Peg Bova, Anna Dyer, Julie Daniels, Sarah Hassenplug, and

other Mohawk women—made contact with St. Regis, as well as with urban Iroquois communities in Utica, Buffalo, and Rochester, and some Tuscaroras from their reservation, and organized a regional Tekakwitha Conference. On a Saturday around All Souls' Day each year the Kateri Committee arranged a mass to honor its ancestors. On a Saturday before Easter (Kateri died at Easter in 1680), they venerated Tekakwitha with a special service. To each of these events they invited their relatives from St. Regis, and together they worshipped with non-Indians from the parish. These masses have become a tradition at St. Lucy's, one that has helped invigorate Catholic worship at St. Regis, especially since Syracuse Mohawks often return to the reservation for marriages, christenings, and funerals. Many Mohawk Catholics worship regularly at St. Lucy's but they also support St. Regis parish. "'This is really our church'" (Marquette. JINNAM. April 1986), they say of the Akwesasne parish, but they receive grace in the urban parish in Syracuse.

Since the middle 1990s, the Fallen Leaves Mass and Feast on All Souls' Day (St. Lucy's Church, November 6, 1993) commemorating dead relatives and friends has become a major event in the liturgical year. People of all races pay $1.00 to the Kateri Committee of the parish for each leaf placed on a tree set before the altar. In the afternoon the names are chanted, and thus sanctified in memory, followed by a mass and feast, sponsored by the Catholic Indians of the parish. Peg Bova is in charge of the Native American Ministry at the church, "home of the first chapel dedicated in honor of Blessed Kateri Tekakwitha," according to her newsletter, *Tekakwitha Notes*. Through the efforts of Ms. Bova—recently elected to the Board of the National Tekakwitha Conference—St. Lucy's has become a center for the cultus devoted to the Mohawk maiden.

The church is almost filled with Mohawks and non-Indians, and the feast following mass is packed with peoples and victuals. Here is an opportunity for the Indians to host their non-Indian neighbors, and if there is any tension between the ethnic groups, it is invisible to an observer. It is also a time for St. Regis and St. Lucy's Mohawks to renew friendships and make plans. At the start of mass the Kateri Committee provides a sweetgrass blessing, "cleansing for mind and body," they exclaim, and the congregation dutifully scoops the smoke to themselves as the ritual leaders walk the aisles with the smoking Mohawk herb. There is a basket of strawberries at the base of the memorial tree, honoring the dead, and Mary George tells the worshippers what the berries mean. Not only do the Iroquois thank the strawberry when it is ripe in June, she says, but at Iroquois weddings the husband gives a strawberry cake to his wife as a symbol of his ability to provide for her welfare. Finally, strawberries are placed along the way of the dead to the other world, according to Iroquois tradition. When an Iroquois dies, it is said that, "You've gone strawberry picking," hence its place at this service.

A platter of food is next to the strawberries. Another Iroquois reads, "At a time when our hearts and minds are as one, the Iroquois remember . . . their dead and share in a feast. With great love, we set aside a plate of food, a gift for those that have died. As we all come together to share as one, this plate is in honor of our dead, for they are not forgotten." Of the several hundred names chanted, many are recognizably Mohawk: Tarbell, Lazore, Cook, Thomas, Papineau, Benedict, Cree, White, Mitchell, George, LaFrance. They also include names of families who have married Iroquois, e.g., the Sacco family of Syracuse. Still others are non-Indians, ancestors of the others in the congregation. At the Fallen Leaves Mass and Feast, located in the Catholic calendar around All Souls' Day, Indians and non-Indians remember their dead together, and they do so under Catholic authority and with a Catholic worldview. The liturgical brochure for the event, for example, states on its cover, "Grass withers and flowers fade, but the word of God endures forever." Thus, despite its Mohawk trappings of symbolism, the message is a Christian one—that God's word outlasts us all.

* * *

Attending the 1993 national Tekakwitha conference is a Mohawk woman from Caughnawaga, brought up within the Longhouse tradition and trained as a storyteller from her youth. She is now working toward her doctorate in American history, writing a dissertation on Catholic boarding schools among Native Americans. As a young adult she determined to separate herself from the Longhouse, partially because she came to regard it as a "new religion" rather than a manifestation of aboriginal Iroquois religiousness. She terms the Longhouse founder, Handsome Lake, a "Quaker dupe," and criticizes the syncretistic conjoining of antagonistic features of Christian and Iroquois traditions in the Longhouse complex.

She felt unsatisfied with her place in the Longhouse and with her Iroquois identity in general, so she sought to assimilate herself to mainstream culture in North America. She wanted to try on one of the Western religious traditions. Protestantism did not suit her, nor did Judaism. Because of her Longhouse background she perceived Catholicism as the enemy of the Iroquois and thus she avoided it.

Conversations with a Catholic nun aroused her interest in faith within the Church. She continued to feel hostility toward Catholicism; however, she began to take instruction from several priests. She challenged them with interrogations that led her toward the conviction that the Church possesses a teaching authority she had never encountered before. The Longhouse had unresolved contradictions between its various parts, and thus lacked *magesterium*, in her view. The systematic quality of Catholic theology had an appeal that won her to conversion. In the twentieth century, when Mohawks have abandoned the Catholicism of their recent forebears for the "traditionalism" of the Longhouse, she turned toward the authoritative teaching tradition of the Church. This "circuitous" route took her five years of searching.

After her conversion and baptism, another Catholic sister "dragged her kicking and screaming" to a retreat led by the Ojibway medicine man and Catholic priest, John Hascall. Father Hascall's goal in ministry has been to make Catholic Indians feel spiritually at home in their Indian culture; it was the last thing on the new convert's mind to embrace Indian practices through the agency of a Catholic cleric. In the company of urban Indians in Milwaukee who sponsored the retreat, she was surprised to find herself drawn, through Catholicism, to Native American spirituality.

At Tekakwitha conferences she continues to blend her newly validated Catholic and Indian religiousness. For all the blending, however, she regards herself as, and indeed is, a "conservative" Catholic convert. She is put off by the feminist flouting of Church authority, and she tells the sisters with whom she travels, to their dismay, that Catholics need to obey even a patriarchal Catholicism. She has chosen not to marry because she will not accept the subservient position of a woman in a Catholic marriage. On the other hand, she cannot bring herself to contradict the Church's *magesterium* and disregard the patterns established through matrimony. She would rather not marry than marry and have to be subservient, but even more strongly, she wants to obey the Church (Shillinger, August 5, 1993).

* * *

In 1995 the Catholic Iroquois of the United States and Canada hosted the annual Tekakwitha conference, ferrying the thousands of participants between St. Regis (Akwesasne) and the Blessed Kateri Tekakwitha Shrine at Caughnawaga (now also referred to as Kahnawake), Quebec. In planning the 1995 gala, organizers such as Elaine Cook and Peg Bova have hoped to bring together Iroquois Catholics from both reserves, as well as the St. Lucy's contingent from Syracuse; simultaneously, they have hoped not to offend the members of the Longhouse by their expressions of Catholicism (St. Lucy's Church, November 6, 1993). The resulting celebrations demonstrate the centrality of Kateri for the Catholic Iroquois and the significance of Iroquois Catholicism to Native Americans in the Church.

At a newly completed hockey stadium on Cornwall Island at Akwesasne, several thousand participants witness a high mass conducted by Bishop Robert La Belle of the Diocese of Valleyfield. "He really loves it here," attests a sister (Murphy, August 5, 1995) who has served as catechist at St. Regis for several years, and so does she. As a white outsider, driving back and forth between the reserve from Montreal, she has experienced hospitality and affection at St. Regis, and at the mass on Cornwall Island she is greeted most warmly by elders and youths alike. The Kateri Circle at the reserve creates a solid core of staunch Catholic faith; the children learn their lessons well and are amply prepared for confirmation. Even the traditionalists seem to look benignly upon professions of contemporary Iroquois Catholicism.

The audience receives the smoky blessings of Indian smudging before mass. Everyone applauds the various Mohawk elders—Cecilia Cree, Mary Herne, Louise Herne, Ruth Herne, Dorothy Jacobs, Elizabeth Jacobs, Harriet LaFrance, Agnes Lazore, Isabel Lazore, Margaret Terrance, Mary Terrance, Agnes Sunday, Father George White, O.M.I., Dr. Solomon Cook—as the litany of their accomplishments is recited. Dr. Cook, for instance, with a Ph.D. from Cornell University and a distinguished record as former chief of the St. Regis Mohawk

Tribal Council, is said to be a devotee of Kateri Tekakwitha. He is a parish council member at St. Regis, a Eucharistic minister, a member of the Kateri Circle, and a charter member of the Knights of Columbus chapter named in memory of Father Michael Jacobs, S.J. (his brother-in-law).

The Mohawk choir of St. Regis and other performers sing the praises of Kateri Tekakwitha, both in Mohawk and English songs of their own composition. "Tewanaton Ne Kateri" ("We Sing of One Named Kateri") contains these verses penned by Peg Bova:

> We sing of one named Kateri,
> A holy maiden of Mohawk tribe.
> Her one true love was Jesus the Lord,
> and chosen was she to be His bride. . . .
> Forbidden by her tribal friends,
> to follow Christ, her beloved One.
> When urged to wed, she heard His call,
> and vowed her love to God's own Son. . . .
> Upon her deathbed came a great light.
> Her pockmarked face was clean and bright.
> Amazed and awed were all who were there.
> They knew they saw a maiden of Prayer.
>
> (St. Regis, August 5, 1995)

At Caughnawaga the public celebration of Kateri is every bit as effusive as at Akwesasne. Although it is reported (Preston, August 4, 1995), that only a few dozen Mohawks attend Sunday mass and that their contemporary expressions of faith are often "lackadaisical," the reserve bears many reminders of Tekakwitha's presence in the St. Francis Xavier Church shrine. There is a school, a hospital, and a park named for Kateri. The traditional chief welcomes the Tekakwitha conference visitors, even though his reserve is more secular than Catholic these days. Its inhabitants are accustomed to the thousands of pilgrims who journey to the Kateri shrine each year, and who leave in the church the photographs of persons, many of them Indians, for whom their prayers are offered in hope of intercession. In recent years the Caughnawaga Mohawks have often resented the pilgrims; however, on this special day of celebration they wave to the busloads of Indian and non-Indian outlanders and sell them their wares.

As the pilgrims arrive, they enter the shrine to pay homage to Blessed Kateri. Monsignor Paul A. Lenz describes the scene:

I stood for a long time in the St. Francis Xavier Church where the tomb is located and watched the steady stream of Native American people pray. The lines were long and lingering and I observed tears in the eyes of many as they showed their love and devotion for Blessed Kateri, the only one with Native American blood who has been honored by the Church. I know the sincere prayers were that she will soon be Saint Kateri Tekakwitha. (*Bureau of Catholic Indian Missions Newsletter* 14, no. 6, August 1995)

Following these personal devotions, Bishop Bernard Hubert of the Diocese of St. Jean-Longueuil leads a Eucharistic Celebration in the church, accompanied by the Caughnawaga Mohawk choir, Knights of Columbus, and various co-celebrants. The Ojibway catechist, Ron Boyer (married to a Caughnawaga Catholic stalwart), prays during a penitential rite—a sweetgrass burning ceremony preceding the mass: "We come here for healing . . . , to get rid of the garbage, . . . the hypodermic needles, . . . the pain of our existence" (Kahnawake, August 4, 1995).

In order to accomplish this goal, the congregation offers its prayers: "God of all peoples, Great Spirit of Life, you made Blessed Kateri Tekakwitha, the Lily of the Mohawks, a sign of your presence among her people." A young girl recites the "Our Father" in Mohawk; a violinist plays a meditational piece as an acclamation of the gospel; and Bishop Hubert evokes the holiness of Kateri's presence. "Her remains rest in this sanctuary," he declares, "and thus this is holy ground which reveals the way of the divine to us." Before the offertory procession of corn, beans, and squash, the participants make a "Native Profession of Faith":

> We believe in the Creator, the Great Spirit, Maker of Mother Earth and Father Sky, Creator of the seasons and of all living things. We believe in Jesus of Nazareth, a man of God, who lived with the courage of commitment, who sacrificed life that the people may live, for all people, for all ages, for us. We believe in the Holy Spirit, the action-love of the Great One and of Jesus, who breaks down barriers between people and empowers us to love one another. We believe in the community of committed and faith-filled people. We believe it is our task to be the salt of the earth and the light of the world, justice and peace-makers, knowing that this calls us to the sacrifice of the cross. We believe in the power of the Great Spirit's presence as it fills our hearts, helping us to reach outward in the Four Directions to all people in need of healing. We believe in a just world, in equal rights for all. We believe in resurrection, and in a more full life with the Creator in the world beyond. We believe! Help our un-belief! AMEN!

Finally, the audience turns its prayerful attention back to its beloved Tekakwitha, "that Blessed Kateri may be recognized as a saint by the whole Church":

> O God, who, among the many marvels of Your Grace in the New World, did cause to blossom on the banks of the Mohawk and of the St. Lawrence, the pure and tender Lily, Kateri Tekakwitha, grant we beseech You, the favor we beg through her intercession; that this Young Lover of Jesus and of His Cross may soon be counted among the Saints by Holy Mother Church, and that our hearts may be enkindled with a stronger desire to imitate her innocence and faith. Through the same Christ Our Lord. Amen. (Ibid.)

At the close of the Eucharistic Celebration, the congregation hears a story of one pilgrimage, said to symbolize the import of Kateri Tekakwitha not only to Iroquois Catholics but to Catholic Indians throughout North America. A dying Native American woman painted a likeness of Kateri to be presented at the Caughnawaga shrine in 1995. "The Tekakwitha Conference has come home," she told her sons, "and I want my painting to be there." After her death, the sons brought the portrait in their car from the United States to Canada. When they were asked at the border, "Do you have anything to declare?" they replied, with a typically Indian mixture of reverence and humor, "Yes. We have a saint in the back seat" (ibid.).

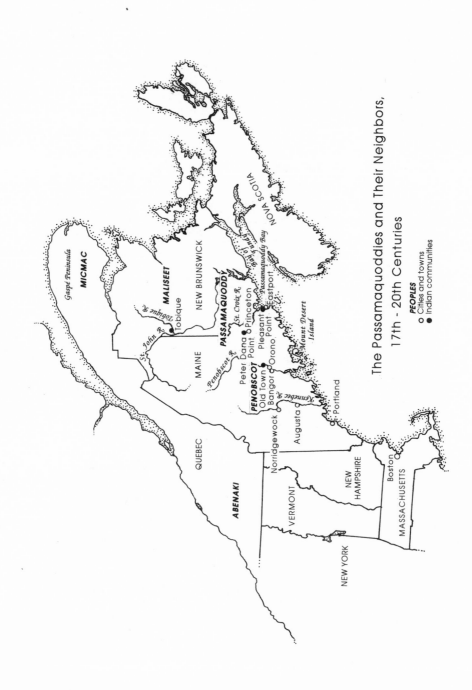

The Passamaquoddies and Their Neighbors,
17th - 20th Centuries

PEOPLES
○ Cities and towns
● Indian communities

MICMAC

Gaspé Peninsula

MALISEET

Tobique R.
Tobique

St. John R.

NEW BRUNSWICK

PASSAMAQUODDY

St. Croix R.
Princeton

NOVA SCOTIA

Bay of Fundy

Passamaquoddy Bay
Eastport
Pleasant
Point

Peter Dana
Point

MAINE

Penobscot R.

PENOBSCOT
Old Town
Bangor Orono

Mount Desert
Island

Kennebec R.

Portland

QUEBEC

Norridgewock

Augusta

ABENAKI

VERMONT

NEW
HAMPSHIRE

Boston

NEW YORK

MASSACHUSETTS

Before the Jesuits encountered the Montagnais along the St. Lawrence River or the Hurons beside Georgian Bay, long before the evangelization of the Iroquois south of Lake Ontario, the process of missionizing had begun among the Indians of New France. In 1610 a secular priest, Jessé Fléché, arrived in Acadia and within three weeks he claimed to have converted twenty-one of the local Native Americans.

These Acadian Indians were Micmacs, Eastern Algonkians, related by language and culture to the Maliseets, Penobscots, Passamaquoddies, and other Indians of the Abenaki Confederacy in what is now New Brunswick and the State of Maine. The Micmacs and loosely affiliated Abenakis, numbering several thousand in the early seventeenth century, were typical of northeastern hunting peoples in their worldview, spirituality, ritualism, and environmental relations. They believed in the creative prowess of their culture heroes, the necessity of communicating with the *manitos*, and the interplay of natural, divine, and human realms. They made tobacco offerings to the spirits and animals; they revered their dreams; each individual was responsible for maintaining balance with all forces, for the sake of good hunting, for the sake of human continuance.

Abbé Fléché preached to a band of these Micmacs under the watch of their leader, Membertou, and within a year the priest had well over a hundred baptisms to his credit, which was a "remarkable achievement" (Jaenen 1976b: 23), considering that he spoke no Indian languages. "For this hasty act," reports a historian, "Fléché was censured in retrospect by his successors" (Grant 1985: 4). Nonetheless, the beginnings of Christianity among the Indians of New France took place at Port Royal (now Annapolis, in Nova Scotia). A correspondent described the proceedings: "Membertou was named after our late good King Henri IV., and his eldest son after Monseigneur the Dauphin, today our King Louis XIII., whom may God bless." Membertou's wife received her name from Marie, the queen regent, and their daughter took the name of the queen, Marguerite. A second son was named for Paul, the pope, "and thus each one was given the name of some illustrious or notable personage here in France" (Thwaites 1896–1901,

1:77). Some of the Micmacs took to wearing crosses on their person, and one sagamore erected a large cross in his village, "although he did not understand a word" (79) of French.

The following year two Jesuits arrived at Port Royal. Fathers Pierre Biard and Ennémond Massé were unimpressed by the progress of faith among the baptized natives. Biard wrote:

> I had them make the sign of the cross; but I was very much astonished, for the unbaptized understood almost as much about it as the christians. . . . When I asked them if they were christians, they did not know what I meant; when I asked them if they had been baptized, they answered . . . "Yes, the Patriarch has made us like the Normans." (1:163)

It may be that the Indians "accepted baptism as a sort of sacred pledge of friendship and alliance with the French" (in 2:89), as the two Jesuits surmised. Without the "unmistakable evidence of a comprehension of the principal beliefs of the Catholic faith," they were wary of christening any Indians, save for "infants with the consent of their parents in the hope that there would be opportunity for their later instruction and adults at the point of death" (Leger 1929: 19).

Nonetheless, Henri Membertou "remembered that he was a christian, and therefore prayed to God" (Thwaites 1896–1901, 1:167) when he was suffering from hunger and again when his son fell ill. When God seemed to deliver him from his bodily needs, he began to exhibit a kind of Christian zeal. "I call it . . . a miracle," wrote Marc Lescarbot,

> that these poor people have conceived such an opinion of the Christian Religion, that as soon as they are sick they ask to be baptized; and, even when they are well, they approach it with great Faith, saying they wish to be like us, fully recognizing their own shortcomings. Membertou, the great Sagamore, exhorts every one of the Savages to become Christians. All bear witness that since they have been baptized they are afraid of nothing, and go out boldly at night, the devil no longer tormenting them. (2:183)

The Christian Micmacs were convinced that the Jesuits possessed power over disease and the hunt and wished to share in their efficacy.

Membertou was an old man and he died before the close of 1611, after receiving extreme unction. He chose to be buried in a Christian burial ground rather than with the bodies of his ancestors. His three sons, Louis, Philippe, and Paul, carried on the family association with Christianity. Soon the priests brought word of Christianity to other Algonkians of the region. These "heralds of the Gospel traversed a

great part of the country. A godly act was performed wherever opportunity allowed; hands were laid upon the sick; parents and children
were conciliated by means of little gifts . . ." (1:215–217).

At the mouth of the St. Croix River (now Pleasant Point, Maine), a
Passamaquoddy chief, Oagimont, wished to renew the friendly relations he had established with the French as early as 1604. Further west,
at Mount Desert Island, Biard christened an apparently dying child,
who recovered. The Penobscot chief requested the priest to establish a
mission (called St. Sauveur) on the island. In this way the Abenakis
joined the Micmacs as French allies and potential Christians. Among
all these Indians the French carried out a policy of "missionizing from
the top" (Krieger 1993:97): converting chiefs and affirming their authority through gifts and symbolic gestures.

In 1613 the English put an end to the French evangelical experiment, shipping Father Biard back to the Old World; however, from
France the Jesuit exhorted others to take up his missionary work. He
did not think that he had made sincere and knowledgeable Christians
of the natives in his two years in Acadia; that goal would take the
resources of a "Catholic colony," and even so it would require "long
patience" (Thwaites 1896–1901, 3:137, 141).

Recollects and Capuchins made attempts to fulfill the expectations
of the short-lived Jesuit effort, the former along the St. John River and
the latter on the Penobscot. An epidemic in 1616 made the Abenakis
receptive to the curative potential of Christian charms, and so these
missions met with some success. The Indians imitated Christian gestures of prayer and urged the priests to intercede on their behalf with
God to combat disease and find food. In the meantime the Jesuits returned to New France and began their efforts among the Algonkians
and Iroquoians north and west of the St. Lawrence.

In 1642 the Montagnais apostle of Sillery, Charles Meiachkawat,
saved several Abenakis following a battle. He brought them to Sillery,
where the Hospital Nuns treated their wounds. The nuns and priests
also instructed the patients in prayer. When the Abenakis recovered,
Meiachkawat accompanied them to their home on the Kennebec
River in order to preach about the Catholic faith. He made a positive
impression on at least one sagamore, who journeyed back to Sillery
with the Montagnais evangelist and received instruction and eventual
christening.

This was the beginning of an Abenaki mission, for in 1646 Father

Gabriel Druillettes, S.J., answered the call of the Abenakis and founded Assumption mission on the Kennebec with the help of the Indian catechist Noel Negabamat. Druillettes learned the Abenaki language and served as an envoy of trade with the French in two stints lasting until 1652.

The Jesuit baptized dozens of Indians at Assumption. He cared for the sick during an epidemic and earned the Indians' praise as a curer and humanitarian. He became a leader among them and was able, without visible opposition, to get the Abenakis to give up alcohol, throw away aboriginal charms, and turn against their shamans. The Kennebec Abenakis embraced Catholic practice so warmly that the process of conversion seemed painless, almost natural. A recent historian writes that the Abenakis "did not compartmentalize traditional and Christian beliefs." Instead, their Catholicism represented "a syncretic intensification of their ancient religious life" (Morrison 1981: 236; cf. 75–87).

Druillettes' presence sparked a religious revitalization among the Abenakis, a Christian revival that lasted for years. The Abenakis became devout Catholics, at least in appearance, demonstrating a "monks' harsh self-discipline" (Conkling 1974: 18). They went to confession frequently; they accepted the Jesuits' authority. They turned to Christian power as if their old religion had none left to offer. Druillettes concerned himself little with theological education; rather, he played the role of the native holyman, conjuring up some moose for the kill with an Our Father, laying blame on shamans for purported witchery. In the Abenaki communities baptized by Druillettes, dreams and visions continued to play important roles, only they took on a Christian content, with visitations from recently deceased relatives reporting on the joys of heaven.

When Druillettes was called to a mission in the western Great Lakes region, following the Iroquois devastation of the Hurons, the Abenakis went once again without a priest. Nevertheless, they maintained their Catholic identity. Some of their numbers continued to travel to Sillery, as they had since the 1640s, to seek asylum, instruction and baptism, and many of these came to live at the reduction until it became, in effect, an Abenaki reserve. Some of the Sillery inhabitants were refugees from King Philip's War, which erupted in New England in 1675. In the late 1670s Father Jacques Bigot, S.J., received consistent aid at Sillery from these refugees in maintaining the devotional quality of life at the reduction. "Conversion to Catholicism followed kinship lines" (Morrison 1981: 253) as they taught one another, chided backsliders, and learned their prayers and hymns proficiently. They seemed especially fearful of the "horrors of hell" impressed upon them by Bigot's "spectacular representations" (in Grant 1985: 62) in song and sermon. In the anomie of their dislocated condition—an impoverished refugee people dependent upon charity from missionaries—Christianity both frightened them and gave them hope. Some escaped and others entered into the sedentary farming life of the reserve. When the soil at Sillery was finally exhausted in the 1680s, the community moved to a new site, St. Francis de Sales, slightly closer to Abenaki country. By 1688 over six hundred Abenakis lived in Canada, presumably as Christians, at St. Francis and other locations (Morrison 1984: 96–98).

Father Bigot resolved in 1688 to reestablish missions among the Abenakis in their own territory, following the lead of another priest of the Foreign Missions Seminary of Quebec, Louis Pierre Thury, who went among the Penobscots the year before. French officials wished these priests to hold the Abenakis as allies in the impending war with England, and in this the priests were largely successful. Until the Capitulation of Canada in 1760, Abenakis served French interests, traveling back and forth from their own villages to the several reserves—St. Francis de Sales, Bécancourt, and others—close to the French. In times of war the Indians could retreat to these reductions, or set out from them to attack the English. The continual contact between reductions and home villages meant a thorough association between Catholicism and the Abenakis. The missionaries tried to keep the Indians from the debauching influence of the French, but the lure of liquor often accompanied the attraction of the gospel.

Perhaps as many as a half dozen Jesuits were appointed in the early 1700s to the territory of present-day Maine and New Brunswick, a territory claimed by England. Cotton Mather referred to their missions as congeries of "half Indianized French, and half Frenchified Indians." He reported that the priests told the Algonkians "that the Lord Jesus Christ was of the *French Nation*; that his mother, the virgin *Mary*, was a *French Lady*; that they were the English who had murdered him. . . . Hence, the Indians should serve Jesus by taking revenge on the English" (in ibid., 146 [emphases Mather's]). In 1700 the Massachusetts

General Court banned the Jesuits from their realm in an attempt to cease their meddling

In the bitter colonial battles between French and English, Sébastian Râle, S.J., played a pivotal role in holding the allegiance of the Abenakis. Other priests spent time among the Penobscots and Passamaquoddies further east, but Râle's activities were the most famous among the French, and infamous among the English. Râle spent thirty years among the Indians, largely at Norridgewock on the Kennebec River, until in 1724, during the war that wrecked the Abenakis, the English "pillaged his church, drove his converts to Canada, and carried his scalp back to Boston . . ." (Axtell 1986: 253).

In the aftermath of this attack, the eastern Abenakis fled their territory and found refuge in the reserves of Quebec, particularly St. Francis de Sales and Bécancourt, where they intermarried with the French over the years. Some of their descendants remain in the Northeast— both in Canada and the United States—to this day, still baptized members of the Roman Catholic Church. In 1980 Bishop John A. Marshall of the Diocese of Vermont wrote that the Abenakis in his state "have intermarried with the French settlers and become general Vermonters. We have no special ministry to Native Americans as they are not a distinct group" (Marquette. DCRAA. 1980). In more recent years, however, these Abenakis have begun to assert their cultural identity.

Other Abenakis in the eighteenth century escaped to the Penobscots, Passamaquoddies, and Maliseets in the Penobscot, St. Croix, and St. John River Valleys, respectively. There they were given refuge and kept contact with Jesuits until the end of the French and Indian War, when the missions ceased.

After the initial appearance of success among the Micmacs, most of that tribe remained unevangelized, and some who were in contact with Christians expressed hostility toward French missionaries. In the 1670s, however, both Micmacs and Maliseets received missions. The Recollect Christien Le Clercq developed a hieroglyphic system for teaching prayers and catechism to the Micmacs in the Gaspé Peninsula. He wrote these glyphs on paper and the Indians treated them with great devotion—as they would their aboriginal mnemonic parchments—by placing them in bark cases with wampum beads and porcupine quills. Through these scrolls, and later through an alphabet developed by another priest, the Micmacs became accustomed to voicing Catholic ideas in their own language (see, e.g., the Lord's Prayer in

Micmac hieroglyphics, Le Clercq 1881: opposite 16). They came to be called "the oldest daughter of the church among North American Indians" (in Krieger 1993: 88–89), although it was unclear in the seventeenth or eighteenth century just how christianized the Micmacs were.

Over the centuries, however, all of these Eastern Algonkians—Micmacs, Maliseets, Passamaquoddies, Penobscots, and the eastern Abenakis—became firmly associated with Catholicism. The Jesuits had entered their traditional worldview as charismatic leaders; the French had become their legendary allies. Without coercion the priests had caused the Eastern Algonkians to be "voluntarily obedient" (Conkling 1974: 2). In the nineteenth century a solitary priest, Christian Kauder, "reactivated Micmac Catholicism" (Krieger 1993: 100) by drawing upon their long-held loyalties. He formed Christian cadres against alcoholism; he had a local chief lead daily prayer services; he made Catholic identity the core of their communal ethos, so that "the harshest" penitence for them, he reported, was "exclusion from common prayer and mass" (in ibid., 99).

Over time "Catholic symbolism pervaded" the culture of the Eastern Algonkians:

> "He who made all" ensured success in hunting, in agriculture, and in warfare. Patron saints, the use of medals and crucifixes as personal power objects, the placement of chapels in the fields, and community prayer—all represent elaborations of the traditional Abenaki belief in a cosmos organized by conflicting, personalized powers. (Morrison 1981: 254)

These Indians "preserved their identity as Catholics, which they have maintained ever since . . . , more than two centuries after the British Conquest" (Axtell 1986: 277).

During the American Revolution the Abenakis and Micmacs saw a chance to renew association with the Church. Since the 1763 Treaty of Paris, the Jesuit mission had retreated to the St. Lawrence, and in 1773 Pope Clement XIV had suppressed the Society of Jesus worldwide. Having resisted Protestant initiatives for a decade, the Indians offered to side with the revolutionists of Massachusetts (after all, the French were their allies now) in return for a promise of renewed Catholic evangelism. A Maliseet spoke in 1775: "We want a Black-gown or French priest. Jesus we pray to, and we will not hear any prayer (i.e., religion) that comes from old England" (in Shea 1855: 155). Orono, the Penobscot sagamore—who had told the New England Congregation-alists, "We know our religion, and love it: we know nothing of you or yours" (156)—joined in the call, as did the Passamaquoddies, who managed to get a brief visit from a French navy chaplain in 1779 when the Massachusetts General Court could not secure a Catholic cleric, despite the agreement.

After the Revolution's end the Bishopric of Baltimore was established in 1790, with the former Jesuit, John Carroll, as the first American prelate. The Passamaquoddies, Penobscots, and Maliseets sent him a cross once belonging to Father Râle and penned the following note to him: "Nous te prions, Père de l'Eglise de cette terre, de nous envoyer un prêtre; nous l'attendons avec un coeur inquiet, espérant que tu nous repondras favorablement" (in Leger 1929: 133). Carroll deployed a French Sulpician, Father Francis Ciquard, who spent several years in Penobscot territory before settling among the Maliseets. He was succeeded by Rev. John Cheverus, who recognized that "The Indians will do anything . . . in order to get a Priest" (139). When he entered the territory of the Passamaquoddies in 1797, he "expressed amazement that the Mass for the Dead is sung in exactly the same tune as is customary among French Catholics, with the correct singing of the kyrie and the responses at the Preface" (138). The following year the General Court of Massachusetts appropriated $200 annually for him to live alternatively among the Penobscots and Passama-quoddies, and when Cheverus became bishop of Boston, he made sure that others succeeded him. In 1804 a Protestant wrote disdainfully of the Penobscots:

> The attempts to civilize these people have been attended with not much more success than those which have been made to christianize them. They say that the religion of the Congregationalists is too simple for them and they are in some measure attached to the Roman Catholic religion, on account of its being more ceremonious, repeating their prayers and crossing themselves at morning and evening. They treat the Roman Catholic priests with great respect, and have children baptized. They have no doubt of the power of the priests to pardon their sins and are cheerfully willing to pay the utmost of their ability for so great and necessary an accommodation. (145)

But from the Catholic point of view at mid-century, the Indians of Maine at three locations—Penobscots at Old Town, Passamaquoddies at Pleasant Point and Peter Dana Point (Indian Township)—were devoted Christians. All three of their churches, manned by Jesuits from 1848, were "dedicated to St. Anne, the patroness of the tribe, which has an unbounded devotion to the Mother of the Virgin, and in distress sends her pilgrims to the wonder-working shrine in Canada" (Shea 1855: 162) at Sainte-Anne-de-Beaupré. Despite the difficult social adjustments of a dwindling population—there were fewer than a thousand Maine Indians in 1855 and incest was a problem as the communities tried to keep to themselves (ibid.)—Church authorities felt proud of their successes.

Sisters of Mercy entered the Penobscot and Passamaquoddy area in the 1870s, teaching and serving as "field matrons. . . . Living as they do in the heart of the Indian villages, while the priests are located from two to twenty miles away," wrote a Catholic observer in 1913 (*The Indian Sentinel*: 12), "the Sisters are the real missionaries among the Indians. In the absence of the priest, the Sisters conduct services in the churches, to which the Indians are very much attracted." This assessment rings true from the documentation within the diocesan archives in Portland, Maine. In 1885 the Passamaquoddy governor at Pleasant Point, Louis Francis, wrote to the Bishop of Portland, "Our Lord & Great Father," from his "children," thanking him for his pastoral care: "Since you became our Bishop our children know how to pray better and are growing good christians since you gave us the sisters, & we, too, know more of religion & are better christians. That we know will make your heart glad" (Portland. May 31, 1885). A visiting priest at

Peter Dana Point described the Passamaquoddies there: "The Indians are, as a rule, docile, and like children. They are peaceable, and never quarrel except when under the influence of 'Firewater' to which, like most Indians, they are given" (1901?). Another priest said, "The Faith and Catholic life of our good Passamaquoddy Indians are a great consolation to me and make me feel that everything should be done to keep them safe from the many dangers threatening their spiritual life on all sides" (May 10, 1901). Letters from the Passamaquoddy governors attested to the success of the sisters (e.g., August 5, 1907) and at least one Passamaquoddy boy was reported to have a possible vocation to the priesthood (April 21, 1935).

Three hundred years after the first founding of missions among the Indians of Maine, *The Indian Sentinel* termed the Penobscots and Passamaquoddies "the happiest people in the world." These Indians were "without a single grudge." They were "the most favored in their treatment at the hands of the Government; among the best cared for in the matter of religion; the most Catholic in their history" (1913: 5). The Catholic missionary organ acknowledged the presence of debilitating alcohol among the Maine Indians; except for this blight, however, their condition was "nigh perfect" (19). Although the Indians had lost almost all their lands to the State of Massachusetts and Maine, they continued to live religious and industrious lives. "Does not justice demand that the State make return for the lands seized or ceded?" asked the Catholic writer, answering his rhetorical question with the claim: "The people of Maine need no outsider to inform them of their duty. They are fulfilling that duty, to the very brim if not to running over" (11). For example, the Knights of Columbus in 1911 erected a stele on Main Street in Orono to honor "Joseph Orono, Catholic Indian Chief" (Orono, August 5–9, 1992). When pastors called for building funds for their Indian parishes, e.g., when St. Ann's Church burned down at Pleasant Point in 1928, people throughout the diocese contributed generously (Portland. July 5, 1928).

It would appear that the Indians of Maine made an adjustment to Catholic life that indicated a successful period of evangelization. "They bear a very good reputation, are of superior intelligence, self-supporting, and sober," wrote a Catholic sister in 1929 (Leger 1929: 5). A priest reported them all Catholic, "wonderfully loyal to their Faith during all this time, despite wars, persecutions, and many other adversities, including deprivation of a priest for considerable intervals" (*Our Negro and Indian Missions* 1941: 40). According to another priest, "Notwithstanding the indolence and sometimes total indifference of certain Indians, the Catholic Faith is preserved and progresses in their midst" (1947: 22).

This judgment, with regard to the Indians' preservation of faith, is repeated in the present day. A Jesuit states that the Indians of Maine, New Brunswick, and Nova Scotia have been thoroughly catholicized over three and a half centuries: "No one remembers what it was like not to be Catholic. They are truly ethnic Catholics" (Marquette. JIN-NAM. February 9, 1984). A Belgian scholar says of the Micmacs that their "traditions were seemingly replaced or discarded in order to take over adapted Catholic ceremonies. No parallel 'traditional' religious set of behaviour seems to exist anymore." They practice "their own Micmac Catholicism" and their "culture as constituted today is a product of missionary influence and their reshaping activities" (Krieger 1993: 93, 100). A diocesan priest with fourteen years of experience as pastor at the Maliseet Reserve of Tobique in New Brunswick remarks upon the "very reverent" (Thibodeau, August 7, 1992) attitude of the Catholic Indians of the old Abenaki Confederacy toward priests, sisters, saints, and sacramentals. He says mass in the Maliseet language, much to their joy. He admits that at Tobique only 20 percent of the Maliseets are "practicing" Catholics. "Of course they're *all* Catholics," he adds. "Don't tell them they're not." Like the Micmacs and Maliseets, the Maine Algonkians are said to have combined their Catholicism and native spirituality in an easy and fruitful blend, without secretive compartmentalization (Starkloff, March 18, 1985). According to various Jesuit commentators, they have maintained a deep and ritual commitment to Catholic forms, proud of the longevity of their association with the Church, and persistent in their devotion to Ste. Anne as a symbol of the divine among them (Egan, July 9, 1989; Stogre, October 13, 1990).

Scholars assent in this judgment of Eastern Algonkian Catholicism. It is fully incorporated into the Indians' culture, including that of the four thousand Indians of Maine (Smith 1976: 119–127; Morrison 1984: 99–101). Their liturgical calendar focuses upon Sundays, Fridays, and the special Catholic feasts at Christmas, Epiphany, New Year's Day, Ash Wednesday, Palm Sunday, Easter, Corpus Christi, St. John's Day, and most importantly, Ste. Anne's Day. Their legends recount the heroic deeds of priests, wielding their crosses as weapons against the forces of evil. Both in ritual and in myth the Indians continue to express the values of their aboriginal culture, but they do so through the culture of Catholicism as a fully integrated aspect of their being, at least according to those who have examined their contemporary faith.

When one examines the archives and visits the communities of the Passamaquoddies, a different picture emerges. At least since the late 1930s there have been patterns of disaffection, violence, and dysfunction that belie the sobriquet of "the happiest people in the world." Instead one sees people who feel abused by the Church, despite their devotional piety; people who often seek the visionary and ritual patterns of the distant past—patterns long gone but now in the process of revitalization—to calm the turmoil in their lives.

In 1938 Rev. James J. Tomlinson, the first modern pastor to live full-time on the reservation, wrote to his bishop about the Passamaquoddies at Peter Dana Point (Indian Township): "I do not know what has happened to the faith of the Indians. . . . They seem to lack all responsibility—They are a loose living group and have been made so by association with a cheap crowd of whites who frequent their shanties. . . . they are a seeming [sic] hopeless people" (Portland. July 12, 1938). When he arrived to say Sunday mass, he found only four Indians present. Two years later he complained that "It seems the priest that is sent to this Mission is the object of pity of all the other priests in the diocese" (February 27, 1940). It wasn't just the cold winter weather, the cracked boiler in the church, the feeling of "exile" on the reservation; there was a growing sense of immorality gone rampant, more than partially as the result of increased contact with non-Indians. "Right now we have an epidemic of hunters," Tomlinson wrote, "who come around this place to hunt the Indian girls" (November 19, 1947). More than one Indian woman ran a "cat house" (March 16, 1952), causing public scandal. Adultery was widespread, according to the priest, with concomitant illegitimacy in births. Alcoholism was becoming a salient feature of reservation life, even among the community leaders. When the clerics tried to assert moral authority, they were met with violence. One Passamaquoddy man burned down a rectory and hit a priest with an axe. A woman—"a savage," steamed Tomlinson—threw an iron at him; in return he "spanked her." After fifteen years of service at Peter Dana Point, Tomlinson was concerned with far more than "fallen away Catholics" from the fold; he was concerned for his life. He concluded

wryly, "There is never a dull moment here." Contemporary Passamaquoddies remember that Father Tomlinson used to carry a strap, a billy
club, and a twelve-battery flashlight, and "he used them" (Gabriel et
al., August 23, 1992). This is reported not as a complaint but rather as
a description of how "rough" the reservation was in the 1930s and
1940s.

At Pleasant Point the clerical evaluation was more ambivalent. The
pastors praised the Indians' participation in benedictions and processions; they recognized the good deeds of sodalities in keeping up the
parish church; they recommended a medal, "Pro Ecclesia," for Syl-
vester Gabriel, who had been the "mainstay of priests and sisters" for
many of his long years. "I am tremendously pleased with our people at
Pleasant Point," said Rev. Thomas F. Coyne. "The loyalty of the tribe
to the faith these hundreds of years surely deserves some form of papal
recognition" (Portland. October 5, 1956). On the other hand, the same
priest was shocked at the "serious problem" of immorality on the
reservation, including prostitution and alcoholism: "Saturday nights
are war nights—wild West. Never saw anything like it—most ap-
palling—the depravity of human nature." He was discouraged "to realize that we have been here these many years, and have not been able to
make a dent here" (February 15, 1955). A decade later another clerical
administrator of the parish found a "lack of parental authority" at
Pleasant Point among the 320 Catholic Indians, out of a population of
335. As for their spiritual condition, it was

> Good, on the whole although there are weak spots due to the inherent
> character of the Indian. Their Catholic faith is strong but it is a childish
> faith. Their religious convictions do not always stand up to the de-
> mands of the Catholic faith, i.e., on the question of Sunday Mass atten-
> dance or on the question of the virtue of purity. Alcoholism is a major
> problem among the people. (March 11, 1964)

Even as recently as 1982 a Catholic sister at Pleasant Point said that the
people's faith was "not up to Vatican II yet." They were "strongly attached to Catholic sacramentals and ceremonies" but most were "leery
about fulfilling lay ministries. They think they are unworthy," she said
(Hutchinson, August 12, 1982: 14). During the middle decades of the
twentieth century the Passamaquoddies at both reservations appeared
to their pastors to undergo a moral breakdown, even though they continued to participate in the life of the Church.

In the 1970s the Passamaquoddies and Penobscots initiated monumental land claims against the State of Maine, resulting in a 1980 settlement of $40 million adjudicated by the federal government. The hard feelings engendered by the claim and the resistance of the state to the Indians' rights created tension between natives and non-Indians, tension that spilled over into relations with the Church. At both Passamaquoddy reservations, but especially at Peter Dana Point, vandalism against Church property became endemic, leading priests to live off the Indian territories. The Sisters of Mercy, so beloved in former decades, were accused at Indian Township of hoarding funds and turning profits. Church spokesmen called for greater Indian leadership in the Catholic communities, as deacons, for example (Portland. June 24, 1979); however, in the spirit of nationwide Indian nationalism, the Church was becoming suspect as an alien institution, centuries after the apparently thoroughgoing conversion of these Algonkian people.

Before the 1980 land claims settlement, the Bishop of Portland, Amedee Proulx, wrote a draft letter, "rejected for now," to the Indian leadership of Indian Township, in which he decried the "vandalism" against Church property and the "constant harassment and verbal abuse against the Sisters who teach the children of your Community" (May 31, 1979). The vandalism continued, including a Christmas Eve break-in at Indian Township, 1979, in which a silver chalice and a ciborium were stolen. Father Joseph Laughlin, S.J., told his parish in the Christmas bulletin that the vandals were "courting excommunication" (December 25, 1979). But "anti-white" (May 6, 1980) developments continued at Peter Dana Point throughout 1980 and 1981, with threats of "sacrilege" (September 26, 1980) against sacraments in the church. The principal of the Indian school, a Sister of Mercy, resigned her post and the Order considered quitting the reservation, although the community gave the nuns a vote of confidence at a public meeting in the spring of 1981. The sisters remained, but Father Laughlin could take no more and left in the fall, after giving a "very strong sermon condem[n]ing the behavior of the Indian Community—number of break-ins" (November 24, 1981).

A Church representative explained the factors underlying the "tension" at Peter Dana Point between Catholic personnel and the Passamaquoddies. He blamed the land claim, the "self-actualization" and "struggle for autonomy" among the Indians, but also the changing values of priests and sisters following the Second Vatican Council. As it was, he wrote, the Indians received a "disproportionate share" of

Catholic resources in the State. In centuries past the Indians had sought out priests and sisters but maybe it was time for them to withdraw, to serve where they were wanted. "The difficulties . . . are beyond toleration," he concluded (January 21, 1981).

Without a resident priest the heads of eighty-five Passamaquoddy families petitioned the diocese for renewed sacerdotal contact (September 26, 1982). A core of Catholics continued devotions to Our Lady and Ste. Anne. They said their rosaries, made novenas, prayed at the Stations of the Cross. They listened to taped sermons and discussed them as a group. On Good Friday there were morning chants, as they identified with Christ's suffering. These acts of devotion were designed to impress upon the bishop their deep Catholic faith. Bishop Proulx was willing to comply with their request, but not without enumerating the "fundamental problems" at the reservation:

> 1. The stress caused by the legitimate desire to preserve their heritage and the need to prepare for a healthy relationship with the rest of American Society.
> 2. Possible lack of adequate ethics to cope with life as they know it today. My theory is that the restriction of this people to life on a reservation has made many of their traditional ethical principles ineffective or inoperable, e.g., lack of discipline in bringing up children. When children needed to learn early in life the art of survival in the wilderness it was important for them to grow up with a sense of independence. Living in close quarters more discipline is required to learn respect for the rights of others. . . . The principles of Anglo-Saxon Christian ethics have not been assimilated sufficiently to fill this void. (October 20, 1982)

Having requested the return of a parish priest, the Passamaquoddies at Indian Township entered a more peaceful period of relations with the Church. With money from the land claim settlement filtering into the community, generalized resentments were softened—though not obliterated—in the economic upturn. In the present day an uneasy equilibrium holds in both Passsamaquoddy reservations.

PLEAſANT POINT

Pleasant Point consists of a hundred acres, almost completely surrounded by water, in Passamaquoddy Bay, the Bay of Fundy. It is virtually the easternmost place in the United States, across from New Brunswick. A population of six hundred and thirty Passamaquoddies crowds into a small area. There is much intermarriage with whites, and some resentment of those whites who marry in. Route 190 runs through the center of the village, and in the early 1970s the local militants tried to charge a toll on cars coming and going to Eastport, an island reached across the narrows by a causeway. With money from the land settlement of 1980 the tribe has been able to purchase land from a neighboring township, and there is much bustle in the community. There are tribal offices and a tribally owned supermarket. Some Indians have organized a language program and a cultural museum. Some Passamaquoddies will say that they wish they never got the money from the land settlement; it has made them "greedy" and "venal," they claim (McCarty, August 21, 1992). On the other hand, the money has helped a very poor community to care for its elderly and to grow in many ways. The reservation has the feel of a busy working-class neighborhood, with brick and wooden houses, trailers, and cabins set along winding streets. A portion of the territory is forested and there are fishing weirs at several points along the St. Croix River, tended by the Indians.

The parish priest shows a visitor St. Ann's Church, a brick structure in some disrepair. Termites are devouring the window frames. The building dates to 1928, he says, after a fire ignited by holiday candles and evergreen wreaths destroyed the previous church on Christmas Day. The tribe has "intimated" that it will provide the $100,000 or more needed to repair the present building, but the funds are not yet forthcoming. The stained glass at the back of the church portrays a missionary priest surrounded by Plains Indians in headdresses and tipis. The side windows include a painting of Kateri Tekakwitha and a statue of the Mohawk maiden stands at the altar.

Father McCarty lives in a run-down trailer, no better than the poorest homes on the reservation. The teaching sisters reside by the church in a small, neat home. The back of the church, formerly the priest's quarters, is now a Montessori school. Despite the lack of riches possessed by the Church personnel, an Indian remarks pointedly that the church is the largest building on the reservation, dominating the landscape (Pleasant Point, August 21, 1992).

Rev. Paul McCarty, S.J., admits that he has not been energetic enough in his years of pastorate at St. Ann's. "I try to be a good guy. I get along with people. I lend or give money. But the services here at church, I've sort of let them go" (McCarty, August 21, 1992). He gets "down in the dumps" now and then and thinks of leaving what he considers a difficult post. The difficulty, he acknowledges, is that he is never at home with the Indian people; after centuries of Passamaquoddy assocation with the Church, the priest is still an outsider to the community, still regarded as an intruder. "I did the sweatlodge thing," he acknowledges. During a recent Tekakwitha conference in Orono he brought Apache Crown Dancers to his church to perform a Native American liturgy. At the same time, he does not feel comfortable romanticizing Indian rituals that have never been part of Passamaquoddy culture. Apache ceremonialism is completely foreign to their traditions, and sweat lodges disappeared from local practice hundreds of years ago. He wonders what kind of Church the Indians of his St. Ann's parish really want.

Maureen Wallace, a Sister of Mercy with over a quarter of a century experience at Pleasant Point, runs the local school. Her Order has served ("and ruled," according to one resident [Pleasant Point, August 21, 1992]) the reservation since the 1870s; today she devotes considerable energy to anti-drug and anti-alcohol components of the curriculum. She also helps adults with recovery from substance abuse. In doing so she attempts to support the local culture, both in school and around the territory. On occasion she "takes flack" (McCarty, August 21, 1992) from some locals who accuse her of stereotyping the Passamaquoddies as alcoholics, but for the most part she is respected as a "very dedicated" (Roderick, August 21, 1992; see Canton, March 1992) public servant, a credit to her Church among a people ill at ease with its institutions.

A local Passamaquoddy woman, Joan Paul, introduces herself laughingly as "Joan Paul, just like John Paul, the pope" (Paul, August 21, 1992). Rosary beads and a cross hang by her dining table; another set of beads dangles from the rearview mirror of her car. She has been a "practicing Catholic all my life," like her mother before her. Her grandmother was a Catholic like virtually everyone else at Pleasant Point, "but not practicing." Ms. Paul adds that there was "no Indian spirituality" on the reservation when she was growing up: "Catholic faith is all I knew." As a girl she considered becoming a sister and to this day she is active in the parish as a Eucharistic minister. She is also a teacher's aide at the community school under Sister Maureen Wallace. She has attended several Tekakwitha conferences, and in 1992 she helped plan the annual Tekakwitha meeting in Orono, Maine.

The Catholic faith of her family, she feels, is fast eroding among the Passamaquoddies. Only thirty or so attend mass each Sunday at Pleasant Point, mostly older and middle-aged persons, not children. She says that this is "not very many, . . . not very much." Religious instruction is "not a priority" for parents and not even a concern for children. Infants receive baptism, first communion, and "that's all you see them." Before school each day there is a half hour of catechesis; however, only a handful show up. Ms. Paul, the sisters, and some other school personnel continue to offer instruction, but "we get discouraged," she admits. In general, she finds, the Church is "not directing the youths' spiritual life anywhere," because their parents do not care one way or another about the teachings of the Church.

Why have her people turned away from Catholicism as a source of authority after centuries of involvement in the Church? She suggests that many of her generation and younger are "turned off to the Catholic Church because of the strict rules. They just want to do what they want to do." They ask, why should they be married in the Church? Why should they not remarry after a divorce? Why should they not live together, unmarried? They have been strongly influenced by the secular culture around them in their values and orientation, and from that perspective the Church appears as a hindrance to their individual desires.

In addition, some of the younger people proclaim, "It's not the Indian way. It's not part of our culture. It was forced on us." By "it" they mean the rules that hinder their license, but they also mean the entirety of the Church. The Passamaquoddies do not usually talk about their faith, or about their resentments toward the Church. These matters mostly go unsaid. Nonetheless, over the past generation there has been a seething upsurge of feelings against Catholicism at Pleasant Point, even among those like Ms. Paul who remain faithful Catholics, and certainly among those who have left the Church behind.

"Some have been really hurt by the Church," she avers. Priests and sisters have wielded "power" over the Passamaquoddies and the Indians have experienced it as "oppression." "I have a personal relationship with Jesus Christ," she states, but "fear, shame, guilt all came along with it," and she resents the feeling of worthlessness she and her people have acquired by being Catholics. For all her participation in catechesis, she is not certain that she wants her grandson to receive Catholic instruction. The whole process of confession is offensive to her: thinking of oneself as sinful and repugnant to God; the threat and fear of punishment in hell. Even the word "confession" disturbs her: "Someone who commits a crime *confesses*, but children?! . . ." She does not approve of the traditional Church practice of "scaring us into being good."

In 1991 she attended a "Catholic liberation workshop" with other Passamaquoddies as part of her attempt to address her resentment. Until then she was "in denial" about her painful participation in the Church. Now she speaks to Father McCarty and others of her "feelings." The priest tells her, "Don't go overboard." "He's afraid I'm going to abandon ship," Ms. Paul adds.

She claims "abuse" by sisters and priests at Pleasant Point in her youth, a charge that is doubted but not denied by Father McCarty. Some of it was "sexual abuse," and there are grown men today, she asserts, whose drinking problems, suicidal impulses, and violent tendencies derive at least partially from molestation in their youth by priests. The clerics appointed to service among the Passamaquoddies were often inadequate, not just as priests but more fundamentally as persons. Indeed, she says, the diocese used to send priests to Pleasant Point and Indian Township "for punishment. . . . One priest disclosed this to my brother a long time ago." Perhaps this is why such abuse took place on the reservation. Moreover, "our being an oppressed people, they may have thought we were easily victimized." Ms. Paul acknowledges that across North America today there are sensational revelations of sexual abuse within the Church; "of course these things happen in other communities," she says. Her point is that the abuse at Pleasant Point became a tradition, a sizable portion of the community culture, a "learned behavior, generation to generation." Treatment

by Church personnel, she says, has had a disabling effect on Passamaquoddy existence.

She complains of "physically and emotionally abusive nuns." The
Sisters of Mercy, she says, used rulers on children's knuckles. "They
grabbed your skin and pinched it; it was so thoroughly oppressive,"
she declares. When people reject the Church, they are rejecting the sisters who represented Catholicism on the reservation. She knows that
generations of non-Indian Catholics tell jokes about the strict sisters of
their youth; at Pleasant Point the treatment is no laughing matter.

It is not funny because the Indians do not think of the priests or the
sisters as part of the community. There has only been one female religious born at Pleasant Point, as far as Ms. Paul knows—everyone "respected their native nun," she exclaims—and so for all the years that
ecclesiastical Catholicism has existed among the Passamaquoddies, its
representatives have always been foreigners. As the Indians have rejected the Church, they have been saying that "they want their power
back." They no longer want non-Indians controlling Indian lives on
Indian land, and abusing them, to boot.

The Passamaquoddy planning committee for the Orono Tekakwitha gathering in 1992 hoped that the meeting would have produced
"healing" by having the bishops of Portland, the Sisters of Mercy, and
the Jesuits make "apologies" to the Indians of Maine for past "abuses."
The fact that this did not happen was a disappointment to Ms. Paul,
who found that her experiences were similar to the "hurts" of other Indians from other parts of North America.

Ms. Paul blames the Church for its part in making Pleasant Point a
"dysfunctional community." The primary symptom of the dysfunction
is alcoholism, which she views as an attempt to "numb the painful experiences" of Church and government. She herself became an alcoholic, she says, because "I didn't feel good about myself." She thinks
that if she and her people had been allowed to live their aboriginal culture, respecting and reaffirming themselves as a people, their lives
would have been better.

She says of her alcoholism, "I'm working on my recovery," and that
process "really has affected my life," including relations with the
Church and traditional Indian culture. At the Alcoholics Anonymous
meeting she attends, the Indians often engage in ritual drumming and
sweats. Within the past fifteen years the Passamaquoddies have been
introduced to these pan-Indian activities through powwows, through

visits from Canadian Micmacs, and even through the ministrations of
Catholic priests like the Ojibway Father John Hascall. Ms. Paul has
been attracted to these "Indian" expressions as means to heal the souls
of her people. At a Tekakwitha conference she found the Southwest
Indian singing "so spiritual" that it "brought tears to my eyes." She is
"quite resentful that we lost this for so long" and that Church authorities called native ritualism "witchcraft."

Ms. Paul has engaged only rarely in the sweat lodges of Alcoholics
Anonymous, yet she views these rituals as a way of "expressing spirituality, who you are." For her they are not "worship," but rather a "form
of prayer," to be used for good like Catholic prayers. She says that for
the Passamaquoddies of today, the Great Spirit, God, the Creator, are
all names for the same divine being, and there are no atheists in the
community. When she prays, she has connection to the divine, and she
can make that connection in a sweat lodge, at mass, or praying alone.
Ceremony is important to her and her fellow Indians, and they have
found that going to church does not provide the full range of ceremonial expressions.

In the past the people at Pleasant Point were devoted to Ste. Anne,
respecting her as grandmother of Christ. They traveled to Sainte-
Anne-de-Beaupré as a mode of religiousness apart from the weekly attendance at mass and the liturgical markings throughout the year:
Easter, Christmas, Palm Sunday, Ash Wednesday, funerals, and weddings. They expected miracles from Ste. Anne, healings for themselves
and their families. In the old days alcoholics would leave their bottles
at the shrine, hoping for a cure from their drinking. Today some elders
still journey to the Quebec shrine, but their hopes against alcoholism
are connected more closely to Alcoholics Anonymous and to demonstrations of Indianness. There are some Passamaquoddies who say that
the only way to heal themselves is to return to the lost old ways. The
Church cannot help because it has been a cause rather than a cure of
the disease that is destroying them.

Can Catholicism help the Indians? Ms. Paul thinks so, through the
kinds of counseling programs offered by Sister Maureen Wallace. It is
possible that priests can offer guidance, although few Indians will seek
or follow it today. A committed Catholic herself, she thinks that the
Church has lost its hold on most of her people.

M. Grace Roderick concurs with the assessment of a slipping
Catholicism at Pleasant Point. During the past generation the public

displays of Catholic piety—the old-time processions, the erecting of personal chapels, holy communions and confirmations made before the whole community—have "really dwindled" (Roderick, August 21, 1992). Now she and Ms. Paul are among the two dozen or so Passamaquoddies who attend Sunday services out of a population of six hundred, almost all of whom are baptized Catholics.

She herself is loyal to the local church. "St. Ann's Church stands for security," she says. "It is our church. We belong. We know everyone." She enjoys the visits by vacationers and other outsiders who like to attend Sunday mass during the summer because she is "proud of our lovely church. . . . I prefer this church, my church." She receives the sacraments, including penance, which she terms the most interesting part of Catholicism. "You come out of confession feeling so light!" she exclaims.

A mixed-blood Indian ("We shared a lot more than corn with Columbus," she jokes), she knows that she is at least third-generation Catholic and probably more. Her mother and grandparents, she attests, were "very good Catholics" who sent her to the Sisters of Mercy for local schooling: "The school here was so good then. We looked up to the priests and nuns." When the experience of prejudice drove her from public high school in Eastport, she left the reservation, married a non-Indian, and brought up her children away from Pleasant Point, which she now calls affectionately, "the end of the earth."

Now she is living in a well-apportioned house she owns, next to the house she was born in. She received her high school equivalency and completed a two-year college program at the University of Maine at Orono, thanks, she states, to the encouragement of the Catholic sisters. She puts her energetic industry into the local school board as well as St. Ann's.

Ms. Roderick does not attribute the falling away of Catholic Passamaquoddies to patterns of abuse or an overbearing emphasis on human sinfulness in the Church. To the contrary, she suggests that the Indians avoid institutional Catholicism because "people here have learned the white man's ways." Many residents of Pleasant Point have lived in mainstream America and have become "streetwise." They have picked up the secular values of an America in spiritual breakdown. They look askance at going to mass or sending children to religious instruction because they do not want a religion that makes moral demands on them.

By no means, in Ms. Roderick's opinion, should Church personnel give in to valueless secularism. Passamaquoddy children come from "dysfunctional" families—single parents, drugs, drinking. They need a strong Church personified by a strong priest. With half the local population under eighteen, there is a need for direction and role models. Although she likes Father McCarty, she finds him "too laid back," too unwilling to take a forceful role in the liturgical or moral lives of the Indians. "The Church is very laid back these days," she says. No one in authority is willing to tell people that they have to attend mass; they need to stop sinning; they must act in certain ways. "They went from one extreme to another," she asserts, "from authoritarian Church to permissive Church. . . . They need stability on this reservation" and the Church should provide it. As it is, the people call upon the priest only when someone is dying. Ms. Roderick would like to have a priestly presence in her community that would regain the loyalty of her people.

Ms. Roderick acknowledges that some Passamaquoddies have turned to sweatlodges and burning sweetgrass to satisfy their need for a native spirituality; however, she declares, "This isn't our custom. It comes from elsewhere, out west, other Indians." She will not gainsay the spiritual benefit of such ritualism among her neighbors—"they want to be Indian, that's fine"—but in her judgment the appeal of "neo-traditionalism" lacks the commanding moral presence of Catholicism, which was the traditional religion at Pleasant Point for many generations, but which seems to be that no longer.

INDIAN TOWNSHIP

At Peter Dana Point (Indian Township), fifty miles from Pleasant Point up the St. Croix River, the position of Catholicism is equally tenuous, although this is not evident at a mass at St. Ann's Church, Peter Dana Point (Indian Township, August 23, 1992), Rev. Thomas Lequin officiating. Fifty Passamaquoddies and non-Indians sing spirited hymns in English and the Indians' language, to the accompaniment of Joan Dana's drumming. George Stevens serves as Eucharistic minister, with the help of his daughter, Ashley, and an altar boy. The Lord's Prayer is in Passamaquoddy; instead of the handshake of peace, Lequin passes around a braid of sweetgrass from one to another, to remind us all of how we are bound to each other. Most smile amiably at one another; most receive the Eucharist; most place their bills in the collection basket.

There are Indian touches around the simple clapboard church: Passamaquoddy baskets on the altar to hold the hosts, an eagle feather fan upon the altar, a statue of Kateri Tekakwitha. A carving by an Italian artist depicts children of various ethnic identities surrounding Jesus. One child is a Peruvian Indian in bowler hat; another is a North American Indian wearing a feather.

Before and after mass Father Lequin greets his parishoners, including a female religious who teaches at the adjacent elementary school, and there is pleasant banter on a summery day. In face and gesture the Indians show their affection for the priest, and he for them. They appreciate his saying the Lord's Prayer in their native tongue and they smile at his sermon—about the narrow gate to heaven—when he jokes about Charlie Brown, trying to go out into the snow but too bundled up to make it through the door. We are like Charlie Brown, he says. We wear too much baggage: things, attitudes, feelings. We need to simplify our lives to make our way through the heavenly gate.

Later the same day Joan Dana confirms an outsider's impressions. Today was the first time that Father Lequin used sweetgrass at mass, and the people found it "touching" (Dana, August 23, 1995). "They loved that," she says. There has been drumming at mass for a decade or more, with almost no resistance from the Indian parishoners. Those who attend mass find it a moving experience. "The drum is like a heart-beat" to the Passamaquoddies, she states. As for Lequin's command of Passamaquoddy in saying the Lord's Prayer, Ms. Dana says it is "coming along," and everyone is proud of his courage to pray in their language.

There are six hundred and forty Indians living on this reservation, isolated along Route 1, north of Princeton, seventy miles from Penob-scot Old Town, where other Passamaquoddies live. "All but three call themselves Catholic" (Lequin, June 17, 1992), says their pastor, and for over the last four hundred years "the constant has been Catholicism" (August 8, 1992), but only about a quarter of them are ever involved in the Roman Catholic Church between baptismal and burial (Dana, August 23, 1992).

The going concern at Indian Township is the economic boom cre-ated and sustained by the 1980 land claims settlement. The tribe sup-ports its members with jobs: firemen, game wardens, teachers, and lumberjacks. It owns businesses such as a restaurant, a bowling alley, a day-care facility, and a gambling establishment. Some Indians com-plain of political and economic machinations on the part of the tribal leaders, but there are many others who say that the settlement brought "nothing but good." It "took the people out of crap and poverty," ac-cording to Father Lequin, making them "a hundred times better off" than they were before 1980 (Lequin, August 22, 1992).

In matters of religion, however, the Passamaquoddies are an aching people. There is virtually nothing left of the old-time spirituality. Some are trying to reinvent it by borrowing from Plains and Great Lakes Woodland rituals. Those over age forty still speak Passamaquoddy; however, the youths have not kept it up. They are more at home with MTV than with hunting or fishing lore (Indian Township, August 22, 1992), and from an "old-fashioned" Indian Catholic's point of view, "they're not interested in anything" (Mitchell, August 22, 1992). In that context, Catholicism is but a minor force in people's lives. A cyni-cal old Indian man comments on the bingo hall standing across the road from a Catholic chapel on Route 1: "Pray for me, pay for me. That's how much goddamn religion we got here" (Gabriel et al., Au-gust 23, 1992).

Father Lequin tries to instill as much Catholicism into the reserva-tion as he can but he plays up his shortcomings. He took his assign-ment with trepidation, hoping to do "as little damage as possible"

(Lequin, August 8, 1992), and fearing the "isolation" of working with "different" people with "widespread dysfunctionalism in the community," including endemic "drugging and drinking" (August 22, 1992). He acknowledges that the Passamaquoddies "have been abused by priests in the past," and that "there are resentments" against the Church (June 17, 1992). He hopes to deliver good homilies and lead meaningful liturgies; then he is ready to move on to the next assignment (which he did in 1993).

Father Lequin comments on the paucity of Catholic devotionalism at Indian Township. The Eucharist was never the primary liturgy here; indeed, not until Father Tomlinson's tenure in the late 1930s was mass offered every Sunday. The Jesuits of the previous eras considered the mass "too complicated" (Lequin, August 8, 1992) for the Indians to comprehend, so instead they encouraged "devotions" like the rosary, which is still said every Sunday afternoon at church. All of the active Catholics have rosary beads and they say them at funerals and other times. "They would rather have that than go church," declares a conservative Catholic in Indian Township. "They like prayer beads better than books, and in church you pray with books" (Mitchell, August 22, 1992). Ms. Delia Mitchell remembers how her grandfather would escape the noise of church—he complained that the choir sounded like a "bunch of crows"—and seek prayerful solitude in his canoe, telling his "prayer beads." Even today older Passamaquoddies like to pray alone with rosaries, outside of church.

The Passamaquoddies come out in sizable numbers on Ash Wednesday and Palm Sunday to "get something for nothing," as Lequin puts it (Lequin, August 22, 1992), to have a concrete sign of their Catholicism in the ashes and palms. Some Passamaquoddies from Indian Township travel to Sainte-Anne-de-Beaupré for Indian day and on her feast day but there is no local celebration of the formerly popular saint. Some of the older Indians recall miraculous cures at the Quebec shrine in their youth, but no one expects such divine intervention in the modern world (Mitchell, August 22, 1992). In the past the Indians used to practice a rite of reconciliation—visiting one another to ask forgiveness for any slights during the previous year—and there are a few who would like to revive the liturgy. Lequin introduced the feast day celebration for Kateri Tekakwitha, attended now by two dozen Indians. Formerly the Assumption was a major day in the liturgical calendar, but this is no longer true. Novenas are a thing of the past. In general, the activities of the Church are not a priority on the reservation.

When the Tekakwitha Conference conducted its annual meeting in Orono in the summer of 1992, some Passamaquoddies, like Joan Paul of Pleasant Point and Joan Dana of Peter Dana Point, were on the local planning committee. They enjoyed working on a joint project and came to feel like old comrades. The most committed Catholics, perhaps thirty from each reservation, attended the events. For them, the coming together of Catholic Indians from all over North America was instructive, even inspiring—hearing mass in Maliseet language, observing the ritual leadership of Native American elders—although for others the bitter feuding that marked the conference reminded them too much of their local squabbles. Most Indians from Indian Township said that it was too far to drive, too expensive, they were too busy to attend the Tekakwitha conference. Father Lequin asked them how many times they drive the greater distance to Bangor to shop, how much money they spend on purchases, and how many times they take a day off from work for more secular pursuits. The fact is, he says, that Catholic forms of religion do not much interest the majority of his flock, particularly the young.

On the same day as Father Lequin's mass, a group of Micmacs from Nova Scotia are teaching the locals about the proper uses of sweatlodges. Several dozen Passamaquoddies are in attendance and even the staunch Catholics express support for the activity. One man wearing a large cross around his neck describes himself as a "serious Catholic" who often sings in the church choir (Gabriel et al., August 23, 1992). He sees nothing strange about Catholics taking sweats, and he supports the Micmacs with cans of corn for their communal soup. Joan Dana, who provides the drumming at St. Ann's, is not averse to investigating the sweatlodges. Although she has never used one ritually, she says that the sweat is "sacred ground" for her (Dana, August 23, 1992). The Eucharistic minister, George Stevens, knows little about the rites, although at the recent Tekakwitha Conference there were sweats conducted by the Ojibway priest, John Hascall. Stevens viewed these as a "positive influence," introducing Indians to a practice of nature-spirituality that was once "part of us. . . . I don't know. They're new here. I'd like to know more about them, about my own background. . . . We need all the help we can get" (Stevens, August 23, 1992). The Passamaquoddies say that "we were Catholic before the Europeans came" (Mitchell, August 22, 1992), meaning that they prayed to the "Great Spirit" in their own pious ways. With Catholicism in decline, some of them are looking to the ancient ways to revive their religious experiences.

Father Lequin cites alcoholism as the foremost factor in deadening the Passamaquoddies to Catholic devotion. Indeed, he regards drinking as a disease which undermines spirituality and keeps it at bay. For generations the Indians have suffered from devastating alcoholism, which in turn has crippled their spirituality. He does not see the Church as a factor in fomenting the disease; however, the Indians are too frightened of "judgmental" Catholicism—calling them to such high standards and condemning them when they fail, which they do in so many ways—to seek succor from the faith. Alcoholism is the number one, overwhelming fact of their lives, according to Father Lequin (himself the offspring of alcoholics, he remarks). Catholicism is not a force that combats the scourge effectively. The faith is but a small portion of the culture, attempting to treat the symptoms of the disease.

Lequin is in favor of whatever might treat alcoholism most effectively. If the drumming and sweats were effective, he would support them. If getting rid of the Church would resolve the problem, he would tear down St. Ann's. On the other hand, he thinks that it is wrong to blame the Church for the deepest disease of Passamaquoddy existence. For him, alcoholism is its own demonic cause (Lequin, August 22, 1992).

Many of the inhabitants of Indian Township are members of Alcoholics Anonymous. On a Saturday afternoon there is an A.A. "Roundup" on the reservation (Indian Township, August 22, 1992) for Indians and non-Indians of the region. They speak openly of their problems and call upon a "higher power" to help them on the steps to recovery. There are some priests who will have nothing to do with A.A. because of its notion that all religions are equivalent versions of one another; however, Father Lequin thinks that the Twelve Steps program has a good deal to teach the Church, especially concerning Indians. He finds that A.A. helps Indians not only recover from drinking but also to accept themselves as flawed persons. Some of them take aspects of their recovery to Church and their Twelve Steps become fused with Catholic spirituality. He finds this appealing. They are regaining spirituality through the impetus of A.A. Catholicism may fulfill some spiritual impulses but the Church seems unable to commence the process on its own. A program in Augusta, Maine, run by the diocese, combines Catholicism and A.A.; a number of Passamaquoddies have attended it, and Lequin applauds the combination of the institutions toward a common end. He also accepts those Indians who will have nothing to do with the Church as part of their recovery. For him, the recovery is the most important goal.

Does Lequin give sermons against alcohol abuse? There are some in his parish who wish he would be more forceful in condemning such behavior (Mitchell, August 22, 1992); however, he feels that the Indians have heard too much condemnation from the pulpit over their lives. At funerals of infants who have died of fetal alcohol poisoning and of adults killed by drink and the accidents caused by liquor, he tries to deliver a sermon that draws out the lessons from *this person's* life and death, which everyone in the community knows intimately. It is his duty to draw the lessons of behavior: this behavior killed this person, caused this suffering. At the same time he does not want to make *these people*—this mother, for example, who killed her fetus by drinking and drugging—hate themselves even more than they do. It is a narrow path to walk, helping his congregation to face their dysfunctional behavior without compounding their guilt.

The effects of alcohol are no more evident than in the life of Joan Dana, mother of ten, grandmother of thirty-nine and counting. She is the pillar of the extended family, housing as many as twenty-two relatives in her home at one point recently. She leads the singing at Sunday mass, holds a big family picnic at her house, then brings the leftovers to feed the Micmacs who are leading sweats in Indian Township. She is a provider for others.

Ms. Dana is also a recovering alcoholic, who attends the A.A. "Roundup" and is constantly aware of the disease's close proximity. Her husband, from whom she was separated long before his death, was a drunk, and she says that she too drank under the stress. "It almost destroyed my life . . . but I had dreams. Maybe someone was praying for me" (Dana, August 23, 1992). She continues to beseech the Blessed Mother and Kateri Tekakwitha for the cessation of alcoholism, for herself and for her family.

In a life of painful events—three white men attacked her when she was a teenager, causing her to be "always afraid" of strangers; her brother died in an accident; she calls her life a continual succession of "hard times"—Ms. Dana's worst trauma came several years ago when her daughter's husband murdered her and then committed suicide in an alcoholic episode. Ms. Dana recalls vividly how her grandchildren came running into her house, their legs bloodied from the violence. She says that they all knelt and wept together.

"I was struggling with my faith and forgiveness when my daughter died," she relates. To heal herself she turned to her dreams. In one dream her son-in-law's jaw healed—the jaw he shot away in the suicide. A hole remained in his throat, but he was able to tell her about the afterworld: "The place is so beautiful for all the little children." She adds, "I'm holding onto that hope every single day." In another dream he fell down and called for help. She tried to fulfill the biblical saying that whatever you bind on earth is bound in heaven; whatever you open on earth is opened in heaven, so she opened windows in her dream. In yet another dream a cross spoke to her, urging forgiveness for the murderer. Through these dreams and others she came to the conclusion, "The pain is there. The tears are there. But we have to keep holding to our faith."

When Ms. Dana speaks of her faith, she is describing a mystical Catholicism and also the spirituality of her Passamaquoddy family. Her grandparents taught her to pray as a child. She remembers getting on her knees at their house, praying to their instruction in Passamaquoddy and English. Her grandmother told her about Jesus feeding the multitudes with loaves and fishes. The woman told her that you can see the handprint of Jesus on the head of the haddock, found in the waters around Peter Dana Point. Whenever she sees a haddock, she thinks of the story and her grandmother. When she hears gospel stories, she can remember her grandmother telling them to her. Hence, her Christian life is interwoven with her familial life in the manner idealized by commentators on Eastern Algonkian Catholicism in the past. No one forced her to be a Catholic; she was raised as one, in the same process as growing up Passamaquoddy. "I get discouraged at times" with the "burden" of her faith, she says, "but I have to hold the cross." She wishes that her family would attend church more often and she chides the girlfriends of her sons that they should be married instead of "living in sin." Nevertheless, she will "let them grow" without her interference. She is happy when her grandsons express interest in becoming altar boys but by and large she is alone in her family as a contemporary Catholic.

Ms. Dana is a visionary, always looking for significance in the world around her. At Pleasant Point several years ago during a Passama-quoddy Kateri Circle, she and others saw a cross appear miraculously in the sky. "Some people were scared," she reports, but she was excited by the revelation of the divine. At a recent Tekakwitha conference in Orono, a bird flying around the arena landed in the crux of a cedar cross laid on the floor. She found the happenstance full of meaning.

When she works she always asks "the spirit to guide my hands." When she sleeps she calls upon the supernatural to speak to her, so that she can help others. She describes her deceased father as a "medicine man" who gathered herbs to treat people. She states that she has fol-lowed in his footsteps, fulfilling his prophecy about her as the healer in the family. "Through Jesus" and the guidance of her father she tries to carry out the role of "medicine man" in her community. Having healed herself, she feels that she has the potential to cure her fellows.

She seeks curative premonition, explanation, guidance, and com-fort in her dreams to help her friends with their "hurts." In one the Blessed Virgin Mary gave her milk-white rosaries; in another the Lord's hand lifted up her family. She remembers hundreds of her dreams and shares them with other Indians, e.g., the Catholic Mo-hawks Peg Bova and Sarah Hassenplug, asking them what they might mean. In turn they ask her to interpret their visionary experiences, as Northeast Indians used to do hundreds of years ago. "It's just amaz-ing," Ms. Dana declares, how much she learns in this way.

Sitting in view of beautiful rapids where she used to come as a girl, and again as a young mother, for picnics, swimming, and fishing, Ms. Dana recounts one of her most meaningful dreams: Jesus was standing by the roadside, calling to her from his tomb. The earth was breaking apart and people were falling in, screaming and groaning. On the other side of the road were soldiers on horses. Jesus pointed to both sides. Then the sky opened and a white-haired, white-gowned man on a throne gave her "my two special commandments, to love thy God and to love thy neighbor." These would appear to contain a straight-forward Christian message; however, Ms. Dana provides a special in-terpretation: "Jesus was calling me from the tomb of alcohol."

Joan Dana receives her calling mystically. George Stevens' religious vocation is less visionary but at least as important to the future of Catholic faith at Indian Township. Born off-reservation, Stevens lived on both Passamaquoddy territories as a youth. After serving in the military during the Second World War, he came to stay at Indian Township in 1946. He lives with his wife and his adopted daughter (actually his biological granddaughter, whom he adopted in order to raise her in a supportive Catholic environment) in a tidy log house built by a son. His children live nearby in small cabins. Every day his wife feeds the entire clan at their lakeside home.

Back in 1946 the reservation was dirt-poor, Stevens says. There were no telephones, no electricity, no sewers. "When times were harder, we prayed a little harder" (Stevens, August 23, 1992), he recalls. "When we were living in shacks, before we had plumbing, there was more sense of community then." More people attended church. Everyone spoke Passamaquoddy ("even the dogs understood it back then"). His extended family life is an attempt to replicate that old community spirit, and he wishes that all Passamaquoddies would live like the "radical group" of early Christians who shared their goods with one another and engaged in a common project. Primitive Christianity is a model for him, as is his idealized remembrance of reservation life of a half century ago.

Stevens was brought up Catholic, but since the Second Vatican Council he has been much more involved in Church, attending mass regularly and feeling encouraged by Vatican II reforms to involve himself in local parish matters. "We had been so much in the background before; it was hard to get involved at first. Before, everything was done by the priests and nuns," he remarks. Most Indians still prefer to be passive in the Church; indeed, Vatican II permitted many Passamaquoddies to retreat to the periphery of the Church when it lost its authoritarian edge. But he wants a more active role in a more liberal Catholicism.

He is a Eucharistic minister, groomed by Father Lequin for leadership in the local Catholic community. "The Eucharist has been a big boost for me," says Stevens, both nurturing his faith and inspiring his participation. "It's hard to get up there, step forward, after you've been back there so long," he comments; however, he wants to share the salvific experience of the Eucharist with as many people as he can.

With so few Passamaquoddies attending mass and with a shortage of clergy, there is always the real possibility that Indian Township will have to share its priest with a non-Indian parish in the area. Father Lequin hopes that people like George Stevens—"faithful leaders, elders, good men" (Lequin, August 8, 1992)—will be raised within the Church to positions of authority. This is a difficult process in a community where people lack "self-love" and "self-confidence," where vocations are virtually nonexistent. Fathers Lequin and McCarty have appealed to the diocese for a diaconate program especially suited for the Indian leadership already present in the communities. The bishop has opted instead for a standard three-year program with training, away from the reservations, in "Western theology." Lequin regrets that decision, calling local Indian leadership the "paramount question" for the future of Catholicism among the Passamaquoddies. This is the "last hurrah for the Church," he asserts. "We've been here for almost four hundred years and we still deliver the Church to them. It is time that they become the Church themselves."

The Society of Jesus functioned not only in French (and Spanish) colonies, but also among the English of nascent Maryland. Lord Baltimore asked the English Jesuits "to attend the Catholic planters and settlers, and convert the native Indians" (in Shea 1855: 484); in 1634 Father Andrew White and several associates tried their hand along the Potomac River. They established contacts among the Piscataways and Patuxents, and in 1638 they began the task of evangelization.

Father White gained the loyalty of the new Piscataway *tayac* (chief), Kittamaquund, who hoped to use the English as supports for his embattled (and, some said, ill-gained) chieftainship. He said that dreams had urged him to accept the English priests and their beautiful white god. When White cured him of a disease by bleeding him and serving him a remedy of herbs and holy water, the *tayac* determined to enjoin the priest's spiritual practice. Kittamaquund received public baptism (as Charles) in 1640, along with his wife (Mary) and their infant daughter (Ann); these were the first native christenings in colonial Maryland. Kittamaquund died a year later, but during his brief engagement with Christianity he demonstrated outward signs of conversion. He abjured various traditional amulets in favor of Christian worship. He was said to delight in prayer and to speak of the transcending value of heavenly reward, contrasting it to the worthless wealth of this world. He abstained from meat on fast days and disposed of his concubines, hence living according to the rules of Catholic culture. He gave his son over to Father White for education, and he himself tried to learn English (as White was learning the Piscataway language) and to dress in English clothes.

With so few priests—there were only three in 1641—the Maryland Catholics could not maintain regular Indian missions. Instead the priests visited the various native villages, erecting altars, distributing fishhooks and other small implements, and catechizing through interpreters. Father White composed a dictionary and grammar in Piscataway, and Father Roger Rigby, S.J., became fluent by 1643. By that time they had baptized as many as 130 Indians, all healthy adults who had received what the priests considered sufficient instruction.

Warfare with Susquehannas and other Indians disrupted the routines of the newly Christianized Maryland natives in the early 1640s. When Protestants took over the colony in 1645, the Jesuits were either murdered or shipped to prison in England. Father White died in an English prison in 1656. In 1648 the priests were banned from any further Indian missions; whatever faith existed among the Piscataways and Patuxents dissipated without record. Charles's daughter married an Englishman and raised a Catholic family in Virginia, but among the remaining Indians, whose numbers dwindled through the colonial period, Catholicism left nary an official trace. For this reason, "the history of Jesuit missions to the Indians in colonial Maryland is quickly told and, it must be said, merits little space" (Axtell Spring 1986: 1), although some Piscataway Catholics continued to worship, unnoticed in their ethnic identity, in several Maryland and Virginia parishes.

In general, the southeastern part of the United States has not been a stronghold for American Indian Catholicism. The Spanish colonial missions in Florida left no lasting heritage and most of the southern states were almost exclusively Protestant well into the nineteenth century. Nonetheless, two groups of Southeast Indians, the Houmas in Louisiana and the Choctaws in Mississippi, have embraced and embodied Catholic faith for many years.

THE HISTORY OF HOUMA FAITH

New France left its Catholic imprint upon the Indians of the Great Lakes and St. Lawrence drainage system. From Maine to Manitoba, many Native Americans embraced Catholic forms of faith and their descendants have maintained and adapted those forms over the centuries. From the upper Mississippi Valley the Jesuits reached out to various prairie Indians. The French also colonized the lower Mississippi; however, their missions there are less well known. If we are to search the southern regions of New France for a continuing tradition of Indian Catholicism, at first we might think there is little or none.

In the city of New Orleans, we are told, there is "no Indian population," and throughout the archdiocese Catholic Indians are "practically nonexistent" (Nolan, July 5, 1990). The Choctaws of Mississippi, as we shall see, owe their Catholicism to nineteenth-century missionary efforts rather than to the French. What other extant Indian populations are there?

In the southern extremity of Louisiana, primarily in the parishes of Terrebonne and LaFourche within the Diocese of Houma-Thibodaux, live the Houma people. The Houmas are Muskogean relatives of the Choctaws, numbering as many as eleven thousand. Of some mixed racial ancestry in a state that has always concerned itself with the minutae of blood quantum, the Houmas have been called "'racial orphans'" (Fisher 1968: 133), regarded as outsiders by both Whites and Blacks. The Houmas, however, have no doubt about their identity. Despite their French names, their native French language, and their mixed ethnic appearance, they are Indians, Houma Indians.

The Houmas live in the coastal area of marshlands and bayous, canals and lakes. The elaborate water network is only a few feet above sea level and is periodically flooded by storms from the Gulf of Mexico. The Houmas earn their livelihood in the local seafood industry, harvesting shrimp, oysters, fish, and crabs. Some own their own boats; others work for non-Houma bosses. Still others work in oil and natural gas rigs set up across their lands. Some trap for muskrats and nutria. Fewer than a thousand registered Houmas have left the state of Louisiana, and most have maintained a steady Houma identity, even

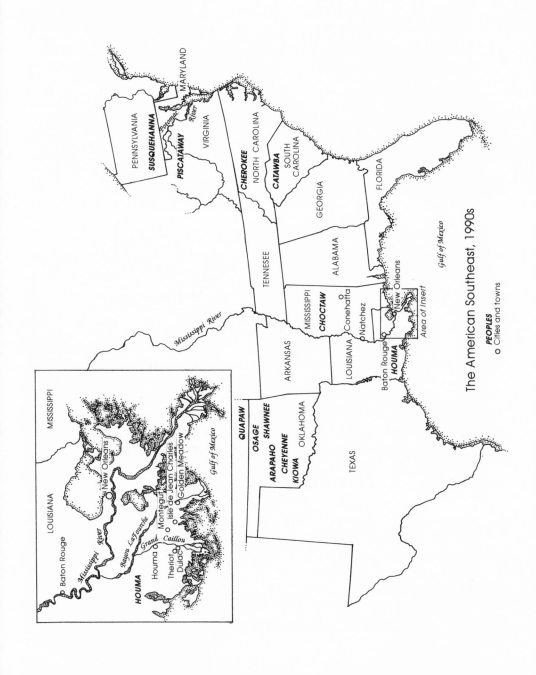

The American Southeast, 1990s

PEOPLES
o Cities and towns

though the United States federal government has never recognized the Houmas officially as an Indian nation (Louisiana granted partial recognition in 1977). Without federal recognition, the Houmas lack palpable sovereignty with its tribal rights to land and resources. Despite state recognition of the existence of the Houma Indians, many people might overlook the Houmas in assessing the conditions of Native Americans in the contemporary United States.

A journey to Golden Meadow, Isle de Jean Charles, Dulac, or Montegut—the major Houma settlements—leaves little doubt of the existence of the Houmas as a people, as an Indian people. And yet their "Indianness" does not consist at first glance of an "Indian" cultural heritage. Houmas speak French (and English these days); the aboriginal Houma language is long gone. They dress like their non-Houma neighbors and their homes bear no marked difference from those surrounding them. Their lack of cultural differentiation has led some ethnologists to deny their Indian status (Curry 1979: 10–11), although most scholars have upheld the Indian basis of Houma identity. In matters of religion, the Houmas seem unlike most Indian communities in the United States, except perhaps the Mississippi Choctaws, who have never ceased to recognize the Houmas as native cohorts. The Houmas say nothing of Mother Earth, sweat lodges, or a Great Spirit. They are not peyotists; they do not burn sage or sweetgrass. If religious affiliation is a means by which peoples maintain identity, the Houmas have not persisted in a "native" self-image. Rather, their "religious affiliation is strongly Catholic, reflecting that of the surrounding population" (9). It would be a mistake, however, to conclude that Houma Catholic identity has subtracted from Houma tribal consciousness. The Houmas have integrated Catholicism into their community existence, their passage through life, their seasonal cycles, their economy, and their familial ties in a manner unlike any other Indian people in the United States. A priest who was pastor of a Houma parish for several years, and is now archivist for the Diocese of Houma-Thibodaux, says that the Houmas are "acculturated" (Boudreaux, August 20, 1990). By this he does not mean that they have ceased to be Indians, or Houmas, but rather that over the centuries they have made adjustments to French Catholic culture, adopting it in large. By intermarrying with French, Spanish, and some Cajuns and Blacks, they have let go of most of their aboriginal cultural traits but without losing their identity as a people. In a Catholic Church that has segregated them until recent years from other ethnic populations, they have made the transition to Catholic identity without being overwhelmed by outsiders. Now that integration has taken place within the Church, Houmas are able to participate in Catholic parish life without feeling themselves as aliens or even as second-class citizens.

René-Robert Cavelier, known to history as the Sieur de La Salle, was the first European to mention the "Oumas"—although he never saw them—when he explored the Mississippi in 1682. The first recorded French contact with them occurred along the great river in 1686, midway between Baton Rouge and Natchez, and was cemented into an alliance by 1699. By 1700, however, half of the Houmas had died of an "abdominal flux" (Curry-Roper and Bowman 1982: 2) contracted from the Europeans. In that year the French Jesuit Father Paul De Ru entered the Houma territory and got a promise from the Indians that they would construct a church in their village square to receive a mission. By the end of 1700 two Jesuit priests were settled among the Houmas, saying mass in the new chapel and baptizing the first Houma, a three-day-old child whom "God took to Paradise a few days later, there to labor for conversion of his parents and of his fellow Indians," according to the Jesuit Relations (Thwaites 1896–1901, 65:148). The Jesuits described the Houmas in some detail—their traditional temples, their female and male chiefs, their agriculture, hunting, warfare, kindliness, cleanliness, and above all, their communal attachment to one another, bound by aboriginal religious devotions.

The Jesuits hoped to elevate Houma culture by christianizing it; however, in 1704 the directors of Louisiana Territory expelled the Society of Jesus, partially because of the distant Rites Controversy in China and partially because of the Jesuit reputation for protecting the indigenes from exploitation. The Society of Jesus did not reclaim the Houmas, although the priests returned a generation later. In the meantime the Houmas had moved southward along the Mississippi to escape attack from the English and their Indian allies. Warfare, disease, liquor, and migration reduced the Houma numbers throughout the eighteenth century, and the Peace of Paris in 1763 left them unprotected from the Spanish and English who gained control of their territory. To avoid these colonists the Houmas continued to travel south by way of Bayou LaFourche, so that by the end of the 1700s they were dwelling in the area now marked by the city of Houma, at the top of the several bayous that traverse the lowlands into the Gulf of Mexico.

The Spanish, as well as the French who succeeded them once again, recognized the Houmas as a people with land titles and chieftaincies, even as the Indians' numbers were dwindling. At the same time, the natives intermarried freely with French soldiers, their offspring often taking the family names of their fathers. In the 1700s Spanish immigrants from the Canary Islands settled among the Houmas, and in the 1780s the large migration of refugee Acadians (Cajuns) entered Houma lands, exerting additional pressures on the living space of the Indians.

At the time of the Louisiana Purchase in 1803 the Houmas numbered perhaps fewer than a hundred. Officials in Washington, D.C. regarded them as a tribe on the verge of extinction. In 1811 the Houma headman, Chac-Chouma, made an unsuccessful bid for federal recognition of his people; in the years that followed, Houma lands were parcelled and sold as public domain and the Indians began to journey even further south into their present domicile, seeking locations beyond the desires of the ever-expanding Americans. Louis le Sauvage succeeded Chac-Chouma, and Rosalie Courteaux followed in turn as Houma chief, purchasing swampland for her people in 1859 and protecting their interests until her death in 1885—at which time formal Houma political organization diminished and "formal consensual decisions by heads of households in the various Houma settlements" constituted the remnant of Houma sovereignty (Campisi and Starna 1988: 36).

At the time of Courteaux's death, the Houmas were said by observers to be extinct. Their intermarriage with the French had made their racial identity ambiguous and they became "free people of color"—not Blacks, not Whites, descended from Indians but not legally Indians themselves. Nonetheless, they maintained their social solidarity, even while becoming demographically invisible to outsiders. Their French family names—Verret, Billot or Billiot, Dardar, Naquin, Solet, Gregoire, Francis, Verdin, Foret, and others—served as clan monikers, and the Houmas all recognized their own identity through those names. When the anthropologist John R. Swanton "rediscovered" (Curry 1979: 9) the Houmas in the early twentieth century, Houma lineages were easily traced through copious baptismal, marriage, and burial records now in the archives of the Diocese of Houma-Thibodaux. Throughout the nineteenth and twentieth centuries the Houmas conserved their identity not only through their

French nomenclature but also through Catholic sacramentalism. Witness, for example, that Mathurin Guillaume Billot was born on November 9, 1848 to Alexandre Billot and Felicite Verdin, and was baptized at St. Francis de Sales Church in Houma. Alexandre Billot (son of Jacques Billot and Rosalie Courteaux) married Marguerite Felicite Verdin (daughter of Alexandre Verdin and Marie Gregoire) on September 21, 1865 at Montegut's Sacred Heart Church. Barthelmy Billot, seventy-eight years old, died on July 19, 1911 and was buried the next day in the Sacred Heart cemetery in Montegut (Houma).

The Billot-Billiot family tree can be traced as far back as 1765, and in the present day is represented, for instance, by John Billiot, born in Theriot in 1934, now living in a New Orleans suburb. Even though the federal government denies the existence of the Houmas, Billiot can trace his Houma ancestry through the sacramental records of the Catholic Church, for "his people have been Roman Catholics since their first contact with Europeans, and their marriages and births have been meticulously documented in the baptismal registries of the various missions and parish churches that have served the Houma nation" (Slind-Flor 1985: 1A).

Catholicism came to the Houmas at first through marital associations with the French. Only in the 1840s did the Diocese of Louisiana extend missionary efforts to the Indians. Rev. Charles M. Menard began the enterprise, establishing stations throughout the middle part of the nineteenth century. In time these stations became missions and in time some attained the status of parish, namely whenever six hundred families in an area could support a priest and church. Father Menard typified the Church's vocation to introduce sacramental Catholicism among the Houmas, devoting his adult life to the endeavor. He also shared in Louisiana racialism, and by no means did he wish to join Indian and White Catholic worship; nor did he intend to provide the Houmas with educational or social services equal to those enjoyed by Whites (Boudreaux, November 17, 1990). The Whites in the vicinity were almost all Catholics, and so the Houmas experienced Catholicism and racism simultaneously as part of a single culture. Catholicism nurtured them spiritually and provided them with a religious identity, but it also kept them at a distance and treated them with a degree of contempt.

In the twentieth century the Houmas continued to farm, hunt, trap, and fish in their marshland milieu in the "back behind" (Fisher

1968: 137), along the southern bayous. They traveled around in pi-
rogues and shanty boats, mostly landless, keeping to themselves to
avoid persecution and to survive culturally as a people. John Swanton
counted fewer than a thousand in 1907; in 1941 another ethnographer,
Frank Speck, tallied two thousand Houmas. The Bureau of Indian Affairs denied them federal recognition repeatedly, beginning in the
1920s. The discovery of oil in their areas dispossessed them further.
The state of Louisiana made it policy to prohibit public education for
the Indians, in order to keep them ignorant of their rights. Methodists
and Baptists in the 1930s opened the first school among them, followed in the next decade by the Catholics. Only in 1954 did the state
permit the Houmas to attend public (and segregated) grammar
schools; integrated schools arrived in the 1960s, in some part due to
lobbying by Catholic clergy.

Catholicism was firmly entrenched among the Houmas in the
twentieth century; however, when the Protestants introduced the first
schools among the Indians, "many formerly Catholic Indians became
Baptists or Methodists" (Fisher 1968: 139). The Indians were interested in education, and if the churches conducted schools, the Indians
attended and became loyal to the sponsoring denomination. "Thanks
to the Baptists" (Ledet, November 18, 1990), the Catholic Church was
thus put on the spot to open its own Houma schools. Interdenominational rivalry served as an impetus to the Church, in fear of losing its
congregation to Protestant competition.

At the same time, however, Catholic priests were reluctant to interfere with the practices of racial segregation in the area. As a contemporary Houma recalls, "Every time priests would come here, the whites
would get them and tell them how to treat the Indian people" (Francis, November 21, 1990). Each church had segregated stalls or roped-
off areas in the rear for Indian use. Some parishes preferred to build
chapels for the Houmas at a distance from the main church, in order
to keep Indians and Whites separate. The priests said mass in these
chapels periodically, perhaps once a month, and the Houmas had
no illusion that they were anything but second-rate citizens of the
Church. One parish went so far as to refuse services to Houmas, even
in their own chapel, in order to distance the Church from the Indians.
At Golden Meadow, Grand Caillou, Montegut, and elsewhere at mid-
century it was said that "the white people generally do not care to associate" (*The Indian Sentinel* 31, no. 2, March 1951: 29) with the Houmas.

The Whites wished particularly to prevent intermarriages that might come about through contact in church. There was "jealousy" on the part of white women, who feared that their menfolk would find the Houma women "sexier" marriage partners (Boudreaux, November 17, 1990); white men abhorred the notion that Houma men might marry white women: "They wanted the satisfaction of marrying Indian women, but not the other way" (Francis, November 21, 1990).

When Houmas began to attend Protestant schools and services, some Catholic priests stopped giving the sacraments to any Indians who communed with such backsliders. Father Felix Miller faced down petitions from the Houmas to his bishop, protesting his withholding of the Eucharist and other sacraments to them. At the same time, the Church persisted in segregation. One Houma remembers being re-fused communion when he went to the altar rail with Whites at St. Eloi Church in Theriot. After mass he confronted the priest: 'Have you got three gods, too, Father, one white, one black, one red?" (in Slind-Flor 1985: 1A). The priest slapped him, leading to a potentially violent altercation. As a result the family left the Houma area for New Orleans, where anti-Indian prejudice was less severe than in Terre-bonne Parish. Indians and Whites into the 1950s were buried for the most part in separate cemeteries, reflecting not only their distinct neighborhoods but also the official segregation within the Church. Houmas did not participate in public celebrations like Mardi Gras and other Church-sponsored fairs. In prayer, in sacrament, in play, and in death, the Houmas were kept at the periphery of the Church.

To this day, some Houmas are reticent to discuss the racism of the Church in the first half of the twentieth century, because to speak too candidly is perhaps to "start a war" (Boudreaux, August 20, 1990). Other Houmas speak freely, and with some heat, about the discrimi-nation of their youth; however, they aver that the Church, as well as society at large, has changed markedly in the past several decades.

If the Church played a role in the institutional racism of the past, it also played a role in changing the institutions and mores of southern Louisiana. When Father Roland J. Boudreaux came to Grand Caillou for a two-year stint in 1950, he helped make public education available to Houmas. Having served as a catechist at Isle de Jean Charles among the most remote Houmas when he was a seminarian, Boudreaux sym-pathized with the Indians. His Cajun sensitivity to persecution was combined with his internalizing of Church social teachings, causing him to declare himself for the "downtrodden," "oppressed," "under-dog" Houmas (Boudreaux, November 18, 1990). Boudreaux also wanted to win the Indians away from the Methodists and Baptists by demonstrating that the Catholic Church truly cared for the natives. He began a campaign to influence white educational officials, with the help of Houma Catholics. When he told the Indians, "We're going to have to go to the law," more than one Houma was willing to join in the effort. John Francis declared, "I'm with you. I'll fight with you" (Francis, November 21, 1990). The result of their lobbying was the integration of Grand Caillou public schools in 1954, an event that is still recalled with pride by the Houmas. In 1990, when Monsignor Boudreaux returned on a visit to Grand Caillou, he was greeted with gratitude and praise by local Houma leaders, some of whom remembered him from their common struggle, others who knew of his important role in Houma history (Houma Indian Communities, November 18–22, 1990).

Boudreaux's efforts helped to alter the place of the Houmas within the Catholic Church, although that change was slow in coming. He was not able, however, to divert the drift toward Protestant affiliation among the Indians. The Methodists and Baptists were joined by the Full Gospel Church and other Protestant denominations, and in many Houma families various members selected their own spiritual paths, apart from Catholicism. With a long history of racial intermarriage, Houmas have not demurred at marrying across denominational lines. While older priests like Monsignor Boudreaux have resisted the ecumenical tendencies of the post-Vatican II Church—Boudreaux says that he is "not ecumenical" and he chides the Houmas for not having "much of a discriminating sense; they don't always make the right decisions" (Boudreaux, November 17, 1990)—many Houmas seek succor and leadership in more than one Christian tradition.

In the Verret family, for instance, John is a Baptist leader in Dulac; his brother refers to himself as a "Methodist Catholic" (Verret, November 20, 1990)—proud of his family's several centuries of Catholic participation, cognizant of the long history of Houma-Catholic association, and trained as a Methodist minister. Their sister and their parents continue to be active members of the Catholic congregation in Dulac, and in fact all family members not only "interact frequently with each other" (Campisi and Starna 1988: 20), but also attend different Christian churches throughout the year. There are interfaith celebrations, and the intense clerical rivalries of the past are out of place among the contemporary Houmas, who are far more concerned about their extended kinship relations than they are about sectarian disputes. Houmas can name dozens, even hundreds, of Houma relatives by name (they tend to omit the non-Houma family members from these lists [6]), and they fight for the honor of their Houma names in the face of perceived insult. Kinship has been their political organization, their means of mutual aid in times of epidemic and flood, their economic lifeline. Catholicism has been part of their kinship identity for generations. Even as some Houmas have strayed from the institutional Church, Catholicism has remained an aspect of familial life.

A generation ago the pressure of living in a racist society tended to make the Houmas deny their Indian identity. To be Indian was to be persecuted, hence the Houmas steered clear of displaying Indian traits. They emphasized their French or Spanish heritage, even going so far as to deny their Indian forebears. As late as the 1950s parents would tell their children "not to say you're Indian or the feds will get you" (Houma Indian Communities, November 18, 1990). For over a century the Houmas had survived in Louisiana and avoided removal through the strategy of a low profile, moving further and further south, out along the swamps where they could fish and trap but where their landholdings were not challenged. Houmas tended to marry within their community, although there was also a long history of intermarriage with non-Houmas.

With the establishment of integration in the 1960s, intermarriage increased. At the same time, the Houmas began to speak publicly of their Indianness, although most of their Indian traits were long gone from their culture. The Houmas began to rise socially, becoming closer to the middle class without losing their identity as a people. Yet with intermarriage their bloodlines were hardly distinct from those of the surrounding community, so that today, as one Houma tells it, "they're so mixed now, you don't know anymore by appearance whose ancestry is whose" (Ledet, November 18, 1990). The last generation has engaged in two supposedly opposite movements: greater intermarriage with non-Indians and greater cultural reaffirmation. In the 1950s they kept to themselves and attempted "acculturation" (Boudreaux, November 17, 1990) simultaneously. Now they express their "dignity" by proclaiming their Indian identity, and at the same time they are becoming even less distinct racially and culturally.

In 1979 the Houmas created a political agency for their unification, the United Houma Nation, Inc., chaired by Kirby Verret. In 1982 they began sponsoring a powwow each August, drawing Indian and non-Indian spectators from throughout the Southeast. The Indians put on a "coming of age" ceremony, a "new fire" rite, sunrise services, story-telling, feasts, footraces, and hunting competitions, as well as social dances and public discussions of tribal issues. None of these events drew upon Houma traditions per se; rather, there was a creation of new traditions for the purpose of the powwow (see Campisi and Starna 1988: 17–18). What then, constitutes traditional Houma culture in the present day? There is hunting and trapping skill; there is rever-ence of the memory of Rosalie Courteaux, who epitomizes the tribe's struggle for identity; there is knowledge of familial names and a tradi-tion of separateness from Blacks and Whites; there is a belief in native healers called "traiteurs" (34). There are still some Houmas who can construct an old-time clay house or make moss dolls. Nonetheless, the Houma language is long gone, except for some Houma archaisms that survive in Cajun French. Houmas like Kirby Verret speak lovingly of their native language, French, rhapsodizing about its ability to paint pictures more expressively than English (Verret, November 20, 1990).

Is it correct to say that Houma culture is extinct? Yes, if what we mean by culture are aboriginal ways of speaking and worshipping and ancient means of production. However, if we regard a culture as a community's shared consciousness of itself as a continuous unity over generations, then the Houmas are far from extinct; indeed, they are thriving as a people. Their peoplehood has persisted. The Houmas have been subjected to racism and they have maintained their own boundary mechanisms to keep themselves identifiable as a community separate from Whites. They have allowed themselves to change—speaking French rather than Houma, worshipping as Catholics rather than continuing their aboriginal religious forms—but these newer as-pects of culture have become their traditional culture and their means of persistence. Just because others around them also speak French and identify as Catholics does not mean that the Houmas cannot identify themselves through these forms. For many generations the Houmas have been Catholics, just as they have spoken French. Speaking French and being Catholic are fully a part of their culture. In the contem-porary world they are speaking English as well as French, and they are participating in Protestant as well as Catholic forms. Nonetheless,

French Louisiana Catholicism is fully integrated into their lives and they continue to embrace it wholeheartedly in a manner far less ambivalent than that of any other Indian group in the United States.

The Church's contact with the Houmas for centuries has been sacramental, with priests baptizing, marrying, and burying the Indians. Indian children received a "small communion" and a "grand communion" (Boudreaux, November 22, 1990), according to a French tradition. For the small communion Indian children dressed up—girls in dresses and crowns as brides of Christ, boys in coats, white shirts, red ties, and three white ribbons on the sleeves, symbolizing faith, hope, and love. Together hundreds of children went through this rite of passage as a societal marker of progress through life. After three more years of instruction, just before confirmation, children received their grand, solemn communion. This tradition has persisted until recently.

During the year, however, the Houmas received the Eucharist infrequently, despite papal exhortations to the Catholic faithful to receive communion weekly. Like other French Catholics, the Houmas were touched by Jansenism, which impressed upon them their sense of unworthiness to receive Christ regularly. Perhaps Houmas had less of a sense of sinfulness than others of Jansenist bent; however, they felt unworthy to confess their sins more than once a year and receive communion more often than their Easter duty dictated. Many Houmas married first cousins, which was against Louisiana law; hence, they did not come to a priest or a judge to be married. Feeling guilty for their marital indiscretions, they did not receive communion regularly and they were too abashed to confess their sins. After all, what if the priest were to tell them to give up their marriage partners? Houmas also felt peripheral to the Church; they regarded themselves as recipients of sacraments rather than active members of Church leadership. As a result, their notion of sacramental Catholic life was to be baptized, receive communion, say some prayers, get married perhaps before a priest, and receive last rites in the Church. Priests were willing to let them sit at the fringes of the sacramental Church. They visited leading Houma families on occasion but in general ignored the daily spiritual needs of the Indians. Some priests were ready to overlook the Houmas' marriage customs so as to encourage sacramental participation. Others were eager to exclude the Houmas from sacramental life.

Beyond delivering sacraments to the Indians, the priests rarely instructed the Houmas in the intricacies of faith, at least beyond the time of confirmation. On their part, the Houmas preferred to drop away from formal instruction—particularly the men, who wished to begin their lives as fishermen and trappers—and so their faith was "devotional" rather than "theological" (Boudreaux, November 17, 1990). The Indians had a sense of God, of Christ's presence in their lives, and of Mary's intercessional powers, but they did not engage in religious speculation. Both Houmas and the priests among them were satisfied with this arrangement, regarding it as proper that Indians should know God rather than to know *about* God. As a result the Houmas developed a generalized notion of Catholic religiousness—"All religions worship the same God" (Foret, November 21, 1990)—and a directness toward worship that could bypass the role of the priest. As an elderly Houma says, "My mamma told me, 'You don't go to church for the priest. You go to serve the Lord'" (ibid.).

The Houmas' relationship with the priests was one in which the clerics ruled and the parishioners followed. Priests would say to a couple bringing their infant for baptism: "Why should I baptize when you don't attend mass?" Or, a priest would question a child: "Do your parents go to mass? If not, why not?" There was a constant assertion of authority over the Indians' lives; there was a constant intimidation that went beyond the normal authoritarianism of Catholic rule. "There is no coordination without subordination," the priests used to say (Boudreaux, November 18, 1990), and it was clear that Houmas were to submit to priestly authority. To this day the Houmas still regard priests with some fear and fascination, regarding them as mysterious, frightening, powerful presences, to be avoided if possible.

Until recently Houmas did not attend mass regularly. They did not feel invited by the priests or the white parishioners. They felt unworthy to receive the Eucharist. Like other poor people, they said that their clothing was not good enough to wear to mass. They resented the segregation within the church and preferred not to attend rather than stand along the back wall, having been denied pews that were bought or rented by the Whites in order to exclude the Indians. Since the integration in the 1960s, however, the Houmas have become church-goers in ways unheard of in the 1950s. Father Boudreaux (November 18, 1990) was shocked upon returning to Houma territory to find the huge attendance of Indians at Sunday mass, although he noted that even today the Indians still tend to sit by choice at the back of the churches. Today there are Houma ushers and members of the Knights of Columbus; in the 1950s Houmas did not think of taking such positions. But in the 1990s there are not only ushers and Knights but even a Houma priest, Father Roch Naquin (whose biographical sketch appears in volume 3 of *American Indian Catholics*), serving as leaders of an integrated parish, and the Houmas are in attendance at mass and other services.

These changes match the progress that Houmas have made both economically and socially. Some own their own businesses, including boats and stores. Some live in integrated neighborhoods. This pleases and amazes Father Boudreaux, who exclaims, "The first shall be last, the last first. It's the Houmas' turn for success in this country, thanks to the civil rights movement" (November 17, 1990).

Priests who have served as pastors among the Houmas in recent decades have never observed "Indian" ritualism; nor have they heard whispers of such. As far as Father Boudreaux could tell, the Houmas of the 1950s were "fairly orthodox" (November 17, 1990) Catholics, not theologically astute but devotionally committed. At the same time, they integrated their Indian identity into Catholic worship, not by enacting aboriginal Indian rituals but rather by making Catholic liturgy an occasion for familial unification. Two scholars report (Campisi and Starna 1988: 14–16) that Christmas and Easter, like the Fourth of July, Memorial Day, birthdays, anniversaries, and funerals, are opportunities for the Houmas to celebrate their own kinship with one another. On these holidays and at other times of the year, they hold family reunions called "cochandiliers" at which they roast a pig (hence the name, from the French *cochon*, pig) or have some other festive meal. They make of the Catholic (or American) holiday a Houma event.

The most important ritual event in the Catholic liturgical year is All Saints' Day, for at that time the Houmas commemorate their own beloved ancestors. Houmas have a great sense of responsibility regarding funerals and will travel hundreds of miles to attend one, taking time off from work to perform their social duty. On All Saints' Day the Houma women go around to the cemeteries to tend the graves of the Houma deceased. They lay out homemade crepe paper flowers dipped in wax on the graves; others bring cut fresh flowers. It is a "disgrace" to have a sloppy grave (Boudreaux, November 22, 1990), and the families go to great effort to make sure that everything is "propre" (Gregoire, Duthu, and Duthu, November 20, 1990), that is, clean and in order. Some families have their own cemeteries; others are part of larger plots. There is a burial mound for the nine hundred or so Houmas who died in the hurricane of 1909, and the Houmas continue to visit this site to pay their respects. On All Saints' Day the priest makes the rounds and blesses the graves, with the Houma families present. Cajuns as well as Houmas celebrate All Saints' Day with this ceremonialism.

Houma women do the cleaning at gravesites rather than the men, just as at funerals the men stay outside the church while the women perform the mourning. In general, Houma women are more ritually active than the men. In the old days Houma men and women sat apart from one another at mass and engaged in separate retreats. Today the men and women tend to integrate their devotionalism.

When Catholic Houmas move away from their home area, they maintain their faith, and if they can they try to return to Houma territory for death and burial. They dread the notion of being buried away from their people, too distant to be visited on All Saints' Day. As Catholics they are marking a day in the ritual calendar. As Houmas they are reaffirming their kinship. The two parts of their identity— Catholic and Houma—are not only *not* in conflict but are cojoined into a single identity. Catholicism provides the Houmas with means of affirming themselves as Houmas.

HOUMA CATHOLICS TODAY

Enter the small, well-kept house of Mary Gregoire, her daughter Lydia, and Lydia's husband, Ted Duthu, all Houmas, all Catholics described by their pastor as "exceptionally spiritual" people (Naquin, November 20, 1990). Lydia is cooking shrimp and rice for lunch. The Duthu and Gregoire children are playing together with video games. The men, Ted and his brother-in-law Julius Gregoire, have been working on their boats.

They speak easily of their Catholic faith, which has been part of their family lives for generations, for centuries. There are no Methodists or Baptists in the family; indeed, they cannot imagine being anything but Catholic. Catholicism is an integral part of who they are and they laugh at the notion of being anything else. Even more foreign to them is the idea of a Houma—woman or man—being irreligious, not engaging in Christian prayer. They regard themselves as typical Houma Catholics and they regard Houma Catholicism as an unyielding norm of behavior. None of them can recall any Indian elements in their Catholicism. Indeed, when asked what special rituals they perform as Houmas, they respond by describing the rosary services that they attend at the local Catholic church, Holy Family. They are baptized; they have received first communion; they have been married in the Church, and their loved ones have been buried through the Church. Catholic participation is to them a lifetime involvement.

They feel at home at Holy Family among their fellow Houmas and neighboring Whites. Moreover, when they are in the city of Houma they attend mass there, feeling completely comfortable in white congregations. They report that Holy Family is a unified parish; there is integration rather than separate worship by Whites and Indians.

According to the Gregoires and Duthus, the Houmas focus their prayers upon their local needs. When they are sick, they pray for curing. They pray for good weather, for successful shrimping, and for protection from life-threatening forces. They pray to God, particularly to Christ, and to His mother Mary. In April they participate in the blessing of boats before the shrimping season opens in May—their primary economic pursuit. Virtually all the Houma men are involved in shrimping, either working on others' boats or their own. The weather is easy in early summer, but in hurricane season the Gulf and even the inland waterways are dangerously rough. So, they pray for protection against storms, decorating each boat with flags and streamers and calling on their pastor, Father Naquin, to sprinkle each boat with holy water. Protestant as well as Catholic Houmas, and Whites, too, seek the priest's blessing, just as Catholic people worldwide have sought supernatural protection and aid in their productive lives. Then they drop a wreath in the water in remembrance of drowned Houma shrimpers of the past. They remember their dead at the same time as they hope for the living.

In spring they seek protection for their shrimpers, and in late summer they pray for defense of the whole community against a season of hurricanes. Living in homes only several feet above sea level, and in some cases well at or below that level, they are in extremely precarious positions in times of storm, and so they pray:

> O God, Master of this passing world, hear the humble voices of your children. The Sea of Galilee obeyed your order and returned to its former quietude; You are still the Master of land and sea. We live in the shadow of a danger over which we have no control: the Gulf, like a provoked and angry giant, can awake from its seeming lethargy, overstep its conventional boundaries, invade our land and spread chaos and disaster. During this hurricane season, we turn to You, O loving Father. Spare us from past tragedies whose memories are still so vivid and whose wounds seem to refuse to heal with the passing of time. O Virgin, Star of the Sea, Our Beloved Mother, we ask you to plead with your Son in our behalf, so that spared from the calamities common to this area and animated with the true spirit of gratitude, we will walk in the footsteps of your Divine Son to reach the heavenly Jerusalem where a stormless eternity awaits us. Amen. (Gregoire, Duthu, and Duthu, November 20, 1990)

They impress upon a listener the fervor of their prayer, connected as it is to the real danger of disaster to the faith they have in the efficacy of prayer, especially to the Virgin Mary. Says Lydia Duthu, "We have a real devotion to Mary, and she really intercedes for us and protects us from storms" (ibid.). She tells how in the 1980s the Houmas all gathered and prayed in the face of a threatening storm, and it turned around and left the community safe. Houma Catholic faith is concerned not only with heavenly but also earthly salvation.

Among the Houmas there are some individuals who are said to

possess the power to cure certain ailments with prayers. These "trai-teurs" (treaters) attempt to alleviate conditions like sunstroke, arthritis, rheumatism, urinary tract infections, and other "doleurs," the painful but not life-threatening maladies of daily existence. Some locals regard the treaters as a vestige of traditional Indian religious practice; how-ever, the term "treater" is of ancient European origin and there are Cajun as well as Houma treaters in the present day. Father Boudreaux regards the phenomenon of treaters as "not particularly Indian" (Bou-dreaux, November 22, 1990), and as a prayerful last resort when other cures have failed. "The Church has looked upon it as a superstition," he says. "It is never discussed publicly, but is regarded as innocent." The treaters themselves are "good Catholics," he adds.

How do treaters work? "They just pray," says a Cajun man married to a Houma (Boudreaux and Boudreaux, November 21, 1990). When he suffered from a case of the shingles, he went to a Houma treater who massaged the sign of the cross on his rash, and then put corn starch on it to keep it dry. He returned to the treater several times, and the rash subsided within a short period of time. An elderly Houma man, John Francis, describes the process: The treaters take bleeding from a cut. They say, "I'll stop this blood." They recite a prayer, differ-ent prayers for different ailments, "Catholic prayers" like the Our Fa-ther and Hail Mary, and they call for the pain to go away with words such as, "I'll stop that pain." Thus, although they use herbs and ges-tures, in the main "they work by prayer" (Francis, November 21, 1990). Mr. Francis pulls out a sheet of paper with a "Powerful Prayer of the Emperor Charles to the Holy Cross of Christ," typed within the outline of a cross. This prayer is said to be "found on the Sepulchre of Jesus Christ in 1709, and was sent by the Pope to the Emperor Charles when he went against the enemies of France at St. Michel, in France." The prayer contains the power to protect women in childbirth and to protect children "from eighty-two accidents." It is used by treaters to "turn everything good to me," according to Mr. Francis; its special ef-fectiveness for him derives from the fact that "it came from France."

Do the treaters employ prayers and gestures other than Catholic ones? Father Boudreaux does not know: "They wouldn't say what prayers were used" (Boudreaux, November 22, 1990). It is true that the Houmas keep from the Catholic priests most of the details of the treater trade. Partially this is because they feel that in the modern age people should seek help from medical doctors. The Houmas "don't care for the traiteurs too much now. They prefer to go to the doctor," reports a Houma woman, "but some still go" to their native curers (Boudreaux and Boudreaux, November 21, 1990). In addition, the treaters are also employed to harm as well as help people—that is, the treaters are thought to be akin to witches—and so the Indians attempt to keep knowledge of their usage from the representatives of the Church: "They would hide it from the priest," even from Father Naquin, the Houma cleric, "if it was evil" (Boudreaux, November 22, 1990). Priests are viewed as too pure, too innocent, to hear of such things. Father Naquin knows the identity of several Houma treaters, but he denies any substantial knowledge of their doings (Naquin, November 20, 1990).

Mr. Francis is less reticent about the interplay between curing and causing harm among the Houmas. His little house is filled with mementos of his married life: his fiftieth wedding anniversary "second marriage" plaque, photographs of his six children ("all Catholics"), forty grandchildren, and his deceased wife, Angelle Solet. "God helped me to raise my children," he states, just as the "good Lord" helped him to catch shrimp, muskrat, otter, and mink for a living over the years. He has always prayed with the rosary, and he still carries one with him wherever he travels. Never would he intend evil toward his Houma neighbors, he says. Nonetheless, there are Houma treaters who use prayers against their fellows. "They are doing wrong," he states with intensity. "I'll tell you this," he avows, contrasting the activities of healing and harming, "they don't use the same prayer for that. They use another kind of prayer" (Francis, November 21, 1990)

A priest, according to Mr. Francis, once warned a fellow cleric to "'keep an eye on the Houma people. The Devil is close to some of them. He feels with them.' I think the priest was right," adds Mr. Francis. "There are Houmas who work with the Devil" (ibid.). He narrates Houma stories of evil: animals who threaten to catch children or who disappear into smoke; devils who entice spouses to kill their marriage partners or who offer to work magic for individuals. There are some Houmas who are "rich and self-serving," willing to accrue property at the expense of others. Houmas live their lives wary of these persons and these powers; yet, they do not speak to their priests of their fears. "I'm scared of these things," he whispers. "A lot of people are scared of them . . . I pray to the Lord."

Mrs. Eva Pierre Boudreaux and her Cajun husband Joseph Norris

Boudreaux (Boudreaux and Boudreaux, November 21, 1990) live in Grand Caillou. On an autumn day he sits on the porch of their home, fashioning an enormous rosary out of netted rope and plastic corks. A crucifix and a wooden shield with a picture of a dove hovering over the earth lie beside him. He attaches them to the rope to complete the rosary. Each year the parish of Holy Family conducts a March of Christ, sponsored by the Holy Name Society and the Knights of Columbus. In 1990 members of the parish carry Mr. Boudreaux's over-sized rosary on the mile-long march, beginning and ending at the parish church.

While he completes the rosary, his wife is baking sweet potato pies for sale to benefit the St. Vincent Society at Holy Family. At $5 per pie ("People will pay anything if the money goes to the Church," she suggests), she is helping raise funds for the poor, not only in but also beyond her local community. The Boudreaux house is decorated with rosaries, crucifixes, paintings of the Sacred Heart, the Passion in the Garden, the Last Supper, statues of the Virgin Mary, and plaques of merit from the Holy Name and the Knights of Columbus (he is a fourth-degree Knight). They show a visitor a photo of flowers whose petals, they proclaim, reveal the image of the baby Jesus.

For this middle-aged couple, as for many of their congregation, Jesus reveals Himself constantly; Catholicism is their spiritual frame of reference. Weekly they attend Sunday services. On Mondays they participate in novenas. They have recently taken part in a Peace Mass which Mrs. Boudreaux calls "real nice." Father Naquin asked her if it went on too long. She says that mass is "never too long for me. I'd rather stay in church than go home to watch TV." She and her husband pray for the sick, asking the Blessed Mother to intercede for the health of the community, including that of Mr. Boudreaux, who is crippled from bone spurs in his spine. One local man who is sick promised a rosary every Wednesday night if he recovered. His health having improved, he prays at the church altar each week, and the Boudreaux couple join him. They are not shy to make petitionary prayer, and before the war began in the former Yugoslavia they had hopes to travel one day to Medjugorje to seek a cure for Mr. Bordreaux's illness. They listened with fervor at Holy Family church one night as a nun who had been to the shrine several times spoke about her experiences. And they are attracted to charismatic services led by Father Naquin every few months. "We hear it is beautiful," they report. "They sing so well, You can fold your hands, you can raise your hands, you can holler, shake and dance. It's all worshipping God" (ibid.).

Mr. and Mrs. Boudreaux celebrate Christmas, Easter, and all the Catholic holy days of obligation. They commemorate Good Friday; they pray on the American holiday of Thanksgiving; they pay special attention to the ceremonies surrounding All Saints' Day in Grand Caillou and in Montegut, where his parents are buried. In none of this are they out of the Catholic or Houma ordinary in their devotional life. Nor are they extraordinary in that both were married before—he in the Church, she before a judge. For many years they lived together without marrying. During that time they went to mass but did not receive communion. She was cooking and cleaning for the local priest, but they were not full communicants until he finally received an annulment (her dissolved civil bond did not pose an ecclesiological problem) and they were married in the Church. During the intervening years, however, they never left the Catholic fold: "We were *in* the Church. We never had it in mind to change our religion," they state.

It is noteworthy that Eva Pierre Boudreaux is a Houma and her husband is non-Indian. They engage their Catholic faith in apparently identical ways and they participate in the Church with Indians, Whites, Blacks, and the many of mixed ethnic origin as if there were no distinctions to be made among them all. They make no reference to Indian Catholicism as a particular species within the universal Church. Nor do they dwell upon the segregationist practices of the not-so-distant past, although they remember that past distinctly.

Mrs. Boudreaux recalls tales of a priest who supposedly told the Indians that he would drown their children if they came to church. Another "bad priest" slapped the face, pulled the ears, and shook the hair of a girl who sat beyond the "Indian benches" during services. "He was *big*. We were so afraid," she reports, and he shouted, "You don't have no business here!" (ibid.). Segregation led to disaffection and was a major reason why some Indians left the Church and joined the Methodists and Baptists, who seemed to care for Indian education. Each time a new priest arrived in Grand Caillou, the white parishioners took him aside and told him that segregation was the rule. Not until the early 1950s did the patterns begin to alter, with the coming of Father Boudreaux and his successors. They took down the bars that separated the races; they invited the Houmas to become regular members of the Church. And the majority of Houmas, like Mrs.

Boudreaux, who had continued in catechetical instruction and sacramental participation, accepted the invitation. "Things have changed,"
she acknowledges. Her husband adds, "They all mix now. Whites
marry Indians. Indians marry Negroes. Some don't like it still, but
things have changed in the last fifty years." When he was first married
at eighteen to an Indian woman, "it was rough." His male relatives
wanted to give him a whipping, but he braved them away. By the time
of his marriage to his present Houma spouse in 1978 there was no
comment concerning interracial unions.

Prejudice against Indians still exists, of course, not only in Louisiana
society but also in the Church. The Boudreaux pair remark upon a sermon delivered by a visiting priest who spoke of how "mean" the Indians were when first encountered by Catholic missionaries. Fights still
break out when Whites refer to the Houmas as "Sabines," a slur of ob-
scure origin that arouses violent reaction among the Indians. In the
Church, however, the Houmas seem to have found their peace, especially with the presence of a Houma pastor with spiritual authority
over Whites as well as Indians. Eva Boudreaux concludes: "I believe
so, a lot of people didn't like the way they were treated in the old days.
Some still have hard feelings. Not me. It's like it never happened.
Those old people from then are dead now. . . . Now we all hug and kiss
at mass. . . . It could have been that way all those years. . . . Such a big
change! . . . God sees everything" (ibid.).

Since the beginning of the annual Houma powwow, some of the
Indians have begun to reflect upon aboriginal religiousness and they
have attempted to express Indian values apart from their Christian
framework. In addition, beginning in 1992 several Houmas have been
attending the annual Tekakwitha conferences, sponsored in part by the
Bureau of Catholic Indian Missions. These Houmas are struck with
how "different" they are from other Indians across the United States
and Canada. One of their members, Pierre Solet from Dulac, comments that his people have taken a path separate from other Indians;
he realizes how little aboriginal culture his people have maintained, for
better or worse. His wife Mary feels the presence of tribal ancestors
when other Indians dance and sing at the Tekakwitha rituals; however,
she and her husband are firmly rooted in their contemporary Houma
culture, including their Catholicism. The Solets are comfortable in the
Church. They love their priest, Father Naquin. They are satisfied in
their home community. The Houmas may have given up their aborigi-

nal ways, but they are anything but culturally adrift. To the contrary, they are moored securely in a Houma culture that includes Catholic identity, piety, and values. Their son is in medical school at Louisiana State University; they have ambition for his social advancement. At the same time they expect him to devote part of his medical practice, gratis, to his Houma people. They see that Father Naquin has employed his priestly training for the benefit of his people, and they wish their offspring to follow that exemplar. In this way they and other Houmas are firmly embedded in their peoplehood; they are committed to perpetuate their culture.

It is ironic, then, to find them at the Tekakwitha conferences, their travel fees paid for by a Catholic bureaucracy, coming into contact with other Indians whose adjustment to Catholicism has been painful and less thorough. At the Tekakwitha conferences Indians from various tribes are encouraged to express their indigenous and pan-Indian culture in a Catholic context. Houma culture *is* Catholic culture, as much as Polish or Italian or Irish culture in America is Catholic culture. Yet, here are Pierre and Mary Solet, encouraged by the Church to participate in sweat lodge ceremonies conducted by Native American religious. Neither husband nor wife has ever heard of a sweat lodge until attending the conference. Neither lasts the full round of sweats. Both of them find the ritual "strange" (Solet and Solet, August 8, 1992). They joke about setting up a sweat lodge behind Holy Family church back in southern Louisiana. What would Father Naquin say? They erupt in laughter at the thought of it.

Between one annual Tekakwitha conference and another, the Houmas have survived Hurricane Andrew in 1992. Grateful for the relief efforts of various Americans, the Houmas organize themselves through the agency of the local Christian churches to deliver aid to Missourians ravaged by the summer floods of 1993. It is emblematic of the Houmas' cultural values that they are eager to reach out beyond their Indian community to help afflicted non-Indians. Their Catholicism has played no small part in prompting such an outreach of charity. At the same time, however, they are intrigued by their specialness as Indians and they seek to embrace the spiritual forms of other Indians without a thought of abandoning their Catholicism.

When they return to the Tekakwitha Conference, this time with Father Naquin in tow, they hope help him "get back to his roots" (Seattle, Swinomish, Lummi, August 5, 1993). After reflecting upon their sweat lodge experience of the previous year, they have decided that it is an enriching spiritual experience, and they want their Houma priest to be likewise "enriched" by various Native American rituals. But when Father Naquin goes back to Louisiana and tries out a sweetgrass service he has learned at the Tekakwitha meetings, his parishioners are turned off. The Houmas who call themselves traditionalists regard it as an unwelcome innovation; the staunch Catholics like it even less (Potsdam, August 5, 1995). In the 1990s the old-fashioned Catholic patterns still prevail among the Louisiana Houmas.

THE CHOCTAWS

The Choctaws were first approached by French missionaries in 1702, a few years after the first French contacts with their distant relatives, the Houmas. Over several decades the Jesuits attempted to interest the Choctaws in Christianity; however, conditions were not conducive to evangelical success in the early eighteenth century, a period of unremitting warfare in the lower Mississippi region. The Jesuits remarked on their lack of headway among the Choctaws, attributing it to the Indians' untractability. One Jesuit wrote that getting the Choctaws to think and speak like Christians would be a long and painful task: "This indeed can only be the work of Him Who knows how, when it pleases Him, to change the stones into children of Abraham" (Thwaites 1896–1901, 68:213).

The Jesuit effort among the Choctaws ceased in the 1700s. In the late eighteenth century Protestants made inroads in most Choctaw communities. Only in the nineteenth century was another attempt made by the Catholic Church to reach the five thousand or more Choctaws still residing in their homelands in Mississippi and Louisiana, the remnants who had escaped the Indian Removal of the 1830s. Rev. Adrian Rouquette's "intense love to be among the Indians" (Rouquette 1842–1885) resulted in a lifetime devoted to the Louisiana Choctaws, particularly in the 1850s and 1860s. However, by the first decade of the twentieth century the small pocket of Catholic Choctaws in Louisiana "had all but disappeared" (Pillar 1988: 290), some having moved to Indian Territory, others having intermarried with Blacks and Whites.

In 1883 a Dutch missionary, Father Bartholomew Bekkers, arrived in Neshoba County, Mississippi, having tried in vain to revive the Louisiana missions of Father Rouquette. With the encouragement of the local bishop and financial support from Holland, he purchased land and set out to create a farming community of Choctaws. The Indians were distrustful of Whites, who were intent upon seizing Choctaw allotments of land, but he won their interest by providing fifteen acres to each Choctaw family willing to live in the vicinity of his newly constructed church.

Rev. Bekkers tried to learn the Choctaw language but could speak
only a rudimentary form in order to explain Christian doctrine. At
first he used religious pictures to supplement his halting discourse:
"trees, fishes, man, woman—God created. —Good man, heaven; always there. Bad men, hell, great fire; never get out. —Me, body; me,
soul. Dog have body; not soul" (ibid., 289). He opened a school in
1884, hoping to draw the Indians to Catholicism through education.
Only eighteen attended during the first year, and the opposition of
Baptist missionaries and traditional Choctaw medicine men kept
Choctaws in large numbers from seeking baptism. Some Choctaw
clans would have nothing to do with relocating near the church. Others feared that Bekkers would allow them to cultivate their acres, only
to confiscate the land once it was improved. Their experience of
Whites had taught them suspicion, and Bekkers broke through their
mistrust only with perseverance. It was over a year before he baptized
even his first Choctaw child, a little girl who was dying. Another six
months went by before an adult, Mary Polk, asked for baptism, and
she, too, died shortly afterward. In 1886 the first surviving adults were
christened.

Bekkers also served the small community of white, mostly Irish
Catholics in Neshoba County. He tried to have them serve as models
of Christian life for the Indians. A Sister of Mercy joined his mission
and taught both Choctaw and non-Indian children. Bekkers' goal was
to teach the Indians English, and he soon ended his attempt to learn
Choctaw. His bishop encouraged him to use the Indian language, but
Bekkers replied, "Dear Bishop, I also wish so very often that I could go
off to the woods with the Indians, leave civilization a hundred miles
behind me and be free from the influence of the whites, but as things
are, that is just a wish and nothing more" (in ibid., 307).

The priest and the sisters were successful in teaching English to the
Indians; however, most Choctaws also retained their native language.
In the realm of religion, they wished to receive baptism before dying;
however, they were not immediately committed to changing their
ways of life—their plural marriages, for example—in order to live as
Christians. Nonetheless, by 1890 there were over two hundred Choctaws attending mass at Holy Rosary Indian Mission, along with fifty
Whites. By the turn of the century the Choctaw congregants had
tripled, and Holy Rosary was becoming a somewhat solid Catholic
community, although it is suggested (see Kidwell 1995: 181–188) that

Bekkers and the sisters secured attendance at mass with gifts of clothing and food.

In 1903 many Choctaws moved under government pressure to Indian Territory to join relatives there. The federal government did not recognize the Indian status of the Mississippi Choctaws, and so their landholdings were insecure, despite the support of the Church, which purchased a 1,400-acre tract where the Indians were allowed to live and cultivate crops, free of rent and taxes. Carmelite priests and brothers who succeeded Bekkers went west with the Indians. In Oklahoma Father William Ketcham translated into Choctaw a catechism of the Catholic religion in 1916, with the help of Catholic Choctaws such as Victor Murat Locke, principal chief, Choctaw Tribe of Indians, Oklahoma. At that time Locke praised the "splendid translation" (in *The Indian Sentinel* 1, no. 1, July 1916: 21) and wrote of his people's cultural changes: "Today the Choctaws are approaching the final act in the drama . . . for the Anglo-Saxonization of the race." He said that the process was "in a measure painful at times," but the translation of the Catholic catechism marked a "happy event" (22) in the tribe's history.

Father Ketcham not only translated Catholic doctrine into Choctaw; he also lobbied as director of the Bureau of Catholic Indian Missions for federal recognition of the Mississippi Choctaws. Recognition was gained in 1918 and as a result, many Choctaws returned from Oklahoma to Mississippi, where reservations were established in Neshoba and Newton Counties. Some Catholic Choctaws stayed in Oklahoma, where they have constituted but one of several Catholic Indian communities in the state, including Quapaws, Osages, Shawnees, Kiowas, Cheyennes, Arapahos and others numbering, all told, close to thirty thousand today (Marquette. DCRAA. 1983). The center of Choctaw Catholicism, however, has been in Mississippi. A succession of diocesan priests and sisters served the Choctaw mission until 1944, when the Missionary Servants of the Most Blessed Trinity—the Trinitarian Sisters—took over within the Diocese of Natchez-Jackson.

Throughout the twentieth century many of the Mississippi Choctaws in their seven different settlements have engaged in Catholic worship and attended catechetical instruction. Some Catholic Choctaws persisted in traditional Choctaw culture. Illa Pintabi, for example, served as a medicine man during the 1930s. For whatever curative powers he possessed in using herbs for doctoring, at least according to the missioners of his time, "he refers all thanks to God." At Sunday mass he sat in his accustomed pew, and the sisters found his "reverence during the Holy Sacrifice . . . "very edifying" (in *The Indian Sentinel*, 15, no. 1, Winter 1934–1935: 14). Some Choctaw leaders, like Wade Billie, established chapels in their homes, where mass could be said as the priests made their rounds. At midcentury the Mississippi Choctaws—Catholics, Baptists, and the remaining pagans—held their harvest encampment near Holy Rosary Mission. Indians from Conehatta and a half dozen other communities converged, and the local church chief, John Charlie, made arrangements for festivities and prayers. There was a great stick ball game—a traditional Choctaw pastime—and a "Ball Play Dance" (30, no. 9, December 1950: 142) fostered solidarity. There were holy hour services for the Catholic Indians (and anyone else who wished to attend), and the bishop of Natchez celebrated mass, with Willie Solomon, the chief catechist at St. Catherine's Mission at Conehatta, translating for the older Choctaws. The priests and sisters continued to make converts, for example, Henry Farmer in 1948 ("kneeling so erect during Holy Mass, and receiving Holy Communion with such devotion" [31, no. 9, November 1951: 119]), and Comeal Polk, baptized as Camille in 1951. Catholicism flourished as a minority religion within the tribe. As a result, in the 1990s over a thousand Mississippi Choctaws, one-fifth of the Choctaws in the state, are counted by the Church as Roman Catholics. Most of the other Choctaws are Baptists.

In recent decades the Mississippi Choctaws have employed their political organization toward economic development. Underlying the political and economic layers of Choctaw society, however, has been the structure of Christian denominational alliance. Through the century the Choctaws have helped one another locally through their churches, Catholic and Baptist, and upon this solidarity they have created community leadership. Like the Houmas, it might appear that the Choctaws have more in common with other rural, non-Indian folk of the deep South than they do with Indians from across America; however, the Choctaws have maintained a clear sense of identity, in no small part through Church activities. Choctaw church chiefs conduct services and each parish has its own elected parish council. There is active participation in Church life, parishioners serve as altar boys, scriptural readers, and Eucharistic ministers. In 1987 the Vatican permitted mass to be said in Choctaw language. Unfortunately, the approved liturgical language is an Americanized, homogenized Choctaw that no one really speaks, although everyone who speaks Choctaw dialects can understand it. The local dialects are still used in prayer and in church parish meetings.

Today, through business growth, the Choctaws are building modern houses where formerly many of the tribe lived in swampland shacks. There is medical care, housing for the aged, and opportunities for employment close to home, as the tribe lures corporations to Choctaw territory with its tax-free land, low salaries, and other benefits to employers. With this development has also come political corruption, according to some (Placilla and Culhane, August 5, 1992). Catholic (as well as Baptist) culture among the Choctaws today provides stability in the face of change. Mississippi Choctaw religious culture may be strongly Christian, but it is also strongly Choctaw, in leadership and ownership. The Indians understand that the non-Indian missionaries are ephemeral to the community, and that Choctaw Catholicism is Choctaw at the core of the community. John Farmer appreciates the Trinitarian sisters (and the Trinitarian priests who remain among the Choctaws), but he says, "You can't become too attached to them. . . . They will move on" (ibid.).

In recent years the Bureau of Catholic Indian Missions has encouraged some Choctaw Catholics to come into contact with other Indian Catholics through the annual Tekakwitha conferences. Like the Houmas and the more recently evangelized Indians of the Southeast, such as the Cherokees and Catawbas, some Mississippi Choctaws have begun to attend the annual conference, beginning in 1992. Accompanied by sisters of the Immaculate Heart of Mary, who replaced the Trinitarians in 1988, Choctaws like John Farmer are encountering other Indian Catholics for the first time and finding their traditional ritualism "strange, but interesting" (Farmer, August 7, 1992). Farmer observes a pipe ceremony conducted by a Crow Catholic, and he observes a parallel from his own community: "We burn incense in church," he says, comparing the Choctaw Catholic burning of incense to the native ceremonial smoke offerings of the Plains Indians. Like the Houmas, the Choctaw Catholics of today feel more at home in the rituals of the Church than they do in pan-Indian ceremonialism.

Passamaquoddies celebrate a feast day in their village in Maine, c. 1913.
Used by permission of Marquette University Library, Milwaukee, Wisconsin.

*A Franciscan missionary displays traditional Ojibway religious
articles given to him by Catholic converts, Bayfield, Wisconsin, c. 1915.*
Used by permission of Sacred Heart Franciscan Archives, St. Louis, Missouri.

The first fullblood American Indian Catholic priest,
Rev. Albert Negahnquet (Potawatomi), poses at St. Louis' School,
Pawhuska, Oklahoma, 1924.
Used by permission of Marquette University Library, Milwaukee, Wisconsin.

Choctaw girls honor Kateri Tekakwitha,
Holy Rosary Mission, Mississippi, 1939.
Used by permission of Missionary Servants of the Most Blessed Trinity, Philadelphia, Pennsylvania.

The Catholic Ladder adorns a government school catechism class in Tulalip, Washington, c. 1941.

Used by permission of Dominican Sisters, Edmonds, Washington; photograph by Sr. Mary Jean Dorcy, O.P.

*Coeur d'Alene women pray the rosary beneath a statue of
Kateri Tekakwitha, Sacred Heart Mission, Idaho, c. 1942.*
Used by permission of Sisters of Providence, Spokane, Washington.

*Rev. Joseph Brown, S.J.
(Blackfoot) celebrates his
ordination mass,
Alma College,
California, 1948.*
Used by permission of the Jesuit
Oregon Province Archives,
Gonzaga University, Spokane,
Washington; negative no.:
819.01.

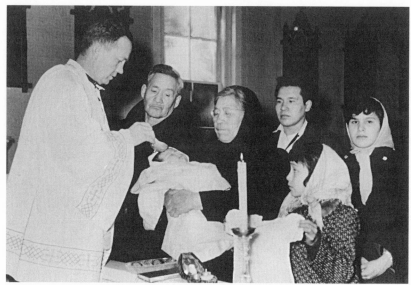

*A Benedictine priest baptizes an Ojibway child,
St. Mary's Mission, Red Lake, Minnesota, 1956.*
Used by permission of St. John's Abbey, Collegeville, Minnesota.

*Passamaquoddy and Mohawk Catholics lead an entry procession at the
annual Tekakwitha Conference, Fargo, North Dakota, 1989.*
Used by permission of photographer Catherine Walsh.

Houma Indians Mary Solet and Rev. Roch R. Naquin bless their church with sage and feathers, Grand Caillou, Louisiana, 1996.
Used by permission of Rev. Roch R. Naquin.

✳ III ✳

The Central Algonkians

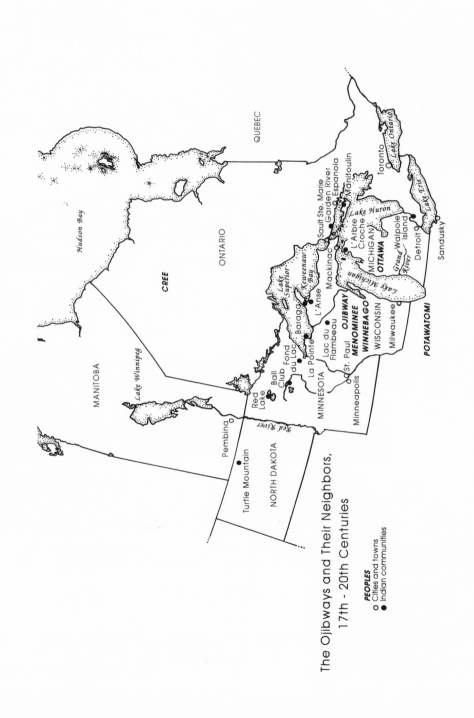

The Ojibways and Their Neighbors,
17th - 20th Centuries

PEOPLES
○ Cities and towns
● Indian communities

CENTURIEƒ OF OJIBWAY MIƒƒIONƒ

The fur traders and missionaries of New France did not give up their goal of expanding westward after the Iroquois destruction of Huronia in 1649. By the 1660s they had paddled and portaged their way to the crucial junction of Lakes Superior and Huron, the rapids they called Sault Ste. Marie. The Indians of that area called themselves Anishinabe, but they have been given several other names over time, including Saulteaux, Ojibway, and Chippewa.

They and their closely related neighbors, the Ottawas, numbered as many as twenty-five thousand in the middle of the seventeenth century, a figure which included Huron refugees who escaped the Iroquois wars further east. The Ojibways were Great Lakes Indians speaking a Central Algonkian language, similar to Potawatomi as well as Ottawa. Indeed, all three of these peoples referred to themselves as Anishinabe. They were hunters, gatherers, and, especially at the Sault, fishers, living in small, autonomous kinship units (the word, "totem" derives from the Ojibway term for a family mark) without anything approaching wholesale political unity. To the north the Anishinabe had linguistic relatives in the Crees, and to the west, in present-day Wisconsin, the Menominees.

The Ojibways may have encountered Frenchmen as early as 1610; by 1670 they were fully involved in the traffic of furs. They obtained all manner of trade goods, including firearms, and traveled further west with the expanding French empire. In their encounter with French culture, they met with Catholicism in the persons of evangelizing priests (see Vecsey 1983: 26–30, 45 ff.).

The Recollects had only touched the periphery of Ojibway territory in upper Michigan between 1615 and 1629. In the early 1640s two pairs of Jesuits got as far as the Sault with their Huron guides but made no visible impression upon the natives beyond planting a cross. Between 1660 and 1690 the Jesuits made more headway around the western Great Lakes and established several missions, some short-lived, others more apparently successful. The names of Fathers René Ménard, Claude Allouez, Jacques Marquette, Claude Dablon, Louis André, and

Gabriel Druillettes became associated with the Ojibway missions for their pioneering work during these three decades.

The patterns of these early efforts differed little from Jesuit activities further east. The priests tried to bring to the Indians a "'knowledge of God' and a more settled condition of life" (Kennedy 1950: 55). They poured baptismal water on the sick, the dying, the infant, the outcast, and the extraordinary (see Thwaites 1896–1901, 46:127–137; 51:61 ff.). They encountered the obstacles of "idolatry, superstitions, legends, polygamy, unstable marriages, and every sort of licentiousness" (51:21), as well as a disdain for the evangelizers themselves, who were seen as worthless disrupters of the social order (see 50:249–305). Intertribal warfare, e.g., between the Sioux and the Ojibways, exacerbated by the disruptive pressures of the fur trade and competition for empire, spelled dislocation for repeated missionizing endeavors. So did competition with native doctors and other religious specialists, some of whom accused the Jesuits of causing diseases with their sacerdotal paraphernalia (Kellogg 1917: 106–107). The priests hung up pictures of universal judgment and hell to frighten the Indians toward conversion; they threatened to leave them and take the fur trade along. Sometimes the natives stole from the priests' bark chapels and wrecked their canoes. At other times they promised to give up their aboriginal religious practices and take Christian instruction (see Thwaites 1896–1901, Vol. 52:205–207; Kellogg 1917: 102–103, 116–118).

The missioners could not be sure of the Indians' intent when they said they were prepared to convert. As one Jesuit wrote in 1668, "Dissimulation, which is natural to those Savages, and a certain spirit of acquiescence, in which the children in that country are brought up, make them assent to all that is told them" (Thwaites 1896–1901, 52:203).

In the uncertainty of the moment, some Jesuits allowed the Indians to continue in their native rituals as long as they made offerings to God instead of their traditional idols (54:181). The priests taught the indigenes how to sing the songs of French Catholicism and how to perform morality plays to supplement native dances (Kurath 1959: 211–212). Along with representatives of the French crown, the priests tried to impress the Indians with gifts and pageantry (Nute 1944: 27–28), and they stationed monumental crosses around the Great Lakes for the Indians to revere (Holand 1933: 159). When one priest brought a "grievous disease" to Sault Ste. Marie, he made public displays of curing the stricken denizens, and hundreds of baptisms took place. Wrote the Jesuit commentator,

> God made use of these very uncommon cures . . . to touch our Savages' hearts; in consequence of which, on the eleventh of October, 1670, all the principal elders of the country repaired to the Chapel in a body, and made a public declaration before all the people that at length the Sault was Christian, and that the God of Prayer was the Master of life. (Thwaites 1896–1901, 55:127)

When Ojibway enemies were defeated or when battle was imminent, the Catholic chapel at the Sault rang with prayers to the priests and their deity: "They are truly our Fathers . . . These black gowns who protect us and give life to the sault, by receiving our women and children into their house, and by praying for us to JESUS, The God of War" (in 57:209).

The Jesuits christened hundreds of Ojibways during the three decades from 1660 to 1690; however, they did not regard these as conversions completed, but rather as steps toward the future. When the Franciscan Louis Hennepin (a critic of the Jesuits, to be sure) observed the Ojibways, Ottawas, and Hurons at Mackinac in 1679, he remarked upon the rudimentary state of progress. He said that the Indians attended instruction out of curiosity, not out of Christian leanings. They listened politely to the Christian creation story and then responded with their own mythic narratives. Baptisms were no more than attempts to procure magical protection or healing. When missionaries gave the Indians pictures, a crucifix, or beads, the natives wore them like jewelry, as if they were charms of wampum. Whereas some accepted baptism, most rejected it adamantly, fearing the promised French afterworld as a place of slavery or starvation. Without a miracle, he wrote in 1683, "so long as Christians are not absolutely their masters we shall see little success" (Hennepin 1966: 338).

In the 1690s the Jesuit presence diminished among the Ojibways. The Society began to lose its fervor for Indian missions, and many of the Indians moved from their aboriginal homes to locations in all directions. The Ojibways established settlements far and wide, from the area north of Lakes Erie and Ontario (in what is now Michigan and Ontario) to the lakes and rivers between Superior and Winnipeg (Wisconsin, Minnesota, North Dakota, and Manitoba), and even north to the drainage area of Hudson Bay. Some Ojibways traveled as far west as the Rocky Mountains, and a small group joined the Mohawk

Catholics to the east at the reserve of Caughnawaga. The Ojibways hunted and trapped for the French, traded and intermarried with them. They acquired the habits, the language, the diseases, and the tastes of their allies, and it is certain that they observed the traders in Catholic religious observances (Bishop 1974: 153).

In dozens of locales the various Ojibway peoples adapted to new environments, creating regional variations of culture that make it difficult to describe the Ojibways as a homogeneous whole. It is certain, however, that for a century they had minimal contact with official representatives of the Church. Fewer than a dozen Jesuits had contact with any Ojibways during the eighteenth century (Shea 1855: 501), and most of these were in the area of Mackinac, where baptismal records were kept ("The Mackinac Register" 1910; Henry 1966: 40, 47, 92). The French lost the war for their northern empire; the British took over and the last of the Jesuits retired from their missions.

When Father Gabriel Richard, the first American Catholic priest in the Mackinac region, passed through the area in 1799, there were some old Ottawas and Ojibways who remembered the earlier era of Jesuit evangelization; however, there were few vestiges of the mission, save an old oak Jesuit cross still standing at a village called L'Arbre Croche (Furlan 1952: 62; Craker 1935: 16). This location had received continuing ministrations. For the Ojibways far afield there were even fewer palpable reminders of New France Catholicism.

During the eighteenth century and into the nineteenth, Ojibways of what is now Wisconsin and Minnesota developed a religious organization called Midewiwin, a formalization of their traditional religious beliefs and rituals combined with portions of Catholicism gained from the French. The cross became a symbol of the Mide Society; a code of ethics resembled the Ten Commandments; birchbark scrolls were consulted like biblical writings. The Mides directed their prayers to a supreme deity resembling in conception the Christian God. In this way Catholicism made its mark on some Ojibways, although not as Catholics. Indeed, Midewiwin developed as a nativistic cult in competition with the Christian missionaries, Catholic and Protestant, who came to convert the Indians in the 1800s. In the early nineteenth century, Ojibways in southern Ontario allied themselves with the anti-White, anti-Christian teachings of the Shawnee Prophet, Tenskwatawa, and his brother Tecumseh, and hardened themselves against efforts to christianize them or remove them from their territories.

Ojibways on the Canadian prairies continued to join themselves economically and conjugally with the fur traders of the Montreal-based North West Company and its competitor, the imperial Hudson's Bay Company. In the fierce rivalry for pelts, one of the Hudson's Bay stockholders established a colony in the Red River Valley south of Lake Winnipeg. In 1818 he hired several Catholic priests in order to attract Frenchmen to his cause. One of the clerics, Sévère Joseph Nicolas Dumoulin, took an interest in the Indians in his midst, mostly Ojibways, and set up a mission at Pembina, now in North Dakota. The instructions to the priests included two primary goals: to reclaim the Indians from barbarism, and to help delinquent Christians. These included Frenchmen who were living like natives, and Métis, people of mixed Indian and Euro-American heritage who formed a distinct ethnic group on the Canadian prairies (Nute 1942: 58, 60).

The Pembina mission under Dumoulin lasted only five years; however, it was reputed to be "much more effective" (ibid., xi) than the Jesuit missions of the 1600s. The priests planted crosses, preached the gospel, prepared pagans for baptism, and made legitimate the "marriages" of native women living as concubines with Christian men. They tried to settle the Indians in villages and teach them to farm, with limited success. They tried to keep the Protestant missioners at bay, and they inveighed against the Indian medicine men. Their efforts netted almost 400 baptisms, 68 marriages, and 49 Catholic burials, according to one estimate (Norton 1930: 43). Dumoulin claimed even greater success: 800 baptisms, 120 marriages conducted or rehabilitated, and 150 first communions. He said that at the time of the mission's closing (when it became part of the territory of the United States), there were many more Indians preparing for the sacraments; "their eyes were beginning to be fixed on this symbol [the cross] of our salvation" (Nute 1942: 415). However, when Henry Rowe Schoolcraft passed through Pembina in 1832, the church was extinct and the half-bloods living in the vicinity were hardly to be identified as Catholics. In the late 1840s a new round of missionizing began afresh at Pembina with the arrival of Fathers George Anthony Belcourt and Albert Lacombe. Thus, in stops and starts, the Red River Ojibways and their Métis kinsmen came to be associated with Catholic institutions.

In other parts of the present-day United States, it was also necessary for missionaries to begin anew the task abandoned by the Jesuits of the colonial era. In the 1820s secular clergy in Michigan restored contact with Ottawas at L'Arbre Croche, aided partially by a band member named Andowish, who had learned something of Catholicism on a visit to Montreal. Another Ottawa layman, Jean-Baptiste Assiginack (Blackbird), educated at the Sulpician mission at Oka in Canada, became a leader of the local Catholic revival.

In Wisconsin various French-speaking priests, including Belgians, Swiss, and Canadians, renewed Church contact with the Menominees beginning in the 1830s. A century later, 90 percent of the two thousand Menominees at an Indian mission in Wisconsin were said to be Catholics (*The Indian Sentinel* 20, no. 7, September 1940: 104). Today about a half of the seven thousand Menominees call themselves Catholics (Marquette. DCRAA. 1983).

The primary impetus to new Ojibway missions came from a Slovene evangelical agency called the Leopoldine Society, founded in 1829. In 1830 the Society funded Father Frederic Baraga's journey from Austria to the United States. The priest learned Ottawa language from an Indian seminarian in Cincinnati (probably one of Jean-Baptiste's sons, who studied for the priesthood) and arrived in L'Arbre Croche in 1831. The work of several other priests over the previous decade had made this village fertile soil for Baraga; hundreds were already baptized, and a forerunner to Baraga said that never had he witnessed "more perfect examples of Christian piety and unaffected devotion" (Baraga, February 11, 1831). Baraga heard that the Ottawas were ever loyal to the French (one of the languages he spoke) and to the priests of the Catholic religion. The Indians would not listen to Protestant ministers, who, "having their wives and children, are men like ourselves; but the *Black gowns* disengaged from these material encumbrances, are left perfectly free to devote their whole time and attention to spiritual matters. . . ." The Ottawas felt that the priests were better suited than the Protestants to serve their "Almighty Master, who is a Spirit himself" (ibid.).

When Baraga arrived at L'Arbre Croche, he established a punctual daily routine, and he claimed that the Indians were faithful to it: Angelus at 5:00 A.M., followed by public prayers led by a chief, then mass. "Very many appear" (August 10, 1831), he reported, for evening services as well: songs, prayers, and catechism, aided after a while by an Ottawa prayer book and hymnal of his own composition. During the day he heard confessions. On Sundays and feast days the Ottawas assembled four times in church, for morning prayers, high mass, vespers, and evening prayers. There were eager converts in those days, bringing Baraga their medicine bags, which he burned as offerings to God. He sent two small bird wings from one bag, formerly the property of a converted chief, to a correspondent back home "as a memento of the triumph of the teachings of Jesus." May this "sensational conversion" attract others, said the priest (ibid.).

And so it did. During his two years at L'Arbre Croche, Baraga christened well over five hundred Indians, including adults and infants (Cadieux and Comte 1954: 15). Without crisis or coercion, independent of the Whites with whom they traded at Mackinac, Baraga stated, "the Christian Indians submit themselves faithfully and readily to the law of the gospel, and the announcer of the gospel is their king" (Baraga, March 10, 1832). He distributed rosaries, crucifixes, and other sacramentals of the Church, and he observed the Ottawas in their settled way of life, growing corn, potatoes, beans, and pumpkins, raising pigs, fowl, cows, and horses, gathering maple sap, hunting and fishing. "The mode of life of the converted Indians of this mission resembles very much the mode of life of the whites . . ." (August 25, 1831), he wrote with satisfaction.

Baraga visited the small communities throughout the Ottawa regions of Michigan, adding to his credit several hundred baptisms. He moved to Grand River in 1833, where he converted close to a hundred Indians within three weeks. He soon had a parish of two hundred, a temperance society (the priest had to lock his door at night to protect himself from drunken brawls), and a loyal Indian following. He wrote that the Catholic Ottawas were improving their behavior; an old violent drunkard became a "gentle lamb" with a rosary around his neck (December 1, 1833). When he heard that the Ottawas were "very much depressed" (June 26, 1834) at the thought of removal forced upon them by the United States, he encouraged them not to cede their territory.

Land speculators tried to have him removed; so did Protestants, who saw in him a dangerous rival. A Baptist missionary instigated a letter to the governor of Michigan, signed by twenty-five Ottawas, complaining of Baraga's doings:

> This is the reason we are lonesome, when we have endeavored to be in health & to love one another, there came among us a foreigner a white man who separated near Friends, now hatred & varience is among us. Everyone that is bad is now in our village. . . . We are all of one mind that sit here in council that you should tell this white man (the

Catholick Priest) to go away from our village. . . . Should you pity us
we shall have joy. . . . This white man the Priest all the time comes to
our houses & tells us we shall be miserable if we are not Sprinkled &
that we shall go to hell & our children. This is the reason we are lone-
some. . . . (May 13, 1834)

The upshot was Baraga's transfer from the Ottawas to the Ojibways
along the shores of Lake Superior. Yet the Ottawa missions continued,
and in 1845 an associate of Baraga's claimed there were almost fourteen
hundred Catholic Indians in the area of L'Arbre Croche (Pierz, February 10, 1845).

On his way to the Lake Superior Ojibways, Baraga thanked his
benefactors for the candlesticks, vestments, and other paraphernalia
with which he was supplied:

> O how amazed and pleased and good Indians will be, who, like children
> are captivated with all that strikes the senses, when they will see such
> beautiful articles in their house of God. What high ideas all this will give
> them about our holy religion, which even in all outward appearances
> strives so very much to attest to our Lord and God the proper honor. —
> And then the beautiful large crucifixes! — How edifying it will be for the
> new Indian converts, who at the sight of a crucifix are very much moved,
> to have such beautiful crucifixes in their houses! (Baraga, March 13, 1835)

At his first stop, La Pointe, there was scarcely a vestige of the mission
buildings or cross left by the Jesuits a century before; however, a priest
from Montreal had visited every few years in the 1820s to minister to
Frenchmen at a trading post. Baraga believed that there were Ojibways
at La Pointe who sought baptism and another sacramental attentions.

He was not wrong. At La Pointe Baraga baptized close to a thousand Indians (Cadieux and Comte 1954: 23) over the next few years.
Even after six months he was able to say, in describing Midewiwin ceremonies, that "the converted Indians now wonder themselves how
they could have been so dumb as to take part in such foolishness"
(Baraga, December 28, 1835). In the same year he journeyed to Fond
du Lac, at the request of a French fur trader who had been teaching the
Ojibways about Catholicism. The Indians liked Baraga's French airs as
well as his sermons, and for many years he visited them, baptizing and
edifying the natives.

After several years of fund-raising and recruiting other priests in
Europe, Baraga traveled in 1843 to L'Anse on Keweenaw Bay. He was
the first priest to come there since René Ménard 180 years earlier. At

L'Anse the priest formed a type of reduction, with as many as thirty Indian families farming their plots of land under his direction. At La Pointe Baraga had become concerned about the half-breed Canadian Catholics who came to La Pointe from their hunting territories in the summer to take Ojibway women as concubines. He wondered if he should keep these wanderers at a distance from his converts, and thus from his Church and from the sacraments. At L'Anse he hoped to keep his catechumens more isolated from bad influences.

Whatever his intentions, Baraga's moves at L'Anse created a row with the Methodists already ensconced at the site. From the early nineteenth century various Protestant bodies had begun their own christianizing efforts among the Ojibways (see Vecsey 1983: 30-37): Methodists, Presbyterians, Baptists, Episcopalians, interdenominational organizations, Anglicans in Canada, and others all vied for control of their mission fields. Ojibways had not only their own native sects like Midewiwin, but also the factions created by denominational loyalties. At L'Anse the fracas was nasty.

Most of the Indians Baraga baptized in his first two months had been Methodists for close to a decade. The Protestant missionary complained of the theft of his congregation to the Superintendent of Indian Affairs in Detroit, who issued a circular that read: *"Wherever a Mission or school has been established, the department cannot permit the interference of another sect and especially among the same band of Indians"* (Baraga, April 3, 1844 [emphasis in original]). This was clearly aimed at the Catholic invasion of L'Anse, so Baraga sent the superintendent a list of several dozen Ojibway students in his catechetical school, which he conducted in the Indian tongue with the help of the French trader's wife. The superintendent still recommended that Baraga move his operation to "some destitute Band," rather than causing "discord and jealousies" at L'Anse (April 15, 1844). Local government employees received their orders to shun the Catholic priest, in order to hinder his work and get him on his way. Baraga would not be budged, however, charging persecution of Catholics and an infringement of his religious liberty and that of his converts.

The Methodist reverend countered that "the establishing of the Catholic mission at this place, has tended, greatly, to unsettle the minds of the indians, and set them against each other" (May 20, 1844). In the course of the controversy Baraga explained that the Indians had invited him to come to L'Anse because a chief named Bineshi had recommended Catholicism—the *"french Religion"* (May 29, 1844 [emphasis in original])—to his relatives before his death. When he passed away, his kin wished to observe his wishes and receive baptism from the "french Priest," as they called Baraga. Now that they were thus christened, former Methodists and pagans alike, Baraga could not abandon them.

A Methodist Ojibway minister named Peter Marksman—by this time there were several such Wesleyan preachers among the Ojibways—told a different story. He said that the invitation had come from the French trader, who perhaps wanted his offspring educated in the Catholic tradition. The trader reportedly told the Indians who traded with him that they would have to join the Catholics when a priest came, the implication being that their trade would suffer were they to remain outside the fold. As for Bineshi, he was a drunk who trafficked in pagan conjurors and earned the wrath of the Methodist powers. His family's alliance with the Catholics was a means of avenging reprimands he had received from the Protestants, according to Marksman.

By the middle of the summer of 1844, Keweenaw Bay possessed two factions of Ojibways: Methodists at L'Anse and Catholics across the bay (at the present site of Baraga, Michigan), where the priest moved his flock to avoid the interdict against two sects at one location. The band was split and feelings were raw; the Methodists were undercutting the French trader with their own post, run by one of the men of the cloth. Baraga organized a petition of half-bloods and Ojibways supporting his mission and asking for the removal of the minister-trader instead. Baraga weathered the storm at L'Anse, and by 1847 the majority of Indians at Keweenaw Bay lived at the Catholic village, joined by French-Indian mixed-bloods.

Unlike the Montagnais, the Hurons, the reduction Iroquois, and the Passamaquoddies—all converts to Catholicism from the Jesuit push of the seventeenth century, whose descendants continued to live primarily within the realm of Catholic culture, isolated to a large degree from Protestant incursions—the Ojibways were only partially touched by Catholic tradition in New France. When the second wave of missions commenced in the nineteenth century in the United States (and Canada), there were other forces competing for the loyalty and orientation of the Great Lakes Algonkians. Nativistic movements had become integral to some Ojibway communities' culture, and Protestant Christianity posed a challenge to Catholicism at every turn. In addition, many Ojibways maintained a substantial involvement in their traditional religion, at least in the first half of the nineteenth century, before the coming of the reservation system.

In 1843 Father Baraga was the only Catholic missionary in the Lake Superior district, amidst what he termed "thirty false prophets" of Protestantism (June 17, 1843). In 1847 he had a handful of European-born clerical associates with whom to plan the future of Ojibway evangelization. He and the other priests continued with catechesis in Ojibway, hoping to produce Catholic Indians who were good for themselves, rather than the Protestant speakers of broken English ("middle-things," Baraga termed them [May 24, 1848]), who were good for nothing, in his opinion. Baraga's use of the Indian language made him appear subversive to the Protestant americanizers of Indians; after all, he was a foreign national, a Roman Catholic, and a supporter of Native American speech.

Baraga was proud of his successes. In his own hand he wrote a missive under the name of the L'Anse band council, regarding the exploits of the Most Holy Name of Jesus Temperance Society, whose members broke a keg of whiskey imported by Wisconsin Ojibways. "We want to tell you," he wrote, "that we the Catholic Indian Congregation have entirely abandoned the use of ardent spirits, and we don't suffer that Indians from the interior who are so much addicted to it, should bring any in our village here" (October 5, 1847). To his sponsors he claimed an overflowing Catholicism among his Indian congregation: "On sundays they are so crowded in the house of God that they can scarcely move, and many are kneeling and sitting on the floor" (June 15, 1848). In the year Baraga became bishop, a Catholic newspaper sang his praise and that of his Ojibway converts: "The Catholic Indians, numbering some thousands, are most exemplary, and rarely sin after Baptism" (February 15, 1853).

Baraga even made peace with the local Indian office and his Methodist brothers in Christ. The Detroit department of Indian Affairs recommended federal funding for the L'Anse Catholic school, with the following accolade: "In the whole range of my official duties, I have found no Indians, giving better evidence of advancement in civilization or in Education, in agriculture and mechanics than those of the Chippewas under the charge of the Catholic Missionaries and Teachers at L'Ance [sic]" (December 8, 1848). The Methodists agreed that Baraga's reduction had become the focal point for Ojibway culture on the southern shore of Lake Superior. It was ironic, then, when Baraga's sister, who had accompanied him to the U.S. in 1837 and opened a girls' school in Philadelphia, became a Protestant. A Viennese colleague of Baraga's remarked that "It was a source of great sorrow to us to hear that the sister of the reverend and pious Missionary Baraga has turned Methodist, to her indelible shame" (March 29, 1850).

In 1853 Baraga was named bishop of the Vicariate Apostolic of Upper Michigan and later, bishop of Sault Ste. Marie. Bishop Baraga carried on his longstanding concern for Great Lakes Algonkian missions almost until his death in 1868. He visited Ottawa and Ojibway Catholic congregations, including La Pointe, L'Anse, and Fond du Lac. He produced an instrumental dictionary in Ojibway (Baraga 1973). He presided over marriages between native and non-Indian Catholics, as Europeans began to settle among the Indians. He reserved land in Indian territory for Catholic churches and gave public lectures about the progress of Catholicism among the Native Americans. Following in the footsteps of the Jesuits Marquette and Allouez, in his three decades of Indian ministry he helped attract many Anishinabe people to Catholic culture. A century after his arrival in America the Ojibways of Wisconsin were still telling tales of his miraculous abilities (Works Progress Administration 1936–1940, 1942: Envelope 3).

His successor in the field was Father Francis Xavier Pierz, a fellow Slovene funded by the Ludwig-Missionsverein of Bavaria. Baraga convinced Pierz to join him in 1835, and Pierz served around Lake Superior in Ojibway and Ottawa missions until the Diocese of St. Paul was organized in 1851, when he moved west. Pierz helped induce Benedictine priests to join his efforts in the 1850s, and he stayed active in Minnesota Catholicism almost until his death in 1880.

Like Baraga, Father Pierz tried to follow the missionary procedures of the pioneer Jesuits: appealing to the native leadership, handing out gifts, providing graphic versions of the good news of Christianity and the need for the salvific Church. He let the Indians discuss his presentation and then he proceeded with further instruction, leading toward baptism. He usually appointed exemplary men from each village as catechists, while he moved on to the next pagan community. He struggled (where Baraga prevailed with relative ease) at learning Ojibway language, and like the Jesuits of yore, he acted as physician to the Indians, administering vaccine to Indians struck by smallpox and teaching homeopathic cures. His first baptism in Indian country came as a result of a recovery from illness following baptism, and another influential conversion took place when pagan parents of a dying Ojibway girl refused her a christening and she hastened toward her demise. "Her blessed death accomplished much good in my mission" (in Furlan 1952: 80; see Pierz 1947–1948: 281–282), Pierz wrote. Like his predecessors, he wished to teach his flock to farm their lands. Like them, he had contempt for unchristianized native culture and eyed with suspicion the power of their sorcery. He thought Christian charms (like the crucifix) more potent than the Indians' magic, and at times he seemed to regard Protestantism as a greater evil than heathen religion.

Pierz's ministry exhibits a pattern common to Catholic missionizing efforts in the nineteenth century. A decade after committing himself to the Ottawas of Michigan, Pierz found himself unfulfilled as pastor among baptized Indians. He thrilled at the struggle against paganism, the dramatic conversion, the clear signs of spiritual progress. But among catholicized Algonkians he found corruption from non-Indian neighbors, the debauchery of alcohol, and a cooling of fervor that left them without spiritual ambition and him without spiritual pleasure. The romantic hopes of the ardent missioner could not be met by the ambiguities of christened Indians with quotidian problems (Pierz, November 25, 1847).

Father Pierz stayed with the Ottawas until 1852. By that time many of the Indians had been removed by the United States government to locations west of the Mississippi. Pierz tried to prevent the removal of Catholic Ottawas by getting them to purchase their own plots, gain legal deeds, and declare themselves educated Christians. In this way the mission saved the homes of its Catholic Indian loyalists. But the priest moved on to Minnesota, where once again he could combat the forces of pristine heathenism, this time among the Ojibways.

In Minnesota as in Michigan, Whites quickly overran Indian territories, and Pierz found himself with the same problem of ministering to Indians whose very existence was in jeopardy. He found himself disillusioned with the wish to establish any kind of primitive Christianity among the natives. He taught them, sometimes cured and fed them, baptized some, and on at least one occasion, during the 1862 resistance led by Hole-in-the-Day, persuaded them to cease their opposition to the encroachment of the "mighty white nation" (McDonald 1929: 122).

Father Pierz had originally dreaded the invasion of Whites on Indian lands, but he came to view their coming as inevitable. In time he even wrote an enthusiastic prospectus to encourage Germans to emigrate to Ojibway country. "Hasten now, my dear German people . . . ," he wrote, "and settle in Minnesota. Do not postpone your immigration. For the sooner you come, the better your chance for settling in the more excellent places of your choice" (Pierz 1947–1948, 41:169). So many Germans flocked to Minnesota that Pierz became pastor to the Catholics among them, leaving the Ojibways to other hands.

While Baraga, Pierz, and their associates were working on the American side, Jesuits, Oblates, and secular clergy were attempting to make their mark among the Ojibways in Canada. The first Indian assignment of the reconstituted Society of Jesus was in the 1840s, at Walpole Island. The Indians living there—Ojibways, Ottawas, and Potawatomis—were unreconstructed nativists, former followers of the long deceased Tecumseh. They would have nothing to do with the missioners (led by Father Dominique du Ranquet, S.J.) except to argue vociferously against Christian doctrine (see Cadieux 1973: 254 ff).

Why should we heed your wisdom, they queried the priests, when we already have ways, passed down to us from our Ancestor, to communicate with the Great Spirit? Since the Great Spirit gave every people their own religion that suits their needs, why should we alter the divine plan? Why should we leave our religion of the heart for yours of the book? The priests replied that all peoples ought to pray to the same God with the same prayer, and they spoke ominously of the last judgment, when Jesus will separate the good from the evil, and those who have rejected His prayer "he will throw into the great fire that will never go out" (Delâge and Tanner 1994: 308). The Indians retorted with a threat of their own, asking the Jesuits to leave them alone: "Sometimes a storm arrives suddenly, without a noise: it brings thunder, rain, and hail: it cannot be resisted. I hope, my brother, that nothing bad will happen and that you will do as I have asked" (313). Five years later the mission burned down mysteriously, like other Catholic chapels among the Ojibways of Upper Canada.

In other Canadian locales the Catholics (and representatives of other denominations) insinuated themselves into Indian communities, sometimes with apparent effect. On the north side of Lake Superior Father Ranquet matched the peripatetic zeal of Father Baraga on the south. After the failure of the Walpole Island mission he served for almost thirty years in other isolated Ojibway communities. His was but

one name among many Canadian Catholic missionaries to the Ojibways during the nineteenth century.

In the United States some secular clergy and Franciscan friars tried
their hand in the Ojibway pastorate, attempting to move forward the
work begun by the Leopoldine and Ludwig agencies. In Minnesota
the Benedictine monks and sisters took up the work in 1878, sponsored
partially by the newly founded Bureau of Catholic Indian Missions. By
this time the United States exerted powerful control over most aspects
of Ojibway life through the administration of federal reservations. The
government supported Christian schools, including those run by the
Benedictines, and pressured the Indians to comply with the schools'
regime in order to acculturate them as quickly as possible. Even tribal
funds were used in some cases to help pay the costs of Catholic education. In this context the Benedictines burned "heathen" (in Berg
1981: 27) items such as medicine bags, as Ojibways sought baptism and
schooling, and the monks refused sacraments to any converts who returned to their traditional religious ways.

In order to further the progress of christianization, the Benedictines
opened "industrial" boarding schools away from the reservations. "We
do not favor education on the respective Reservations," wrote the
teachers, "because parents interfere too much and cause great irregu-
larities" (Order of St. Benedict 1887: 3). The monks and sisters taught
boys and girls at separate institutions, with a curriculum typical of the
Indian boarding schools of their day. Besides their academic lessons
the children learned gender-based skills: farming, carpentry, and other
aspects of shop for the boys; sewing, cooking, laundering, and garden-
ing for the girls. Parents were not allowed to withdraw their children
once enrolled, giving the Benedictines full control over their young
charges. Even so, progress was slow, according to the Benedictines.
"We made no wholesale conversions among the Indians," one monk
wrote. "Soul after soul had to be gained by hard fight, patience, and
prayer, and many . . . only after years of hard work" (Berg 1981: 46–47).

About half of the Ojibways in the United States and Canada (and even a greater percentage of Ottawas) were christened Catholics by the year 1900. Five thousand of the nine thousand Ojibways in Minnesota were Catholic; three thousand were pagan, and a thousand Protestant. Three thousand of the nine thousand Ojibways in Ontario were Catholic, along with four thousand Protestants and two thousand pagans (Gilfillan c. 1911). Whatever residue of Catholic faith and identity had lasted from the French colonial era to the early 1800s, virtually all of the Ojibway converts came to the Church during the nineteenth century, the majority of them after Ojibway freedom was curtailed in the reservation era.

In an earlier book I argued that Ojibway "conversions to Christianity came in large numbers only after Ojibwa[y]s had lost their political autonomy to whites and were subject to diverse pressures from whites to abandon their old religious ways" (Vecsey 1983: 45). The Ojibways were dispersed across a large portion of central North America and too diverse for a summary characterization of their Catholic participation. Let us look, instead, at the varieties of Ojibway conversions in the nineteenth century and the catholicized elements of non-Christian Ojibway culture during the same period, in order to see the patterns of Ojibway Catholicism.

In 1846 a traveller in Lake Superior country commented that in Ojibway beadwork and other ornament, "A prevailing idea of the cross is observed, probably imitated from the vestment of the Catholic priests who first settled among them, from whom also they have acquired many usages. . . ." He added, "It must be conceded . . . that the Catholic missionaries have been most successful" (Ducatel 1877: 371, 377).

In the same year Rev. Otto Skolla witnessed a Midewiwin ceremonial at Fond du Lac, during which the village chief exhorted his people to resist the priest's teachings: "My children, do not join the faith of those living men who are in black clothes and preach the Cross, but faithfully guard your household gods, as did your fathers, so that our tribe will not be scattered among other nations or utterly broken up or exterminated" (in

Skolla 1936: 239). An old Ojibway woman from the same period and place admitted that the priests had taught her people more about God than they had ever known before, but in the process her people had lost their powers. She was grateful, however, that catholicized Ojibways were troubled less in dreams by the evil spirit under the waters than they had been in former days (Kohl 1860: 370).

Father George Antoine Belcourt and other missionaries along the Red River in the mid-nineteenth century heard the oft-told Ojibway tale of a baptized Indian who died and was refused admission to the Christian heaven because he was an Indian (Aldrich 1927: 37). In other versions the deceased Indian was then refused admittance to the Indian afterworld because of his Christian identity. The narrative ended with the admonition to Indians against having anything to do with Christianity (see, e.g., Kohl 1860: 277–278).

George Copway became a heralded Native American in the nineteenth century by publicizing his 1830 conversion to Christianity in a series of books, speeches, and newspaper articles. He became a Methodist minister and devoted a good portion of his adult life to converting fellow Ojibways and other Indians to his Protestant faith. Before his death in 1863, however, he had become a broken man, and in his last days he took baptism as a Roman Catholic, at least partially to curtail his alcoholism (see Smith 1985). Another Ojibway, John Smith, converted to Catholicism in the late 1800s at the advanced age of ninety-eight, because his wife had done so on her deathbed. From the time of his baptism, he said, he never drank alcohol again (Smith [1919]: n.p.).

A full-blood Catholic Ojibway from Pembina by the name of Joseph Abita Gekek came to Red Lake Indian Reservation, Minnesota in 1882. He persuaded many of the pagan Indians to convert to a version of Catholic practice which he instituted. He recounted his visions and dreams; he held councils and powwows, and taught the Ojibways what he called the Prayer Dance. The men danced with rosary beads around their necks; drummers used an instrument blessed by a Catholic priest; the women chanted Catholic hymns. These Indians sought and received baptism and then proceeded to perform their Prayer Dance, until another priest caught sight of them in their Catholic regalia. He slashed the drum with a knife and railed against their "Catholic" movement (see Fruth 1958: 15–16).

Andrew Blackbird, an Ottawa whose brother died on the eve of ordination to the priesthood, formulated twenty-one precepts or moral commandments of traditional Ottawa and Ojibway Indians, rules which syncretized native and Christian concepts. They included diverse commandments, e.g., against stealing from one's neighbor or coveting his goods, mocking or mimicking the thunderers, whose purpose is to fight evil underground monsters, or eating with women during their menstruation; and in favor of honoring one's father and mother (so that you will live a long life), and chastising one's children with a rod. The ultimate reward for following these rules, Blackbird wrote, was to attain heaven (Blackbird 1887: 103–105).

Around the turn of the twentieth century a non-Indian musicologist attended an all-night wake at Garden River, Ontario, at which Ojibways of various Christian denominations sang hymns. The white man recognized the basic melodies as Catholic hymns; however, the leader sang them in Ojibway style, making their European origins almost unrecognizable. Upon questioning, one of the singers acknowledged that the Indians had had trouble learning the Western hymns, and so created a kind of "half breed music" (in Burton 1909: 137).

These examples suggest a range of Ojibway adaptations to Catholic presence in the nineteenth century. Pagan Ojibways continued to resist Catholic inroads, although some appreciated aspects of Catholic teaching or practice. Some used Christian concepts, like the all-important idea of a heavenly realm, as a means of counter-offensive against evangelization. Others combined Catholic and native values, or seized upon Catholic sacramentals such as the cross or the rosary as cultic objects. Still other Ojibways viewed participation in Catholic tradition as a means of reforming personal behavior or creating solidarity with their loved ones who had already converted. Great Lakes Algonkians had a reputation for individualism without strong political cohesion. In their responses to Catholicism the Ojibways demonstrated a variety of personal stances, even when half of them were identified by baptismal records as members of the faith.

This range of associations with Catholic tradition has continued to characterize Ojibways in the twentieth century, even to the present day. In 1913 a Catholic author wrote, "Like other Indians, the Chippewas are naturally a religious people, and with few exceptions have a truly remarkable and deep faith in the Catholic religion. They are very particular about baptism and the last Sacraments for the dying" (*The Indian Sentinel* 1913: 31). A Benedictine monk, after twenty-one years of contact with the Ojibways of Minnesota, concurred: "A large percentage of our Catholic Chippewas lead morally a better life than the fifty millions of 'civilized' Yankees in the United States, who believe in no positive religion, attend no church on Sunday, do not even have their children baptized . . ." (1910: 40); however, he found them a fickle and unreliable people, especially in their family life. "Another century will elapse," he said, "before our Chippewas will understand the nature of the matrimonial contract the same as white Catholics do" (39).

A decade later a Dominican sister in Minnesota acknowledged that the tug of heathenism still pulled hard on the Ojibways, creating "grave moral problems" (3, no. 2, April 1923: 56) amidst the penances and masses, the rosaries and benedictions. Pagans competed with Catholic devotions by holding all-night powwows, and it was hard for some christened Indians to "resist the call of the tom-tom" (57).

The pagans themselves resisted the missionaries' call, saying, "I worship the one true God in my way and you worship Him in yours. I want to die worshipping Him in my way" (in ibid.). But a Catholic bishop claimed that "Often at the hour of death many of the pagans, even the chiefs, summon our missionaries and die a holy death" (*Our Negro and Indian Missions* 1931: 42). Even in their dreams the Great Lakes Algonkians at times of personal crisis found it hard to escape the Catholic imagery they encountered in school and public proselytism. One Ottawa told in 1926 of a dream he had as a boy, before his father's death:

> Both of us knelt down and as we looked up we saw a place like a Cath-olic church in front of us. God sat on one side. He had long whiskers. Jesus sat on the other side, and there was a little white bird in the mid-dle. Jesus held a ball in his palm. God, Jesus, and the bird sat on some-thing raised high from the floor. Christ made the sign of the cross to us and we did the same. (In Radin 1936: 255)

Death was the glue that cemented native and Catholic cultic activ-ity. In Wisconsin in the 1930s and 1940s the Ojibways held a Spirit Dance on All Souls' Day eve, continuing the annual feasting for the dead which Jesuit priests witnessed as early as the 1640s. The Indians prepared foods for a long night of eating in a ceremonial hall. They also brought clothes as offerings for the dead, and if poor folks needed the apparel, they could take them as gifts, as representatives of the de-parted souls. Following grace and an Ojibway song, the feast com-menced. "The general idea," said an Ojibway, "is to feast the souls of those who have gone before, and if the relatives cared anything for their departed they would assist in the preparation of this feast on All

Souls' Day" (Works Progress Administration 1936–1940, 1942). Dancing concluded the commemoration. Pagans and Christians joined in the feast together and danced to their tribal drums. Said another Ojibway, "The pagans . . . celebrate according to their ancient tribal beliefs and intentions; the Christians regard it as a memorial feast and offer prayers for the happiness of the deceased" (ibid.). In earlier times the Ojibways used to sit up all night with the corpse, feasting its ghost before sending it on its way. The Indians constructed a shelter over the grave with a totem marker, where food might be left for the deceased. In the 1940s "remnants of these customs" (Kinietz 1947:148) persisted in some locations, "even among the Christian Indians. . . ." On the Catholic graves the Indians set up a wooden cross instead of a totem marker, or perhaps the two stood side by side. Pagans sometimes hung gifts on the cross or pole, "even on a Christian burial but Christians are not supposed to do it" (ibid.). Many did nonetheless.

Catholic authorities praised the devotional events of the annual Chippewa Catholic Congresses, begun in 1912 by the Benedictines. At these summer gatherings Ojibways received the sacraments and gave speeches against divorce and in favor of Catholic Indian education. In school Indian children answered their catechism questions and read Catholic periodicals like *St. Anthony's Messenger* and *Sacred Heart Messenger*. In their houses Ojibways displayed pictures of Jesus and the saints ("and movie actresses" as well, [Barnouw 1950: 11]). Ojibways could count among their numbers a Roman Catholic priest, Father Philip B. Gordon (whose biography appears in volume 3 of *American Indian Catholics*), and several sisters, including Sister Cordula and Sister Florence. The missionary organs sang of "sincere Catholics" living among Ojibways who "hold tenaciously to their pagan practices" (*The Indian Sentinel* 27, no. 4, April 1947: 54–55), and of "staunch Catholics, in spite of persecution of all kinds by their pagan neighbors" (28, no. 1, January 1948: 16). An Ojibway woman walked thirteen miles through the snow to obtain a priest to deliver last rites to her parents; others made similar treks to fulfill their Easter duty. More than one priest and sister "were touched by their piety" (30, no. 4, May 1950: 55).

Other Church officials evaluated Ojibway spiritual progress differently. One Canadian priest at mid-century remarked that "very often, Christian sacramentals, such as medals and rosary beads, are accepted by the Indian rather as a talisman or charm against evil than as something of spiritual significance." He added, "This is but natural in a world where you are almost overwhelmed with evil" (Sieber 1950: 129). A sister in the United States warned of spiritual devolution among Ojibway youths in locales where Christian evangelism had undermined native religious structures:

> Like so many of the white girls whom they imitate, many of the young Ojibwa girls have no strong religious ties. With the disappearance of the old Midé religion, with its noble teachings and high moral standards, many Indians have accepted no religious code to take its place. Rather, they spend their time attending cheap dance halls and amusement centers provided by white people. (Coleman 1947: 115–116)

Sometimes these young Ojibways—cut loose from their traditional religious moorings but drifting free of Catholic loyalty—committed acts of "sacrilege" against Church property: breaking into chapels in search for wine, strewing beer cans around the aisles and pews. An anthropologist concluded in observing these acts that "loss of Ojibwa[y] religious beliefs has not always meant Christianization" (James 1961: 728). As recently as 1980 a Benedictine father asserted that the Ojibways of Minnesota "are split by a cultural schizophrenia that finds them in many cases bereft of the best of the old values in their society, while captive to the worst of their new discoveries" (Marquette. DCRAA. 1980).

Such has been the refrain of social scientists studying the Ojibways of Wisconsin and Minnesota in the middle of the twentieth century. One historian wrote: "In terms of the aboriginal past, Chippewa culture is a shambles, so much have the people everywhere had to accommodate to the new conditions imposed by their relations with Euro-Americans" (Hickerson 1970: 17). In many Ojibway communities there was a high degree of intermarriage with non-Indians, among the highest of federally recognized tribes in the United States (Paredes et al. 1973: 159), leading to a loss of traditional culture without necessarily a commitment to Christian norms. An observer found bits and pieces of old culture, but no coherent system. "By the mid-1970s," he wrote, "knowledge of traditional religion, folklore, music, and herbal remedies was found only among a few old people." Indeed, acculturation was said to be so severe that anthropological reports "read like coroners' verdicts" (Danziger 1978: 201–202).

In Michigan a different picture emerged, namely that Ottawa and Ojibway Catholics (as well as Methodists and other Protestants) who embraced Christianity without turning completely from native traditions. The Church had permitted some old-time customs to continue, e.g., family feasts and mourning practices, which did not seem at odds with Catholic doctrine. To an extent these became enmeshed in the Indians' lives. When the more conservative Indians made their feasts for the dead, or first fruits offerings, or naming ceremonies with native songs and dances, the Catholic priests paid little mind. In the main the Indians presented a picture of adjustment to white culture, a transition aided by Catholic conversion, and the priests did not regard the Indians' Christian identity as merely nominal. An ethnologist stated in 1955 that, "the more native gatherings and practices evoke little faith or none at all, while the acquired religious patterns dominate the lives of the modern Indians" (Kurath et al. 1955: vol. 5, chap. 12: 4).

Kurath has examined the prayers and hymns of the Michigan Algonkians, finding a clear translation of Christian concepts into the native language. God was the great or benevolent spirit, lord, chief, our father. Jesus was the Great Spirit's son, or simply Jesus the intercessor. The Holy Spirit was the superlatively clean ghost. Mary was regarded as the all-protecting female and the saints were called blessed. The Christian Indians referred to the aboriginal deities as false gods, and evil spirits were termed powers of darkness. Satan was the evil one. The Ottawas and Ojibways had words in their own tongue for soul, ghost, heaven, sin, and sinner (a poor person), as well as prayer, communion, belief, penance, and redemption (ibid., vol. 3, chap. 8: 21–24; cf. Kurath 1954: 313–314). Referring to Michigan Ottawas and Ojibways, the author concluded:

> Three centuries after their sight of the first blackrobe missionary they color their Christianity with pagan fragments, but they have effectively submerged this paganism. A generation ago all of the Catholics celebrated semi-pagan feasts on Catholic holidays and sang perplexing hymns in their native language. Now only the older people know the hymns, confined to wakes and family feasts. (Kurath 1957: 31)

In the more isolated areas of Ontario and Manitoba, Ojibways held onto their native beliefs, despite their official connections to Catholic, Anglican, and other denominational bodies. In many aspects of their lives, they responded to white pressures to acculturate with a strategy of outward compliance. The Saulteaux of Manitoba "developed a 'dual behaviour' pattern," according to two social scientists. "They adapted themselves partially to the newly-developed behavioural pattern set out for them by the agents of change. Their attitude was patient, placid, friendly, and co-operative toward the official programmes. However, they persistently retained their traditional pattern of behaviour among themselves" (Shimpo and Williamson 1965: 111). In religious matters the same patterns prevailed: "They relied upon their own traditional belief system while they were nominally registered as Christian" (109). In the northern forests of Ontario the same patterns were observed:

> Due to a certain lack of pride in the aboriginal culture, certain aspects of contemporary life are shrouded in secrecy. Religion is probably the most conspicuous of these. Outwardly the people profess to be Christian, but underneath they hold many non-Christian beliefs and are unwilling to discuss these freely. (Rogers 1962: 5).

In the late 1900s individual Ojibways and Ottawas have responded to Catholicism in diverse ways. Some have continued to reject its tenets and practices; some have been drawn to the Protestant varieties of Christianity. As many as half of modern Ojibways have been baptized within the Catholic Church, about twenty-five thousand in the United States alone, according to a tally in 1979 (Beaver 1979: 161–167, 189–192). A generation ago there were fifty thousand Ojibways in Canada and thirty thousand in the United States (Ritzenthaler and Ritzenthaler 1970: 4); today the combined numbers, including non-registered persons of recognizable Ojibway descent, might be as many as three hundred thousand in all of North America (Thornton 1994: 463), making the Ojibways perhaps the most populous of all Indian peoples north of Mexico. In the United States alone there are over two dozen different Ojibway reservations, as well as numerous urban communities from Michigan to Montana, with a total population of about a hundred thousand, in addition to perhaps ten thousand Métis in North Dakota of partial Ojibway descent. There are ten thousand Ottawas in the United States, 90 percent of whom are baptized Catholics, many of them in the Diocese of Gaylord, Michigan (Marquette. DCRAA. 1976–1986). It should come as no surprise that these far-flung Anishinabe Catholics display an array of characteristics.

Rose Barstow, who teaches Indian Culture at the University of Minnesota, was baptized Catholic because her mother requested it before she died. The elders of her family were not Catholics, but they baptized her anyway, and she attended White Earth Catholic boarding school between the years 1923 and 1930. One day she was staring at a book illustration, in which Indians were assaulting Whites. A nun happened by and said to her,

"You know, *you* are an Indian." The girl denied it vehemently but learned the truth from her grandfather. Throughout her life, an author says, "Rose claims to have never been reluctant to accept Catholic teachings, finding parallels to them with the teachings at home. Rose and her grandparents practiced both the Ojibwa[y] and Catholic religions, seeing no real conflict between them" (Berg 1981: 177).

Marie Spruce was born in 1919 at Lac du Flambeau Reservation in Wisconsin. Her parents were tribal members who met the priest each week when he arrived at the reservation by train, and put him up at their home when the weather was bad. As a girl, Marie took catechism from Franciscan sisters each summer. She attended boarding school and graduated from a vocational high school in Lawrence, Kansas. At age twenty she left the reservation and stayed away for thirty-two years. She worked for the Bureau of Indian Affairs among the Jicarilla Apaches in New Mexico. When her marriage went bad, she drifted from the Church, and when she remarried she was too frightened to seek an annulment. Finally in 1978, after having returned to Lac du Flambeau in 1972, she reestablished contact with the Church and received the dispensation from her first marriage. Since that time she has been a practicing Catholic. After her second husband's death in 1990, she confided, "My faith is holding me together" (in Lucero, April 26, 1990: 3).

Marilyn Johnson is a Métis from central Ontario with strong Ojibway loyalties, but also French, English, and Swedish heritage. She was baptized and raised a Roman Catholic because her Ojibway-French mother was Catholic. Her father was Protestant. She believed at age five she inherited her great-grandfather's spirit power when the old Ojibway died. She became a visionary and a specialist in ecstatic flights of the soul. Her mentor was an Ojibway named John-Paul Early Morning Light from Manitoulin Island (a baptized Catholic himself), who regarded St. Benedict as his patron saint. He pinned a medal of the saint on his apprentice to keep her safe during her spiritual journeys. He had a picture of Jesus on his wall but there was nothing Christian about his training. Indeed, he had repeated run-ins with Catholic priests over his paganism. Ms. Johnson says, "I no longer consider myself a Christian; I am a follower of the modern Pan-Indian religion. The central ritual is the pipe ceremony" (Johnson 1983: 1).

At Ball Club in the Chippewa National Forest in north-central Minnesota, Larry Cloud-Morgan, Loon Clan member, greets his relatives at an Ojibway powwow (Ball Club, July 19–21, 1991). Dancing men display the symbols of their animal spirit guardians, parading with badger skin, bear head, turtle shell, eagle feathers, lynx skull, and other regalia, while women wear dresses bedecked with conical metal bangles. Old men are blessing children by touching deer antler staffs to their heads. The "dancing spirits" of the aurora borealis keep the powwow dancers company in the northern sky. On the dance ground the Indians chant a prayer in their language over a young man dying of cancer; then they perform an honor dance for him.

"We've always had powwows," says Mr. Cloud-Morgan, an artist, peace activist, and former seminarian (see volume 3 of this work for a biography), "and this is a traditional one, expressing our tribal identity." Another Ojibway man adds that the powwow is a sign of the old-time values of the local Ojibway culture. Whereas twenty years ago the traditional religion seemed moribund—everyone was nominally Catholic or Episcopalian, and a whole generation of adults had been weaned of Ojibway language in boarding schools—in the past generation many portions of the old Ojibway religion have resurfaced. Vision quests, medicinal practice, Midewiwin membership, and funeral customs have all returned to Ball Club. The powwows, which had never disappeared, are presently flourishing as cultural and religious ceremonials which call people back to their Ojibway traditions.

A Catholic mission has existed at Ball Club since the nineteenth century, and the elderly pastor is well liked; however, his congregation consists primarily of the very old. The young are either disaffected from all religion or drawn to the revival of Ojibway religiousness on their reservation. A middle-aged man tells a visitor at the powwow that he considers himself a Catholic; he appreciates the good deeds of the parish priest, but he never participates in mass. Cloud-Morgan concurs that the Church at Ball Club is more of the past than it is of the present. Youngsters are not likely to obey the priest's strict dictum against "living in sin" before marriage; nor will they refrain from drumming all night at funerals, after the priest has gone to bed. In one of the Ball Club cemeteries there are crosses and headstones along with Ojibway grave houses with clan markers and holes in which to place offerings. In the cemetery as well as throughout the reservation, the two religious traditions exist side by side.

In 1991 Sister Eva Solomon, an Ojibway Sister of Saint Joseph, and Father Achiel Peelman, an Oblate priest, organized several meetings north of Lake Superior in Ontario in order to discuss with Native Americans the idea of an Amerindian Christ. At one meeting an Ojibway woman speaks of her Catholic upbringing. When she underwent serious illness and psychological turmoil, she received a revelation in a dream to take up Midewiwin, which she had never known first-hand as a youth. She abandoned Catholicism in order to join the Mides, but still she was not fulfilled. A Catholic nun convinced her to return to the Church, which she did, but now she missed her Midewiwin participation. After many years of fluctuating between the two religious organizations, she listened to the advice of two old women in her village—both of them lifelong Mides—who told her that "the Midewiwin and the Catholic religion are two ways which lead to the one and the same God" (in Peelman 1995: 103). Since then she has treated the two religious ways as portions of a single path in life.

Dominic Eshkakogan, Ojibway medicine man and Catholic deacon in Ontario, says that Jesus is still difficult to incorporate into an Anishinabe worldview. Because Jesus did not come physically to the Americas, he is still a stranger to their physical experience. Eshkakogan's Ojibways refer to Him as "Jesus-Nosse" (Jesus-Father), in order to connect Him to the supreme divinity whom the Ojibways have always known. Another way in which Eshkakogan makes sense of Jesus is to think of Him as a healer, a spiritual aid to the traditional curing ceremonies he performs. "I am more and more discovering the profound correspondence between the teachings of Jesus and our own traditional teachings," says the deacon (in ibid., 121). Like other Ojibways, for whom medicine men have continued to play a central role in the community, Jesus is best appreciated for His curative properties.

The Ojibway artist, Blake Debassige, paints the "Tree of Life," which portrays a cedar tree upon which Jesus is crucified, only in the image Jesus is within the tree; He *is* the tree; His body is the tree's trunk and he shares in the tree's medicinal properties. Jesus also has male and female sexual characteristics, and in his outstretched hands he holds wild roses, symbols of blood and beauty. In the crown of the tree an owl reminds the viewers of their mortality. From the earth two serpents represent the dark potentiality in life. The branches of the tree are full of birds and faces, like the spirits of Midewiwin, who display their presence and power. All told, the "Tree of Life" represents an Ojibway appropriation of Jesus' life-giving force within a native idiom (ibid., 194, 211).

The Church of the Immaculate Conception on Manitoulin Island is a symbol of syncretism. Several years ago when an explosion destroyed the old church—parish house to the Anishinabe of the area—the local priest had the new building constructed in a manner which he considered appropriate to the Indian clientele. It is circular, mostly underground, with a raised smokehole. Anishinabe floral motifs intertwine with Christian symbols. There are clan totems on the doors and color symbols throughout in order to promote "effective syncretism" (Smith 1993). There are also "eclectic" elements: totem pole designs from the Pacific Northwest, Iroquoian turtle patterns, a powwow tipi derived from the Plains. A local Anishinabe artist, Leland Bell, designed the Stations of the Cross in the mode of contemporary Woodlands art. He is a committed member of Midewiwin, not a Christian, but he accepted the priest's commission to produce the work. At first he was reluctant to portray pain and death, but he determined that by adding a fifteenth station—Jesus Risen from the Dead—he would make his commission a celebration of life over suffering.

Non-Indians flock to the church these days, inspired by what they see as native symbolism; however, some of the local Catholic Anishinabe cannot bear to see Indian symbols in church. These are elements they were once taught to reject as "demonic." The Mide practitioners resent the Catholic appropriation of Indian symbols, saying that the priest has no authority to traffic in meanings he knows little or nothing about. It's just "whoring," declares one Ottawa woman. To a scholar observing the interplay of native and Catholic at Manitoulin, "the integration of the two has limits" which have been exceeded in the church (ibid.). An Ojibway native of Manitoulin agrees that the Church is trying too hard to ingratiate itself to the Great Lakes Algonkians (Jacko, October 14, 1990).

North of Manitoulin Island by Espanola, the Jesuits have built the Anishinabe Spiritual Centre, where since 1979 they have conducted Indian retreats once every month. In the midst of Ojibway and Ottawa
communities, the Centre draws several dozen Anishinabe Catholics to
its monthly sessions with its sweat lodge, chapel, and dining hall. Father Mike Murray, S.J., the architect of the program, leads the Indians
in the Spiritual Exercises of the Jesuit founder, Ignatius Loyola. Fellow Jesuit Carl Starkloff conducts a theological dialogue with the native Catholics. Many of the Indians have been coming to the Centre
for a decade or more and their knowledge of Catholic faith is profound.

Father Starkloff, a veteran of Indian ministry in the United States,
says that when he first came to the Centre in 1981, his goal was to train
Anishinabe leadership "for a renewed Church" (Starkloff 1989: 6)
among the Indians. The native Catholics wanted nothing to do with
expressions of traditional spirituality. They thought of it as superstition and witchcraft and the doings of the antichrist, and they were dis-
tressed at the notion that native and Catholic religious forms could be
in dialogue with one another. They were committed to Marian devotions; they made pilgrimages to Medjugorje in Yugoslavia; they had
put aside Indian religiousness and meant to keep it that way (Starkloff,
October 14, 1990). For those Ojibways who practiced some aspects of
traditional religion, it was imperative to maintain "a solid wall standing between" native and Catholic ways (Starkloff 1991: 1). Starkloff encouraged a meeting of the two traditions, while training the locals
toward degrees in Sacred Theology through Regis College of the
Toronto School of Theology.

On a particular day (Anishinabe Spiritual Centre, October 13, 1990)
he and the Indians discuss Avery Dulles, Mircea Eliade, Gerardus Van
der Leeuw, and other theologians in an attempt to relate Catholic sacramental theology to native spirituality. They treat questions of power,
will, and form in uncovering the phenomena that imbue Anishinabe
religion, and they discern between good and evil aspects of their religious traditions.

They begin with *power*, discussing the Ojibway words that convey its various aspects, including knowledge, physical capability, and spiritual endowment. The Indians have been talking about these terms in their home communities, and one Ojibway woman, Margaret Toulouse, tells how her neighbors focused in their conversation upon fearsome mystery. They thought that Ojibways had experienced this power long before the coming of Christianity, in the practice of healing. The Ojibway deacon, Dominic Eshkakagon, states that good and evil medicine spirits have always existed in relation to one another; it is necessary to make a discernment between the two. He himself once studied with a bad medicine man and learned about powers that hurt people. He knows that these things still exist among the Ojibways today on his reserve. Teenagers have been engaged in cults in which they manipulate the blood of small dogs and other animals. Some Ojibways have had upsetting experiences of bad medicines and so they want no part of their tribal ways. Eshkakagon wants his people to reflect upon the good medicines of their tradition. Another Ojibway man, Peter Johnston, who counsels drug addicts and alcoholics, discusses power and suicide. He wonders out loud if suicide is the result of bad medicine, or if it is a manifestation of powerlessness. Chemical abuse, says Joe Fox, another Ojibway deacon, is a "cunning, baffling power," a mighty adversary to those who want their community to thrive.

The Indians ask: How shall we live in relation to powers? What shall be our will, which is bound up in our freedom and our desire, as well as in the blessings and the vocations we receive? We must not give in to the powers of chemical abuse; on the other hand, letting go of one's individual will, for example in a sweat lodge or in the Spiritual Exercises, can be empowering, they say. You let go and allow the Holy Spirit to enter your life. We have the power in the sweat lodge to relax, to trust the Creator and the spirits. We must discern the powers around us and treat them according to their nature.

Throughout the discussion the Indians ask what mediums there are for power. Whose will shall be done? They refer to current events in their communities, the politics of Indian existence in Canada, and their healing ceremonies. They quote from the Bible and translate terminology between Ojibway and English, aiming for precision and nuance in comparing Christian and native notions of power. They try to discern between manipulating nature or the scriptural word of God, and preparing the way for God's will. That is, they distinguish between magic and religion, spiritualism and spirituality, as modes of religious life, fully affirming the existence of supernatural power in all its mystery, and searching for the ways—in Christian or Indian form—of gaining the power to help their people.

In their meditations regarding *form* the Anishinabe theologians reflect upon the encompassing traditions, the repetitions, patterns, rules, visions, and values that affect a people's whole being. To them form is the means of gathering all of one's learning experiences into a shape that makes sense. If we are created in God's image, what does God look like? What do *we* look like? What does the traditional Ojibway culture hero, or Jesus, or Kateri Tekakwitha, look like? These are questions that their fellow Anishinabes ask them because they are confused culturally.

Dennis Wawia says that when missionaries came to the Indians, they tried to replace the culture of the Indians; they took away the *form* that Indians used to have. They took away the image of God that existed in traditional religion, and in so doing they took away the Indians' *gestalt*. Ojibway deacon Ron Boyer comments that in the first half of the twentieth century the old Indians had come to find meaning in the Latin mass. It gave them form and security. God was made identifiable through that mass and they were empowered through it. Many of them did not want to lose the old mass with the Vatican II reforms. They resisted change, and even today some Anishinabe people speak of the Tridentine rite as the "Indian Mass" and ask permission to perform it on occasion. Mr. Wawia replies that some Ojibway Catholics have gotten over the loss of the Latin rite and are feeling comfortable in playing an active role in shaping a new form, a new Ojibway Catholic culture, out of retrievable parts of their past. They are not trying to bring back the aboriginal religion as a whole, or the Tridentine mass, but rather they are cojoining the pieces into a new form, one which they can identify with because they are creating it for themselves.

In creating a form for their Indian Catholicism, the Ojibway theologians are wary of stepping beyond the bounds of the "almighty Church," as they call it. Several of the men are deacons and regard themselves as representatives of the ecclesia; they even hope one day to become priests through special episcopal dispensation (since they are married). They think with the Church on matters such as abortion; indeed, they compare it to the human sacrifice of the ancient Aztecs. Mr. Eshkakagon offers the idea that North Americans abort their fetuses "as sacrifices to their own comfort." Mr. Boyer calls abortion "out and out murder."

They are uncomfortable with mainstream Catholicism, with what they see as its callousness and its complacency. Ursula Jacko says that she went to a rich Toronto parish, where people who never experienced hunger or poverty made up the form of worship and morals. No matter how much they claim that they want to help the poor, she finds them untrustworthy. She wants to practice her Catholicism with other Anishinabe people, whose experiences are more like her own.

She and other Ojibways find meaning in natural symbols from their own environment: particular stones, metals, mountains, trees, and bodies of water, the color of the sun and the shape of the sky in their own land. Catholic sacraments are also meaningful, but the local experiences must be incorporated into the form of their spiritual life for their religiousness to be satisfying. Several of the women say that the feathers, the pipe, the wampum, the native leaders themselves, are agents of spirituality, making the experience of Catholicism more acute. They are grateful to the ongoing sessions at the Anishinabe Spiritual Centre for opening their senses to their native sacramentalism

"One of the greatest experiences of my native spirituality," says Mr. Eshkakagon, was performing a sweetgrass ceremony for Pope John Paul II in 1984 at the Shrine of the Canadian Martyrs, where the Huron mission once stood in the seventeenth century. After the sweetgrass ritual he received the body and blood of Christ at the Eucharistic celebration, in which he served as deacon for the pope. "I felt real acceptance of my traditions by the Church, personified by the Pope," he adds. He tells how the Ojibway word for sweetgrass combines references to hair, earth, and mother; to burn it ritually is to celebrate the nurturing femaleness of the world. Mary Lou Shawana responds that we would not have sweetgrass without God. "We spend too much time, we natives, in focusing on ourselves and our particular desires. There is too much 'I,' too many 'I's' in our worldview. We look at our cultural symbols but we need to look through the symbols, to God," she exclaims.

During their Spiritual Exercises (Anishinabe Spiritual Centre, October 12, 1990) the Ojibways speak with fervor of their religiousness. One woman tells how she meditates upon every word of the Lord's Prayer. Another woman focuses upon the sorrowful, joyful, and glorious mysteries of the rosary. "The miracle in my life," she exclaims, "is Jesus, placed at the center of my existence." A third woman explains that for five years she has come regularly from Sault Ste. Marie to the

Centre, to pray, to be with her Catholic friends, to find time for God in a schedule filled with familial responsibilities. These women embody the Church among their people.

Another woman tells how the Centre has made her comfortable not only with her Catholicism but also with Anishinabe spirituality. She sees the positive effects of native religious practice and it complements her Catholic participation. Still another woman relates her recent experiences with native therapists involved in what they call the Good Red Road, a combination of Native American herbalism, ethical teaching, and bio-feedback technique. The Spiritual Exercises, she states, are the "same thing" as this therapy; both are good for people who need direction in their lives.

One of the Jesuits talks of dreams he has had of Anishinabe spirits. He says that his spiritual life has been enriched by native mythology. The Indians respond by recounting their own visionary experiences. The session closes with a woman telling how, at a Tekakwitha conference, she was watching Dennis Wawia as he spoke. He looked to her like a baby; then his face elongated into the shape of a wolf's visage. She did not know what to think of this, so she mentioned it to him, and he told her one of his own experiences.

Mr. Wawia, ordained a deacon in 1986, was at the Anishinabe Spiritual Centre in the summer of 1990. He got up early to lead a sunrise ceremony for an Indian group in attendance, but he was the only one who arose at the proper time. The night before at the closing of a sweat, he had felt something coming toward him from the woods, but he had become frightened and had entered the Centre dormitory and gone to sleep. Now he was out to welcome the sunrise, and after conducting a ceremony by himself, he felt himself taken by a "holy wind." He walked to the Four Directions and addressed each orientation. Then he came to a hollow in the woods when he had the sudden urge to urinate, which he did. Only when he looked at himself, he had one leg up, like a wolf. He looked around, embarrassed, hoping no one had seen him; however, he continued to feel very much like a wolf. He then went to the lake and cleaned his "paws" and face, like a wolf. At the lake he saw a highway to the sky, yellow like gold, like butter, up to the yellow sun. He saw in the sky four bands of color—white, red, yellow, black—beautiful beyond belief. He saw a church in the sky with Anishinabe people in front of it, and he realized that he was being told to bring about devotion to Our Lady of Guadalupe. When this realization ended, he washed his wolf paws again. It occurred to him then that the wolf was his spiritual guardian. He was abundantly happy with the sign he had received.

Mr. Wawia concludes his narrative by affirming the reality of his experience; it was not a mere dream. He looks at his audience of Jesuits, fellow deacons, theological students, devout Anishinabe Catholics, and female religious, and he gives a good, loud, lupine howl. Then he laughs. No one engaged in the Spiritual Exercises seems the slightest bit unnerved by the narration; indeed, they seem to appreciate the spiritual wonder of it all.

In the 1990s there are still Ojibway communities that are traditionally Catholic. Their idea of ritualism is saying the rosary in Ojibway with their French Canadian relatives on Sunday afternoons (Bucko, September 29, 1991). The Little Shell Chippewas who work as ranch hands in Montana—descendants of a band of Ojibways who refused to sign a ten cent treaty over a century ago and were thus evicted from their reservation at Turtle Mountain, North Dakota—are "very strong Catholics" (Campisi, August 31, 1991). They attend the local Catholic church and a local sister helps them with their social needs. They are loyal to a Church which fed, educated, and disciplined their children during winter starving times for generations. In the Turtle Mountain region of North Dakota is an enclave of Métis—descendants of French and Ojibway, Catholics now for many generations—who continue to celebrate the feast of St. Ann every July 26th with a special novena. They have also developed devotions to Kateri Tekakwitha over the last half century. There are Ojibway priests in the present day who are deeply involved in Indian ministry. John Hascall and Paul Ojibway are perhaps the most prominent (see volume 3 for sketches of their life and work). Ojibways attend and even host Tekakwitha conferences (for example, in 1994). Ojibway Catholics participate in urban parishes in Milwaukee and the Twin Cities of St. Paul and Minneapolis.

At the same time there are Ojibways who have taken other spiritual roads—in Protestant denominations, in Midewiwin and other native movements, and in syncretistic practices—and those who have turned away from religion entirely. Their paths of faith are as widely scattered as their population but the spirituality of their tribe endures.

FOUNDATIONS OF POTAWATOMI CATHOLICISM

A third of the Anishinabe peoples, members of the the Three Fires Confederacy along with the Ojibways and Ottawas, were the Potawatomis, the People of the Fire. Their aboriginal homes were along the southeastern shore of Lake Michigan, where the Frenchman Jean Nicolet saw them in 1634. By 1670 they were also living on the far side of the great lake, beside the Menominees and Winnebagos near Green Bay. Father Claude Allouez found them agreeable subjects for his missionary work and he traveled with them between their homes on the east and west shores of Lake Michigan. When he planted a cross near one of their villages, their elders "manifested much joy" according to the Jesuit; "they notified all by public proclamation . . . that they must *all* pay . . . respect to the holy cross, planted in their country as a symbol of the Christianity which they desired to embrace" (Thwaites 1896–1901, 58:39). In 1690 another Jesuit, Father Claude Aveneau, established the first permanent mission to the Potawatomis, named for St. Joseph, in what is now Michigan.

The Potawatomis were eager for French trade; hence, they showed hospitality to the priests. They also intermarried with French traders and produced mixed-heritage offspring. French military commanders like Nicolas Perrot encouraged Potawatomi interest in Catholicism, telling the Indians that God had shown pity on them by letting the French come among them. When they marveled at the Frenchmen's ability to work iron into knives and hatchets and regarded Perrot as a divinity, making him offerings of homage and tobacco, he attributed his (and his countrymen's) abilities to the Catholic deity (Kellogg 1925: 74–75).

For thirty years the Potawatomi missions thrived, until clerical numbers declined and warfare with Great Britain made a permanent outpost impossible to maintain. Métis kept some knowledge of Catholicism afloat through the eighteenth century, even following the expulsion of the Jesuits in 1764. However, after decades of neglect the early nineteenth-century Potawatomis retained little or no Catholic piety, except at St. Joseph Village and in the area around Detroit.

By the 1800s Potawatomis were ensconced in several dozen villages around the lobe of Lake Michigan, to the south of their Ojibway and

Ottawa allies. They had participated in Pontiac's rebellion in 1763, hoping to maintain their French connections against the British ascendancy. During the American Revolution and the War of 1812 they had sided with the British, perceiving the Americans as threats to their landholdings. Like the Ottawas and Ojibways, some Potawatomis had joined Tecumseh's nativist movement; however, vestiges of Catholic loyalty persisted among them. When the Baptist minister Isaac McCoy attempted to evangelize the St. Joseph Potawatomis in 1822, some of their old people still remembered Catholic prayers; they reported to the reverend that "'they had had water put on their faces,' as they expressed it" (McCoy in Buechner 1933: 292). McCoy reported that some Potawatomis craved contact with Catholic ceremonies and that they revered the blackrobes. Hence they made pilgrimages to Quebec and other Catholic centers in order to perform their Easter observances and to receive blessings from Catholic priests. They valued their relations with half-bloods, who spoke French and could pass on to them Catholic ideas and practices.

In 1830 a delegation of St. Joseph Potawatomis visited Father Gabriel Richard in Detroit, seeking instruction and asking for a permanent priestly presence among them. The Bishop of Detroit, Rt. Rev. Frederick Rese, journeyed to their village during the summer of that year, and upon examination he determined that a dozen of the Indians were worthy of baptism.

Among the christened natives was Pokagon, a secondary chief already in his fifties, who received the Christian name of Leopold. Pokagon was probably born an Ojibway or Ottawa, but he was already prominent among the Potawatomis by the 1820s as a warrior and protector of their land rights. At the same time as he fought the removal of the Potawatomis from their homeland, serving as a treaty negotiator, Pokagon urged an adoption of white culture as a tactic of survival. He was interested at first in Rev. McCoy's mission because he hoped that his people might maintain their territories through a process of "civilization," which would make them more palatable to the United States populace. When McCoy supported Andrew Jackson's removal program, however, Pokagon and other Potawatomis turned to the Catholics, who seemed distinct from mainline American culture. Some American Catholics spoke French, as did some Potawatomis, and the Church representatives declared themselves publicly against removal. Pokagon's Métis in-laws introduced him to Catholicism in the late 1820s, and the

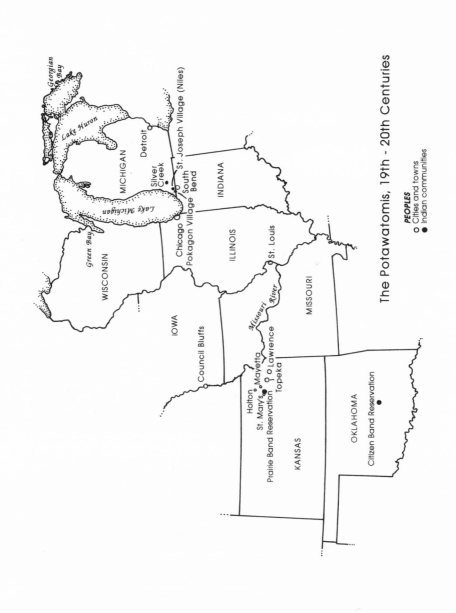

The Potawatomis, 19th - 20th Centuries

PEOPLES
○ Cities and towns
● Indian communities

chief determined to gain a permanent Catholic mission among his people so as to solidify their claims against American encroachment.

After Bishop Rese's visit, Leopold Pokagon beseeched him to send a priest. His missive was quoted in the annals of the Propagation of the Faith in the Vatican:

> Father! Father! . . . I come to beg you to give us a Black-gown to teach us the word of God. We are ready to give up whisky and all our barbarous customs. Thou dost not send us a Black-gown, and thou hast often promised us one. What, must we live and die in ignorance? If thou hast no pity on us men, take pity on our poor children, who will live as we have lived, in ignorance and vice. We are left deaf and blind, steeped in ignorance, although we earnestly desire to be instructed in the faith. Father draw us from the fire—the fire of the wicked manitou. An American minister wished to draw us to his religion, but neither I nor any of the village would send our children to his school, nor go to his meetings. We have preserved the way of prayer taught our ancestors by the Black-gown who used to be at St. Joseph Village. Every night and morning my wife and children pray together before a crucifix which thou has given us, and on Sunday we pray oftener. Two days before Sunday we fast till evening, men, women and children, according to the tradition of our fathers and mothers, as we have never ourselves seen Black-gowns at St. Joseph. (In Buechner 1933: 299; Shea 1855: 394)

A historian suggests that Leopold Pokagon "really wanted to become a priest and to so serve his own people" (Clifton 1984: 67). He was an intensely spiritual man in the Potawatomi mold, fasting frequently and seeking supernatural power for himself and his community. Equally he saw the potential of Catholic schools and chapels as institutional symbols of permanence which might prevent removal from their homelands.

While Protestants like Reverend McCoy were persuading Indians to accept removal and go west, Bishop Rese sent missionaries to establish a station among the St. Joseph Potawatomis. Rev. Stephen Theodore Badin arrived in 1830, followed by Sisters of Charity. The Indians quickly constructed a chapel on the fifty-acre plot which Badin purchased for the mission, and Pokagon served as "'coadjutor'" (Buechner 1933: 299) to the priest, encouraging his fellows to receive instruction and baptism. Pokagon composed melodies by which the Indians might memorize and express the Apostles' Creed and the Ten Commandments. He used his oratorical prowess in exhorting his comrades to confess their sins and to treat one another as relatives. Badin was impressed by the primitive spirituality of the people. He wrote of them in 1830: "Accustomed to a hard life, they fear neither the penance nor the fasting which all impose upon themselves voluntarily, even the infidels, for to honor the Master of Life and to invoke quite ordinarily their Manitous, . . . who manifest their will through dreams" (in ibid., 302). He asked them to devote themselves to the Good Spirit rather than to their aboriginal divinities. Some replied that the Good Spirit need not be appeased with prayer and offerings, whereas their traditional gods required constant attention so as not to harm humans. Still, the Potawatomis began to turn from their pagan practices. Badin reported one old man who "brought me all the things and contrivances with which he previously practised his superstitions; I threw them immediately into a fire; he was pleased with this. . . ." (in Baraga, February 11, 1831). Within two years Badin had baptized all the St. Joseph leaders, 360 adults, and a hundred children in the region. By the following year over six hundred Potawatomis were baptized (Clifton 1984: 68–69). One of the sisters wrote in 1834, "I could not believe that such piety existed among them. . . . I am now convinced of their sincerity and simplicity" (in Buechner 1933: 297). Thus, within a few years the local Potawatomis were enfolded in the Church: "Conversion to the basics of Catholic forms and rituals came quickly, . . . soon replacing ancient Potawatomi religious institutions, if not the private belief and practice of all individuals" (Clifton 1984: 53–54).

Between 1790 and 1832 the Potawatomis had agreed to various cessions of land in the Old Northwest. Under persistent pressure from all sides, the Indians made what appeared to be a final extinguishment of their title east of the Mississippi in the 1833 Treaty of Chicago. The United States made plans to remove all the Potawatomis to western lands; however, an appendix to the treaty mentioned the "religious creed" (ibid., 48) of one Potawatomi band which wished to be removed rather to the northern peninsula of Michigan, to reside among the Ottawas at L'Arbre Croche. The "religious creed" was Catholicism and the band was the St. Joseph Potawatomis under Leopold Pokagon's leadership. Pokagon wept in signing the 1833 treaty, but he hoped at the least to save his people from removal to Indian Territory, using their faith as a justification to remain in the traditional realm of the Anishinabe. Through his doing the Treaty of Chicago seemed to exempt all of Michigan's Catholic Potawatomis from removal, guaranteeing their right of local residence.

Immediately afterward, however, the Ottawas and Ojibways of northern Michigan made their own land cessions, leaving the Catholic Potawatomis with nowhere to go; therefore, Pokagon used tribal treaty payments to purchase 874 acres in southwestern Michigan. He aimed to save his people's home not only by marking them with Catholicism but also by making them citizens of the State of Michigan (Clifton 1985). The St. Joseph Village site was lost in the Treaty of Chicago; however, during the 1830s the Catholic Potawatomis—engaging in daily masses, prayers, catechism, and canticles, eschewing alcohol and proclaiming their faith—established new homes in a neighboring county, where local Whites helped them raise a new church. Father Badin left in 1833, replaced by other priests and deacons, who found the Catholic Potawatomis "all fervent, and eager to gain and instruct their pagan brethren" (Shea 1855: 397), at least partially in order to save them from the impending removal.

In 1838 federal troops compelled most of the Potawatomis to move, including many who had received Catholic instruction. Church authorities baptized and confirmed some of these in the midst of the forced removal, but the ritual acts did not save them from deportation. One of these Indians wrote to a priest: "We had a church, we have been Driven from it. We had land, but it has been stolen, and we are Driven from the home of our childhood. . . . Life is misery. Death is a Pleasure. We are consumed by grief" (in Baroux n.d., 1:27). Leopold Pokagon did not give up his efforts, however, and he was able to rescue several hundred of his citizen Potawatomis from arrest. A local judge exempted them from removal in 1840 and they set themselves to reestablishing their community. Father Louis Baroux instructed them in plow agriculture and got them to dress "like the people of Christian nation," telling them that they could not come to church except in a "civilised condition" (1:33). They wore their new clothes, even though they could not stop laughing at each other's appearance and were "ashamed of themselves" (ibid.) for wearing pants and other American garb.

Sartorial innovation was insignificant compared to the changes wrought by their patterns of landholding. As citizens the Catholic Potawatomis were expected to own their titles as individuals. Tribal identity became difficult to maintain, and before Pokagon died in 1841 he was worried over the collective future of his people. Before his death he tried to transfer his title to the entire Potawatomi acreage to various individuals of the tribe, but he managed to transfer only two hundred acres. He had promised forty acres to the Catholic Church for a school and chapel, recognizing Catholicism as a major force for Potawatomi unity.

Between 1841 and 1848, however, the Catholic bishop of Vincennes, René Laurent de la Hislander, and the local priest, Stanislaus A. Bernier, had been "secretly promoting the removal of the Catholic Potawatomi to Kansas" (Clifton 1985: 23). The two sought ownership of all the land still untransferred, over six hundred acres, and Pokagon's heirs had to fight the bishop and priest for the heritage. In 1848 the Michigan Supreme Court found the two men guilty of fraud and awarded Pokagon's widow, Elizabeth, and son, Simon, the full title.

With the Pokagon family in control of most Potawatomi acreage, the majority of the Indians moved to other sites in the area, maintaining some communal relations for years to come, even "to the present day" (ibid.), but refusing to recognize the leadership of the Pokagon clan.

Despite the schism, most of the Potawatomis remained true to their Catholic identity. When Elizabeth Pokagon died in 1851, a priest recorded her last words to her family:

> First word. I am going to see my dead children to whom I will be united. Second word. It is dangerous to love this world. God has opposed it. Third word. My children, love God with all your heart, all your mind, and all your strength. This is the first and greatest commandment. Fourth word. God wills to see me. Fifth word. My children, you must all go to confession and baptize your children. Sixth word. The Great Spirit is in Heaven. He is a Good Father to us. (In Buechner 1933: 315)

Her son attended Catholic school at Notre Dame and spent a good portion of his life as interpreter and aide to the priests who served the Catholic Potawatomis in Michigan. He and some of his fellows became "lax in church attendance" when the diocese transferred their pews and altar to a parish of Whites, and when Simon Pokagon married a divorcée, "he excommunicated himself" (328). Nonetheless, his granddaughter remembered him as a faithful Catholic, always singing Church hymns, and he received Catholic burial alongside hundreds of other Potawatomis. Indeed, his Catholic loyalties seem to have outlasted his tribal fealty. Before his death in 1899 he wrote about "the Problems of His Race" with this recommendation: "Break up as soon as possible the last vestige of tribal relations. Teach them to know that they owe allegiance to no man on earth except the great chief of the United States" (in ibid., 325–326).

His descendants have maintained both Catholic and Potawatomi identities in several parishes of southwestern Michigan. They are still aware (and so is the Diocese of Kalamazoo) that the Sacred Heart of Mary Catholic Church, Silver Creek, stands on the forty acres donated by Leopold Pokagon; part of the church is built over his grave. The cemetery, still in use, contains the remains of many Catholic Potawatomis and is considered sacred ground by many. The Catholic-Pokagon relationship "ebbed" (Marquette. DCRAA. 1985) from the mid-1800s; however, some of Pokagan's people have continued to worship in the Catholic tradition without ceasing to be aware of their Potawatomi heritage (see "A Brief Sketch of Chief Simon Pokagon's Life" n.d.; Brown 1949; Potawatomi Indians 1939). Numbering only in the hundreds, these people have maintained a Potawatomi identity, thanks in no small part to their Catholicism. Indeed, "the Catholic Church has served the Pokagons as a center for social and political gatherings . . . , providing the opportunities for socialization that have kept the Potawatomi identity and cultural knowledge alive" (Topash and McClurken 1994: 468).

THE PRAIRIE POTAWATOMIƧ

Some Catholic Potawatomis from Wisconsin and Michigan escaped removal by journeying to Anishinabe communities on Lake Huron's Georgian Bay in Canada. A handful of reserves became refuges for these Indians, who have maintained their Catholic Potawatomi identity over many decades under the guidance of Jesuit priests. Although aboriginal religious traits have survived—burning tobacco during thunder storms, making offerings to the spirits, smoking their pipes— these Canadian Potawatomis have remained Christians. Some became Methodists, thus creating a split in the community. Others have looked back with longing at their pre-Christian spirituality, comparing it favorably to Catholicism (Vanderburgh 1977: 188–189). Nonetheless, Catholic faith has survived among these Canadian Potawatomis.

The majority of Potawatomis, however, marched west to Indian Territory under the command of federal troops. Between 1835 and 1837 the Potawatomis from the prairies of Illinois and Wisconsin made their relocation; in 1838 they were joined by their woodlands tribespeople from Indiana and Michigan, following their forced removal. Together the exiles migrated first to Council Bluffs on the Missouri River, then to present-day Kansas, where a treaty established their reservation at St. Mary's in the 1840s. In the following years other Potawatomis joined the community from their homes back east. Together they were known as the Prairie Band of Potawatomis, numbering about three thousand at midcentury.

Catholic priests accompanied some of the Potawatomis on their westward journey, e.g., Father Benjamin Petit, who chronicled the "Trail of Death" from Indiana (Barrett 1988: 2). Other priests met them in Indian Territory, including the Jesuits Christian Hoecken, Pierre Jean de Smet, and the "Guardian Angel" (St. Dominic. September 18, 1938), Maurice Guilland, who taught them farming techniques and scriptural study, spending thirty years among them. Sisters of the Sacred Heart opened a school and helped to reestablish rudiments of Catholic culture in their new homes.

Father de Smet found the Potawatomis in 1838 with little apparent evidence of Catholic faith. Even the French half-breeds among them were almost totally without knowledge of Catholicism, according to the Belgian missionary; however, within several months he claimed several dozen baptisms, young and old (Chittenden and Richardson 1905, 1:157–158, 168–170). He attested to the anarchic state of Potawatomi affairs, as government agents tried to remove them from their new settlement at Council Bluffs to Sugar Creek. A year after beginning his ministrations, he claimed over two hundred baptisms, mostly among the half-breeds, with forty receiving the Lord's Supper. Nonetheless, there was constant drunkenness among the Potawatomis, accompanied by acts of murder and revenge (171–178). Under such conditions he preferred a ministry among "unspoiled" western Indians rather than the demoralized Potawatomis.

At Sugar Creek the Potawatomis received a visit from Mother Rose Philippine Duchesne, canonized in 1988 for her saintly missionary work among American Indians. Although she remained only a year among the hundreds of Potawatomi Catholics, she established her Sisters of the Sacred Heart and earned the Potawatomi title of "Quah-kah-ka-num-ad—Woman who always prays." A memorial marks her association with the hundreds of Potawatomis who died at Sugar Creek, victims of forced migration, disease, and dissolution.

Jesuits and Sisters of the Sacred Heart maintained St. Mary's Potawatomi Mission for several decades, writing prayer books, grammars, and other devotional literature in French and Potawatomi. When Father de Smet visited St. Mary's in 1858, he commented on the reduced number of Potawatomis, from four to three thousand, of whom (he said) two thousand were Catholics. Increasingly surrounded by Whites, the Potawatomis looked toward a "sombre and melancholy" future, despite the ministrations of the Jesuits (Chittenden and Richardson 1905, 3:1198).

In the 1860s the Catholic Indians with a strong French component formed a "Mission Band," which accepted U.S. citizenship and purchased land in what is now Oklahoma. These Indians became known as the Citizen Band Potawatomis and from their numbers came some notable Catholic Indians, including the first fullblood Indian priest, Albert Negahnquet (described in volume 3 of *American Indian Catholics*). Benedictine priests and Sisters of Mercy ministered to these Catholic Potawatomis around Sacred Heart Abbey, and many of the Oklahoma Potawatomis attended St. Gregory's College. Their advanced education furthered the process of acculturation and their population dispersed.

In the late twentieth century there are close to eighteen thousand enrolled Citizen Band members, some of them Catholics; however, they live all across the United States and do not constitute an Indian community.

In nineteenth-century Kansas, pagan groups maintained their resistance to Christianity. Beginning in the 1880s, Kansas Potawatomis began to engage in a new religious movement, the Drum Religion, an amalgamation of Christian and traditional elements which originated among the Sioux in the previous decade. The Indian agent encouraged it as an antidote to drunkenness, and it took root in Prairie Potawatomi culture alongside the Catholic elements that remained viable. The Drum Religion began with prophetic expectations; however, by the twentieth century it was transformed into a more quotidian means of solidifying Potawatomi cultural identity. Christian and non-Christian Potawatomis alike came to associate the Drum with the traditional values of their tribe; it constituted a force in opposition to Catholicism.

Throughout the late nineteenth century non-Indian communities encroached upon the Kansas Potawatomi lands, reducing the reservation from thirty to eleven square miles. Some of the newcomers established Catholic parishes which drew priestly interest away from the Indians. In the 1870s there ceased to be a Potawatomi mission in Kansas; the sisters left and the Jesuits maintained only peripheral interest in the spiritual welfare of the Potawatomis. The Indians felt unwanted by the surrounding Catholic Whites and even by the priests themselves. Hence, they nurtured their own brand of Catholicism apart from their white neighbors. Some Potawatomis would travel to St. Mary's by wagon and spend the night at the seminary, in order to appear at Sunday services. More frequent were rosaries and hymns in the Indian tongue, performed without clerical presence and sustained by feasts of their own providing.

In 1901 these Catholic Indians acquired four acres of ground for a cemetery and conducted Christian burials for their numbers, often without a priest. In 1912 "good Indian carpenters" (Clinton 1987) among the Potawatomis began to build their own church, called Our Lady of the Snows (completed in 1915), which received periodic visits from local pastors and summer retreats from Sisters of Charity. In 1916 the Ojibway priest, Philip B. Gordon, "gave a very successful mission" (*The Indian Sentinel* 1, no. 1, July 1916: 15) to the Potawatomis from his base at the Haskell Institute in Lawrence, Kansas. He noted that the attachment of the Indians to the Church was weakened by the infrequent sacerdotal visitations, no more than once a month for weekday mass. When a local parish priest began more regular visits in 1918, the Potawatomis greeted him warmly and attended the sacraments in faithful numbers.

In 1942 the Jesuits from nearby St. Mary's College reclaimed the Potawatomis as their responsibility. At that time there were said to be nearly 350 Catholic Potawatomis among the seven hundred on the reservation. A Jesuit reported that the Drum Religion still had its adherents, but in faltering numbers (he thought), thanks to the parish devotions at Our Lady of the Snows. The same priest said that traditional religious practices, such as vision quests, faith in guardian spirits, and "antagonism to Christianity" were decreasing. Whereas "many of the non-Catholic Indians for some inexplicable reason would shun a priest," one of the leaders, Chief Francis Marshno, gave his house over to the Jesuits for organizational meetings (ibid., 21, no. 8, October 1941: 116). Persistent Catholic faith was exhibited in the lives of men such as Francis Regis Jackson Wapinummit, a full-blooded Potawatomi who was baptized at the Sugar Creek mission in 1840 at age two, and who died on the reservation at age 104 in 1942 (22, no. 3, March 1942: 47). Anthropological observers in the 1940s might observe the persistence of non-Christian religiosity among the Prairie Potawatomis (see Landes 1970); however, Church officials saw eversteady progress in Christian faith.

In 1953 a Jesuit reported on the Kansas Potawatomis, as two dozen of them received the sacrament of confirmation and sang hymns in Potawatomi. A majority of the Indians, the priest wrote, had "successfully integrated themselves into ordinary American life" (Karol 1953: 367). They had intermarried with non-Indians; served in the armed forces and in defense plant work during World War II; some were beginning to relocate to nearby cities such as Topeka. "It is noteworthy," he wrote, "that the Catholic Potawatomi have, in many cases, been the first to become integrated and have been the most successful at it," so much so that the federal government planned to terminate the reservation, making it "part of the county." The Jesuit envisioned a future in which Our Lady of the Snows church would serve both Whites and Indians together. At that time the Church could well say to the Potawatomis, "Mission accomplished."

A newspaper account from the same period recorded a Drum

Religion funeral for two Potawatomis who died in a car accident. Although there were two hundred Indians at the funeral, chanting and
dancing to the four sacred songs of the Drum, inviting the spirits into
the room of mourning, the author called the religious complex an "old
and dying religion" (St. Dominic c. 1952). A Drum Religion adherent
compared his songs to the Lord's Prayer; both traditions, he said, were
attempts to bring about "Thy kingdom come," and he acknowledged
that his faith had "incorporated Christianity with the old tribal ways"
involving the Indians' relationship to Nature. The Potawatomi man
also noted that the children of his tribe were receiving education from
Whites and soon would "have no use" for the old-time religious practices (ibid.).

Although churchmen, journalists, and even Potawatomis predicted
the demise of the Drum Religion and the smooth transition of the
Kansas Indians into a catholicized, acculturated future, the next decades did not prove them right. One scholar came to Kansas in 1962
expecting to find the Potawatomis "deculturated and assimilated." Instead he discovered "one of the most stubborn people I had ever
met—firmly, bitterly, and successfully resistant to enforced cultural
change, outside domination, and assimilation. So far as they were concerned," he found, "the great melting pot was a place to cook fried
bread, not to lose one's identity in" (Clifton 1977: xv).

Rev. Leo Cooper, pastor of St. Dominic's Church in nearby Holton
from 1954 to 1958, reported a "religious revival" (Cooper, November 26,
1991) on the reservation. He joined the Jesuits and the Legion of Mary
from Holton in ministering to the Catholic Potawatomis—officiating
at their funerals, saying mass at Our Lady of the Snows, validating
their marriages (which, for the most part, were enjoined without reference to the Church), teaching catechism, and encouraging the Indians in their reception of the sacraments. At the same time, however, he
recognized that the Indians, including the Catholics, were still practicing their own religious rituals. When he finished his tasks at the funerals, he left the Indians to bury their own dead. They marked the faces
of the deceased with red and blue designs (symbols of the traditional
moiety system); they sang and orated in their native language, as they
directed the spirit of the dead to the afterworld. The priest was well
aware that Catholic Potawatomis participated in Drum Religion rituals, particularly in the tribal cemeteries, which were "sacred places" for
them (ibid.). Had they asked his permission, he would have said no;

however, they maintained their own counsel and he was content to permit their dual religious participation.

At St. Dominic's Church itself, a virulent "race hatred" (ibid.) kept the Potawatomis from attending services. The Catholic Potawatomis on the reservation, numbering about seventy in the 1950s, were steady in their faith at home, particularly the women, but only if Church officials came to them. When they left the reservation to live in Holton, Topeka, and other nearby cities, they were too "shy" (ibid.) to join the Whites in their parishes and so fell away from the Church. Father Cooper was willing to maintain contact with the urban as well as the reservation Potawatomis; however, the Jesuits said that these Indians were "beyond our reach" (St. Dominic. March 10, 1955). At the same time they ordered the St. Dominic's pastor to leave the Topeka Indians alone: "Our Lady of the Snows is no longer their church and you are no longer their pastor. . . . The only effective answer . . . will be integration into their new parish" (March 11, 1955). Integration did not prove so easy. Neither Whites nor Spanish-speaking Catholics wanted the Indians in their midst, so the Potawatomis moved from parish to parish, which "caused some to just drop the whole idea of trying to practice their Faith any further" (January 17, 1958).

In the early 1960s a survey of religious affiliation on the Prairie Potawatomi Reservation indicated that about half of the several hundred Indians were baptized Catholics. At least as many were Drum Religion adherents, with a small number of Protestants and peyotists. Some of the baptized Catholics engaged rarely in Church services; others attended Catholic, Drum, and peyote rituals serially. Those who left the reservation were even less attached to the Church (ibid., n.d.). Another Church census in 1965 found a similar pattern, with many Indians alternating between Catholic and Drum Religion participation. One Potawatomi man told the census-takers "some of his philosophies & they were truly beautiful & seemed so Catholic. He seems to believe in old Indian religion. Said . . . he was Catholic till a priest yelled at him" (Yokules and Hess [1965]).

By this time the Jesuits were closing their nearby college, St. Mary's, and so they ended their association with the Potawatomis. The new pastor at St. Dominic's could not maintain an active ministry on the reservation—particularly because the Indians could not support a priest financially—and hence Our Lady of the Snows was shut down. "So it is all wrapped up now," said a Jesuit treasurer in his final report.

"I do think this is for the better," with Our Lady of the Snows becoming "a shrine" (St. Dominic. June 8, 1966) rather than a mission.

When the parish priest announced the closing of Our Lady in 1965, the Catholic Potawatomis "felt so hurt, they just dropped out" (Puckkee and Patterson, November 24, 1991); with their own congregation in limbo, "they left the Church" (Klepac, November 24, 1991). Some lacked the means of transportation to attend services in nearby towns. Many "couldn't afford nice Sunday clothes" (Clinton, November 24, 1991). More important, "they sensed they weren't welcome," either by white parishioners or the priests themselves. "People looked down on us," according to one Potawatomi woman. The priest told her mother, who dressed for mass in her long Indian-style dresses, not to come to church without proper clothing, and not without money for the collection plate.

Some of the Indians made the weekly trek to the local churches. Mary LaClair, one of the pillars of Our Lady of the Snows, recalled, "My own heritage was as much white as it was Indian" (in Cavanaugh, January 9, 1987). "But I have to admit that some Indians just couldn't make the adjustment and stopped going to Mass at all when the shrine closed." Some of them continued to say their prayers in private on the reservation. Priests managed to come for funerals and the community held its own Indian wakes, singing hymns all night. Lacking catechetical training, however, a whole generation of Potawatomis grew up without Catholic religious instruction. Despite "a very staunch Catholic strain" (in ibid.) among the Potawatomis, the closing of the church turned many of the Indians from their Catholic faith. By the time the shrine reopened, "most Potawatomis had gone back to the Drum" (Martinez and Thackery, November 24, 1991).

In 1985 Father Robert Hasenkamp of St. Dominic's parish determined that Our Lady of the Snows merited a rebirth. With financial help from Church agencies both local and national, the Catholic Indian community has rebuilt itself. Sister Therese Klepac, S.C.L., became the administrator for the Potawatomi ministry, and under her leadership the Indians have shown great enthusiasm for the renaissance of Our Lady. The Indians refurbished the church and cleaned up the Ship-Shee cemetery, burial place for several hundred Catholic Potawatomis since 1901 (including Mary LaClair in 1991). Sacramental life returned to the reservation. At baptisms, confirmations, marriages, and funerals the church is full. Sister Klepac's photo album contains mementos of

Memorial Day mass at Ship-Shee, catechism at the Summer Vacation Bible School, parish picnics, Christmas plays, and several visits to the community by the Most Rev. Charles Chaput, O.F.M.Cap., a Prairie Potawatomi bishop who grew up off the reservation (a biographical sketch appears in volume 3). Indians from the parish have traveled to Rome for the canonization of Rose Philippine Duchesne in 1988, and they helped dedicate the Duchesne shrine at Sugar Creek, where plaques tell the story of the Potawatomi removal and the initiation of the Catholic mission to the refugees in Kansas.

The Indians credit Sister Klepac with the renewal of their Catholic community. "Oh, sister is a worker!" (Puckkee and Patterson, November 24, 1991), says one woman. The sister in turn praises the "pride" of the community in rebuilding their church. "There are families that won't talk to each other but they cooperate in church," she says. They hold bake sales and bingo games to raise money for the church and they support her as much as they can in her efforts. "I feel very welcome by the people," she attests, and very much "in charge," since a priest says mass at Our Lady only once a month. When a new priest replaced Father Hasenkamp in 1991, one of the Potawatomis asked Sister Klepac, "'When is your new helper arriving?'" (Klepac, November 24, 1991).

Sister Klepac socializes with all the Potawatomis—five hundred on the reservation and several hundred in the immediate area—not only with the Catholics. In 1987 she helped conduct a joint Catholic-Methodist Christmas pageant, and she views ecumenism as a way of life on the reservation. When she is invited to Drum ceremonies, she attends happily, and she says that she is proud of Catholic Potawatomi leaders who are speakers at Drum services. She finds nothing contradictory between Catholic and Drum theologies. "As a white woman," she is disturbed by a "patriarchal" hierarchy in the Drum Religion ("just like my own tradition") and taboos against pregnant and menstruating women; however, she withholds public judgment. Equally, she has nothing against the quarterly prayer meetings of the Native American Church. She often attends when these peyotists hold prayer services for the sick and dying.

Sister Klepac has encouraged Potawatomi devotions to Kateri Tekakwitha. She accompanies a delegation of her parishioners to the annual Tekakwitha conferences, and she helped organize a Kateri Circle on the reservation. Some of the Indians have credited miraculous cures to the Mohawk Lily, and they pray that these miracles will lead to her canonization. When these Indians attend the annual Tekakwitha conferences, they observe other Indians blending Indian and Catholic ritualism, and Sister Klepac has fostered such liturgical inculturation at Our Lady of the Snows. The Indians burn cedar and sage before mass. There are Potawatomi Woodland designs on the pall, on the cover for the lectionary, and in other areas of the church. When a Potawatomi woman, Shirley Shoptese Munoz, donated a painting of Kateri to Our Lady, the sister hung it in the church. Some of the Potawatomis have resisted the "blending of the two ways," says the sister (Klepac, November 24, 1991), but upon experiencing Potawatomi aspects in the services, they have come to appreciate it. "I think they're for it now," adds a Potawatomi woman (Clinton, November 24, 1991).

Sister Klepac is impressed by the "folk piety" of the Potawatomi Catholics. "Theirs is a very simple faith. It is not my way," she adds, "but I respect it." They believe in miracles and visions. They practice great devotions. They aren't too sophisticated to go to confession," as many secularized American Catholics are these days. The pious and the drunkards all confess their sins regularly; they believe in the efficacy of the sacraments. "Who are we to criticize" she asks (Klepac, November 26, 1991), because the Indians maintain their belief in the supernatural and the power of faith? Indeed, she notices that their faith draws local white Catholics to Our Lady of the Snows services. The non-Indians recognize goodness in the Potawatomis' devotions and sometimes wish to emulate them.

Sister Klepac recognizes that the future of Prairie Potawatomi Catholicism rests not in her hands but rather in the community itself. As an administrator her goal is "to work myself out of a job" (Klepac, November 24, 1991). She tries to prepare various people to take over all her tasks. She trains one woman in the care of the sacristy. She takes others with her on her rounds, so that they can see her job in action. When people come to her for advice, she tries to throw the questions back on them, getting them to solve their own problems. She knows that she will not be present on the reservation for many more years—the Church outsiders always move on, whereas Drum Religion leaders arise from the community and serve for life—and so her projects must become their projects, or the church community will dissipate when she leaves.

CONTEMPORARY POTAWATOMI CATHOLICS

Catholic Potawatomi leadership is not difficult to locate. In Lawrence, Kansas, Gerald Tuckwin is an education administrator at Haskell Indian Junior College. He has sponsored a Catholic student association at the college and helped secure a center adjacent to the campus where students attend mass and receive religious instruction. A member of the Prairie Band Potawatomi, Tuckwin is presently the president of the National Tekakwitha Conference and is active in Catholic circles nationally.

Milton LaClair's ancestors on his late mother's side—Potawatomi and Métis—"got their Catholic faith" in the early nineteenth century in Michigan, before removal. His great-grandfather, James Blandin (cf. Clifton 1977: 362–366), donated the ornate altar to Our Lady of the Snows when it was first built, and Milton was an altar boy in his youth. (He still peppers his speech with Latin phrases like "deo gratias.") He remembers the Jesuits of his youth with fondness— "They were the priests we liked the best"—and he recalls the journeys to St. Mary's to fetch the priests for reservation funerals. All of his five children were baptized at Our Lady. LaClair's father was a convert to Catholicism. "The whole family was praying for him to convert . . . and their prayers were answered," reports the son (LaClair, November 27, 1991).

LaClair lives alone in a well-equipped mobile home, a quarter mile from his birthplace. Like other Potawatomi men he spends many of his days hunting on the land he knows so well. A member of the Thunder Clan, one of the five clans still extant on the reservation, LaClair has "come full circle," in his words, having traveled around America and around the world during his lifetime. He spent senior year of high school at a Catholic boarding school in Marty, South Dakota—a "hilarious year" in which he had "a lot of fun." He loved working in the carpentry shop and still enjoys building things for his house and for Our Lady of the Snows. He was constructing a church in Marty when the Japanese attacked Pearl Harbor in 1941. He enlisted in the U.S. Army, participating eventually in the D-Day Normandy invasion, where he lost his right leg at Omaha Beach. He lived in Topeka for twenty-seven years, working as a dispatcher for the police department; then he ran a halfway house for Indians in Topeka. For several years he labored in the Pacific Northwest for the National Institute on Alcoholism and Alcohol Abuse (Department of Health, Education and Welfare), overseeing Indian sobriety programs. He went to a business college and worked for a construction company. Finally, after a stint in the University of South Dakota graduate school, he returned to the reservation to live in 1980.

LaClair refers to himself as a "recovering alcoholic" who developed the habit as a police dispatcher. He decided to leave the "constant pressure" of the police department because he found that he was consuming a "fifth of the hard stuff" after hours with his work mates every day. After treatment at a veterans administration hospital, he determined to help Indian alcoholics like himself. He remarks that "a lot of Catholic Indians became alcoholics. . . . They became ostracized, castouts, castoffs. They felt different and suffered a loss of identity." Despite his Métis heritage and Catholic upbringing, he, too, was torn between "traditional" and "dominant" ways. He stayed away from institutional Catholicism during his travels. Only in more recent years has he come to understand that he can "use the best of both ways," and so he "wears two hats" (ibid.) in his daily dealings with Whites and Indians.

In the intervening years he turned to native spirituality, particularly sweat lodges, in order to attain "faith renewal" and to "set goals for myself." He attended pan-Indian sweats in the state of Washington, where he enjoyed the comradery of Native Americans "all praying for the same thing" in the spirit of "kinship," and to this day he attends sweats on his home reservation "every now and then," when he is "troubled." He tries not to "overdo it"; however, he acknowledges the spiritual benefit he has drawn from participation in sweat lodges over the year and he speaks with awe of the feats of mental telepathy and premonition achieved by sweat lodge leaders and even by himself. "That is our Indian way of communicating," he states (ibid.).

Does he receive similar solace and communal satisfaction from Catholic rituals? LaClair says yes. When his mother died, he felt the "warmth" of the "straight Catholic" service, with hundreds of relatives and acquaintances, Indian and White, saying the rosary together in the funeral home in Mayetta, attending the funeral, and feasting at the Mayetta church hall. "That was a load off my shoulders," he attests, whereas his sister, who has avoided Catholicism for many years, was "broken up" (ibid.), with no tradition to turn to for spiritual comfort.

LaClair has a lifetime of association with death—in the army, the police, in his family—and he speaks of deaths with a matter-of-fact quiet: a daughter and a son both killed in car accidents, a brother by suicide (the priest at St. Dominic's got a special dispensation for a church funeral). On several occasions, he says, LaClair has foreseen death in the eyes of people, right before they died. He says that the Potawatomis have focused their "traditional Indian way of being religious in public" at funerals. Whether conducted according to the rituals of the Drum, peyotism, or Catholicism, a funeral is a "happy occasion—not for us but for the one who has left us" (ibid.). For that reason Potawatomis come together at funerals, overcoming the temporary sectarian boundaries. Even his steadfast Catholic mother went to Drum services now and then, primarily at the death of loved ones.

Milton LaClair points out that the Drum Religion has provided a means of public leadership for Potawatomi men; this has been one of its enduring strengths in the community. He himself has preferred to take a role in the parish of Our Lady of the Snows, where his mother was a cornerstone. It is "primarily grown-up women" (Klepac, November 24, 1991) who constitute the parish, athough some men and youths are "coming back" in small numbers, according to Sister Klepac. A Potawatomi woman, Mercedes Degand, states that women compose the core and future leadership of the tribe's Catholicism. "Men want to hunt their way into heaven," she says with a chuckle (Degand, Gillespie, and Holstein, November 24, 1991). LaClair does not concede that Catholicism attracts more women than men, but he does recognize that women outnumber the men at mass on Sunday. "They outlive the men, that's all," he avows. "Anyway, Potawatomi is a matriarchal society. Always been" (LaClair, November 27, 1991).

Among Potawatomi Catholic women one can locate a range of religious patterns. There are some who were "chased away" from the Church by racist, abusive, or alcoholic priests, or by the twenty silent years at Our Lady. "Of course many of them were looking for an excuse to leave," according to Ms. Degand (Degand, Gillespie, and Holstein, November 24, 1991). Donna Holstein, the daughter of a former Oblate novice, lives far from the reservation and rarely attends Catholic services, except when visiting at home. She says that she likes to worship in the church of her mother's youth, expressing the filial sentiment common to Potawatomis.

Some Potawatomis attend mass at several churches in Topeka, where they are integrated, more or less, into parish life. They say that they experience none of the racist rebuffs of previous generations; there is "nothing like that today," according to one woman (Clinton, November 24, 1991). Still, some of them prefer to attend Our Lady of the Snows on the third Sunday of each month, when there is mass. Zelda Martinez was born in Mayetta. Her mother, who was Catholic, died when Zelda was six. Her father "belonged to the Drum" (Martinez and Thackery, November 24, 1991). She received Catholic instruction while attending government boarding schools, and when she moved to Topeka in 1943 she went to Our Lady of Guadalupe, the Hispanic parish where she met her future husband, a Mexican. "We were glad to put our two daughters through twelve Catholic grades and our two sons through eight grades in Topeka," she affirms with pride. Still, she says that she "feels more at home" at mass in Our Lady, where her grandfather once donated some land for the church. "I think it's home," she adds.

Martinez's daughter, Laura Thackery, wandered from the Church in her late teens, but she has returned to the Our Lady of the Snows with an "authentic faith, informed by questions" (Klepac, November 24, 1991). She studies biblical history and interpretation and she wonders about supernatural manifestations near and far. She asks whether the spirits of Nature and the dead really inhabit the Potawatomi territory, and whether the Blessed Virgin Mary really appears to visionaries and pilgrims. Sister Klepac tries to guide her between "faith and superstition."

Jane Puckkee and Sarah Patterson are sisters, children of a French Catholic father and Potawatomi mother who understood Catholicism but was an adherent to the Drum Religion. Both girls received Catholic instruction in their youth and attended compulsory mass at Haskell Indian School. "Military, school, church, they all worked hand in hand," says Ms. Puckkee (Puckkee and Patterson, November 24, 1991), to produce conforming, straightlaced, Christian women out of "ornery" girls like themselves. Both have stayed close to the Church in their adulthood and they contribute to parish life both at Our Lady of the Snows and at the nearby towns of Holton and Mayetta. "We are expected to donate there as well as here," says Ms. Patterson, without resentment. "The Church and the faith have been a great help to me," says her sister. "When I am depressed, . . . I'm never alone. . . . Jesus and the Blessed Mother comfort me." So do Kateri Tekakwitha and Saint Philippine Duchesne, two more recent foci for devotions. Both women attend Tekakwitha conferences and pray for Kateri's canonization in their local Kateri Circle.

Some Potawatomi Catholics complain of their strict upbringing: the sermons of hell which "scared us to death" (ibid.), the priests who always seemed distant and condemnatory of Indian ways. Others are pre-Vatican II Catholics who have trouble adjusting to the new ways of the Church. Two young women have joined an arch-conservative Catholic group at St. Mary's. They tell other Potawatomi women that they better wear something on their head at mass; they better not wear pants; they better say the rosary. They attend Latin mass and regard themselves as more Catholic than the pope, according to Puckkee and Patterson. "These people believe in the old way" and do not want to change. But Puckkee and Patterson are satisfied with Catholicism as it exists today at Our Lady of the Snows. They are especially fond of the recent blending of Catholic and Indian religious elements in liturgies.

Babe Bell has lived most of her adult life on the reservation, after long years of training at a Catholic boarding school. She says, "I know where I belong" (Bell, November 24, 1991), and by that she means the Catholic Church as well as the Potawatomi community. Although she does not remember the boarding school discipline "fondly," she states that the constant, enforced prayer and regimen of farm chores prepared her for life, giving her the "drive" that today makes her a potential leader of Catholic Potawatomis. Some Indians say that Catholicism was "drummed" into them and they want nothing more to do with the Church; not Ms. Bell, who has taught Confraternity of Christian Doctrine both on and off the reservation and who is presently a Eucharistic minister at Our Lady of the Snows. She delivers communion to the bedridden and tries to help train Potawatomi youths, including her own grandchildren, in the faith.

When her first husband died in 1983, she discovered that the prayerful life of Catholicism was a solace to her. "I had to open my heart and let Jesus in. . . . Christ is in my life very much" (ibid.) these days, as she cares for her second husband, a white man and a Vietnam War veteran who requires daily medication and tender affection. In her personal and community ministrations she tries to live in imitation of Christ and with a mind to His teachings.

Like other Catholic Indians, Ms. Bell finds "oppressive" (ibid.) elements in the Catholic Church, including its patriarchal structure. At the same time, however, she would not object to playing a greater role of leadership among Potawatomi Catholics, and Sister Klepac is eager to pass her own responsibilities to the woman. However, both acknowledge that "jealousy" within the community makes it difficult for one of its members to achieve lasting authority. Sister Klepac is perceived as "objective" by the tribal constituents because she belongs to no one family, whereas Ms. Bell, and anyone else, would be suspect to those outside her lineage.

Like many other Catholic Potawatomis, Ms. Bell is also involved in the Drum Religion, which is so thoroughly enmeshed in the fabric of their Indian identity. "Before I went away to mission school and received my first communion, I knew the Drum and lived in its sacred ring. . . . I was Indian first, Catholic second" (ibid.). Being an Indian, for her, has meant staying close to natural cycles, fitting into the universe. Nothing in that project conflicts with her Catholicism; indeed, both Indian and Catholic ways have "seemed right" to her over her lifetime. She still feels that "being Indian makes me a better Catholic," because of the humble attitude that an Indian expresses toward Nature and other human beings. She tries to bring what she considers Indian piety into her Catholic faith, producing what she hopes to be a life of respect toward others.

She observes the similarity of Catholic and Drum funeral procedures. Both traditions, she says, remind the living that there is a spiritual realm beyond the material world. They both express a "gladness" at a time of mourning; both provide a ritual through which the community of the living can find it in its heart to let go of the dead. "We hold the soul of the deceased for a while; then we release it" (ibid.). In daily life, too, the Drum and Catholic symbol systems are similar, according to Ms. Bell. In Catholicism the bread of the Eucharist is parallel to the sacramental corn, pumpkins, berries, and water received at Drum services. Both sets of symbols remind us of our "basic sustenance," our dependence upon the world which God has made. Thus, they are only different expressions of the same spirituality.

Both Ms. Puckkee and Ms. Patterson share this view. Their mother used to say that the Drum Religion was just like Catholicism. The incense was the same as the smoke; the prayers were the same type of spiritual communication. They themselves are not members of the Drum but they "pay respects" to the religion: "We're more or less spectators" (Puckkee and Patterson, November 24, 1991). They appreciate the "comfort" which the Drum rituals give to mourners—the communal feasts, the gifts to the bereaved—these things "make your sorrow lighter," they say. But the sisters find the same condolence in Catholicism, with its assurance of an afterlife. In actuality, on the Prairie Potawatomi Reservation the two religions work in harmony, mourning, feasting, and consoling the same people. Some Drum people come to Catholic services; many of the Catholics go to the Drum. At funerals the two are side by side. After a century of interaction, Catholicism and the Drum Religion are cooperative partners rather than competitors in Potawatomi life.

Perhaps nobody harmonizes Catholic and Drum religious forms with more sensitivity than Catherine Clinton, a Potawatomi woman living in Topeka. Her Indian name is Oshewa, Away Over There. She received this name as a child in memory of an old woman of the community who had lived a long, honorable life. Thus, she bears the names of two saints, one Christian, one from her Indian people. She identifies herself as "a Catholic" (Clinton. July 8, 1977). "My folks used to go to Our Lady of the Snows," she says (November 24, 1991), and she still finds worship attractive in that rustic hall. When she is at mass there, she can still hear the voice of her late father singing hymns in Potawatomi, especially since the chanting of these hymns is "coming back" (Martinez and Thackery, November 24, 1991) in recent years. She has tried to pass the Catholic tradition to her children, sending them to Catholic schools and providing a Catholic family life at home.

Ms. Clinton is ardent enough in her Catholic devotions to have made a pilgrimage to Medjugorje in the former Yugoslavia in 1990, along with a dozen other Catholic Kansans. Her daughter paid for the journey as a present. Clinton was not able to climb all the way to the site of Marian apparitions; however, she spoke to some of the pilgrims who reported visions of the Blessed Virgin during Clinton's stay in the country. "My visit was a tremendous experience for me. . . . I'd like to go again. . . . God is real. Jesus is real. The Virgin is real. She walked the streets where I walked" (Clinton. November 24, 1991).

Ms. Clinton states of her Catholicism, "My Indian beliefs enhance my religious faith" (July 8, 1977). As a Potawatomi she believes in prayer. She and her people have always sought quiet places, usually in natural settings but even in the home, in which to meditate and communicate with the divine. They have always made sacrificial offerings of food as a type of communion with each other and the spirits. They have always believed in the spiritual efficacy of fasting. She and her fellow Potawatomis have brought these aspects of religiousness to their Catholicism, thus enhancing their religious practice and the Church itself. Clinton tells a legend of her people, about a man who came to speak of ultimate matters to humans. When he left, he rose " 'straight up'—the people could hear His bells for a long, long time and could see the clouds envelop His Person"(ibid.). She identifies this legendary personage as Christ; therefore, in her view, the Potawatomis have always had a revelation of Jesus' coming to earth. Some might say that the legend is of an origin that postdates Christian contact, or that it has been interpreted through Christian Potawatomi lenses. Nonetheless, Ms. Clinton sees the foundations of Catholicism in her tribal people's traditions.

For this reason she sees no dissonance between Catholicism and the Drum. Both traditions teach of the gifts from our Creator, the Great Spirit, to humans; both carry on the practice of prayer, the human response to God. Both foster a piety of thanksgiving and sharing. At least the way Potawatomis engage their faith, there is always feasting— at Drum and Catholic ceremonies alike—in order to fill up the personhood of the congregation that is continually depleted by death. "Eat, eat together, make life, fill up your being. . . . I believe in that," avows Catherine Clinton (November 24, 1991).

One of the Drum leaders taught Ms. Clinton how to perform a service for the dead. This Catholic woman of Catholic parents (her father would go to Drum rituals "from time to time") was so moved by her new knowledge that all she could think of saying to her mentor was, "I'm sorry for having taken so long." He replied that her ancestors forgave her; now she could honor them by helping to console the living. "My feet didn't touch the ground for a week," she adds with some passion (ibid.).

Like many other Prairie Potawatomis on or around their reservation, Catherine Clinton, Oshewa, "belongs to the Drum." She is also a baptized Catholic. In both cases she has been initiated into a community of faith; in both cases she belongs. "I feel at home with the Drum," she states. "I feel at home with the Church" (ibid.).

✳ IV ✳

To the Northwest Coast

A RITUAL AND ITS MYTH

In 1986 the organizers of the annual Tekakwitha conference in Bozeman, Montana culminated their meeting with a pageant celebrating the first appearance of Catholicism in the American Northwest. They reenacted the prophecies of a visionary named Shining Shirt, who foretold the coming of evangelizing blackrobes. They portrayed the activities of a Catholic Iroquois named Ignace Lamoose, who brought to the Flatheads and other related Salish Indians a talismanic metal cross and who spread the word of Christian faith.

Under Lamoose's tutoring, the Salish "hungered after this religion. We sang the hymns, prayed the prayers, walked the paths" (Bozeman, August 10, 1986) of Catholic ritualism, but Lamoose exhorted them with the promise that "there is more" to the religion than his own rudimentary teachings. As a result, four Indian men traveled hundreds of miles to the east, seeking a priest to instruct their fellow Indians. On their way they met with death among their enemies.

Shortly thereafter a Protestant missionary arrived instead of a priest, but the natives were not interested in his proselytizing. He wore no black robes; he carried no rosary. So, another delegation went out, and then a third, but still no priest arrived and each time the emissaries were lost to their tribe.

A Flathead girl named Mary, suffering from disappointment and disease, had a vision of arriving blackrobes. She told her people not to lose hope, and although she died shortly thereafter, her encouragements led to a fourth delegation to the east. As a result, the "prophecy of Shining Shirt, . . . the teachings of Ignace, . . . the vision of Mary . . . and the death of twelve braves" who had journeyed to bring back the Catholic religion were all rewarded.

The Church appeared in the person of Father Pierre Jean de Smet, S.J. (played in the pageant by the Most Rev. Donald E. Pelotte, S.S.S., newly ordained Native American bishop of Gallup, New Mexico; his biography appears in volume 3 of *American Indian Catholics*). He taught the Flatheads the shaking hand ritual and song, which they still perform at mass. The Flatheads at the pageant led the audience in the

handshake of peace, as they celebrated the mythology of Catholic Indian faith in the Northwest.

Like all myths the Flathead pageant expressed much truth; however, it hid the complexities of history. Within the past two centuries
Catholicism has entered the mountainous areas now constituted by
the states of Montana, Idaho, Wyoming, Oregon, Washington, and
the Dakotan northern plains. The various peoples of these regions are
the Siouian Lakota, Assiniboin, and Crow, the Algonkian Blackfoot,
Gros Ventre, Cheyenne, and Arapaho, the Shoshone, the Kutenai, the
Sahaptian Nez Percé, Umatilla, Wasco, and Yakima peoples, and the
many Salishan tribes: Flathead, Coeur d'Alene, Pend d'Oreille, Kalispel, Spokane, Colville, Okanagan, Lushootseed (including Swinomish,
Tulalip, Suquamish, and Snohomish), Lummi, Squaxin, the Wailat-
puan Cayuse, the Chinookan Cowlitz, and others. They have encountered Catholicism and adapted many of its forms and loyalties. The
encounters and adaptations have not come easily, and present-day Indian Catholicism in the Northwest exhibits great variety, as the next
several chapters will illustrate.

Northwest Indian Catholicism has taken several forms (see Burns
1988: 499–500), not only from tribe to tribe but also within each
group. There was no overarching political organization in the area, despite a long prehistory of intertribal trade and intermarriage. Each eth-
nicity possessed its own aboriginal forms of religiousness; even the
shared patterns of spiritual behavior—the seeking of visions and indi-
vidualized power and the giving away of personal property—tended to
produce variety when the natives encountered Christianity.

The encounter of faith took place shortly before the onset of the
great westward migration that began in the 1840s, symbolized by the
emigrants along the Oregon Trail. Fur traders of French descent and
European priests barely had time to introduce their faith to the Indians of the Northwest before Americans (including Protestant missionaries) entered the area and sought to wrest the richest ecological zones
from the natives. The ensuing disruptions lent a chaotic character to
Catholic Indian adaptation, as factions, nativistic cults, and syncretistic and prophetic movements made their appearance and as Catholics
and Protestants vied for Indian loyalties.

Catholicism drew upon and transformed the individualistic, visionary tendencies and the seasonal ritualism of the Northwest hunters
and fishers. A recent study suggests that there was a "conjunction of vi-

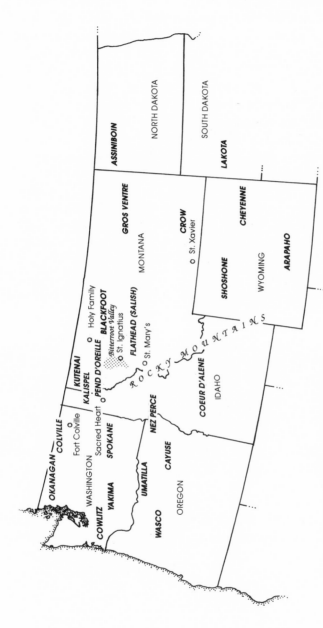

The American Northwest, 19th Century

PEOPLES
o Cities and towns

sions" (Peterson 1993: 23) between the Catholic missioners of the nineteenth century and the Indians of the Northwest Plateau. There was "a shared sense of the miraculous and the interpenetrability of the human and the sacred." Catholic devotionalism, the sacramental power of chants, the liturgical calendar, the values of generosity, community, respect for family, the use of water and incense, the feast days, the processions—all these Catholic elements made sense to the Northwest natives, and so they were attracted to the first priests. This attraction was not necessarily "to be mistaken, however, for the desire . . . to convert to Christianity" (ibid.). Rather, the Indians took up and altered Catholicism in various ways. The next several chapters will examine these varieties of Catholic Indian experience.

CATHOLICIƧM COMEƧ TO THE ROCKY MOUNTAINƧ

Jesuits had taken part in the fur trading enterprise of New France in the seventeenth and eighteenth centuries. With the defeat of France in 1763 and the interdictions against the Jesuits, the old alliance of Church and State fell into disarray. The English took over the trade and pushed westward toward the Pacific coast without the priestly presence. Frenchmen living under British rule formed their own fur trading companies (e.g., the North West Company), which in turn were swallowed up by the expansive Hudson's Bay Company. The French Canadians, many of them of mixed Indian descent, then came under its employ.

Among these Francophone voyagers were "devout Catholic Iroquois" (Burns 1988: 494), descendants of Caughnawaga and other reduction populations. These were said to make up as many as a third of the fur trading employees in the Northwest in the early nineteenth century. As they traveled westward, they acted as incipient missionaries of their Catholic faith among the Indians who trapped, traded, and intermarried with them. During this period "the most influential Indians in the Pacific Northwest were the Iroquois" (Carriker 1985: 109).

The most famous were twenty-four Caughnawaga mission Iroquois under the leadership of Ignace Lamoose, who settled among the Flatheads in about 1816 and piqued their interest in Catholic forms of religion. Ignace acted as prayer leader among the Flatheads, speaking often of priestly sacramental efficacy and the good news of God's love and heavenly afterlife. Under his influence the Flatheads observed Sunday devotions, baptized children, and placed crosses on the graves of their dead. "For some" Flatheads, it is remarked, "this was high medicine, indeed, the deep secrets of the spirit world" (Schoenberg 1982: 3).

It would go too far to say that the Flatheads became Catholics under Lamoose's influence. Little is known of the Iroquois man's intense Catholicism and there are hints that it was unorthodox in itself (Grant 1985: 121–122). What the Flatheads and their neighboring tribes made of Lamoose's displays can only be conjectured or reconstructed from later evidence. Nonetheless, they were excited enough by its spiritual possibilities that they came to yearn for greater contact with its clerical specialists.

During the same period the Northwest natives were first coming to know of western cultural elements. They had obtained horses though trade and capture from other tribes. They secured firearms, ammunition, and the technological products of metallurgy and weaving through the fur trade. These innovations stirred the imagination of Indians and several prophecies began to circulate among them regarding the blessings soon to be theirs (see Spier 1935: 30–35).

One prophet was a messianic figure named Shining Shirt, perhaps a Flathead or an Iroquois. Some say he lived in the early 1700s, before the advent of horses and fur traders (Schoenberg 1982: 2–3); others suggest that he was Lamoose's contemporary (Burns 1966: 14–16). The Coeur d'Alenes have their own legends of a similar prophet named Circling Raven. Shining Shirt foretold the providential coming of blackrobes with their power to attain horses, defeat enemies, and live to an old age. He had a metal talisman that Flathead Indian warriors kissed or bit before battles and the hunt.

Present-day Salishans still tell of Shining Shirt, employing the perspective of their contemporary understanding:

> In those early days the Salish would band together with the Pend Oreille and with other tribes and travel to hunt buffalo. On one of these journeys there was a family, a young boy and his parents. When they went to hunt with the rest of the people, the mother and father were killed, and the boy came home an orphan.
>
> Then he had a vision. He was told to go into the mountains, to pray and to mourn. He stayed there for many days, and one night in a vision he was told that when he grew older he would be taught a new dance, a jump dance or medicine dance, and that when he did this dance, he would be able to help his people. In his vision he was told he would grow to be a strong medicine man and that, when he died, lightning, thunder, and hail would shake the earth. So the young boy went back among his people, and he became a strong medicine man and a prophet known as Shining Shirt. . . .
>
> Shining Shirt was given a vision about the future. He prophesied the coming of fair-skinned men wearing long black robes who would teach the Indians a new way of praying and a new moral law. The Black Robes would bring peace, he predicted, but their arrival would also mean the beginning of the end of all the people who then inhabited the land. (In Peterson 1993: n.p.)

The prophecy of Shining Shirt, indeed the prophetic culture that prevailed throughout the Northwest Plateau in the early nineteenth century, fostered the gains of Catholicism in later decades. In that context the teachings of Ignace Lamoose and the Indians' imitations of his devotionalism were truly forerunners of a future faith (see Schaeffer 1937: 229–231).

Lamoose not only taught the Salishans the "French prayer" (Point 1967: 21), but he also exhorted them to seek permanent association with Catholic priests. In 1831 a delegation of four Flatheads arrived in St. Louis. The Catholic authorities greeted them and baptized two of them ("Narcisse" and "Paul"), who died there (Schoenberg 1982: 4), but the clerics did not realize that the object of the Indians' visit was to obtain a missionary. The other two Flatheads headed back home but they disappeared along the way.

In 1834 and 1835 two delegations of Protestant missionaries approached the Flatheads, but the Indians spurned their evangelical overtures. Instead, old Ignace took two of his sons, Charles and Francis, on a journey to St. Louis to try once again to obtain Catholic priests for the Flatheads. Jesuits baptized the two youths; Ignace confessed his sins. He told the priests of the thousands of Indian souls from several nations, all desirous of sacerdotal contact. Despite promises by the local bishop, however, Ignace's 1835 delegation accomplished nothing. So again in 1837 old Ignace and four companions (including one Nez Percé) set off for St. Louis. This time, however, the Sioux intercepted and killed them all.

Two years later a fourth delegation, led this time by Ignace the younger and another Iroquois named Left-handed Peter, set off eastward. At Council Bluffs they met the Belgian-born Jesuit, Pierre Jean de Smet, who was mightily impressed by their fervor. The following year de Smet journeyed to the Rocky Mountains and established the first Catholic missions in the Northwest.

The Society of Jesus conducted these early missions. Suppressed (but not completely disbanded) by the papacy in 1773, the order had been restored in the early nineteenth century. In 1833 the Second Provincial Council of Baltimore recommended to Pope Gregory XVI that the Jesuits be assigned the task of American Indian missions, a duty accepted by the Jesuit superior in Rome. Priests like the young de Smet came to the United States in the 1830s and 1840s, especially as anti-clerical forces gained power in Europe and America appeared as a land of spiritual opportunity.

De Smet had arrived in St. Louis in 1823 and became a naturalized U.S. citizen in 1833. His disappointment with the dissolute Potawatomis of Indian Territory only sharpened his excitement in his first encounter with the Flatheads. Having received his commission, he accepted their invitation and in 1840 he faced well over a thousand of them, along with their Pend d'Oreille and Nez Percé allies, in what is now Wyoming. Big Face, a Flathead leader, welcomed the Jesuit and bade him to instruct the Indians regarding Christianity. After a brief catechetical discourse, de Smet baptized several hundred. Then he returned to St. Louis in order to collect Jesuit recruits to effect the conversion of the Flathead "elect of God" (Chittenden and Richardson 1905, 1:327).

In 1841 de Smet, along with the priests Gregory Mengarini and Nicholas Point and three Jesuit brothers, initiated a Flathead mission in present-day Montana. The Indians had been saying their prayers in de Smet's absence, and a dying Flathead girl had received a vision of the Blessed Mother, who told her to construct a house of prayer in her name; hence, the Jesuits called the mission St. Mary's.

De Smet had plans. In 1829 the Jesuit superior in Rome had directed his priests to study the methods used by the seventeenth- and eighteenth-century Jesuits in Paraguay. Their reductions were to serve the nineteenth century as models of missionary goals. Using Luigi Muratori's *A Relation of the Reductions of Paraguay* as his textbook, de Smet and his fellows set out to create a wilderness kingdom of God in the Rocky Mountains. With St. Mary's as the hub, they planned to establish as many as a dozen reductions, separated from white contact insofar as possible. The "Border Tribes" of the Midwest, like the Potawatomis, were too spoiled by white contact. Here in the mountains were Native Americans who had the potential to become exemplary Christians under hermetically sealed Jesuit care. Even if the Flatheads and their neighbors could not be weaned from their nomadic hunting ways and settled permanently in reductions, at the least these religious centers might teach them the rudiments of Christian civilization in isolation from other Christians.

The small number of Jesuits was in no position to enforce Christian practice on the Flatheads and other Indians they encountered. As superior of these new missions, de Smet set an example of liberal evangelism among the natives: employing their terminology for the divine, permitting them to persist in indigenous ritualism, even joining them in their hunting parties. "Accommodation was inherent especially in the Jesuit's 'incarnational' attitude—that all human good was potentially Christian" (Burns 1966: 38). Thus the priests tended, at least at first, to regard Indian spirituality as a road rather than an obstacle to conversion. Such an attitude did not imply a latitudinarianism which permitted all things. Indeed, according to one historian, the missioners only "half-heartedly tolerated the grafting of Christianity onto Indian religious beliefs in order to win converts. At the same time, they attempted to discredit their rivals, the medicine men, and to put a stop to Indian religious ceremonies, saying they were evil and the work of the devil. Priests told converts to throw away their medicine bags, and many did" (Peterson 1993: 115).

Over time this was certainly true. One Jesuit wrote in 1861 that he had seen Kutenai shamans commanding animals to death in magical feats which the priest considered frighteningly real: "Ah, Mary save us! the medicine-men have power from Sathanas" (in Chamberlain 1901: 97). In retrospect, wrote another Jesuit, "The Indian, before the advent of the whites, was a wild creature, steeped in moral and material barbarism" (Palladino 1922: 105). It was the task of the missionaries to educate and uplift them, as they would any "helpless little savage" (ibid.). In 1841, however, de Smet spoke differently of his ambitions. He saw the Flatheads as "a model for other tribes,—the seed of 200,000 Christians, who would be as fervent as were the converted Indians of Paraguay" (Chittenden and Richardson 1905, 1:327).

Father Point was less glowing in his reports. Between 1841 and 1847 he lived among the Flatheads, Coeur d'Alenes, Blackfoot, and other Indians, and found among virtually all of them "an unrelenting spirit of independence, laziness, a passion for gambling, cruelty to the vanquished, very little regard for women, forgetfulness of the past and improvidence for the future" (Point 1967: 12). His desire was to remake these peoples through the grace of the Holy Ghost, to cleanse them of their sinfulness. Using his skill as an artist, he presented to them vivid scenes of the mysteries, sacraments, precepts, prayers, and virtues of Catholicism. In one such painting, the "Way of Heaven," he depicted the progression of time, the succession of laws, the Old Testament and the New, and a summation of Christian doctrine. He found the Flatheads to be an eager audience for his instruction. In those first few months the Indians were still rejoicing in little Mary's vision of the Virgin Mother. For hours on end they learned their catechism and recited their lessons. One man saw an apparition of St. Francis Xavier on his feast day. A little Flathead boy learned his instruction miraculously when he saw in the chapel several paintings of Mary, the serpent, and the apple. When Point accompanied the Flatheads on their buffalo hunt, they recited prayers at sunrise and sunset each day. They said their rosaries and attended services on Sundays and feast days. They received baptism, and by Easter of 1842 they were preparing themselves for their first communion. They created a little wooden statue of Our Lady of Peace, to which they conducted pilgrimages. During 1842 they held their first processions of the Blessed Sacrament of the Feast of Corpus Christi. Benedictions took place, as well as devotions to the Sacred Heart. Father Point recorded this liturgical progress in his sketchbooks (51–56), and he wrote that "since their baptism an admirable transformation has taken place in their entire manner of life" (12).

The Flatheads sang hymns to rejoice in their new religious fervor: "He is coming down from the star, The great Chief, With us he is living, The infant Jesus Christ" (in Peterson 1993: 99). When their hunting was successful, they professed their devotion to the powerful God of the Christians. Father Point wrote that the killing of buffalo or deer was like the miraculous catch of fishes accomplished by St. Peter in the gospels: "To remove the great obstacle to the conversion of the most obstinate, the hand of God had to become visible" (Point 1967: 180). "Now we see very well," they told him, "that the prayers of the Blackrobes are more powerful than ours. Father, you may baptize us when you wish. Here we are" (in ibid.). In 1843 de Smet met with Pope Gregory XVI to discuss the expansion of missions in the Northwest. He brought a message from a Flathead chief to the pope: "If the Great Chief of the Christians is in danger, send him a message from me. We will build him a lodge in the middle of our camp; we will hunt game that he may be fed; and we will be his guards to protect him from the enemy" (in Killoren 1994: 81).

By 1843 Father Point had journeyed to the Coeur d'Alenes to found the Mission of the Sacred Heart. These Indians seemed unlikely converts and Point encountered stiff resistance, especially when their hunting and fishing seemed to falter in his presence. His adversaries charged him with bringing deathly powers, but when two baptized Indians recovered their health after receiving the sacrament, the tribe became more willing to accept the priest and his faith. Within several years he baptized nearly two-thirds of the five hundred Indians and convinced the majority of these to burn their traditional medicines. Christian Coeur d'Alenes competed successfully with their gentile relatives in bagging game and some of the leading men were willing to give up the practice of polygamy. When Father de Smet visited the Sacred Heart Mission, he found saintliness widespread among the populace. Nonetheless, Father Point grew discouraged in his inability to convince the Indians to settle into a reduction and cease their hunting way of life.

He and de Smet tried their hand with the Blackfoot and found them apparently eager for ministrations. In particular, these Indians wanted to gain the Christian powers they had seen demonstrated among their enemies, the Flatheads. The Flathead warriors had bent their knee and prayed before a successful battle with the Crows, and they had not lost a single life in the fight. "Perhaps the Black Robe could intervene on their behalf with his Master of Life," the Blackfoot asked de Smet, "and make their lives better—thus the invitation to visit them in their village" (Carriker 1995: 92). The Blackfoot had suffered recent defeats from the Flatheads, and smallpox had spread in some of their communities; therefore, they looked to the medicines of the Jesuits as a panacea.

"It is rare, at present," wrote de Smet in 1847, "to find any Black-Feet, even among the most vicious tribes, who are not convinced that the Black-gowns desire their happiness" (Smet 1847: 391). The Blackfoot regarded Point as a medicine man, whose baptismal potency rivaled the rites of the sweat lodge. They called him Thunder Chief and represented his likeness among the thunderbirds, snakes, antelopes, the sun, and the moon (Ewers 1971: 231–237). A medicine man reported that Point had the power to make the thunder roll and the earth quake, and that the priest's medicines could prevent native charms from working. Point regarded such attitudes as superstition, and he refused to baptize the many warriors who sought to be inducted into his mysteries.

When de Smet first encountered the Flatheads, their Christian leanings were already imbued with the same sense of God's power in warfare. When they defeated a large party of Blackfoot after praying in the manner taught them by the Catholic Iroquois, they became convinced of the military efficacy of the new religion. In the winter following de Smet's first visit in 1840, they carried his church ornaments like an ark on their winter hunt. De Smet seemed unaware at first of their motives. Like the Blackfoot, they thought of Catholicism as a source of earthly success, particularly in warfare.

THINGS FALL APART

The Jesuits bemoaned the chronic violence among the Rocky Mountain tribes. They hoped that their reductions would put an end to the cycle of revenge and bloodshed. Perhaps the Indians would all unite under the single banner of Christian piety. On the contrary, the presence of the missionaries served to exacerbate the thirst for battle, as each group felt itself possessed of supernatural potency. The Flatheads became more and more arrogant as they gained knowledge of Catholic rituals, considering themselves immune against injury.

When de Smet and Point went to the Blackfoot to spread the word of God, the Flatheads were angry that "De Smet, their Black Robe, extended to their traditional foes the spiritual power they believed belonged to them and them alone. For the Jesuits to do such a thing, in their estimation, amounted to a betrayal, the moral equivalent of an arms merchant supplying both sides in a war" (Carriker 1995: 86). Having played the role of miracle-workers, at least in the eyes of the Indians, the Jesuits were now suspected of delivering the miraculous to the enemy. The Flatheads turned against the missionaries, leading Father Point to abandon his post in 1847. Despite the depictions of Flathead devotions, their faith quickly dissipated and by 1850 St. Mary's Mission was closed, due to the Indians' disinterest and even hostility. The Jesuits sold their property to a fur trader, and when they renewed their missionary effort in 1854, they chose another site, which they called St. Ignatius Mission.

In a decade the hopes of both the Flatheads and the Jesuits had been dashed. For a generation the Indians had pined for a supernatural deliverance promised by the Catholic Iroquois. Instead, they experienced a marked disruption of their way of life. Whites filed into their beloved Bitterroot Valley, bringing with them diseases and destruction of the traditional way of existence. As invaders took over Indian territory, recriminations flew against the Jesuits—from the Indians for arming their enemies, and also from the Protestants, who considered the Catholics to be agents of a popish plot to usurp the American West. Wars spread throughout the Northwest, and despite the Jesuits' view of themselves as peacemakers, they were part of a process that led to Indian disarray.

The Jesuits were stripped of their illusions of a wilderness kingdom of reductions. There was no room to insulate the Indians from each other or from the white invaders. The Jesuits could not prevent the Indians from traveling far and wide into each other's territory and instigating fights. Nor could the priests control the influx of Whites; indeed, de Smet functioned as a bellwether for ranchers and other settlers who grabbed Indian lands. The Jesuits found the influence of these Whites, albeit Christians, to be a detriment to Indian spiritual progress. "Because it was covetous desire which led these white Catholics to the lands of the Flatheads," wrote one priest (Mengarini 1977: 217), "it is almost impossible to find among them any who are loyal in the practice of their faith." Father de Smet was even more emphatic in charging that "all the degrading vices of the whites have caused the greatest havoc" (Smet 1847: 89) among the Indians. He sympathized with the "ill-fated tribes that have been swept from their land, to make place for Christians who have made the poor Indians the victims of their rapacity" (125).

Despite their sympathy for the Indians of the Plateau, the Jesuits did little to persuade United States officials to divert the tide of the white invasion. Indeed, the priests, most prominently de Smet, worked with the government to pacify the Native Americans and make way for their acculturation on reservations. By the 1850s "Catholic missionary work among the tribes was less concerned with social justice," according to one of de Smet's biographers. "Indian rights would seldom be stressed, and native customs were usually discouraged. Christ's teachings were still presented, but the salvation promised through Christ became identified with civilized life" (Killoren 1994: 100).

Within the reductions de Smet's reforms were attractive at first. The Flatheads were intrigued by the notion of planting crops, and they became fond of potatoes, corn, peas, beans, turnips, and carrots. On the other hand, they had no desire to stay at home and tend their gardens. They persisted in their summer hunts, where "more sins are committed," said one Jesuit (ibid., 207–208), "than during three full years of village life." Nor did the Flatheads intend to alter their marriage customs—their practice of polygamy and divorce —despite their reverence for the Jesuits' supernatural propensities. Their most intimate social arrangements were sacred to them and the Jesuit reforms appeared "subversive" (Schaeffer 1937: 250) to their way of life. For all his affection for the Indians, it never occurred to de Smet that "in bringing Euro-American civilization to the Indians he tacitly encouraged the destruction of the natives' own culture" (Carriker 1995: 242–243). Neither he nor the other Jesuits understood that Flathead marriage customs were institutions which supported a culture, reinforced by beliefs, gift-giving, values, and public opinion. Marriage was a contract between two families, who then lived together, hunted together, and shared food in times of want. Good hunters needed more than one wife to prepare skins, dry meat, and store goods. Often a husband took younger sisters of his first wife, and thus solidified the affinal and familial bonds. For all the Flatheads' affection for de Smet—and he did appear to have had a "unique relationship" (Killoren 1994: xiv) with the Indians—they became disillusioned with his Jesuit colleagues.

Perhaps de Smet gained the initial interest of the Flatheads by arousing too many expectations. He was "too eager to please the Indians with lavish personal promises" (ibid., 91). At the same time he was too eager to move on to the next group of Indians, leaving behind neophytes without sufficient training to grow in their faith on their own. He taught Indians the catechism:

Q. Are there several gods?
A. No, there is but one God.
Q. Are there several persons in God?
A. Yes, there are three persons in God, the Father, the Son and the Holy Ghost; this is called the Holy Trinity.
Q. What is the Holy Trinity?
A. The Holy Trinity is one God in three persons . . .
Q. Are the Father, Son, and Holy Ghost three gods?
A. No; three persons, but one God.
Q. Why are the three persons only one God?
A. Because the three persons are equal in all things . . .
Q. Do the three persons differ from each other?
A. Yes, they differ; one is not the other. (Smet n.d.: 151–153)

However, the lessons did not have time to sink in. "'How can one just baptize here and there—and then run off?'" asked his Jesuit superior in 1845 (Carriker 1995: 108). De Smet's rhetorical flourishes were effective in spreading the fame of the Plateau missions. He raised substantial sums of money in his European journeys and attracted priests and sisters to join the missionary enterprise in the American Northwest. Nonetheless, his reports were "deliberate publicity releases. His widely publicized letters, designed to gain support for his reduction project, emphasized specific positive achievements. . . . The really negative factors, however, were not recounted" (Killoren 1994: 88; see Tinker 1993: 69–94).

The most negative factor was the incessant pressure upon the land of the Flatheads and their allies. In the 1855 Hellgate Treaty, the Washington territorial governor, Isaac I. Stevens, bullied the Flathead chiefs to give up twenty-five thousand acres in the Bitterroot Valley for a reservation surrounding St. Ignatius Mission, to be shared with the Kalispels, Pend d'Oreilles, and Kutenais. The Flatheads refused to budge, however, and so the Jesuits reestablished St. Mary's Mission in their midst. In 1872 the U.S. Congress passed an act of removal and two Flathead subchiefs signed the agreement. Another generation passed before the Flatheads finally were "escorted" by the military in 1891 to their new home, against the wishes of Charlo, their head chief and a devout Catholic. Before leaving St. Mary's, the Indians held an all-night prayer vigil and feast and then gathered before the church for their removal. Along the march of seventy miles, they sang the Catholic funeral dirge, *Dies Irae*—"The Day of Wrath" (Peterson 1993: 140). To this day the Flatheads still make pilgrimages to St. Mary's each September. Agnes Kenmille, a Salish woman says,

> My mother was three years old when they had to leave the Bitterroot. They were bitter, the people. . . . They still talk about it. They think about what happened because that was the Indians' church. That's where they go to Mass on Sunday, whenever they have wakes or something like that. That's where the cemetery is, right there for the Indians. (In ibid., 173)

The same pattern of events prevailed among the other Indians of the Northwest. The Nez Percés, the Coeur d'Alenes, the Blackfoot, and the Crows all lost lands rapidly in the second half of the nineteenth century, while portions of their tribes embraced forms of Catholicism. The changes came so quickly and were so unsettling that it is difficult to assess the religious conversions on their own. Among all these tribes the initial attraction of Catholicism was its promise of prowess. The Indians hoped that the crosses, medals, and other sacramentals would serve as medicines and talismans. The mass itself was to them an empowering ceremonial, the central symbol of the Catholic priest's communion with the Great Spirit and a source, the Indians hoped, of divine aid in earthly pursuits. "Converted Indians added prayers to the customary harangue before a battle," wrote one priest (Point 1967: 156), believing that warriors lacking the protection of the cross would be killed.

A difficult task ensued for the Jesuits, including Italian as well as French priests, to transform these supernatural, even supersititious longings into Catholic faith. Among all these tribes the Jesuits met resistance to attempts to transform married life. Diseases spread resentment against the priests and other Whites, as did the the reduction of Indian lands to reservations, where several tribes often vied for scarce resources. Factionalism in the reservations was exacerbated by sectarian disputes among Protestant and Catholic denominations. In addition, new religious enthusiasms arose: prophets and visionaries led their people in cultic movements which promised new powers or a return to the old ways. These sectarian stirrings often made use of Christian paraphernalia, gestures, and ideas; however, they agitated against Christian institutions and the inroads of the Whites.

These factors prevented Catholicism from solidifying itself quickly as a religious force among the Plateau Indians. Nevertheless, in the late nineteenth and early twentieth century, when reservation authorities began to prevent aboriginal religious practices—the dances, giveaways, and other rituals—the Indians found their only freedom of expression in Catholic ceremonialism. Protestant missionaries were more unyielding than the Jesuits in forbidding any combination of traditional and Christian worship, and so the Catholic missions served as oblique means of passing down tradition, albeit in Catholic shape.

"Many thousands of Indians lived a Catholic life" in the Northwest between the 1840s and the close of the nineteenth century. There were examples of feverish devotion, often followed, however, by dissolution, especially under the pressures of the white invasion. For those Indians who received Catholic baptism the question remains, how deep was their faith? "The historian unfamiliar with religious psychology easily misconstrues the evidence," writes a Jesuit historian (Burns 1966: 57). "Judgments by the resolutely pious or the doctrinaire secularist tend to emerge as a few confident simplicities." Another historian states, "Baptism, despite its importance to the missionaries, had little actual effect upon the inner or outer world" of the Northwest Indians. "It was the destruction of the Indian world between 1850 and 1900 that made possible further penetration by the white man's medicine" (Harrod 1971: 38).

Jesuit missionaries among the Blackfoot worked hard to destroy the fundamentals of Indian culture: polygamy, medicine bundles, and tribal rituals like the Sun Dance. In 1890 they established a boarding school at Holy Family Mission, Montana, in order to remove Indian youths from their parental influences and to enculturate them into the ways of Catholicism. By the early twentieth century, however, the Blackfoot as a people were a long way from Catholic culture. Despite baptisms, despite catechism, confession, and communion, despite novenas, processions, feast day celebrations, and devotions to the Blessed Sacrament and the Sacred Heart, despite the Indians' desire for last rites and burial in the Catholic graveyard, Blackfoot individuals persisted in their traditional culture. Even on their deathbeds the men often refused to repent their polygamy and the priests therefore denied them Catholic burial. "How could a priest refuse to bury one," the Indians asked in a particular instance, "who previously to his death had called for a priest? The refusal caused great excitement," reported the Jesuit priest (Holy Family Mission Diary, June 20, 1909) but he would not relent.

Native medicine men urged their Blackfoot fellows to spurn the sacraments; the priests searched the Indians' homes for medicine bundles and exhorted the natives to throw them out if they wanted to receive the blessings of the Church. "Eternal separation most probably!!" (November 14, 1908), wrote a Jesuit about two brothers: one a medicineman who died without last rites; the other baptized on his deathbed by a Catholic relative. A boy died shortly after a sickbed baptism, and at his funeral, "father urged that all should help to have children instructed in their religion as at the hour of death it appears how grevious is the fault of having neglected it." The priest continued, "The boy had never been at school and hence had never had the opportunity of instruction and had to appear before his Savior he scarcely knew" (September 12, 1913).

The Jesuits wanted the Blackfoot to attend communion and other liturgical services. They wanted to apply last rites to the dying and to bury the dead according to Catholic tradition. However, they found many Blackfoot resistant to these minimal concerns. Many of the Indians would not give up their medicines for Catholic sacramentals. At the same time the priests found it "morally impossible to abolish all dances" of the Blackfoot, and so they tried to encourage a few rites, like the Grass Dance—which seemed to the priests not to have overt "superstitious motives" (July 4, 1910), and which they hoped would continue at the expense of others like the Sun Dance. In the early twentieth century, "Jesuit sacramentalism had little power to transform entirely Blackfoot religious culture. Rather than transformation, there was a blending of the two cultures, and at this time religious behavior was often only minimally Christian" (Harrod 1971: 99).

Father Aloysius Soer, S. J., sermonized to the Blackfoot about the eternal opposition between God and the Devil and the Indians' place in that struggle: "There are two classes of people in the world: the good & the bad; those who belong to God & those who belong to the devil; those who are on the road to heaven & those who are on the road to hell. Now who are those who wish to be on the side of God?" (in ibid., 196). Nevertheless, the priest recognized the Blackfoot ambivalence toward Catholic faith. They wanted their children baptized but they also wanted them to grow up in the midst of "superstition and familiarized with its instruments—medicine-bags, otter-tails, bear-paws, medicine pipes. . . . Thus," according to Father Soer, "the children imbibe superstitions so naturally and so deeply that they grow up with the conviction that they can be good Christians while devoted to the vain observances of paganism" (in ibid.). This "inconsistency" led one Blackfoot to reprimand another for relying solely on Indian medicine, "whereas he should divide his service and his hope between God and pagan practice" (*The Indian Sentinel* 1910: 19).

Similar patterns held for the Kutenai living on the Flathead Reservation in Montana, where it was said in 1901 that the Roman Catholic missionaries had diverted some energy from the Winter Dance to Christmas preparations. "But while they celebrate the Christmas of the whites, these Indians have not altogether forgotten the festival of their forefathers" (Chamberlain 1901: 96). The priests fostered the practice of community reconciliation on New Year's Day, encouraging the Kutenai to make peace with anyone with whom they had fought during the year. The Indians took temperance vows, recited Catholic hymns and prayers, and shared a common feast in the spirit of Christ's birth; however, tribal religiousness played a role in the spiritual commonweal.

Evangelization among the Crow Indians "was considered an impossible task" (*The Indian Sentinel* 2, no. 6, April 1921: 252) when St. Xavier Mission was founded in 1887. Despite Father de Smet's earlier optimism, the Crows had not embraced Catholicism and they mocked the ministrations of Father Peter Paul Prando in the late nineteenth century, despite support for him within a couple of Indian families. When two Crow men, Benedict He-Does-It and William John Bull-Bird, converted, they became pariahs among their own people for receiving baptism. The tribe repeatedly petitioned the federal government to remove the priests; however, with the aid of Ursuline sisters who conducted a boarding school, the Jesuits gained influence among the Crows, and by the twentieth century about half of the two thousand Crows were at least nominally Catholic. Still, the Jesuit successors to Father Prando had to track down Crow apostates who had attended the mission but married without Church sanctions and put aside their Catholic connections. Some Crows turned to Protestant institutions; others became disillusioned with Catholicism, especially when the boarding school lost federal financial support and enrollments dropped off. Aboriginal Crow religion continued to hold a great appeal for many of the Crows. The Jesuits hectored Crows to have their marriages "rectified" and to become "staunch Catholics and apostles" (1909: 35). Nonetheless, Catholicism became but one of "a variety of overlapping religious sects" (Hoxie 1995: 225) in the Crow community.

The Shoshone remained indifferent to the Church, despite the influence of Catholic traders in their midst. The Nez Percé Indians mostly kept their distance from missionary efforts. The Church had a far greater impact upon the Coeur d'Alenes by the turn of the century. "The entire tribe is Catholic," the missionaries proclaimed, "and Catholic in all that the name—honor, dignity and responsibilities—implies." The six hundred Indians at Sacred Heart Mission on the Coeur d'Alene Reservation in Idaho displayed devotions to Christ and the saints, and they graced the liturgical year with apparent fervor. "Can you find a more faithful portraiture of primitive Christianity?" the missionaries asked. "Can you recall a scene more Scriptural, more in harmony with the teachings and spirit of Holy Church?" (*The Indian Sentinel* 1903–1904: 21, 25).

As for the Flatheads and their Kalispel, Spokane, and Pend d'Oreille neighbors at St. Ignatius Mission, the missionary enterprises of the late nineteenth century rekindled an interest in Catholicism. These "one-time savages . . . have been won to Christianity," claimed the missionaries in the early years of the twentieth century (1904–1905: 10–11).

The faith and fervor of the Indians are most edifying. Every day, winter and summer, year in and year out, at the first tap of the bell which summons them to Mass and instruction early in the morning, and to instruction again and night prayers in the evening, you see them all, men, women and children come out of their log cabins or tepees, and move toward the church. On Sundays and feast days of obligation or of special devotion, thrice in the day are they called to their devotions, and the bright, gay colors of their wrappings lend additional cheerfulness to the festive character of the occasion. (Palladino 1922: 98)

Ursuline Sisters joined Sisters of Providence from Montreal at the Indian boarding school. The Jesuits oversaw a general court conducted by the Indians in order to maintain societal discipline on the reservation. Adultery, abandonment of one's wife, lying, stealing, slander, drunkenness, violent anger, were the offenses punished by flogging. Disorderly conduct at church services was added to the list as the Indians at St. Ignatius became stolid Catholics. In this way the Church became part of the Indians' system of authority.

In the early twentieth century, however, when the United States withdrew support for mission schools, the Church's influence began to wane. In 1909 the federal officials opened the reservation to white settlement and "close contact wrought havoc" among the natives, destroying their "high religious and moral standards and reputation" (*The Indian Sentinel* 1, no. 14, October 1919: 4). Drunkenness, vice, and divorce entered their ranks and they "reached the depths of moral depravity." Furthermore, Whites took over St. Ignatius as a parish and treated the Indians as a "contagion" (ibid.); consequently, the Indians ceased to attend church, except several times a year for festivals and at the occasion of death.

Faithful Flatheads remained in the Catholic fold, including some of the offspring of old Ignace Lamoose, the founder of their faith. One of his sons, Francis, died in 1919 at the age of ninety-seven, a lifelong Catholic, having been baptized in St. Louis in 1835 (see Schoenberg 1982: 4–5). His younger brother Louis died at an advanced age in 1927. Chief Baptist Kakaeshe was an infant when Father de Smet baptized him in 1841. As an adult he carried the banner of the sacred heart and kept order in church during mass. The octogenarian died in 1923 (see *The Indian Sentinel* 3, no. 2, April 1923: 86–87).

However, in general the continuing pressure on reservation lands by overwhelming numbers of Whites spelled the demise of self-contained

Catholic Indian communities at St. Ignatius and elsewhere throughout the Northwest. "As a result," a mission organ stated in 1936 (*Our
Negro and Indian Missions*: 29), "large portions of the old mission fields
have become small, struggling white parishes with a few Catholic or
heathen Indians on their margins. The Indians may be gradually ab-
sorbed by intermarriage and acculturation," the report predicted. "In
the meanwhile, most of them have become social problems." By the
early decades of the twentieth century, "Indian missions became a
footnote to the White church, institutionally a failure but in terms of
individual Indians a continuing success" (Burns 1988: 499).

We continue to read in the mid-1900s of pious Catholic Indians in the Rocky Mountain states. An eighteen-year-old Flathead, Stephen Matt, died a sanctified death at St. Ignatius Mission in 1939, clutching a crucifix and kissing it with the words, "Sweet Jesus, mercy. Jesus, into thy hands, I commend my spirit" (in *The Indian Sentinel* 19, no. 2, February 1939: 27). Other obituaries attest to Flatheads who "died a good Catholic death" (23, no. 5, May 1943: 79; cf. 21, no. 3, March 1941: 47; 33, no. 9, November 1953: 141–142). Hundreds of Flatheads "have a special love of the Way of the Cross" in their Lenten devotions, wrote one Ursuline sister (20, no. 4, April 1940: 54). They sang the *Stabat Mater* in their own language every Friday in Lent. On Good Friday they converted the sanctuary of their church into a replica of Mount Calvary and carried a statue of the crucified Jesus in procession before laying it in the sanctuary amidst sobs and tears of the Indian Catholics. "What goes on in the soul of each God alone knows," a Jesuit wrote (26, no. 5, May 1946: 68). "This we know—many of the Indians . . . devoutly made their Easter duties."

The Kutenai on the Flathead Reservation were no less pious at mid-century; however, the customs of these "God-fearing, law-abiding people" were said to be "an interesting blend of age-old practices and Catholic beliefs" (23, no. 3, March 1943: 44). For example, on New Year's Eve the Kutenai men and women took their respective sweat-baths. Then, after the priest heard confession, they gathered for a night of prayer—rosaries, hymns, and catechetical lessons—at their chief's house. The next morning they greeted the sunrise with Hail Marys and gun salutes. Then everyone shook hands with one another in order to forgive and forget old enmities. Everyone received communion at mass, followed by a feast and a tribal dance. At wakes the Kutenai Catholics gathered by clans, smoked their pipes, told their rosaries, and sang their keening dirges, reminding their Irish priest of his Celtic homeland. Following a funeral mass two groups of Kutenai mourners faced each other and chanted in call and response. The first group wailed, "I am in purgatory. The only thing that can help me is prayer, the Mass and the Rosary." The other group answered, "Our

Father in heaven help those in purgatory so that they may be soon on the road to heaven" (in 23, no. 7, September 1943: 101). At a feast for the dead that followed, the Kutenai paid all monetary debts to and from the deceased. The immediate family of mourners dressed in dirty old clothes; everyone else wore finery, as the deceased's earthly possessions were given away as "almsgiving for the benefit of the soul of the departed" (24, no. 4, April 1944: 56). The missionaries did not try to stamp out these mourning rituals, embedded in the giveaway traditions of the Northwest, but tried instead to place within them a Christian interpretation.

Catholic priests were able to locate the "worthies," "old reliables," and "old dependables" (23, no. 6, June 1943: 89) among the reservation populations of Crows, Nez Percés, and other Indians of the Plains and Plateau, but even among these one could find aspects of old-time culture intertwined with Catholic practice, in many cases producing an estimable spiritual whole. A Jesuit noted that Crows practiced a custom called "fasting" (39, no. 2, March–April 1959: 31) during the last three days of Holy Week. Those who performed this activity came to church on Holy Thursday morning and stayed until late Holy Saturday evening. They were fulfilling a vow made during the year in return for some divine favor. During the three days they ate and drank nothing, not even water, and they did not sleep. They participated in all church services during the time. In this way they marked their Lenten duty with the zeal of aboriginal Crows, who fasted strenuously for spiritual potency, often in fulfillment of vows. They turned their ancient Crow fasting into Catholic devotion.

The Coeur d'Alenes appeared to the missionary fathers of mid-century to be both the most normative and zealous of Catholics. When they lost their church building to fire, they "wept aloud and their lamentations were to be heard for long afterwards." They begged their bishop for a new church, causing their parish priest to comment, "It was truly a moving spectacle to see how these poor Indians love the Church" (*Our Negro and Indian Missions* 1940: 35). In 1843 they celebrated the centennial of their first contact with Father de Smet, thankful—according to their Jesuit pastor—to missionaries of the previous century who "foresaw that the country would be filled one day by white people. The Indians must accordingly be trained in new ways of living" (*The Indian Sentinel* 33, no. 10, December 1953: 149). "The entire tribe has long since become Catholic," said John J. Brown, a Jesuit scholastic of the Blackfoot tribe (36, no. 9, November 1956: 140), and it had been many decades since these people had tried to combine tribal ritualism and Catholic worship. The Coeur d'Alenes sang hymns in their language and dressed in Indian regalia for ceremonial occasions; however, their church was much like any other rural parish, celebrating the same masses, sacraments, and devotions, organized in groups like the Sacred Heart Society, taught through the Confraternity of Christian Doctrine, reading Catholic periodicals, and attending a day school taught by the Sisters of Providence. Kutenai, Spokane, and Kalispel students boarded at the school, and according to Rev. Brown, "Some of them beg to remain over the Christmas holidays and even during the summer vacation" (141).

Among the Blackfoot the patterns were far more ambiguous. Even though they were said in 1960 to be 88 percent Catholic, and despite their apparent pride in having taken the initiative in seeking Catholic ties in the 1830s and 1840s, large numbers of baptized Blackfoot were no more than "nominal" or "folk" Catholics (Spitzer and Spitzer 1960: 21). For over a century Catholic priests had tried to incorporate Blackfoot into the sacramental life of the Church, and yet Blackfoot Catholics seemed more attracted to sacramentals than to sacraments. Holy water and candles, kept in their homes like the medicine bundles of old, were more important to them than confession or holy communion delivered by the priests. One might perceive "a steady shift from Indian to Christian religious values" (28), as the Blackfoot attended retreats and recited the rosary, and the Indians were cordial to their priests. The pastors remained tolerant of Blackfoot practices, including prayers offered in their native tongue and even attendance in the Sun Dance, "insofar as they are not in active conflict with Christianity" (25). The priests were even willing to describe the Virgin Mary in a litany as Queen of the Sun. And yet the fathers reprimanded a medicine woman for her active role in the Sun Dance. When she became ill, they told her that she would have to make a public retraction of her Sun Dance vows before she could receive last rites. The priests were willing to permit the Sun Dance's validity as a "traditional ceremony rather than as worship" (32), but they would not take seriously the notion that Blackfoot ritual acts—like the consumption of the sacred buffalo tongue during the Sun Dance—had any validity in comparison to the holy communion of Catholicism. Smarting from the priests' criticism, some Blackfoot concealed their tribal religious allegiance. The pastors claimed that the ancient spirituality formed but a facade on the edifice of Catholic faith; however, others perceived Catholicism to be the "overlay" (34) on the older patterns:

> There is a range from deep faith, through superficial allegiance, to a combination of sacred and folk elements, some Indian, some Catholic, which forms an institution inclusive within the Catholic framework. . . . It would appear that, despite the activity of formal Catholicism, the need for the past and the resurrection of Indian practices from time to time have deeper roots than the concept of a facade would indicate. (33)

The experiences of the past generation have not altered dramatically the religious portrait of Catholic Indians of the Rocky Mountain states. Dioceses have introduced Cursillo, diaconate training, youth ministry, and other post–Vatican II leadership programs. Indians have increased their devotion to Kateri Tekakwitha and many attend the annual Tekakwitha conferences. Catechesis and parish outreach have been matched by Indian-run spiritual enterprises like the Pilgrimage among the Blackfoot, which attempts through a system of retreats to overcome alcoholism. Amidst poverty and alcoholism—the residue of the rapid routing of aboriginal culture—Catholic Indians have maintained their faith despite their isolation from Church institutions. A third of the eight thousand Crows, half of the thirty thousand Blackfoot, most of the Flatheads, Pend d'Oreilles, Kalispels, and Kutenai (known collectively as the Confederated Salish and Kootenai Tribes, numbering about six thousand), and almost all of the one thousand and more Coeur d'Alenes regard themselves as Catholics and come to church for weddings, baptisms, and burials. Catholicism is a part of their cultural lives. When Clarence Woodcock, a Pend d'Oreille Indian, speaks of living "a real traditional life" as a child, he remembers "every night, especially during Lent, we'd have to pray the whole rosary sometimes, of course in our Salish language. Church every Sunday and sweats all the time" (in Peterson 1993: 175). In Oregon there are Catholics among the Umatilla, Cayuse, and Wasco peoples.

And yet on occasion, anger strikes out among the Indians of the Northwest against their Catholicism. Vandals damage church property. Words of resentment often find their way into conversation about religious matters. Even the Coeur d'Alenes, regarded as the most solidly Catholic of the Plateau tribes, are described as "a broken people" (Bartholomew 1990: 15), 98 percent Catholic but 47 percent below the poverty line. The faith of the young is not strong, and people feel abandoned by the Church since the Sacred Heart school closed in 1974, due to lack of funding. Today, "many of these people are untouched by the Church except at Christmas and Easter when they attend Mass. Others are confused and bitter about the changes they have seen in the Church since Vatican II" (16).

Among the Confederated Salish Catholics, including the Flatheads, there is ambivalence toward their Church and faith. "When the Black Robes got here is where my ancestors were run out of their home-land," says Frances Vanderburg. "But they still hung on to the Catholic ways. They used the sweat house, they used their medicine dances, but kind of on the sideline and then they'd go to church. My amazement is that after all that happened, they still stayed Catholic." She concludes, "It made some people strong" (in Peterson 1993: 177).

THE OBLATEſ OF WEſTERN CANADA

The 1840s were a decade of expansion for Roman Catholic missions to North American Indians. As Father de Smet and his fellow Jesuits were establishing the first missions among the Salish and other Indians of the Rocky Mountains, the Red River colony in what is today Manitoba and North Dakota received an influx of priests, members of the Missionary Oblates of Mary Immaculate. Oblates spread Church missions across western and northern Canada and the United States through the rest of the century.

What the Jesuits were to New France in the seventeenth century, the Missionary Oblates of Mary Immaculate were to nineteenth-century Canada. Founded in France, the order epitomized the ultramontanism of Roman Catholicism, a "highly structured, authoritarian, centralized, and disciplined international movement bent upon saving humanity from the spiritual perils that threatened from every quarter" (Choquette 1995: 5). Like the ultramontanists who produced the doctrines of papal primacy and infallibility, and the condemnation of liberalism, nationalism, secularism, and modernism of every stripe, the Oblates regarded themselves as troops in combat with the forces of Protestantism and heathenism. Between 1845 and 1900 nearly three hundred Oblate priests worked in Canada's greater Northwest, converting Indians, ministering to the Métis, and establishing Church structures which have lasted to the present day.

When the Oblates began their Red River missions in 1845, they looked westward toward the various native peoples from the western end of Lake Superior to the Rocky Mountains, including Ojibways, Blackfoot, and Crees of the Algonkian language family, and the many Northern Athabaskans such as the Chipewyans, Hares, and Beavers. These Canadian Indians of the northern prairies and lakes numbered about sixty thousand. On the Pacific Northwest there were another hundred thousand Indians of numerous linguistic families, including more Athabaskans (e.g., the Chilcotin and Carrier tribes), Kutenai, Salishans such as the Shuswap and Lillooet, and many others. In the far north were thousands of Inuits, the Eskimoan-speakers of the tundra. Across the prairies were fifteen thousand Métis, already somewhat

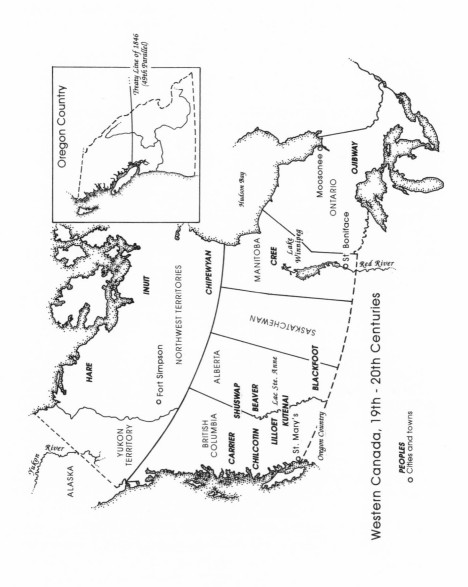

Western Canada, 19th - 20th Centuries

PEOPLES
○ Cities and towns

familiar with aspects of Catholicism, as well as four thousand Whites, most of whom lived south of Lake Winnipeg along the Red River. The Oblates saw the French-speaking Métis as their first line of contact, among whom they hoped to play a "civilizing role" (Giraud 1986, 1:177–186). The order of priests established a diocesan capital at St. Boniface, Manitoba, and from there expanded north and west into Saskatchewan, Alberta, Northwest Territories, and the Yukon. By 1847 there were Oblates in Oregon Territory, and in the 1860s Oblates were stationed as far west as the Yukon River and as far north as the Arctic Circle. Accompanied at times by the Sisters of Charity (the Grey Nuns) of Montreal and other orders of sisters, the Oblates established schools, parishes, and sacramental life for thousands of Indians.

In the 1880s missions began in Alaska among the Athabaskans and Eskimos, manned primarily by Jesuits from the Oregon Province. Sisters of St. Ann opened schools. As the United States hierarchy formed dioceses, Native American Catholics became part of the northern Church. By 1928 there were twenty-seven mission stations conducted by Jesuits in Alaska, minstering to almost five thousand Native American Catholics (*Our Negro and Indian Missions* 1928: 28), one-fifth of the native population (1933: 26). A survey in 1979 counted eight thousand Indian and Eskimo Catholics in the Diocese of Fairbanks, two thousand in the Archdiocese of Anchorage, and five hundred in the Diocese of Juneau (see Beaver 1979: 141–146). In the succeeding decades the numbers have continued to grow slightly. Both Fairbanks and Anchorage have developed special native ministries and diaconate programs.

The Oblates, like the Jesuits, excelled in evangelical training, preparing in advance the methods they were going to employ and mastering numerous Indian languages. Many of them received their first missiological lessons from the Sulpician priests working among the Iroquois Catholics at Oka. From there they gained experience among the Ojibways at Red River. Finally, they were ready to enter their own widespread mission fields, where they attempted to create dictionaries and grammars and to translate prayers and scriptures into native languages. In this way the missionaries served incidentally as keepers of Indian culture, although as one scholar says, the "missionaries in general were ignorant of the cultural values held by native societies" (Whitehead 1988: 12).

The Oblates had a low opinion of Canadian Indians, regarding the

natives as liars, idlers, and gamblers, sexually lax and irresponsible as
children. Oblates could hardly speak of the Indians' having a religion;
their myths were merely fanciful tales with no religious worth. Hoping
to establish "a missionary-controlled agricultural community" (Gresco
1973: 151) in each of the locales in which they placed themselves, the
priests were determined to change the tribes' basic ways of interacting
with the environment, the spiritual world, and with each other. The
missioners were willing to tolerate some Indian participation in native
rites in the short run, expecting that under catechesis the aboriginal
paganism would die out over time and the Indians would devote themselves entirely to God. Even at the outset, however, the Oblates tried
in vain to forbid religious practices like spirit quests, shamanistic cures,
and potlatches (ritual giveaways). Most importantly, however, the
Oblates attacked particular aspects of Native American culture which
they found abhorrent. The priests attempted to prohibit polygamy,
sexual contact outside of marriage, infanticide, drunkenness, and gambling. The missionaries also tried to ameliorate the status of women
in their communities. According to the priests, the Northern Athabaskans treated their women like dogs, using the same word for "my
daughter" as for "my dog" (Hermant 1948: 16). The Oblates wished to
revolutionize gender relations, even though the Indian women could
hardly believe that the Catholic faith was for them, so accustomed
were they to degradation from their men.

The Oblates and Grey Nuns appealed to Indians as carriers of spiritual power, and the natives perhaps hoped to translate that prowess
into worldly goods. "The fact is that the Indian looks upon Priests and
Nuns as rich," reported one Oblate. The natives thought that the missionaries "only have to send a little bit of paper into the 'Great Countries,' and it will bring them back a cargo" (Duchaussois 1919: 77). For
this reason some of the priests referred to their early converts as "tobacco Christians" (in Grant 1985: 116), seeking whatever goods they
could from the white newcomers.

For all their appeal, however, in their early days of mission work the
Oblates could not enforce their reforms. Indeed, they faced competition not only from traditional tribal authorities but also from native
prophets who took the Christian message to be their own personal
calling, and who tried to transform Christianity into a native cause. In
1855 Father Vital Justin Grandin faced an Athabaskan Indian who
claimed to be "the Son of God." The Indian got his followers to burn

their tents and give away all their worldly possessions. He said that he had come to earth long before and that white men had killed him. Now he was rejecting Whites and making the Athabaskans his "chosen people" (Hermant 1948: 26). Father Grandin confronted the prophet, calling him a fraud who could speak neither Latin nor even French, and who was incapable of working the wonders of an authentic Indian Christ. The Indian's followers soon rejected him and rejoined the Church. Several years later Grandin faced another Athabaskan vision-ary, a young Chipewyan, who called upon his people to give up Catholicism, saying that all the Indians needed to know was that "eter-nal life is from the earth and sun" (in Grant 1985: 117). At one point he assaulted Grandin. In 1861 Father Isidore Clut had to deal with an-other Chipewyan prophet who heard confessions of Indian women by having them take off their clothes and "join their confessor in bed" (Choquette 1995: 68). Father Clut excommunicated the Indians and then engaged in fisticuffs with the man's family, in order to establish his clerical authority.

The most infamous of the Indian prophets, of course, was the Métis seminarian Louis Riel, whose insurrections against Canada and the Protestants in 1869–1870 and 1884–1885 were fueled by his mes-sianic and politicized interpretations of scripture. The Oblates disap-proved of Riel's violent outbursts, but he caused their efforts to be suspect throughout Canada. Catholics came to be perceived as danger-ous revolutionists, inspired by a clergy whose loyalties were only to Rome. The Oblates did not have good relations with the Canadian In-dian Department in any case. They sought to gain as much local con-trol over their Indian charges as they possibly could, away from governmental interference.

In order to establish that control, the Oblates created the Durieu System, named for Father (and later Bishop) Pierre Paul Durieu. Fa-ther Durieu's scheme was an imitation of the famous Jesuit reductions of Paraguay, like the experiments attempted by Fathers de Smet and Point among the Plateau Salishans in the United States. Durieu and his fellow Oblates first worked out their plan in Oregon Territory, at Fort Colville and along the Puget Sound; however, they put it into ef-fect most assiduously in British Columbia.

The Durieu System assumed that the Indians of the Northwest were deficient in their cultural development; the Oblates planned to under-mine the traditional culture and replace it with an authoritarian Christian one under their clerical control. As Father Adrian Gabriel Morice, O.M.I., explained it, the Indian was "a grown-up child" (Morice 1910, 2:351), who needed constant policing and public penance in order to act properly. "A degraded creature, who partakes more of the child than of the adult, without being blessed with the innocence of the former or the control over the passions of the latter," wrote Father Morice, "the redskin must be treated with the firmness, the prudence and the foresight required by the government of youth" (2:350). The Durieu reductions were completely controlled Indian settlements, ensuring constant indoctrination of the inhabitants. Another Oblate described the system:

> . . . it consists in the applications of the proper ways and means to protect an Indian against himself and against evil-doers and to confirm him in Christian life. The Indian is weak in mind and heart. . . . he must be paternally and effectively guided and strengthened against moral inconstancy. . . . Bishop Durieu knew every fibre of the Indian nature. . . . He knew that the Indians bitterly resented the interference of white people in their intimate affairs. . . . The Indians are only big children who can be naughty sometimes. . . . the Indian must be ruled by religious motives; if these fail we have lost our grip on him. (Bunoz 1942: 193–194)

In short, Durieu's regimen was an attempt to produce rapid and thorough acculturation and to prevent opportunities for backsliding.

Among the Coast Salish and other Indians of the Pacific Northwest, the Oblates tried to establish themselves as equivalents of the native elders and nobles. They represented themselves as personal emissaries from their God, the "Chief of the Above," and set up a political order among the Indians which answered only to the priests. In these reductions only adults could be baptized. "Catholic Indians had to be more than 'païens lavés'" (Gresco 1973: 152); they had to obey whatever the priests told them to do.

Indians were kept busy in spiritual and manual labor. The bells rang at dawn. In the morning the Indians prayed, chanted, attended obligatory mass. In the afternoon there was catechism, in the evening, more prayers and songs. Each day the Indians painted houses, washed floors, tended gardens, and kept to a strict regimen of work. There were, indeed, "monastic rules in Indian villages" (Bunoz 1942: 205). Indians were not allowed to play games, either traditional ones or those introduced like football. Instead, Durieu's system had them filling in swamps, working constantly in public works projects. Sundays were days of physical rest, when Indians sang in their choirs, made their confessions, and attended two required masses.

Their entertainments were religious pageants in honor of the Sacred Heart, the Blessed Sacrament, and the Virgin Mary. The Indians engaged in processions in honor of the feast of Corpus Christi. There were grand celebrations at Christmas and Easter, and other holidays for the Indians to witness cannon salutes, fireworks, brass bands, and European-style ceremonialism of all sorts. The Indians joined confraternities and sodalities, where they were permitted to gather, shake hands, and perfect their Christian lessons.

Several times a years the Salishan Indians under Oblate direction at St. Mary's Mission in British Columbia celebrated the Blessed Sacrament by building altars, lighting candles, and setting up pyrotechnic displays representing the Sacred Heart and the Virgin Mary. Each time the displays were completely destroyed and then rebuilt for the next celebration. Once every year the Indians at St. Mary's performed an elaborate passion play which they rehearsed throughout the year, drawing audiences in the thousands—both Indian and White— from near and far. This performance became known as the Canadian Oberammergau. As the Indians portrayed several tableaux, dressed as Jews and Romans witnessing Christ's passion, the Indian multitudes kept up a mournful chant, "The Christ is dead—the Christ is dead" (in Hughes 1911: 334).

In the 1880s at Lac Ste. Anne, Alberta, the Oblate priest, Jean-Marie Lestanc, instituted a pilgrimage in honor of Ste. Anne, in commemoration of the saint's miraculous appearance to cure an ailing Indian girl. This pilgrimage site came to rival Sainte-Anne-de-Beaupré in Quebec. Thousands came to bathe in the healing waters of the lake named for the grandmother of Jesus.

In all of the Oblate reductions the Indians were kept in constant awareness of their sinfulness, especially those sins "most commonly committed among the Indians" (Bunoz 1942: 198). Father Durieu published a book of sexual ethics, which became the standard by which morality was enforced. Indian catechists appointed by the priests read public examinations of conscience; Indian watchmen pried into all manner of personal behavior and reported to the Oblates in charge; Indian captains enforced the Oblate laws and meted out punishments. If the residents of the reductions did not obey the strictures of Durieu's ethical codes and tone down their native spiritualism and ritualism, they were dealt with at courts of moral and religious offenses, presided over the priests and their delegates, the captains, watchmen, and catechists. Public humiliation and flogging were common penances. Thus it was said that throughout the Durieu System, "it is not rare to see Indians, tied up or free, kneeling down or standing up in front of the whole congregation as a means of atoning for public delinquencies" (352).

Catholic boarding schools connected with the Durieu System were employed throughout western Canada to wean children away from their old life in their family circles. The schools taught by rote and by discipline, training the Indians to value obedience to Catholic authority; that obedience was not meant to apply to indigenous leadership. Watchmen made it nigh impossible for the youths to play the truant or to run away, and over time the children began to regard their families as strangers. This was the goal of the residential schools, and it had its effect in harming the Indians' familial and social cohesion.

The residential schools were Oblate means "for retaining and strengthening the Indians' Catholic faith; this goal, not assimilation, was the Oblates' primary concern" (Whitehead 1988: 57). The missionaries wanted the Indians to become Catholic, not Canadian. The priests were at odds with secular and Protestant culture and were trying to inculcate Catholic rather than nationalist values and loyalties. Thus the Oblates tried to keep Protestants and other Whites at a distance from the Catholic Indians. This became difficult as white Catholics joined the missionary invasion of British Columbia and the Oblates were required to serve them, too. The missionaries tried to keep the Indians and Whites apart, in order both to maintain reduction authority and to keep the secret that many Whites were both irreligious and morally corrupt. Over time, however, the world could not be kept at bay. Indians within the Durieu System came into contact with Whites, and although they were none too fond of them, they also learned to imitate them.

Father Nicolas Coccola was a Corsican Oblate who spent over fifty years as a missionary to British Columbia Indians and Whites, including eighteen years with the Kutenai. Like the other missionaries among the Indians, he was "determined to revolutionize their world" (ibid., ix). And like other Oblates, he "entered British Columbia knowing virtually nothing of the Indian peoples," which did not prevent him from attempting "massive cultural disruption" according to what he and his fellow Oblates imagined a "'perfect' conversion system" (12, 13). Coccola practiced the Durieu System, teaching white models of agriculture, medicine, and child care, and conducting both residential and day schools.

The Corsican priest was a theological conservative who was frustrated in the difficulty of teaching the Indians Catholic theological concepts, e.g., the notion of transubstantiation. He received approval from his Indian audiences when he spoke of the goodness of a Supreme Creator, but as soon as he mentioned the punishments of hell, they hissed at him and said that he must be a denizen of the infernal region, since he knew so much about it. Their medicine men argued with him, asking why should there be churches in a world in which Nature is the perfect place for the Great Spirit. Father Coccola replied that churches are for humans, who would be too distracted from prayer outdoors. Why are there jails, a medicine man asked? The priest's answer: to protect society from bad men. The Indians tried to make sense of Catholic theology through the lens of their own spiritual concepts, asking about ghosts, guardian spirits, and the travel of souls. Are there spirits over all things? There are angels, Coccola retorted, both good and bad. What kind of spirit is in me?, a medicine man asked. Is it good or bad? At this Coccola balked at answering. If he said a good spirit, the man would say that he did not need a priest to guide him. If he said a bad spirit, the man would threaten everyone with his evil. The next day the medicine man led his people against Coccola, preventing him from saying mass.

Father Coccola preached sermons about prayer and work as the means of accumulating property and physical comfort. If you pray and work regularly, he said, you will be both successful and godly. He made a census of sins, fining Indians and whipping them, or having Indian sheriffs perform the tasks. Those guilty of gambling, drunkenness, theft, and other antisocial acts were, according to an eyewitness, "tied down on a robe, hands and feet secured by rawhide thongs to stakes placed in the ground, and soundly flogged, regardless of age or sex" (in ibid., 21).

The Indians challenged Father Coccola, not only in his theology but also in his associations with the Whites who soon entered the Kutenai territory. These Indians, Coccola said,

had no love for white people for the reason that the majority of those
they had seen were drunkards, blasphemers, trying to corrupt the
women, being themselves religiously inclined, sober and moral. On one
of their gatherings, the question was: "Where are the white people
coming from? not from God surely to judge by their ways of living."
. . . The priest was not considered a white man by them, but as some
one sent to them direct from heaven. (In ibid., 107, 119)

Coccola's celestial origins were suspect, however, when he used his authority to persuade the Kutenais to sell their lands to the white invaders. His association with the Canadian military and with the white
Catholics of the incursion made him a force for uprooting the very
people he was charged with protecting in the reduction. As a result, he
was obliged to move on to other mission fields in British Columbia.

From the 1860s to the 1890s the Durieu System flourished as what
Bishop Louis D'Herbomez thought "a very effective system for keeping the Amerindians on the straight and narrow path" (Choquette
1995: 196). In 1888 one of the Oblates wrote of the progress accomplished under their rule: "The most savage and barbarous customs
have been softened. The most ferocious nations have given up their
cruel habits. Traditional wars among the enemy tribes have ceased.
There is no more fighting, no more scalping, no more enemy whose
blood is desired" (in Carrière 1973: n.p.). In British Columbia the system resulted in "the relatively complete Catholicization of the tribes
within a very short period of time" (Lemert 1954: 23).

In 1892 Father Eugene Casimir Chirouse, O.M.I., was arrested and
convicted of abetting an assault upon a seventeen-year-old Lillooet
woman in the British Columbia mission system. He had overseen the
"sentencing" of the woman, who was accused of a sexual offense, to a
flogging (fifteen lashes), although he was not present when it was administered. The Lillooet chief and two assistants were charged with
the actual assault. Chirouse's trial and conviction made public the oppressive aspects of the mission system, and the Protestant authorities
were not eager to see the system continued. Father Chirouse was released from his one-year sentence under sharp lobbying by the Oblate
bishops, including Pierre Paul Durieu himself; however, the Durieu
System was doomed, despite an Oblate defense of the corporal punishment (see Morice 1910, 2:390–392). "Ambivalence" (Whitehead
1988: 73) to the Oblates arose among the Indians, and by 1910 the
priests were virtually unwelcome in British Columbia.

Between the 1850s and the end of the nineteenth century, Oblate priests (as well as Protestant ministers) imposed themselves, their faith, their notions of village planning, authority, social order, and architecture on the Indians of British Columbia. By the turn of the century most of the twenty-five thousand remaining Native Americans in the province were declared Christians, over eleven thousand of them Catholics. These Indians built churches under the direction of the Oblate missionaries and seem to have submitted to their wills for decades under the Durieu System, despite initial resistance. By the 1930s, however, the Durieu System had broken down. The System had made it possible for headstrong missioners like Father Morice, and even homosexual pediphiles like Father Émile Petitot and other such "problem cases" (Choquette 1995: 197), to ply their unsavory trades among the captive audience of Indians. The power the Oblates held over the Indians served to infantilize the Catholic Native Americans and disrupt their social solidarity, making them resentful of Catholicism as a whole. When the Indians were finally released from the reductions, many of them left active participation in the Church and rebelled against the priests (Lemert 1954: 27). Agents told the Indians that the whippings were illegal and could not be enforced. White inroads brought alcoholism. Land was lost and the communities broke apart.

CANADIAN INDIAN CATHOLICI/M

In 1939 a British Columbia census listed 57 percent of the Indians as Catholics and only a score of natives as still holding aboriginal beliefs (see Whitehead 1988: 71). These figures, however, were misleading. Many of the Indians once deemed secure in the Catholic faith have reverted publicly to traditional beliefs and practices, which were forbidden in Canada in the late nineteenth and early twentieth century. "Many people believed that it was possible to take on the ways of the church without dishonouring the ways of our grandfathers," said an Indian from British Columbia. "They hoped that the Mother Earth and the Mother Church would be sisters and friends" (Manuel and Posluns 1974: 61). Given the opportunity, converts often took up their traditional ways once again.

According to the 1981 census, over 50 percent of Canadian Indians and Inuits—over two hundred thousand, in addition to most of the hundred thousand Métis—were Catholics. Anglicans represented another 25 percent, and the remaining native peoples were designated as members of other Christian denominations. According to a recent report (Frideres 1988: 160), "no information has been gathered regarding the extent to which Native people still adhere to pre-Christian religious beliefs. Apparently, a significant percentage of Natives have retained their indigenous religious beliefs." Even though the majority of Indians in Canada are identified as Christians, this does not mean that the aboriginal religions have disappeared.

Indeed, according to one Oblate, Rev. Achiel Peelman, "Christianity has not been able to displace the traditional Amerindian religions" (Peelman 1995: 15). His sober assessment of Canadian Indian Catholicism states that churchmen "must recognize that the reception of Christianity by a large number of Amerindians (their yes) was indeed a sublime form of the rejection of Christianity, at least in its western, cultural expressions. *Their yes was also a no!*" (67, his emphasis). He finds that some Indians have achieved "full conversion," whereas most others have taken the paths of "dual acceptance, religious dimorphism, syncretism" (66). Even a full generation after Canada ceased to be missionary territory in the eyes of the Roman Catholic Church (in 1967

the missionary period begun by Jacques Cartier in the 1500s came to
an end when the Apostolic Vicariates of Canada were upgraded to
archdioceses and dioceses), Indian Catholics in their local churches
still bear the marks of missions: passivity and apathy. More significantly, Peelman finds,

> the Amerindians have not become Christians *like us* and . . . they have
> not spontaneously joined our western churches. After their conversion
> they managed to create their own expressions of Christianity on the
> fringe of the official churches and often in opposition to them. They
> often reinterpreted the Christian faith from the cultural vantage point
> of their own religious existence. Some have turned their back on the
> church while others commit themselves to the Amerindian renewal of
> their Christian communities. (82–83, emphasis his)

Twenty years ago a scholar interviewed Oblates ministering in the
Canadian north and west among Indians and Inuits. He was disappointed to find that the attitudes of the previous century—the condemnation of native culture and the belittling of aboriginal religious
heritage—were still extant. The Oblates' "dominant theological motif
operative in missionary consciousness," he wrote, "is that of exclusively revealed Christian truth which implies a hostile theological
judgement on indigenous faith" (Gualtieri 1980a: 310). Much like their
predecessors in the nineteenth century, the modern Oblates expressed
the notion that "there was little or no religion worthy of the name"
among the natives before the arrival of the missionaries, and that the
old culture "no longer exists" in the present. As a result the modern
Oblates were loathe to attempt any program of indigenization of
Catholic ritual or belief. "To press for cultural adaptation," the priests
said, "might amount to nothing more than an additional instance of
white paternalism prescribing what it deems best for natives according
to white fantasies of archaic culture" (299). The Catholic Indians
seemed to share the Oblates' evaluation of their traditional spirituality,
and there was very little evidence of synthesis between native and
Christian religious expressions.

In more recent years some Oblates like Father Peelman as well as
other representatives of the Church have embraced the project of inculturation among Catholic Indians, even joining the Indians in their
sweats and vision quests, and encouraging them to create for themselves images of Christ and Christianity which are appropriate to native culture and worldview. A Catholic priest in British Columbia,

Terry McNamara, has even been initiated as a spirit dancer among the Salish Indians. He regards his participation in native ritualism as part of his Indian ministry (Hilbert, January 11, 1990.)

Other Oblates continue their far-flung ministry, albeit in less experimental ways. Bishop Jules Leguerrier, O.M.I., of the Diocese of Moosonee, ministers to twelve thousand Crees and Ojibways in northern Ontario over an area of five hundred thousand square miles. By airplane and dogsled and with the help of a dozen or so Oblate priests, he reaches a wide area.

Many devout Canadian Catholic Indians still participate in the ceremonial life established by the Oblates. The annual pilgrimage to Lac Ste. Anne in Alberta still takes place, with as many as thirty thousand pilgrims arriving each summer to land held by the Oblates, in order to honor Christ's grandmother and to bathe in the lake's sacred waters. Indians from across Canada perform liturgies in their native languages—from Dogrib to Cree—and many bring back bottles of the water to their homes and reserves. In 1993 one Chipewyan woman walked almost a thousand miles over two months to Lac Ste. Anne, saying the rosary and collecting money for her local Catholic church (*Tekakwitha Conference Newsletter* 12, no. 3, September–October 1993: 19).

Nonetheless, the Oblate heritage among Canadian Indians is a mixed one. One recent writer says, "In the end the Missionary Oblates of Mary Immaculate served to liberate the Indian people of Canada, but did so within a context of ethnocultural subjugation of the Indians driven by the Euro-Canadian conquest of Canada's North and West" (Choquette 1995: 236). The Oblate Father Peelman finds this assessment too sanguine. He states that Oblates (and Jesuits and other Catholic missionaries) were participants in the conquest of Native North America, even when they opposed the abuses of their governments, and it was they who often subjugated the Indians they were said to serve (Peelman 1995: 86). Peelman recites the sorry statistics of contemporary native life and death in Canada: the disappearing languages, the unemployment and economic dependency, the low life expectancy and high infant mortality, the rates of suicides and violent deaths (32–35). He recalls that a Shuswap Indian from British Columbia, Frank Manuel, first coined the phrase "Fourth World" to "designate the legitimate but dispossessed peoples who had become the 'internal colonies' of nation states such as Canada and the United States of America" (180). Indeed, Manuel makes it clear from the perspective of an Indian whose community was transformed by the Durieu System and the residential schools, that the Church helped create the "laboratory and the production line of the colonial system" (Manuel and Posluns 1974: 63).

In 1984 and again in 1987 Pope John Paul II visited Canada and met with thousands of Indians, Eskimos, and Métis, both at the Shrine of the Canadian Martyrs in the old Huron region of Ontario and also, in 1987, at Fort Simpson in Northwest Territories, 350 miles south of the Arctic Circle. Both times he delivered a speech in praise of traditional Indian culture and in sympathy with Indians' economic plight. Some Native Canadian activists wished in 1984 that he had made a stronger statement about their political rights. One Indian complained that the pope's emphasis on spirituality eclipsed all-important material needs: "he's blind in one eye and can't see out of the other" (in Martin, September 16, 1984). At the same time he received acclaim for voicing the notion of an Indian Christ.

In 1984 fog had prevented the pope's airplane from landing at Fort Simpson, but three years later he kept his promise to complete his northern journey. The natives of the subarctic performed a "spirit dance" (in Burns, September 20, 1987) to assure suitable conditions for his flight, and when he said mass he wore vestments of fringed and decorated leather, dressing in effect like a western Indian.

Some Indians wept in appreciation "that the pope had traveled into the backwoods to demonstrate his support for people who struggle with some of Canada's highest rates of poverty, of alcoholism and of family break-up" (Burns, September 21, 1987). Yet in private Indians spoke to the pope of their "concerns . . . about the church's history here, its slowness in adapting the liturgy to traditional Indian forms, and its policies on matters that have prompted unrest elsewhere, such as the bans on married clergy and on artificial birth control" (ibid.). In particular, the Indians complained of the past—the Durieu System, the boarding schools, the prohibitions against native languages, the forbidding of traditional cultural forms in Catholic liturgy. John Paul II spoke of the Indians' "dignity," "destiny," and "worthy traditions"; however, he defended the missionary heritage. Rather than apologizing for the Church, the pope said that "the Indians owe much to the missionaries, particularly for the preservation of their culture" (ibid.). In a homily in which he warned against materialism and the politicization of contemporary Indian discourse, he declared:

I come to you as many missionaries have done before me. . . . They proclaimed the name of Jesus to the peoples who lived in Canada, the Indians, the Inuit and the Métis. They taught you to love and appreciate the spiritual and cultural treasures of your way of life. They respected your heritage, languages and customs. Truly the missionaries remain among your best friends, devoting their lives to your service as they preach the word of God. (In ibid.)

The pope "seemed to say that the Indians themselves, as much or more than the missionaries, are responsible for the troubled state of the church, which faces a pattern of an aging priesthood, shrinking church attendances, and a lack of interest among Indians in the priesthood, which has no Indians in its ranks in Canada" (ibid.). However as we have seen, there are also profound historical reasons for Native Catholics' lack of involvement in the structure of the Canadian Church.

When the fur trade brought French Canadian Catholics to the Pacific Northwest with the Hudson's Bay Company in the 1820s, colonists formed an agricultural community along the Willamette River and wanted the succor of priests for themselves and their children. In 1834–1835 they appealed to the bishop of St. Boniface, Red River, the nearest ecclesiastical authority, and he communicated with the bishop of Quebec, Joseph Signay, who appointed Father Francis Norbert Blanchet the Vicar General of Oregon Country (under joint British and American jurisdiction) in 1838. Blanchet took along Father Modeste Demers on his evangelical mission to his new post, and before the year was out they had arrived at Fort Vancouver on the Columbia River.

Although there were desultory Spanish visits in the late eighteenth century, there had been no official Catholic contacts since the British raised their flag in the northern Pacific coast in 1794. Some scattered Iroquois Catholics, employees of the Hudson's Bay Company, had settled among the Coast Salish tribes in the 1820s, and Métis traders took Indian wives in Oregon Country. In order to block Protestant inroads among these people, the bishops wished to establish a Catholic presence in the fur trading communities. The chief trading-post factor, Dr. John McLoughlin—a Protestant who soon converted to the Catholic faith—was interested in securing priests in order to foster employee morale, and so he welcomed the clerics. They set up mission stations at the Cowlitz portage and along the Willamette River, saying the first mass in the territory. In 1839 Father Demers visited Fort Nisqually, another Company post on the southern tip of Puget Sound. There he met with a delegation of twenty-two tribes, including the Lushootseed chiefs Tslalakum and Goliath of Whidbey Island, who invited a visitation from the priests. In 1840 Father Blanchet planted a huge cross on Whidbey Island and baptized over two hundred willing Native Americans. The same year a Yakima chief arrived at the mission near Fort Vancouver and received three weeks of instruction in Christian fundamentals.

Bishop Signay stated in 1838 that his priestly emissaries to Oregon were meant not only for the "poor Christians living in the region" but also for the Indians of the area (Office of Minority Ministries 1988: n.p.). Most of the Hudson's Bay Company employees in the Northwest were Catholic, and they treated the priests with respect. Seeing the high status of the clerics among the trading hierarchy, the Indians looked up to them, too, and responded positively to their first ministrations. Listening through translators using the Chinook Jargon, the trading argot of the Northwest, the Indians heard the priests speak of the "medicine" of the sacraments (ibid.; Thomas 1986: 134), and they witnessed the pageantry of Catholic ritualism. "The sight of the altar, vestments, sacred vessels, and great ceremonies were drawing their attention," wrote Father Blanchet (in Thomas 1986: 133), and the priest took advantage of their interest to lure them from the sermonizing of Protestants.

The various native leaders who journeyed to Fathers Blanchet and Demers asked for something to bring back to their people as a sign of the priests' teaching and authority. In response the priests designed for their "untutored minds" (Blanchet 1859: 1) a stick with marks indicating Christian ideas, e.g., a cross symbolizing the Crucifixion. Like priests before them for several centuries—for example, Paul Le Jeune in 1637, who attempted to instruct the Algonkians of New France by marks made on the ground (Thwaites 1896–1901, 2:151–159)—Blanchet and Demers created a mnemonic device for catechetical purposes.

The Indians called it the Sahale (Heaven) or Soul Stick in Chinook Jargon. The stick was four feet in length and two inches squared, with bars and dots which represented the creation, the fall of angels and of Adam and Eve, the birth and death of Jesus, and the mission of the apostles. In addition, illustrations of a church, a cross, and a star filled in the catechism. Father Blanchet commissioned Chief Tslalakum of Whidbey Island as his catechist, following eight days of instruction, at which time the Lushootseed chief and his fellows were said to be "'masters of the subject'" (Hanley 1965: 40). Blanchet reported that the delegates returned to their people like the first twelve apostles.

Within a year Chief Tslalakum, "the first recorded Indian catechist" of Oregon Territory (Whitehead, July 1981: 99), had already made a copy of the stick and was spreading his version of the Christian message among his people around the Puget Sound. From these first sticks Father Blanchet soon concocted what he called a Ladder, like that seen by the patriarch Jacob in his biblical dream, from which the Lord spoke. It was a pictorial catechism, a chart of ink on paper with linen backing, many feet long. The priests and the Indians hung these charts from trees as the reference points for instruction. The ladder made it possible to expand upon the rudimentary message of the Sahale Stick. After explaining its use to his bishop in 1842, Blanchet manufactured many copies of the ladder and it spread not only among the Indians but also the children of the Catholic colonists

The Catholic Ladder marked Christian history with bars (centuries) and dots (years), from Adam through Christ to 1842, from the beginning of time to the present day. It pictured biblical scenes: Adam and Eve in the Garden, the Tower of Babel, Noah's Ark, Sodom and Gomorrah, the Commandments at Mount Sinai, Solomon's Temple, and so on. The appearance of the Star of Bethlehem introduced salvific history, followed by representations of the Virgin Mary and Jesus, His life, death, resurrection, and ascension. The Holy Roman Catholic Church appeared with its sacraments, commandments, and prayers, as well as its creeds. St. Peter's Basilica represented Catholicism at the core. A branch veering from a central path showed the heretics leaving the true Church, from Martin Luther and John Calvin to King Henry VIII and Joseph Smith. Other markings represented the doctrines of Catholic theology: the Trinity, the Incarnation, Redemption, God's eternity, immensity, providence, and power. Creation was indicated along with angels both good and wicked. Heaven and hell were pictured, as were the tree of knowledge and the Fall.

In consultation with Father Pierre Jean de Smet, who journeyed to Fort Vancouver in 1842 to coordinate Northwest missionary efforts, Blanchet honed his pictography in subsequent editions, and from these came several imitations, published in Canada, France, Spain, and the United States. There were even Protestant pictorial catechisms based on Blanchet's model. The most famous of all the Catholic imitations came from the hand of Father Albert Lacombe, an Oblate missionary among the Blackfoot in western Canada. In 1865 Father Lacombe used burned-out embers of a fire to draw catechetical pictures on a buffalo hide stretched between two poles. The Blackfoot responded favorably to these illustrations and Lacombe continued to perfect his drawings, until in 1872 the sisters of the Congregation of Notre Dame in Montreal produced a colored edition.

Lacombe's Ladder was organized around two paths, ascending in parallel lines, one toward heavenly reward and the other to eternal damnation. The point of the ladder was to illustrate "all life on our pilgrimage to Heaven" (Goutier n.d.: 1) and the diametric opposition between that road and the one to hell. This was its genius, for it made graphic the crucial choice facing all who looked at the chart, either to walk the path of the Church to communion with God, or to orient one's life toward the Devil.

The Oblates encouraged the dissemination of Lacombe's Ladder. When Pope Pius IX saw a copy, he had several thousand made, to be distributed among the missions to the "savage tribes" (Hughes 1911: 203, fn. 1) worldwide. In 1896 Lacombe updated the Ladder and it remained in constant use in Native American evangelization for at least half a century. Even after writing became common among missionized Indians and Catholic priests turned to the "picture machine" (*The Indian Sentinel* 2, no. 12, October 1922: 541) — photographic slides — the "two roads catechism" remained popular and effective in Native American missions. Even in the days preceding World War II, Indians on the Puget Sound, e.g., at Tulalip, were receiving instruction in the pictorial catechism originating with Father Blanchet. The great-grandchildren of Tslalakum's Lushootseed people still encountered Catholic doctrine through these mnemonic devices (21, no. 5, May 1941: 67–68). And in the present day one of Blanchet's earlier versions hangs in the church of St. Paul on the Swinomish Reservation (Swinomish Indian Reservation, January 14, 1990).

In 1984 Father Paul O'Bryne of Calgary commissioned a modern version of the pictorial ladder, specifically for the use of Indian Catholics. It tells the story of Catholic faith but with many Indian symbols, in order to facilitate inculturation. An Indian named Standing Alone created the painting, entitling it "Come to Me . . . I am the Way" (in Goutier n.d.: 1), and including on it a peyote altar and a Sun Dance pole, as well as the Virgin of Gualalupe and several tipis. A chart makes it clear that Indian rituals have sacramental value, for instance, "an Indian symbol of sacrifice and penance: the one-hundred willow sweat lodge. Just like the two roads, one side is painted red to signify good, the other side is painted black to signify the bad. The one hundred willows signify the years of happiness for which we pray" (10).

"Nowhere," wrote Father de Smet (Smet 1847: 98), "does religion make greater progress, or present brighter prospects for the future, than in Oregon Territory." In 1843 Father Blanchet became bishop of the Vicariate Apostolic of Oregon City. In 1846 the United States and Great Britain settled their territorial dispute in the Northwest through the Treaty of Washington, establishing a boundary line at the forty-ninth parallel and thus ushering in an era of territorial consolidation and settlement. When Washington Territory was carved from Oregon Territory in 1853, the Church created the Diocese of Nisqually (later known as the Diocese of Seattle) to administer this, the most north-western region of the United States. After a century of administrative shifts, the Archdiocese of Seattle was formed in 1951 in the far west of Washington State.

In Oregon the Church initiated missions among the Umatilla, Cayuse, and Wasco Indians. Along Puget Sound in Washington lived ten to twenty thousand Salishan-speaking Indians, including Nisqually, Squaxin, Puyallup, Muckleshoot, Suquamish, Duwamish, Snoqualmie, Samish, Snohomish, Swinomish, and Skagit (all members of the Lushootseed language group, from south to north), and north to the Canadian border, the Nooksack and Lummi tribes. These linguistic relatives of the Flathead, Coeur d'Alene, and Kalispel peoples of the Rocky Mountains inhabited villages in the cedar forests and harvested salmon from the rivers and sea.

The aboriginal Coast Salish villagers paid close attention to the identity, social status, and responsibility carried by their family names. Noble clans and individuals were expected to look after their less fortunate relatives with gifts and hospitality and thereby gain names of great esteem. Giveaway ceremonials extolling the names of the living punctuated the long winter ritual season. So did feasts at which ancestral names were honored and passed down. The Lushootseed Indians looked forward annually to renewing their kinship with the dead, and they burned food and other goods as symbols of communion with their forebears in the spirit world. It was a duty of the living to "spread the table," to "care for" (Hilbert, January 13, 1990) the ancestors, re-

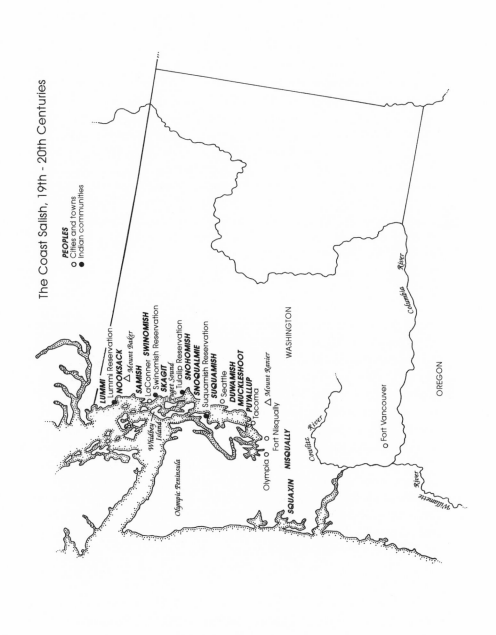

The Coast Salish, 19th - 20th Centuries

PEOPLES
o Cities and towns
● Indian communities

LUMMI
Lummi Reservation
NOOKSACK
△ Mount Baker
SAMISH   SWINOMISH
LaConner
SKAGIT   Swinomish Reservation
Whidbey   Tulalip Reservation
Island   SNOHOMISH
SNOQUALMIE
Suquamish Reservation
SUQUAMISH
o Seattle
DUWAMISH
MUCKLESHOOT
△ Mount Ranier
PUYALLUP
Tacoma
Fort Nisqually
Olympia o   o
WASHINGTON
SQUAXIN   NISQUALLY

Puget Sound

Olympic Peninsula

Cowlitz River

o Fort Vancouver

Columbia River

Willamette River

OREGON

minding them of their continued importance in the world, and to bring their names back to life in the present generations.

In the summer season the Indians greeted their staff of life—salmon returning to their waters—with prayers and offerings. Thanksgiving to the Creator accompanied the honor paid to the fish: "The food that you gave us," the Indians intoned, "causes us to come together, binding ourselves together" (in Petius, May 20, 1977: 12).

Individuals gained supernatural power by seeking guardian spirits in vision quests. Families sent their children to designated places in order to engage in "spiritual bathing" (Hilbert, n.d.: 17), which preceded visitations from spirit protectors. Those who attained especially potent guardians were thought capable of extraordinary feats. They could locate missing objects and recover lost souls. They had the ability to "stroke people with words" (Hilbert, January 11, 1990), soothing and restoring them in times of sickness. A renowned Skagit healer once remarked, "Good words are medicine, our elders said. Good words are medicine for someone in sorrow, someone ill, someone feeling sad. It uplifts one, fixes him up when he hears these good words" (Petius, May 20, 1977: 10). Secret societies of these practitioners engaged in rituals to cure, comfort, and admonish their communities, sometimes traveling in spirit canoes to recover lost or stolen souls. Every winter individuals celebrated their spirit protectors by chanting their songs. In the longhouses spirit dances occurred throughout the entirety of the winter months. Dancers adorned in red and black "expressed" (Hilbert, January 20, 1990) the spiritual potency in the natural world to harm and heal.

Thus, the Indians of the Puget Sound reminded themselves year round of their connections to their human, natural, and spiritual relatives—connections contained in their names. The Coast Salish paid especial attention in the old stories to their relation to the sky world, which was imagined as a source of creativity and community. The Creator lived in the sky world, and the all-important legends of Starchild and Diaperboy (the moon and the sun) delineated the many ways in which the sky world served as a locus of meaning and an example of proper behavior for humans on this earth.

Always alert to new sources of spiritual relationship, the Coast Salish had sent emissaries to Cowlitz Valley when Hudson's Bay Company personnel arrived there, and even before their famous delegation of 1839 the Indians had learned something, however vague, of Catholic belief from the French Canadian fur traders. In the early 1840s the Indians of Whidbey Island greeted several visiting priests "with enthusiasm" (Schoenberg 1962: 14). The Indians sang Christian hymns and repeated the lessons from their pictorial catechism. They were attentive during the celebration of the mass, leading Father Demers to weep with hope that "an infinite satisfaction had been offered to God for the sins of these poor people" (in Blanchet 1932: 89). Inspired by the potential of this new religion, the natives constructed a great cross—which still exists in the 1990s as a historical monument to the first conversions in the area—and a house of worship on Whidbey Island, and Bishop Blanchet filed a land claim for legal possession of the site.

It is suggested (see Collins 1980: 33–35) that the Coast Salish had already adopted aspects of the Plateau prophet dances, and that their interest in Catholicism derived from their millenial enthusiasm. At least one Skagit leader developed a religious cult in which his followers knelt in prayer, made a sign of the cross before meals, observed Sundays, and prayed for divine aid in the imminent end of the world brought by white people. This man's house served as a church but also as a location for traditional guardian spirit dances during the winter. Over time the Indians of the area combined Catholic and native elements to create several new religious movements.

Blanchet and Demers were in no hurry to baptize the Indians to whom they preached. Recognizing the difficulty of translating theological terminology and the long process required for sufficient conversion, they were willing to proceed deliberately. Even Chief Tslalakum took four years of instruction, during which time he served as a catechist, before receiving baptism. Blanchet insisted on no more than the following profession of faith from the native catechumens: "Yes, we believe in God who created all things. Yes, we believe in Jesus Christ, who came to redeem us. Yes, we believe in the seven medicines to make us good" (in Thomas 1986). As for the converts, the pioneer missioners made few initial demands: "To shun warfare as far as possible, to marry one wife, to have the children baptized and confirmed, and to die in the arms of the Church was as much as could reasonably be expected and usually more than could be attained" (Warner and Munnick 1972: n.p.).

In 1848, the Oblates established the first permanent mission among the Squaxin Indians of the Puget Sound, near the present site of

Olympia. Father Pascal Ricard was the superior of the Oblate enterprise; however, Father Chirouse, the same Chirouse who worked years
later in British Columbia, was the most effective missioner in the field.
Ordained by Bishop Blanchet in 1848, Father Chirouse served in several locales in Oregon Territory until he was appointed to the first
Tulalip mission (St. Francis Xavier) among the Snohomish and Snoqualmie Indians in 1857. Over the next several years he initiated missions among the Suquamish (now St. Peter's), the Swinomish (now
named St. Paul's), and the Lummi and Nooksack (now St. Joachim).
In 1861 he was named U.S. government teacher at Tulalip.

By this time the Territorial Governor, Isaac I. Stevens, had already
conducted several treaties with the Indians of the area, reducing their
landholdings and opening the region to economic exploitation. Saw-
mills, commercial fisheries, and hopyards were soon to overtake the
remnants of the fur trade as Washington moved swiftly into the
modern era. As with their Plateau relatives, the Salish Indians of the
Northwest were overrun rapidly and their population diminished;
Catholicism constituted part of the trauma as well as providing succor
in their travails.

Father Chirouse established Catholic religious life on the Puget Sound reservations. He baptized several thousand Indians, including four hundred at Tulalip in the month of May 1859, inducing the converts, it is said, to give up "gambling, conjuring, fighting, and murdering" (*The Indian Sentinel* 1, no. 7, January 1918: 11). "If you are sick, you are going to die," he told the Indians. "If you are not baptized, you will not reach the good country" (in Collins 1980: 36). He employed "statues, pictures, bits of wood, carvings, allegorical and symbolical pictographs" (*The Indian Sentinel* 1, no. 7, January 1918: 12), including Blanchet's Catholic Ladder, and he used his skill as a storyteller to edify the Indians with biblical legends. He had no patience with the "sorcerers and jugglers . . . vile hellish wretches," who, in his view, were agents of the devil and kept their people in the darkness of "superstition." He preached to the Indians of the "only true God" who "alone has full power over your souls and bodies" (46–47), and he challenged the native religious practitioners to test their spiritual powers against his own. To prove his prowess he vaccinated thousands of Indians against smallpox in 1863 and became a veritable medicine man to the Puget Sound natives. To demonstrate his victory over his native rivals, the Catholic converts "piled the paraphernalia of the medicine men at the feet of Father Chirouse" (Office of Minority Ministries 1988).

Father Chirouse was an authoritarian, although not to the degree he would become in later years in British Columbia. Like his associate, Father Durieu, he seized both civic and religious power in order to transform the several thousand Native Americans under his charge. He received appointment as Indian agent at Tulalip during the U.S. government's Peace Policy of the 1870s, when reservations were entrusted to Catholic and Protestant missionaries among the American Indians. He "soon became a power among them" (*The Indian Sentinel* 40, no. 2, Summer 1962: 23) and had them praying and singing morning and night. "We soldiers of the Creator, we shall fight the devil until we die" (in Metcalf 1954a: 73), was a hymn well remembered by the Indians he instructed. He instigated the destruction of any native institutions he deemed inimical to Catholic lifeways, e.g., the Suquamish communal building, Old Man House, which he said promoted immorality (Forsman, January 16, 1990). When the Nooksack Indians moved to Lummi in the 1870s at Chirouse's request, "they did not like the strict regime Chirouse had instituted" there (Amoss 1978: 22). They left the reservation and would have nothing more to do with the Church. The Puget Sound Indians were no strangers to discipline and authority; however, they would have found no attraction in the corporal punishment employed by the Oblates in their reductions (Hilbert, January 9, 1990).

On the other hand, Father Chirouse learned the Lushootseed languages, translating Christian concepts and texts into their tongue, and they respected him for his talent. If we observe his translation of the Lord's Prayer into Snohomish (or Skagit), and conveyed into English by the contemporary Lushootseed linguist Vi Hilbert (see Vecsey 1992), we can observe the priest's technique in planting the seeds of Catholicism along the Puget Sound:

The Lord's Prayer

(From a translation by E. C. Chirouse found on page 6 of the "Prayer Book and Catechism in the Snohomish Language" compiled by Father J. B. Boulet October 15, 1879, Tulalip, Washington)

1. gʷəɫ dibəɫ dəgʷi ʔal kʷi šəq.
   Our father you who are up high.
2. haʔɫ kʷi gʷəshuyutəbs liɫdᶻixʷ haʔɫ tə ʔadsgʷaʔ ʔadsdaʔ.
   Good that it be made first good that which is your name.
3. dəgʷi gʷəsixʷsiʔabčəl
   You are our leader (our honored one).
4. haʔɫ kʷi gʷəsčalatəbs tə ʔadsgʷaʔ ʔadsčəɫx̌əčəb ʔal ti swatixʷtəd.
   Good it would be that it be followed your thoughts
   on this land.
5. x̌ʷulab ʔə kʷi gʷəsčalatəbs ti ʔadsgʷa ʔadsčəɫx̌əčəb al ti šəq.
   Just as it would be followed that which is your thoughts/wishes there up high.
6. tiʔiɫ sʔələdčəl ʔal kʷi bək̓ʷ sləx̌il ʔadsʔabyitubuɫ ʔal ti sləx̌il.
   That which is our food each day is your gift to us on this day.
7. ƛub čəxʷ ʔubaliicyitubuɫ ʔə tə dᶻək̓ʷadədčəɫ.
   Let it be that you forget for us that which is our sins.

8. x̌ʷulab ʔə tə sbaliicyidčəɬ tə ləli ʔaciɬtalbixʷ ʔə tə dᶻək̓ʷadads dxʷʔal dibəɬ.

   Just as forget for them the other people that which is their sins toward us.

9. ƛub čəxʷ ʔucəlalik̓ʷtubuɬ dxʷʔal gʷəɬ bək̓ʷ dᶻək̓ʷadadčəɬ.

   Let it be that you let us be winners toward all of our sins.

10. huy čəxʷ ʔuliltubuɬ tuiˀʔal k̓ʷi bək̓ʷ saʔ.

    Then you remove us from all that is bad.

11. ƛub ʔəsʔistə.

    Amen.

Retranslated in literal form by ṯaqʷšəblu—Vi Hilbert, 3-4-84.

The Christian prayer is to "our father," with whom we have a bond of kinship. The term Chirouse used is literal and mundane, referring simply to someone's father, nothing more. But the importance of kinship to the Indians cannot be overemphasized; thus the prayer's opening provides a proper meeting ground—the dimension of kinship—between Christian and Lushootseed spirituality.

"You who are up high" ends the first phrase. There is no mention of heaven, and the phrase does not refer explicitly to the Skagit mythological notion of a world above the sky. It refers only to "up there," with no connotation of the sacred. What meaning could this have to the nineteenth-century Indians trying to learn Christian theology? Vi Hilbert suggests that "our father . . . up high" makes no sense in her language unless you know there is a prayer going on, and it is a Christian prayer. She explains that the priest did not try to say something sensible to the Lushootseed worldview, but rather used Lushootseed words that would say something mysterious (and therefore, religiously appealing) about the Christian worldview. Who is this father of ours, up high? To answer this question, the Indians had to turn to the catechism, the sermon, the missionary message as a whole about God.

If Lushootseed Indians were referring to the Creator of their mythology, they would use a religiously charged term, *xaʔxaʔ*, which means both "sacred" and "forbidden." Father Chirouse, it appears, did not wish to associate the Christian God with the Lushootseed concept of spirit power, which was a force both extremely helpful and extremely dangerous. The Oblate wanted to introduce a new spiritual orientation, rather than to build upon the aboriginal one.

"Good that it be made first, good that which is your name": the first half of this phrase refers to a name that is first among names, a name that has the highest social status. For the Puget Sound Indians, class rank has always been very important. The priest was appealing to Indian values while avoiding the word *xaʔxaʔ*, which might be used for "holy" or "hallowed." The second half of the phrase indicates that it is a good name, both morally and pragmatically: an ethically good, usefully good name. That which is *xaʔxaʔ* is too electrified to be called merely good. The Catholic translator avoided the Lushootseed reference to something supernaturally powerful, choosing instead to call this father up there high-class and good.

The third phrase, usually said in English as "thy kingdom come," says nothing about kingdoms or kings. These are Christian terms with a long sociological pedigree based on Western political structures, none of which make any sense to the Indians of the Puget Sound with their attachment to local kinship and interconnected village structure. Instead the phrase reads, "You are our leader (our honored one)," a high-class person deserving tender regard and respect. There is also no implication here of Judeo-Christian eschatology, the messianic kingdom to come, either on heaven or earth. The expression is in straightforward present tense, "You are our leader," now.

Since the nineteenth-century Lushootseed had no concept of heaven (although there was a sky world for them), the fourth phrase does not attempt to establish God's will "as it is in heaven." Rather, it is said that "good it would be" if His thought were followed "on this land," our territory, this earth, as it would be "there up high."

The sixth phrase establishes the nobility of our father because he gives us "that which is our food each day." Gifts and gift-giving were highly valued by the Skagit and Snohomish Indians. That our father would provide a gift of food means that he is high-class, a noble person. That fits what was said about him as "our honored one." Chirouse did not choose to employ a word for salmon, which might carry for the Lushootseed all the sacramental qualities of bread as food for the early Christians, and instead used a word for food in general, thus transcending the local context of Indian culture.

Phrase seven expresses the hope that our father will "forget for us . . . our sins." The verb is "forget" rather than "forgive," and thus the priest did not use the term that is central to the good news of Christianity: God's forgiveness of human sinfulness. In the prayer the word for "sin" is one that means to travel and stray, a departure from rules, like a trespass. The term carries judgmental overtones, but without any notion of sinful nature. In Lushootseed there is no positing of sinful nature and therefore no need for divine grace to overcome human depravity. The whole reason for the good news is missing in Lushootseed language and thought. It was the task of the Christian missionaries to convince the Indians that they were sinners by birth. Otherwise the Indians would feel no need for the Christian promise of salvation. The priests told them that their maladies—their blindness, their arthritis, etc.—constituted a divine payment for their sinfulness. The Indians found the idea cruel. Yet in this prayer the concept of ontological sinfulness, original sin, human depravity, is missing.

So is the notion of debts. The Puget Sound Indians have long been concerned with debts—canoes, horses, such things are terrible to owe—but the prayer in phrases seven and eight makes no use of a concept that might have carried powerful overtones of Puget Sound Indian economic and societal forms.

"Let . . . us be winners toward all of our sins" carries in Lushootseed the connotations of gambling games—stick games, tugs of wars, and the like. These games required discipline and concentration; hence, the phrase calls the Indians to be winners over self-indulgence, laziness, and laxity toward rules, although it is doubtful that Chirouse meant to evoke gambling here. In phrase ten, "remove us from all that is bad," the word for "bad" does not mean "evil" but rather "useless." It does not carry a Christian moralistic message, but rather completes the pragmatism of the previous phrase regarding "winning."

The word for "amen" is a perfect affirmative, "let it be that way," but what was it that the late nineteenth-century Puget Sound Indians were affirming in the prayer? Father Chirouse understood native usage well enough to graft Christian ideas onto aboriginal meanings when they seemed appropriate to him. In translating "The Lord's Prayer," he avoided, for the most part, explicit, exclusive aspects of Christian culture: God, heaven, sinfulness, the kingdom of Christianity, messianic hope. At the same time he steered clear of spiritually loaded Lushootseed terminology. He seems to have attempted a culturally neutral, quotidian translation that would represent something (but not everything, not even the forgiveness of human sinfulness) of Christianity without presenting a theology so foreign as to be repellent to the Indians. He used several Lushootseed ideas (most prominently, our

Father's social primacy) without embedding the prayer in Indian culture. After all, he wanted to move the natives to a new cultural life, ori-
ented to Jesus and the Church, without perpetuating their traditional
worldview.

We cannot tell for certain what the Puget Sound Indians thought of
the Catholic prayers they learned and recited; however, thousands of
their diminishing numbers received baptism. It is suggested today
(Forsman, January 16, 1990) that the first Catholic converts were impressed by Catholic ritual displays and desirous of trade goods brought
by the Hudson's Bay Company. Diseases weakened the Indians' faith
in their aboriginal religion; the yearning to gain new sources of spirit
power made the Indians open-minded to Catholicism. Many others
joined the Protestant cadres.

When Chirouse built churches at Tulalip, Lummi, Swinomish,
Suquamish, and Muckleshoot, he appointed "local, dusky vicars" (*The
Indian Sentinel* 1, no. 7, January 1918: 10): native prayer leaders, cate-
chists, and singers who led their fellow converts in the forms of
Catholic worship. Some of these, like Sahl-pud at Tulalip, also known
as Father Joe, maintained their posts, leading prayers according to
Chirouse's translations many decades after the Oblate had moved on.
We should not think of the early converts as disinterested neophytes.
Indeed, many Coast Salish Indians "accepted Christianity because it
inspired their interest and, in many cases, their respect; they demonstrated this by their willing participation in the missionary process not
only as followers but also as active exponents of the newly accepted religion" (Whitehead, July 1981: 98).

Coast Salish Indians who have reflected on the conversions of the
first decades of missionary activity suggest that their ancestors were
attracted to Catholicism because it seemed so much like their traditional faith. It posited ritual means of communicating with the spirit
world; it was concerned with propriety in behavior, social responsibility, and the curing of diseases through sacramental medicine (Hilbert,
April 29, 1989). Martin J. Sampson, a Skagit elder, commented that
"Catholicism was, and is, the major adopted religion of the Indians of
Skagit Country." His aboriginal religion taught of a spirit world, a
Creator, and an afterlife, and so did the Catholic priests. "The Indian
observed the similarity of the two doctrines—the life unseen with bodily eyes, the spirit in man, the life that never dies, but lives beyond the
grave—and was readily converted" (Sampson 1972: 13). "The priest,

Father Chirouse, said to them, he said this, 'it is the will of the heavenly father, though your body dies, your soul will live. It just returns from whence it came.'" This was "Christ's message" to the Puget Sound Indians. The Indians replied, "'We believe the same thing. Our breath leaves us. Our bodies return to the earth, yet our souls live.' . . . The beliefs were the same, they thought the same thing. The press yourself religion [so called for the sign of the cross] and their own" (Sampson 1977: 2).

The Indian and Catholic ideas about the spirit world were not the same. The Coast Salish religion was concerned with the retrieval of souls and journeys to and from the other world, which was thought to be just to the west, beyond the waters: "Yet where the Indians went was close. Where their souls are . . . There is nothing but summer there. The Indians are always singing there. They are always happy. Someone with spirit power will go there." Father Chirouse spoke to them of purgatory, heaven, and hell, and these were new concepts to the natives. For all the differences, however, the Indians felt that "the beliefs are the same" (ibid.).

For those Indians who were initiated into Catholic life in their youth, the memory of traditional spirituality and values became combined with Catholic beliefs; however, it would appear that the Coast Salish instilled their aboriginal ideas into the practice of their new faith. An aged Skagit, Ruth Shelton, was recorded saying,

> The son of the Creator said, when he walked here on earth, "There are just two big sins which will cause my death." This self-importance, wishing to become most important leader. Someone wanting money . . . Is selfish with that money. Doesn't give toward the poor. Two, there are two that are foremost of sins. (Metcalf 1954a: 59–60)

She kept to her parental, familial, and ancestral teachings—never to lie, to respect all beings, to send out good thoughts from a good mind—and made them part of her practice of Catholicism. "It is not only that I practice Christianity," she said. "If someone meets misfortune I feel bad. If someone is ill, this makes me unhappy" (64). To her, Jesus was the Changer, a clever inventor of technology and ritual, whose ways one would be wise to follow. Nevertheless, her notion of religiousness was an attitude of reverence which she associated, rightly or wrongly, with the traditional ways of her people.

For Indian peoples for whom the extension of kinship was a

supreme value, the catholicity of the Church appealed to them. They heard the priests saying, "'We are all (brothers & sisters) one people, everywhere on this land. . . . In the beginning we were all one people.' . . . So they accepted this (religion)" (Sampson 1977: 1). They affirmed that "it is just one land that we go to" (Metcalf 1954b: 15), and they admitted their sinfulness as the priest had taught them: "Acknowledgement is made that the supernatural power is compassionate to you[. This is the reason] that you are doing penance here on this poor earth. It is just sin" (ibid.). Still, they attributed their long lives to faith in the ways of their ancestors.

When the Oblates ordered Father Chirouse to quit Washington Territory for British Columbia in 1877, the various Indians of the Puget Sound petitioned the Church that he stay with them. "We Swinomish Indians," read one missive to the local bishop, "all come to pray you to not take away our good father Chirouse. . . . Please tell the pope to not let us perish and to not take our father our Saviour" (Seattle. April 23, 1878). Receiving no change in orders, Chirouse departed in 1878, leaving behind him approximately twenty-five hundred baptized Indian Catholics. In the early part of the twentieth century, Puget Sound Indians were still intent upon continuing the lessons he taught them. One Indian man, for instance, refused to allow his arm to be amputated because "he would no longer be able to make the Sign of the Cross" taught his forebears by the Catholic priest (March 3, 1974). Over a century after Chirouse's departure a Tulalip Indian still recalled the Oblate: "We still have a great love for Father Chirouse. He was a great man. He loved us, and we loved him" (Office of Minority Ministries, April 17, 1988).

In the second half of the nineteenth century the Indians of western Washington met the full force of the white invasion. The newcomers, changers all, erected their webs of telegraphic lines and occupied the sacred spaces of the Coast Salish peoples, crowding them out, taking their land, separating one people from another and forcing others to-gether in tight quarters. The high-class families suddenly became poor, as their forests were denuded and their waters polluted. Those who had secured reservations had at least a buffer against the wave of in-truders. Those who had not, like the Skagits and others, were forced to rely on the generosity of other tribes or fend for themselves as land-less squatters on their own territory, gathering, fishing, even hunting in the old haunts.

The Indian converts quickly suffered a similar fate, becoming minor figures within the institutions of Northwest Catholicism. As early as the 1860s Whites had established their own parishes throughout Wash-ington Territory (which became a state in 1889), and the reservation missions retreated to the backwater of Church consciousness. The Puget Sound missions were incorporated into diocesan assignments, and the progress of Catholicism among the Indians, once deemed so hopeful, soon became "disappointing" (Burns 1988: 498).

Some Puget Sound Indians became disenchanted with the Catholic Church and sought other spiritual avenues, including Protestant de-nominations. Others took elements of Christian practice and belief and reworked them into new religious movements. The most impor-tant of these was the Indian Shaker Church, begun in 1882. In that year a Squaxin man, John Slocum (baptized a Catholic), experienced super-natural revelation. When his wife, Mary, prayed over him in an ecstatic trance the following year and seemingly saved him from death, their followers constructed a church and began to spread the new faith throughout the area. In 1892 they incorporated their church legally in the State of Washington, and by 1900 the new sect was known in In-dian communities around the Puget Sound and into adjacent British Columbia. In the early twentieth century Indian Shaker missioners spread their faith into Oregon and as far south as the Hoopa Indian

Reservation in California. Thousands of Northwest Indians took part in this religious movement; a century after its founding there were said to be a thousand active members (Amoss 1990: 639).

Indian Shakerism had its roots in the shamanistic healing traditions of the Northwest Indians; it also possessed a strain of millenialism associated with the Prophet Dance of the Plateau region. In its ritual, theological, and ecclesiastical aspects, however, it evidenced Catholic (and other Christian) influences. Shaker worship featured lighted candles, rung bells, a communion table, and the repeated sign of the cross. When healing, Shakers brushed away evil, employing a gesture similar to that of their traditional curing rituals; however, in prayer services the Shakers repeatedly signed themselves with the cross, intoning, "In the name of the father . . ." (Lummi Indian Reservation, January 22, 1990), in keeping with the Lushootseed name for Catholicism as the "'press yourself religion' (sign of the cross religion)" (Sampson 1977: 1). Shakers believed in an almighty God, Jesus as His son, and Mary as the mother of Christ. The Indian Shakers appointed bishops and created an ecclesiastical structure like other Christian bodies, so much so that the Catholic hierarchy regarded the Indian Shaker Church as a rival denomination. "The great schism of Shakerism," wrote one representative of the Diocese of Seattle, "still continues to wean many from the fold, but, thanks to God! they generally return at the hour of death" (*Our Negro and Indian Missions* 1926: 40). Well into the 1950s Catholic churchmen throughout western Washington sought ways of protecting Catholic Indians from the influence of the Indian Shakers and regarded the movement as a threat to the Catholic faith. Indeed, in 1938 when Whites were buying up waterfront property on Whidbey Island and displacing the gravesites of Tslalakum, Goliath, and others of the first Lushootseed converts to Catholicism of the 1840s, the Catholic authorities feared that the Shakers would seize the initiative in exhuming and reburying their remains. The bishop, Gerald Shaughnessy, directed his clergy to "assume the lead rather than fall into line with some pagan or civic celebration" (Seattle. March 1, 1938). The parish priest responsible for the Swinomish Indians assured the prelate that "the destruction of Shakerism" (February 28, 1938) was his goal, and he officiated at the reinterment services, keeping the Shakers at bay.

From the time of northwestern Indian treaties of the 1850s and the formation of the Puget Sound reservations, Whites had expected aboriginal religions to fade away under the pressures of Western institutions. Bureau of Indian Affairs agents discouraged or even forbade traditional dances and giveaways. Schools both on and off the reservations attempted to inculcate American values and habits. Indians without reservations to call their own were enveloped by populations of non-Indians and seemed to lose their native identity. With the forests denuded and the fishing areas captured by non-Indians, the traditional economy collapsed and the religious life was endangered. The Church played a significant role in acculturating the Coast Salish, e.g., in providing boarding schools such as Our Lady of Seven Dolors, conducted by the Sisters of Providence at Tulalip from 1869 until 1901, and St. George's School in Tacoma, founded as a government contract school in 1888. In 1891 St. George's became a free mission boarding school; by 1933 over three thousand Indians had attended it. Many Indian parents, particularly those of mixed ethnic heritage, were glad to send their children to St. George's, even though the youths spent a good deal of their time at the school trying to run away (see Seattle. 1930s). It served as a force in adapting Northwest Indians to modern existence.

A Suquamish elder, Lawrence Webster, remembered being sent there with his siblings in the first decade of the twentieth century when he was five years old. His mother figured, "It's going to be a hard winter, and she thought she'd send us over there to cut down on expenses" (Suquamish. March 22, 1982). His parents had been teaching him about gaining spiritual power: fasting at night in a secluded spot on the reservation. Schooling put an end to the training. He attended St. George's through grammar school and when he returned home, Whites were everywhere at Suquamish and the opportunities for vision questing were nil. The place was too crowded to find a secluded spot, and anyway, he recalls, Church authorities and officials of the Bureau of Indian Affairs wanted to put an end to spirit quests and spirit dancing. "They didn't want any more of that. We were supposed to give it up and learn to be Christians." Webster suspected that people in his village would inform the Whites when a ritual had taken place; if you were caught, you had to perform arduous labor for a week or so.

Nonetheless, Puget Sound Indians, including many baptized as Catholics, continued to take an interest in the old-time religion, and when they were able to circumvent the prohibitions on their ceremonials, they kept them up or even revived them. Webster recollected the potlatches held in secret: "Just what they were doing, I'd never be able to tell you, but they all wound up so happy" (ibid.). The pastor of a parish neighboring Lummi warned his bishop in 1936:

> Since 1920 or thereabouts an abuse has grown up amongst the Indians which is pagan in its origin and in its performance. It is known in modern times as a "smoker" but is essentially a rite to a pagan god, calling on his aid to protect his people from sickness and other necessary evils. This affair begins at sundown on Jan. 22 and continues to Friday even or most likely Sat. morning. Besides the religious ceremony of which I know little apart from the fact that some of them become "possessed" and foretell the future, cure illness and so on, it consists chiefly of feasting and much drinking, dancing in a most vulgar manner and each Indian is costumed after the manner of his ancestor, a dog a pig etc. etc. Many if not the far greater majority of the Catholic people attend these doings and thus cause grave scandal and must offend their Creator seriously. I have spoken to them time and time again and intend repeating myself on Sunday as it will be the last opportunity given me before this "smoker" occurs. (Seattle. January 8, 1936)

There were Catholic Indians, he reported, "who abhor and detest" this event and they wished that the bishop would assert his authority by ordering "the practical Catholics at least to abstain from this pagan celebration." For the priest the setting posed an occasion of sin as dangerous as the paganism of the ritual: "This shed is one room perhaps 45 by 30 feet, all sexes of all ages are housed together in this place and it has been reported that grave immorality exists amongst them which if true, must give unspeakable scandal to the young." Despite the bishop's promise to take "stringent methods" (January 10, 1936) against the spirit dance, it persisted as an annual feature of Puget Sound Indian culture and is known these days as Treaty Day.

The Lushootseed Indians recount the legend of the Treaty Day's origin in the early twentieth century. U.S. government officials had banned spirit dancing, so several longhouse representatives met with the Indian agent to plead for their religious rights. He said that if they could prove any truth of their religious claims, he would allow them one night each winter to perform their rituals. A Skagit man sang his power song and a cougar appeared in the agent's room. "All right," the agent conceded, "now I believe you; make it go away" (in Hilbert 1985). From that time onward the Puget Sound Indians, including many baptized Catholics, have danced to their spirits under the disguise of a supposed Treaty Day commemoration.

In the 1930s the Diocese of Seattle counted almost two thousand

Catholic Indians of a total of more than three thousand Indians living throughout the diocese (see Seattle. 1933). Some lived on reservations, such as Lummi, Tulalip, Swinomish, and Suquamish, where they received religious instruction and sacraments at their "so-called reservation churches" ([c. 1933]). Others, like the Skagit, Snoqualmie, and Duwamish peoples, were scattered in various parishes, where the local pastors were encouraged by the bishop to look after them as best they could. Catholic Indians also lived in other areas of the State of Washington, most prominently at Yakima in the south and at Colville in the northeast, as well as at various sites around the Olympic Peninsula on the Pacific coast.

At Tulalip, where Father Chirouse had focused his ministry for two decades, the practice of Catholicism did not meet the standards of priest or bishop in the 1930s. The Indians at Tulalip, wrote Bishop Gerald Shaugnessy, "are all of Catholic stock, well instructed by the original Fr. Ch[i]rouse but greatly neglected around the year 1920 and adjoining years, so that the generation of that period has grown up almost entirely non-instructed and not appreciative of Church Law" (Seattle. September 12, 1935). In particular, the Indians at Tulalip refused to obtain marriage licenses and kept no baptismal records. On Saturday nights they attended dances of a social nature, imbibing alcohol and neglecting the duties of Sunday mass. The several hundred Indians "are supposed to be practically all Catholic, but as with other Indians Shakerism and indifference militate very strongly against a practical Faith," wrote the bishop after his annual visitation to the reservation (April 24, 1939). Even though Tulalip youngsters seemed interested in catechetical instruction, their parents offered no encouragement. In the late 1940s the local priest counted close to two hundred baptized Catholics at Tulalip; however, he reported, "many are lapsed" (September 3, 1948).

The same general picture held true for Lummi and Swinomish. Father John Baptist Boulet had served the Puget Sound Indians for four decades, from the removal of Father Chirouse until 1919. He was less beloved than Chirouse. For instance, at Lummi, it was said, "the Indians frequently forget and at other times refuse to convey him by wagon to the reservation and the Christian instruction of the children has been in many instances neglected" (October 29, 1913). When Boulet died, a shortage of priests spelled the ebbing of Catholic participation at Lummi. The 1930s saw an increase of sacerdotal attention and the bishop found the Lummis "very much attached to their Church" (May 16, 1936). Nevertheless, the bishop noted that "they exhibit the same defects as other Indians, being inclined to Shakerism and indifference" (April 21, 1939). When Bishop Shaughnessy visited Swinomish, "a large number of the crowd went to Communion. The Indian children answered well my questions on the Sacraments," he wrote (April 1939). "All the Indians on the Swinomish Reservation, excepting one family, consider themselves Catholics," reported a priest, although a score of old people "call themselves Shaker & Catholic" ([1948]).

The Suquamish Indians across the Puget Sound from Seattle found that their greatest obstacle to Catholic participation was the presence of Whites who took over the Indians' church in the 1930s. Vacationers and weekenders from the city attended mass at St. Peter's Church, where the Suquamish Indians had buried their dead for several generations, and the natives resented the intrusion by their non-Indian Catholic brethren. Bishop Shaughnessy found there a "serious situation inasmuch as surely the Indians have first right to ministration here, and yet seem to be in the process of being shunted aside, not through the fault of the priest but rather through that of the people" (September 6, 1938). A Jesuit wrote of Suquamish a decade later: "It is very difficult to get any response from the Indians. They are not well organized, they are scattered over the whole of the parish . . . , and there are very few family units." He added that "the few who do come faithfully to Mass are exemplary Catholics," but his ministry was received with indifference by those who were "nominally Catholics at one time." He concluded, "I feel that a good deal of their apathy to the church is the result of resentment that the whites have moved into their church in such numbers that they have practically taken it over. That is what a couple of the old-timers have told me" (August 16, 1948).

The Archdiocese of Seattle wished to hold onto its Indian parishioners. Indeed, the Church authorities tried to accomplish the goal of "parishization" (August 28, 29, 1957)—"to help and encourage them to become active, integrated members of their local parishes" (November 22, 1960), and to make the parish priest the center of Indian community life both on and off the reservations. However, the Indians at Suquamish were outnumbered by Whites and the parish priests needed to direct their attention to the largest numbers of Catholics. By

1956 St. Peter's no longer served the Suquamish Indians of the vicinity; the parish priest said of them, "Most of the Indians are Shakers. Only a very few Indian families go to the Catholic Church" (August 21, 1956).

During the 1960s and 1970s disaffection from the local church made the Suquamish people susceptible to the questioning of old moralities and worldviews which became current throughout North America. In a general environment of permissiveness, Indians found it easy to say no to mass, to priests, to the Church, to religion itself. Some took to the smokehouses, reasserting their tribal identity through spirit dancing. Half of the Suquamish might continue to call themselves Catholics; however, only a small percentage maintained any active association with Catholicism (Forsman, January 16, 1990).

"I was raised as a Catholic," Lawrence Webster recalled in 1982, but the Suquamish religion seemed a more adequate faith, in retrospect. It had its own moral rules and the people tended to keep them. As for the golden rule of Christianity, "we don't follow it very well." When Webster looked at the behavior of Christians and the policies of supposed Christan nations, producing atomic weapons or permitting racial discrimination, for instance, "I begin to think the old Indian was right" (Suquamish. March 22, 1982). According to Webster, "old Indians believed that you're just going on to another world and that you will be back. You're not going away forever, you'll return. If not bodily, your spirit will come back." Consequently, Indians were not afraid of death. "They're just going on to another world. You came from the earth, you return to the earth." Webster did not reject all of the Catholicism of his youth. He remembered "really beautiful" hymns translated into his language by Father Chirouse and he appreciated the Christian emphasis on a "Supreme Being." Nonetheless, he had his questions: "Whether there's a true religion or not, I don't know. I begin to wonder about so much of it."

Suquamish old-timers, interviewed in the early 1980s by young Indians more interested in recollections about the longhouse religion, told of their fond but fading memories of their Catholic youth. Martha George talked about the "wonderful priest, the one that . . . learnt the Indian language and he taught them how to pray in Indian." She sang "Angels We Have Heard on High" in Lushootseed and translated it into English: "Angels are over at the prairie singing. . . . they were singin[g] about God coming to earth, you know, an[d] lived here a while an[d] then went to heaven" (January 13,

1982). She tried to bring to mind the Catholic prayers of her youth: "I used to know the Hail Mary in Indian, but I'm even forgetting that, now" (July 23, 1982). Bernard Adams said, "I used to be an altar boy that could say these long prayers in Latin. Of course I didn't know what I was saying, but I could do it" (March 24, 1982). John Loughrey, whose father was neither Indian nor religious, remembered his upbringing:

> Oh yeah, we were . . . Catholics but we were . . . never church-goers. . . . my mother was a good Catholic, in fact she was buried as a Catholic. . . . she had the priest with her when she died. . . . she wasn't religious . . . , she didn't overdo things. But she believed. . . . Well, I do too, as far as that goes. . . . I think there's someone that takes care of us, there must be. (November 4, 1982).

According to non-Indians who lived among them, "the Suquamish Indians were all Catholics, invariably they were all Catholics" (September 1982). In the most recent decades, however, the culture of the Church was a matter of ambiguous memory among the venerable and the young were looking elsewhere for their religious fulfilment.

The same kind of pattern developed at Lummi. Even though the Lummis helped celebrate the centennial of St. Joachim's founding in 1961, the church was less and less associated with the reservation. By 1967 the parish priests reported a "very grave situation," in that the Lummi Indians felt "discriminated against" by the fact that there was no resident priest among them. Most of those attending St. Joachim's were tourists and other Whites. Before long, the priest wrote, "we will have lost all of our Catholic Indians there" (July 27, 1967) to the pull of Mormons and the traditional Indian religion.

At Swinomish, too, in the 1960s, St. Paul's stood "locked each Sabbath and only a handful cross the Swinomish Slough Bridge for Mass at Sacred Heart Church, LaConner, a mile away" (Wyne, October 4, 1968: 6). Laura Edwards explained that the few hundred Swinomish, Skagit, Samish, and Snoqualmie Indians living on the reservation "didn't feel we were wanted in LaConner when they stopped having Sunday Mass at St. Paul's" (in ibid.). Archbishop Thomas A. Connolly determined to reopen St. Paul's in 1968, following a five-year hiatus brought about by a shortage of priests, and the new priest of the "mission-parish," Father Michael J. Cody, set out to reestablish ties between the Church and the Swinomish Reservation. "I have to share with them," he said. "I have to sit down and eat with them. I have to go to meetings and listen and share myself with them. . . . I have to feel I'm growing as a priest with them. Taking what they have to offer as a culture makes one a better person and a better Christian" (in ibid., October 25, 1968: 6).

The Swinomish were receptive to the attentions of the Church. Dewey Mitchell, the tribal chairman, acknowledged the presence of Protestant bodies on the reservation: "It's funny," he said of his people, "they may go to other churches, but they still regard themselves as Catholics." Even though, as he noted, "in the past 20 years a lot have been Catholic in name only," they were willing to build a new altar adorned with Indian images. Father Cody attested that "they should know as soon as they enter that they are in the church on the Indian reservation. It has to be totally different and totally beautiful" (in ibid.). The priest had in mind a new church building on the model of a Northwest Coast Indian longhouse, fronted by a totem pole with a crucifix on top. In a proposal to the Catholic Church Extension Society for $150,000 (Seattle, January 13, 1969), he claimed a potential congregation of two hundred adult Catholics on the reservation.

The grant of money did not materialize. Neither did the large number of Indian parishoners. In 1971 Father Cody admitted to his archbishop that mass attendance at Swinomish averaged only three dozen each Sunday, only half of those being Indians. Most of the native churchgoers were small children, unaccompanied by their parents. Cody conducted only one baptism in three years, and no marriages. He tried to conduct religious education on Saturdays, using Indian legends as a basis for understanding Catholicism. A dozen children attended these lessons erratically. "I consider only six families on Swinomish to be anywhere near a standard concept of active parishioner" (January 19, 1971). "Tribalism," the priest wrote, and a "fragmented culture" prevented any progress on his part in creating a "genuine Christian community." He found his initiatives blocked by one family or another, and although at first he sensed acceptance as a spiritual leader to the Swinomish people, he now felt rejected. "[I]t is impossible," he declared, "for a white Catholic priest (probably also an indian Catholic priest) to function in his leadership role as pastor" on the reservation. Lacking a staff with anthropological and psychological training, Father Cody asked his Archbishop Connolly for "permission to quietly close St. Paul's church" and have the faithful Catholics of

Swinomish attend services in LaConner. "[I]t galls me to have to admit defeat," he concluded. "However, this is the reality."

In March 1971 Father Cody announced the closing of St. Paul's. Immediately, members of the Swinomish community, non-Catholics as well as congregants, petitioned the archbishop to keep the church open. Such a breaking off of services, they argued, would be experienced as an example of the "ravaging power" of Whites over Indians, and the "spiritual hurt will be long lasting and, with our cultural spiritual beliefs virtually extinct, we find this action of closing the church extremely difficult to accept as an act of God." One Indian man recalled that in the past, "when the priest stopped coming then the people began not to go to church." A Swinomish woman pleaded, "We would miss having Mass every Sunday and keeping our children in touch with God—right here on our own reservation. . . . I would not know what to do without having to visit God every Sunday." The petitioners concluded, "We pledge earnestly to attend Mass as often as it is possible for us to do so in the future" (March 18, 1971).

Petitions notwithstanding, the archbishop decided to discontinue regular services at St. Paul's, although the prelate promised the community that mass would be said there "when circumstances permit" (March 24, 1971). Connolly attempted to find another priest—it was a time of clerical shortages—to take the assignment, but clergy "failed to materialize" (March 30, 1972) for the assignment. It was not until 1985 that the archdiocese found another priest, Father Patrick J. Twohy, S.J., to offer a regular ministry at Swinomish.

MODERN RENEWAL

Father Twohy came to Swinomish with experience in Indian ministry, having served on the Colville Reservation for several years. Before accepting his new job on the Puget Sound in 1985, he penned these words:

> We missionaries can play the game of fitting our lives and the lives of the Peoples we intensely love into categories of meaning and purpose that slake the institutional Church's thirst for numbers, order, correct forms, "growth," and "progress." But it is only a game. The categories never really fit. The Spiritual Life of the Indian People is too wide and powerful, their hearts have suffered too much to be understood by Western European modes of thinking. . . . They must be allowed to be who they are, to do what they want to do . . . , or they must be exterminated. (in Office of Minority Ministries 1988)

Having experienced "turmoil" (Swinomish Indian Reservation, January 14, 1990) in Indian ministry, he asked himself what his role should be among Indian peoples. He suggested that he would do best to be a good neighbor without pretending that he had anything of value to offer them. "When a Jesuit comes to live with Indian people," he mused, "it is better if he comes to listen and to learn. This can make him very anxious for it is not our usual way. But whatever he does know will probably fail him, so it is better that he learn to let what he thinks he knows go on by. Gradually," Father Twohy concluded, "the People will help him to know what he is to share with them. This can take many years" (Office of Minority Ministries 1988, June 27, 1985).

With the help of several sisters—two Dominicans and a Sister of St. Joseph of Peace—Father Twohy tried to locate elders at Swinomish and Tulalip who might commit themselves to lay leadership in the local churches. Rather than establishing himself as the authoritative representative of Catholicism on the reservations, Twohy sought to draw out the leadership already present in the community, asking both women and men to serve as Eucharistic and educational ministers to their own people. In the nineteenth and early twentieth century the Coast Salish Catholics had provided their own catechists to the Church; Twohy attempted to recreate that stewardship as part of a formal Indian ministry in the Archdiocese of Seattle. Understanding that the Puget Sound Indians wanted religious activity to affirm themselves locally as a people within the Catholic Church, Twohy emphasized the specialness of the Catholic forms they themselves would create. Recognizing their suspicion of anyone trying to intervene between the individual and the divine, he encouraged an autonomy of the spirit among his Indian congregants. At powwows Father Twohy felt inspired to perform in full regalia the fancy dances he had learned at Colville. At Treaty Day ceremonials he blessed the spirit dancers' costumes and sat in as an appreciative audience to their native religiousness. In church services he led as little as possible, turning to locals such as Robert Joe, Landy James, and Eileen Charles to preach and distribute communion. Before too long the Swinomish and Tulalip Catholics were said to feel "empowered" (ibid., February 25, 1988) by Twohy's ministry. Catholic elders testified that the new Indian ministry was an answer to their prayers after more than a decade of neglect by the Church, and even non-Catholic Lushootseed Indians were calling him a "sweet," "darling" man (Hilbert, January 10, 1990), greatly "loved" (April 4, 1987) by the Indians of the Puget Sound area. Some of the Indians thought of him as a lost soul, searching for comfort and spiritual guidance and a good meal. People took him in, fed him, told him old stories, and allowed him to participate in their rituals because they felt pity for him, an unmarried man living by himself, and they empathized with his gentle, humane, searching spirit (see Hilbert, April 29, 1989).

Father Twohy's Indian ministry was part of the archdiocese's attempt to accommodate the various ethnicities of the region (including many Asian nationalities) in the spirit of the Second Vatican Council's commitment to inculturating the Catholic faith. In the 1970s a series of Indian masses took place in Seattle and Tacoma as the archdiocese began to take stock of the Catholic Indian population in its midst. It was estimated in 1979 (Beaver 1979: 187–188) that the Archdiocese of Seattle had approximately four thousand Indian Catholics. (The Diocese of Yakima had a thousand, mostly Yakimas; the Diocese of Spokane had three to four thousand, primarily Salishan and Sahaptian tribes on the Colville Reservation.) In 1983 Archbishop Raymond G. Hunthausen reported close to seven thousand Catholic Indians in his archdiocese out of a total population of well over thirty thousand Indians—many of them Native Americans from across the northwest

United States and western Canada. The five main populations of indigenous Puget Sound Indian Catholics were at the Lummi, Tulalip,
Swinomish, Suquamish, and Skagit reservations, totalling about five
thousand baptized Catholics (Marquette. DCRAA. 1983), with a thousand or more Indian Catholics, e.g., Puyallups, in the Tacoma area. In
1988 the archdiocese counted over eleven thousand Indian Catholics,
roughly 25 percent of the total population of Indians in the region. Beyond the reservations Indian Catholics represented from 1 to 4 percent
of the congregations in nineteen parishes throughout the archdiocese,
including rural and urban locales (Office of Minority Ministries 1988).

In 1987 Archbishop Hunthausen commissioned a study of the
Catholic Indians within his domain. At the same time he took the lead
in signing, along with nine other Christian denominational leaders, "A
Public Declaration to the Tribal Councils and Traditional Spiritual
Leaders of the Indian and Eskimo Peoples of the Pacific Northwest"
(ibid.). Addressed "in care of" Jewell Praying Wolf James, a Lummi
who was spearheading efforts to protect American Indian religious
freedoms nationwide, the declaration constituted "a formal apology
on behalf of our churches for their long-standing participation in the
destruction of traditional Native American practices." The signatories
affirmed the rights of Indians to engage in traditional ceremonies and
to gain access to sacred sites on public lands, and they asserted that
"the spiritual power of the land and the ancient wisdom of your indigenous religions can be, we believe, great gifts to the Christian
churches." And in closing, "May the God of Abraham and Sarah, and
the Spirit who lives in both the cedar and Salmon People be honored
and celebrated."

In order to reach out to the Indians of the Puget Sound, "many
with strong cultural ties to the Catholic Church" (Office of Minority
Ministries 1987), Hunthausen created in 1988 a Pastoral Ministry to
Native Americans, headed by Father Twohy and Sister Barbara Bieker,
O.P., and an advisory group made up of native and non-native lay and
religious, coordinated by Joan Staples-Baum, a part-Ojibway living in
Tacoma. The director of the Office of Minority Ministries for the archdiocese, Esther M. Lucero, told the archbishop that "despite neglect
and outright hostility, the Indian people have remained faithful to the
Church and hungry for the Word of God." These included, she said,
"the children of people who were severely beaten in the mission
schools for speaking their own language, or denied the Sacraments by

priests who refused to serve the missions in their parishes. A great deal of healing is needed" (Office of Minority Ministries 1988, May 12, 1988).

The archdiocese determined that a special ministry was necessary for the Puget Sound "Indians of Catholic heritage,"

> because many Indians consider themselves Catholic although they are not currently practicing. This is due to the lack or unpredictability of Masses, confusion over the Church's attitude toward multiple marriages, and the concurrent practice of traditional cultural and religious ceremonies. There is also a deep respect and reverence for the Catholicism of their grandparents, and memories of the Oblate Fathers such as Reverend Chirouse continue to be treated with great love and respect. (Ibid.)

Some of these Indians on reservations felt that the Church did not care about them; others living off the reservations, including Indians who had moved to the Puget Sound region from elsewhere, felt lost in their non-Indian parishes. "I speak as an Urban Indian," wrote Joan Staples-Baum (ibid., April 20, 1988), "when I say that it is very lonely to be a Catholic Native American in the Archdiocese of Seattle. I have to go North to Tulalip, . . . Lummi or . . . Swinomish if I want to pray with my Native People. We have churches that serve the Blacks, Hispanics, Asians, etc., why not the Native American Indian?" For all these Indians the Church wanted to provide the opportunity of special inculturative liturgies. "The old ways have not been lost," one report said, "but are used to give expression to the Catholic sacraments in uniquely Indian ways" (Office of Minority Ministries 1987). Although Indian liturgies might offend some non-Indian Catholics, and even Indian Catholics would need to adjust to native elements in Catholic rites, the archdiocese seemed committed to create a special ministry to the Native Americans. Many of these Indians, wrote one pastor near Tacoma, "will not enter into a white setting nor attend Mass with people in the white community. It seems essential to develop some kind of liturgies for them apart from the white community so that they can enter into worship in the Catholic way" (Office of Minority Ministries 1988, March 28, 1988).

The last decade has witnessed a growth of Catholic activities throughout the Puget Sound area. There have been conferences in honor of Kateri Tekakwitha, retreats for teenagers, classes to prepare people for the sacraments, Easter vigils, ecumenical feasts, a women's

Cursillo, powwow masses, and the like. Father Twohy has blessed the burgeoning fishing enterprises in the various Indian communities, and he has attended traditional namings, burnings, and other rituals throughout the region. Catechists like Barbara James and elders such as Laura Edwards have provided stability to the native understanding of Church tenets and worship. Catholic practice at Swinomish, Tulalip, and Lummi has grown markedly in personal commitment if not in numbers of weekly communicants. Robert Joe, a Eucharistic minister and pillar of the Swinomish church, has exhorted his people: "We need more young people in the churches. We've been kind of lax in getting around to ask people why they aren't in church. The reservation has a lot of Catholics. If they all came, it would fill up the church" (Office of Minority Ministries 1988, February 29, 1988). Landy James has added, "The smokehouse is growing because people need something to identify with, to reach out for. We need to show that there are many parallels between the Church and traditional religion . . . , that there is no conflict with traditional religion." And Bertha Dan of Swinomish: "We have to prove that our God is real. Not some weak-kneed something that will let us sin one day and preach before the people the next. . . . We're not as strong as our mothers and grandmothers. We *had* to go to church. . . . Landy's grandmother . . . used to preach fire and brimstone. . . ." At Tulalip Rachel Hood has said, "Our oldest traditions are gone, but have been replaced by the Catholic traditions. They are now our oldest traditions" (April 17, 1988).

At Lummi the faith has progressed despite several obstacles. By the late 1980s, when the Archdiocese of Seattle conducted interviews with Indian Catholics, many of the Lummis were reported to have "fallen away" from Catholic participation. "Maybe they don't understand the new Church," one woman said. "They all show up for funerals and other gatherings. We need to work out their differences with the Church" (April 7, 1988). A Lummi woman suggested that "a lot of people fell away because traditional dancing was banned at church." Another Lummi woman said, "In Canada, they do a Shaker and Catholic service together. I would like to see that happen here."

"Our core of Christians has been brought up to be antitraditional" retorted Bill James, a Lummi tribal archivist. "Even though they want to be traditional now, they don't know how to be" (ibid.). He missed the old pageantry of the Church: the Corpus Christi processions, the Gregorian Chant. "I'm not too happy with the contemporary

Church. . . . There are a lot of people who feel that way. . . . I remember the high Latin Masses, the mystery of the Church. Now it's lost its mystery. . . ." In his younger days, he said, there was catechetical training. People knew what to do in church, how to behave. There was discipline. Now, he suggested, the young people do not have "training in the Church" and so they do not bring their children in for baptism. Other Lummis stay away from the sacraments, suggested Rena Ballew of Lummi, because of confusion regarding the rules of matrimony. "I think there are a lot of married people who would like previous marriages annulled," she said. "Maybe there could be a workshop on it. My daughter was married by a minister, now can't remarry in church."

Father Twohy has attempted to open the lines of communication between the Archdiocese and the Catholic Indians at Lummi, and to some extent he has been successful. Although he has been a greater presence at Swinomish and Tulalip, he has also helped make Catholicism more vital among the Lummis. Whatever strengths Catholic faith has at Lummi, it must coexist with other religious organizations. For example, when the Lummi elder Norbert Charles died in 1990, his funeral was held in St. Joachim's Catholic Church. The night before, however, the community put on a lengthy prayer service in the reservation gymnasium, conducted jointly by Catholic lay prayer leaders, drummers from the local longhouse, Indian Shakers, and representatives of a contemporary religious development from Yakima called the Seven Drums Religion. Each of the religious organizations provided its own form of consolation to the living and aid to the deceased. Each denomination sang its prayers and exhorted the hundreds of Indians in the audience, performing separately and sequentially. When it was time for the feast of elk meat, all of the worshippers ate together in honor of the dead. At Lummi as well as throughout the Puget Sound region, the Coast Salish recognize the helpful validity of several religious traditions, Catholicism among them. A recent widow, not a baptized Catholic but adorned with rosary beads at the spirit dancing of the Swinomish Treaty Day, publicly thanked Vernon Lane, the Lummi Catholic prayer leader, for the comfort he had given her a month before when her husband died (Lummi, January 22, 1990). For her and for the other Coast Salish people, attending prayer services for the dead is a preeminent act of religiousness, more significant than attending to the weekly calendar of Christian masses. The Indians come out in large numbers to mark the periodic crises brought by death. To pray together, in the manner of Catholics, Shakers, longhouse members, etc., is more spiritually significant than the chronic obligation to Catholic liturgy. These Indians are still on "Indian time," meaning not that they are unobservant about time, but that their "clock" is the timepiece of the beating heart. They come together when a meaning-ful event occurs in their community, not merely when the bells ring at ten o'clock on a Sunday morning.

A Swinomish altar boy tolls the bell in the short steeple at St. Paul's church, calling the faithful to Sunday mass (Swinomish Indian Reser-vation, January 14, 1990). The reservation comprises ten square miles on an island across the bridge from the artists' colony of LaConner. On the mainland where cedar forests stood tall not so many decades ago, there are now Victorian farmhouses and flat muckland, where non-Indians raise flowers and vegetables for market. On the reserva-tion fish nets hang in the yards, next to neat wood houses. The road passes a churchyard, a bingo hall, the Longhouse Restaurant, a fish processing plant, and a mini-mart. Across from the church is a school, tribal headquarters, senior citizens' housing, and a gymnasium. Up the road in the moss-covered woods is a Shaker church made of cedar shingle.

Inside the entryway to St. Paul's is the visage of Kateri Tekakwitha, sided by a version of the Catholic Ladder. Next to the old altar is a big yarn eye of God with feather pendants. A Mexican blanket covers the altar and several Pendleton blankets lie on the floor ready to be worn and given as gifts. Even as the bell rings for mass, Father Twohy and his Swinomish right-hand man, Robert Joe, are still on their way from celebrating mass in LaConner. Sister Barbara Bieker, O.P. greets the congregants as they arrive and Beverly Peters, the Swinomish music director, hands out the hymn books. Half a dozen native matriarchs arrive; little children, young adults, non-Indians, and visitors collect. By 10:30 the little church is filled (perhaps half of those present are Na-tive Americans), and the celebrants have arrived. Father Twohy says mass here every other Sunday, alternating with Tulalip. On alternate Sundays there is a communion service led by Robert Joe, who is also tribal chairman and leader of the longhouse. There is also a bible study group every Wednesday evening.

Father Twohy and Mr. Joe say mass together. They walk out in tan-dem with the altar boy. Mr. Joe heads the Mass of the Word: leading prayers, reading the gospel, delivering a homily. Father Twohy also gives a sermon and performs the Mass of the Sacrifice, handling the bread and wine; however Mr. Joe is at his side, reciting the incantation at the Transubstantiation along with the priest. When Father Twohy elevates the host, Mr. Joe enacts the same gestures, empty-handed. It would be wrong to say that they hold equal performative power at the mass—the priest is the sacramental authority—but Twohy and Joe share as much of the duties as possible within the strictures of canon law. Mr. Joe glances out occasionally to his Swinomish audience, chuckling slightly as if he were playing an awkward role on stage.

On this Sunday there are two special events, both concerning non-Indians associated with the parish. Two local Whites who call this church "a refuge" for them are renewing their wedding vows, accompanied by their family. The Indians treat them warmly and give them the Pendleton blankets as gifts. "We wondered about you two at first," Mr. Joe jokes in his speech of witness to their matrimonial union. There is also a memorial service for an English woman who spent her last years in the senior citizens' home on the reservation. Her relatives, strangers to the Swinomish, appear uncomfortable throughout the ritual. This is an Indian church to be sure; however, it ministers to non-Indians as well. The gifts of blankets, the speeches of witness, are both native traditions worked into the service; both serve the non-Indians as well as the Native Americans. The Indians act as hosts in the church to the non-Indian outsiders, welcoming them hospitably. One Indian man says at the mass that he expresses his faith by trying to transcend any ill feelings he may feel toward Whites who have taken his people's lands. Being a Catholic for him means "going beyond bitterness" and honoring those whom one is tempted to hate. In like manner, Mr. Joe serves as Eucharistic minister in LaConner among the Whites as well as in his home community.

In his sermon Mr. Joe speaks about opening the door to the spirit, to God. He uses the imagery of God—the Spirit—"shining around" certain people, e.g., the married couple and the deceased woman. He refers to the service as "helping" the soul of the dead to "reach" the afterworld. The language is suitable for Christianity but it comes from a longhouse member whose ideas of spirit are in harmony with traditional Coast Salish concepts. When he addresses the congregants, he calls them "beloved," an expression of tender affection familiar to the gospels but also very much at home in the Lushootseed terminology of respect. As a Coast Salish man, Mr. Joe is cojoining his native and

Catholic expressions of spirituality and endearment, creating a single mode of public religiousness. Mr. Joe is not so much combining Lushootseed and Catholic forms as he is employing a language which is expressive of both religious worldviews.

Father Twohy's sermon meditates on Jesus' baptism. He states that there was nothing special about Jesus. He wasn't rich or powerful—things the world thinks highly of—but he was a man of spirit and compassion. The priest tells his Indian audience in effect that they are like Jesus: seemingly poor and powerless but endowed with spirituality and solicitude. He says that when he first listened to Petius (Isadore Tom), a recently deceased Coast Salish healer, he thought he was hearing the gospel of John with all of its sympathetic phrases. Now he finds it hard to listen to his fellow white priests; their language is so blunt and aggressive compared to the caring language of Mr. Joe and his kinsmen. Father Twohy exhorts the Swinomish at mass to live up to the ideals of their ancestors and the values of their native tongue.

After mass the "wandering padre," as the Swinomish refer to Father Twohy, joins in a meal with the churchgoers and the old-timers at the senior citizens' housing, where he lives. They demonstrate their joy in his presence, and he in theirs. In conversation he attests to his goal of making Catholic worship at Swinomish an articulation of local culture. He must also be faithful to Catholic rules; however, he wants the Swinomish to feel at home in their own Catholic church at St. Paul's. He has no desire to import pan-Indian ritualism from elsewhere in Native North America; the Tekakwitha conferences jar his sensibilities with their combination of ceremonial elements from the Southwest, Plains, and so on. Here on the Puget Sound he encourages his congregation to express themselves religiously in ways that feel appropriate to them.

"Never back the Indians into a corner," a Blackfoot Catholic priest once told Twohy. Never insist that they do this or that. They won't say no but they might not want to do the thing you demand, and so they will resent your imposition. Father Twohy makes suggestions but he spends more time listening to Indians as they work out their own modes of Catholic expression. If they transpose ideas or utterances among their longhouse, Shaker, and Catholic locales, so be it. Twohy does not try to initiate syncretistic ritual; nor does he pretend to hold authority in religious realms beyond the Catholic Church, or obstruct the local manufacture of a religious life which combines aspects of native and Catholic spiritual culture. When Robert Joe wears his black paint face at Treaty Day, Father Twohy offers no objection. He blesses the Treaty Day fire and paraphernalia; he observes spirit dancing; he adds his words at prayer services for the dead. But he tries to let the Coast Salish Catholics be themselves, by themselves. If Sunday mass is not the central ritual of their religious lives—many more of them attend the Treaty Day spirit dancing and the round of funerals—he is content for them to celebrate the religiousness that is theirs.

In the Swinomish longhouse before an audience of more than a thousand Indian Catholics and Church personnel from across North America (Seattle, Swinomish, Lummi, August 5, 1993), Father Twohy proclaims the meaning of "traveling in deep waters." He invokes the image of salmon swimming in the depths and suggests that we are all fellow travelers, searching for salvific wisdom.

> I think of the profound respect that Isadore Tom, holy man, and Vernon Lane, Catholic prayer-leader, kept for each other up at Lummi. I think of the bond between Kenny Moses, a healing man among all of the People here, and myself, a priest. Whether we are at the Smokehouse or Spiritual Centre doesn't really matter because the depth at which we are swimming is far beneath the surface where ignorance, fear, anger, and resentment always tear at the waters. (*Tekakwitha Conference Newsletter* 12, no. 3, September/October 1993: 16)

Father Twohy has tried to establish a new epoch of good will between the Coast Salish and the Church, and with more than a little success.

The missionaries of an earlier age did not seek the good will of the Indians; they sought their conversion and their obedient loyalty to the Roman Catholic Church. Today the relationships between the Puget Sound Indians and the Church are more ambiguous than the pioneer missioners would have wanted. This is an era—truly a new, ambiguous age—in which large portions of popular culture esteem traditional Indian spirituality more highly than they do the mainline faith of the missionary fathers. This is an epoch in which Church authorities like the late Archbishop Hunthausen apologized for the missionary past and in which a priest like Father Twohy praises the values of native healers, even to the disparagement of his fellow clerics.

In St. Peter's churchyard on the Suquamish Reservation lies the grave of Chief Seattle, a nineteenth-century Duwamish leader who is currently an object of some veneration to non-Indians. His speeches, or least texts of an ecological bent purporting to be such, have been on the best-seller lists in recent years (see Egan, April 21, 1992). Seattle's grave has a cross upon it and a wood monument surmounted by two canoes, carved by a local troop of boy scouts. There are offerings upon the grave—stones, a carrot, a bandana, remains of a fire—left by Whites who regard Seattle's life with romantic nostalgia (Hilbert, January 10, 1990).

To his own people his reputation is far less glorious. They recall that he was one of the first of the Puget Sound chiefs to receive baptism, taking the biblical name of Noah in the 1840s. As Indians and Whites vied for land, Chief Seattle befriended the Christian invaders and played a pivotal role at one point by warning the Whites of an impending Indian attack. For that deed the city of Seattle bears his name. The scattered Duwamish have not forgotten that they are a landless people, thanks in part to the turning of their renowned chief's loyalties. Nor have the other Puget Sound Indians forgotten. "This is why (Chief Seattle) was so highly honored by the white people at Seattle," a Skagit woman once said, "because he saved them from being killed. It was not because he was a leader that you folks know about him" (Metcalf 1954a: 50). Nevertheless, the Coast Salish also regard Chief Seattle with reverence befitting an ancestor of noble title and spiritual power. His name has been passed down through the years and is currently held by Jewell Praying Wolf James, the Lummi activist. Puget Sound Indians continue to sing his spirit power songs, treating them as mighty hymns and cultural treasures.

The cross upon his grave and his resting place in a consecrated churchyard indicate that when he died in 1866 he was still considered a Catholic. Even among his Lushootseed people in the twentieth century he has been remembered for a speech he once made to them, in which he seems to advance the cause of conversion: "You folks observe the changers who have come to this land. And our progeny will watch and learn from them now, our children and they will become just like the changers who have come here to us on this land. You folks observe them well" (in Hilbert 1985; cf. Hilbert 1991).

Chief Seattle made another speech, however, at the Treaty of Point Elliott in 1855—a treaty in which the governor of Washington Territory, Isaac I. Stevens, proposed (and gained) land cessions from twenty and more tribal groups around the Puget Sound. Among his spirit helpers Seattle had Thunder; for this reason he could be heard a half mile away when he delivered his Lushootseed orations.

Translators conveyed his 1855 speech into Chinook Jargon. Over twenty years later a white man who heard the talk wrote it down for the first time. It has become a classic of American Indian oral literature, a timeless Native American address not only to Governor Stevens but to all Whites:

> 1. Your religion was written on tablets of stone by the iron finger of an angry God lest you forget. 2. The red man could never comprehend nor remember it. 3. Our religion is the tradition of our ancestors, 4. [t]he dreams of our old men, given to them in the solemn hours of the night by the great spirit and the visions of our leaders[,] and it is written in the hearts of our people. 5. Your dead cease to love you and the land of their nativity as soon as they pass the portals of the tomb; they wander far away beyond the stars and are soon forgotten and never return. 6. Our dead never forget this beautiful world that gave them being. 7. They always love its winding rivers, its great mountains, and its sequestered vales, and they ever yearn in tenderest affection over the lonely-hearted living and often return to visit guide and comfort them. 8. We will ponder your proposition, and when we decide we will tell you. 9. But should we accept it, I here and now make this the first condition that we will not be denied the privilege, without molestation, of visiting at will the graves, where we have buried our ancestors, and our friends, and our children. 10. Every part of this country is sacred to my people. Every hillside, every valley, every plain and grove has been hallowed by some fond memory or some sad experience of my tribe. 11. Even the rocks which seem to lie dumb as they swelter in the sun along the silent seashore in solemn grandeur thrill with memories of past events connected with the lives of my people. 12. And when the last red man shall have perished from the earth and his memory among the white man shall have become a myth these shores will swarm with the invisible dead of my tribe; 13. and when your children's children shall think themselves alone in the fields, the store, the shop, upon the highway, or in the silence of the pathless woods, they will not be alone. In all the earth there is no place dedicated to solitude. 14. At night when the streets of your cities and villages will be silent and you think them deserted, they will throng with returning hosts that once filled and still love this beautiful land. 15. The white man will never be alone. Let him be just and deal kindly with my people for the dead are not powerless. 16. Dead—did I say? There is no death, only a change of worlds. (Hilbert 1985; cf. Hilbert 1991)

For some Coast Salish people as well as non-Indians, Chief Seattle's famous speech stands as an unassailable argument for aboriginal sensibilities and against the hunger of Whites for lands and conversions.

In spite of his Catholic identity, Chief Seattle is best remembered today as an exponent of native spirituality.

A Skagit knowledgeable in his people's traditions of spirit power songs—and also a baptized and confirmed Catholic—has remarked on the shrinking availability of natural resources upon which to support the oldtime religion of his people:

> Only if it is good ground, sacred ground would there be spirit powers present. That is no longer possible today, because if you were to go to camp at Mr. Rainier, or Mt. Baker, in the morning there you would find, there a beer bottle, and over there, and there, no more is there a good place. There are no spirit powers there any more, because the white people who come here have caused them to be no more by what they bring there. . . . It has become polluted, the earth is contaminated now. (Sampson 1977: 21).

In this degraded spiritual environment the traditions of Catholicism have seemed to him almost ameliorative. "Christianity gives us strength to this day," he has said. It "stands us up" in the way a Skagit healer does to a sick person in order to get the patient to sing of the spirits and thereby recover health. "If it were not for Christianity there would be no Indians today" (17).

What kind of Indians are they, and what kind of Catholics? There are Coast Salish Catholics who still feel the hurt of the missionary insistence that their traditional culture was reprehensible. The priests said, "You are sinful, vile," and the Indians wondered, "What have I done?" (Hilbert, April 4, 1987). Some have accepted the notion that Christianity is the modern fulfillment of the aboriginal spirituality; however, many others have returned to native practices once outlawed and considered moribund. Some attend mass and receive the sacraments, but many of these wear the native facepaint on Treaty Day. Many have transcended their bitterness toward the Church; others have turned away from Catholic institutions and are irreconcilable to them. Their association with their own Catholic identity has been ambiguous for many generations now, and continues to be so.

Several years ago Father Twohy invited Robert Joe to address a gathering of Jesuits in Seattle. The Swinomish Eucharistic minister told the following story (cf. Vecsey 1992: 53), which is a favorite of his when addressing Catholic audiences (Seattle, Swinomish, Lummi, August 4, 1993):

A priest came to an Indian village. He performed religious instruction and baptized the whole village, except for one elder, who resisted conversion. So, the priest visited him and finally baptized him, giving him a new, Christian name.

The priest told the elder that there were three rules he was compelled to follow: go to mass on Sunday, confess your sins on Saturday, and abstain from eating meat on Friday.

Pretty soon, however, the priest found the elder on a Friday, cooking venison in a pot. He asked him, "Why are you eating deer meat rather than fish?"

"I am eating fish," the elder replied.

"Don't lie to me," said the priest.

"I'm not lying," said the elder. "This *is* a fish. When I killed a deer, I took it down to the river and baptized it, and I changed its name to 'fish.'"

BIBLIOGRAPHY

ARCHIVAL SOURCES

All citations of archival sources in the text list archive name, file name (if applicable), and date with a period after the archive and file names (e.g., Marquette. DCRAA. 1980).

APS	American Philosophical Society Library Archives, Philadelphia, Pennsylvania
Houma	Historical Research Center, Diocese of Houma-Thibodaux, Thibodaux, Louisiana
Kansas City	Chancery Archives, Archdiocese of Kansas City in Kansas
Lushootseed	Lushootseed Research Archives, Seattle, Washington
Marquette	Department of Special Collections, Marquette University Memorial Library, Milwaukee, Wisconsin. Files include: BCIM (Bureau of Catholic Indian Missions); DCRAA (Diocesan Corrrespondence, Reports, and Applications for Aid); JINNAM (Jesuits in North American Ministry); TCA (Tekakwitha Conference Archives).
Notre Dame	The Archives of the University of Notre Dame, Notre Dame, Indiana
Ogdensburg	Chancery Archives, Diocese of Ogdensburg, New York
OMMS	Office of Multicultural Ministry Services, Archdiocese of Seattle, Washington
Portland	Chancery Archives, Diocese of Portland, Maine
Seattle	Chancery Archives, Archdiocese of Seattle, Washington
Smithsonian	Bureau of American Ethnology Archives, Smithsonian Institution, Washington, D.C.
St. Dominic	St. Dominic's Church Archives, Holton, Kansas
St. Regis	St. Regis Church Archives, St. Regis, Quebec
Suquamish	Suquamish Museum Archives, Suquamish, Washington
Wisconsin	The State Historical Society of Wisconsin, Manuscripts, Madison, Wisconsin

REFERENCES

"A Brief Sketch of Chief Simon Pokagon's Life." [Cornelia Hulst, *Indian Sketches*?] N.d. Notre Dame.

Aldrich, Vernice M. 1927. "Father George Antoine Belcourt, Red River Missionary." *North Dakota Historical Quarterly* 2:30–52.

Amoss, Pamela T. 1978. *Coast Salish Spirit Dancing: The Survival of an Ancestral Religion*. Seattle: University of Washington Press.

———. 1982. "Resurrection, Healing, and 'The Shake': The Story of John and Mary Slocum." *Journal of the American Academy of Religion, Thematic Studies* 48:87–109.

———. 1990. "The Indian Shaker Church." In *Handbook of North American Indians*, vol. 7, *Northwest Coast*, ed. Wayne Suttles, 633–639. Washington, D.C.: Smithsonian Institution.

Anderson, Karen. 1991. *Chain Her by One Foot: The Subjugation of Women in Seventeenth-Century New France*. London: Routledge.

Angus, Josephine, and Cecilia Cree. September 13, 1987. Interview by author, Phoenix, Arizona.

Anishinabe Spiritual Centre, Anderson Lake, Espanola, Ontario. October 12–14, 1990. Author's fieldnotes.

Archambault, (Sister) Marie-Therese, O.S.F. August 5, 1989. Interview by author, Fargo, North Dakota.

———. 1991. "The Time for Turning Around." Unpublished ms. in author's possession.

Artscanada. 1973–1974. *Stones, Bones & Skin: Ritual and Shamanic Art*, nos. 184, 185, 186, 187.

Axtell, James. 1975. "The European Failure to Convert the Indians: An Autopsy." In *Papers of the Sixth Algonquian Conference, 1974*, ed. William Cowan, 274–290. Ottawa: National Museums of Canada.

———. 1986. *The Invasion Within: The Contest of Cultures in Colonial America*. New York: Oxford University Press.

———. Spring 1986. "White Legend: The Jesuit Missions in Maryland." *Maryland Historical Magazine* 81:1–7.

Baegert, (Rev.) Johann Jakob, S.J. 1979. *Observations in Lower California*. Trans. M. M. Brandenburg and Carl L. Baumann. Berkeley: University of California Press.

Bagley, Clarence B. 1932. "The Catholic Ladder." In *Early Catholic Missions in Old Oregon*, ed. Clarence B. Bagley, 2:117–122. Seattle: Lowman & Hanford Company.

Bailey, Alfred Goldsworth. 1969. *The Conflict of European and Eastern Algonkian Cultures 1504–1700*. Toronto: University of Toronto Press.

Balikci, Asen. 1956. "Note sur le Midewiwin." *Anthropologica* 2:165–217.

Ball Club, Minnesota. July 19–21, 1991. Author's fieldnotes.

Bandy, Peg Bittel. November 17, 1974. "Tekakwitha." *Syracuse Herald-American*, pp. 4, 6–7.

Baraga, (Rev.) Frederic. 1831–1868. Correspondence, Notre Dame.

———. 1973. *A Dictionary of the Otchipwe Language, Explained in English*. Minneapolis: Ross & Haines. Original publication 1878.

Baribeau, Jean. 1980. "L'Influence de l'Évangélisation sur la Conception de la Vie et de la Mort chez les Têtes-de-Boule au Dix-neuvième Siecle." *Studies in Religion* 9:201–216.

Barnett, H. G. 1957. *Indian Shakers*. Carbondale: Southern Illinois University Press.

Barnouw, Victor. 1950. *Acculturation and Personality among the Wisconsin Chippewa*. Menasha, Wisc.: American Anthropological Association.

Baroux, (Rev.) Louis. N.d. "Forty-three Years in the Life of a Missionary Apostolic in Europe, Africa, Asia and America." 2 vols. Unpublished manuscript, Notre Dame.

Barrett, Patricia Sulcer. Spring 1988. "*Hownikan*: The Story of a Tribal Newspaper." *Native Press Research Journal*, pp. 1–11.

Bartholomew, Marianna. February 1990. "A Legacy of Faith." *Extension* 84:14–17.

Bayou Catholic, 1990 Catholic Directory, Diocese of Houma-Thibodaux. January 31, 1990.

Beaver, R. Pierce, ed. 1979. *The Native American Christian Community: A Directory of Indian, Aleut, and Eskimo Churches*. Monrovia, Calif.: Missions Advanced Research and Communication Center.

Béchard, (Rev.) Henri, S.J. 1976. *The Original Caughnawaga Indians*. Montreal: International Publishers.

———. 1994. *Kaia'tanó:ron Kateri Tekakwitha*, trans. Antoinette Kinlough. Kahnawake, Quebec: Kateri Center.

Bell, Babe. November 24, 1991. Interview by author, Potawatomi Reservation, Kansas.

Berg, (Sister) Carol, O.S.B. 1981. "Climbing Learners' Hill: Benedictines at White Earth, 1878–1945." Ph.D. dissertation, University of Minnesota.

Betsiamites, Quebec. July 27–28, 1990. Author's fieldnotes.

Bigtree, John. July 9, 1989. Interview by author, St. Regis, Quebec.

Bischoff, (Rev.) William N., S.J. 1945. *The Jesuits in Old Oregon 1840–1940*. Cadwell, Idaho: The Caxton Printers.

Bishop, Charles A. 1974. *The Northern Ojibwa and the Fur Trade: An Historical and Ecological Study*. Toronto: Holt, Rinehart & Winston of Canada.

Bittle, Celestine N., ed. 1934–1935. "Father Anthony Maria Gachet, O.M.Cap." *Wisconsin Magazine of History* 18:66–76, 191–204, 345–359.

Blackbird, Andrew J. 1887. *History of the Ottawa and Chippewa Indians of Michigan, and Grammar of Their Language*. Ypsilanti, Mich.: The Ypsilantian Job Printing House.

Blanchard, David. 1982. ". . . To the Other Side of the Sky: Catholicism at Kahnawake, 1667–1700." *Anthropologica* 24:77–102.

Blanchet, (Most Rev.) Francis Norbert. 1859. *The Key to the Catholic Ladder*. New York: T. W. Strong, Printer.

———. 1932. "Historical Sketches of the Catholic Church in Oregon 1838–1878." In *Early Catholic Missions in Old Oregon*, 2 vols., ed. Clarence B. Bagley, 1:6–149. Seattle: Lowman & Hanford Company.

Blegen, Theodore C. 1963. *Minnesota, A History of the State*. Minneapolis: University of Minnesota Press.

Blessed Kateri Tekakwitha, North American Indian. N.d. Great Falls, Mont.: Tekakwitha Conference National Center.

Bluhm, Donald A. June 17, 1989. "The Hunt for the True North." *Milwaukee Journal*, pp. 8H,10H.

Boudreaux, Eva Pierre, and Joseph Norris Boudreaux. November 21, 1990. Interview by author, Grand Caillou, Louisiana.

Boudreaux, (Msgr.) Roland J. August 20, 1990. Telephone interview by author.

———. November 17–23, 1990. Interviews by author, Louisiana.

Bowden, Henry Warner. 1981. *American Indians and Christian Missions: Studies in Cultural Conflict*. Chicago: The University of Chicago Press.

Boyer, Ron. August 11, 1986. Interview by author, Bozeman, Montana.

———. October 14, 1990. Interview by author, Anderson Lake, Espanola, Ontario.

Bozeman, Montana. August 6–10, 1986. Author's fieldnotes, Tekakwitha Conference.

Brown, Beatrice. January 3, 1949. "Church Endures as Memorial to Pokagon. Indians Still Worship on Historic Site." *South Bend Tribune*, section 2, p. 1.

Buckley, (Rev.) Cornelius M., S.J. 1989. *Nicolas Point, S.J.: His Life & Northwest Indian Chronicles*. Chicago: Loyola University Press.

Bucko, (Rev.) Raymond, S.J. September 29, 1991. Interview by author, Madison, New York.

Buechner, Cecilia Bain. 1933. *The Pokagons*. Indianapolis: Indiana Historical Society.

Bunoz, (Most Rev.) E. M. 1942. "Bishop Durieu's System." *Études Oblates*, 1:193–209.

Bureau of Catholic Indian Missions Newsletter. 1981–1996.

Burns, John F. September 20, 1987. "For Arctic Indians, a Papal Promise." *The New York Times*, p. 30.

———. September 21, 1987. "Pope Ends Trip at Mass beneath Arctic Rainbow." *The New York Times*, p. B12.

Burns, (Rev.) Robert Ignatius, S.J. 1966. *The Jesuits and the Indian Wars of the Northwest*. New Haven: Yale University Press.

———. 1988. "Roman Catholic Missions in the Northwest." In *Handbook of North American Indians*, vol. 4, *History of Indian-White Relations*, ed. Wilcomb E. Washburn, 494–500. Washington, D.C.: Smithsonian Institution.

Burton, Frederick R. 1909. *American Primitive Music with Especial Attention to the Songs of the Ojibways*. New York: Moffat, Yard and Company.

Cadieux, Lorenzo. 1959. *Au Royaume de Nanabozho*. Sudbury, Ontario: Université de Sudbury.

Cadieux, Lorenzo, ed. 1973. *Lettres des Nouvelles Missions du Canada, 1843–1852*. Montreal: Les Éditions Bellarmin.

Cadieux, Lorenzo, and Ernest Comte. 1954. *Un Heros du Lac Superieur, Frederic Baraga*. Sudbury, Ontario: College du Sacré Coeur.

Cadot, (Rev.) J. C., S.J. 1920. "Bruce County and Work among the Indians." *Ontario Historical Society Papers and Records* 18:22.

Campeau, (Rev.) Lucien, S.J. 1967. *La Première Mission d'Acadie (1602–1616)*. Monumenta Novæ Franciæ, 1. Quebec: Les Presses de l'Université Laval.

———. 1979. *Établissement à Québec (1616–1634)*. Monumenta Novæ Franciæ, 2. Quebec: Les Presses de l'Université Laval.

———. 1987a. *Fondation de la Mission Huronne (1635–1637)*. Monumenta Novæ Franciæ, 3. Quebec: Les Presses de l'Université Laval.

———. 1987b. *La Mission des Jésuites chez les Hurons, 1634–1650*. Montreal: Les Éditions Bellarmin.

———. 1989. *Les Grandes Épreuves (1638–1640)*. Monumenta Novæ Franciæ, 4. Montreal: Les Éditions Bellarmin.

———. 1990. *La Bonne Nouvelle Reçue (1641–1643)*. Monumenta Novæ Franciæ, 5. Montreal: Les Éditions Bellarmin.

———. 1992. *Recherche de la Paix (1644–1646)*. Monumenta Novæ Franciæ, 6. Montreal: Les Éditions Bellarmin.

Campion, Owen F. October 8, 1989. "Alaska: The Church in 'The Great Land.'" *Our Sunday Visitor*, pp. 6–7.

Campisi, Jack. August 31, 1991. Interview by author, Oneonta, New York.

Campisi, Jack, and William A. Starna. March 14, 1988. "Response of the United Houma Nation, Inc. to the Letter of Obvious Deficiencies and Significant Omissions of May, 1987." Unpublished ms. in author's possession.

Canton, Don. March 1992. "Sister Maureen Wallace: Teacher and Friend of Maine's Native Americans." *St. Anthony Messenger* 99:12–17.

Carrière, (Rev.) Gaston, O.M.I. 1972. "Contribution des Missionnaires à la Sauvegarde de la Culture Indienne." *Études Oblates* 31:165–204.

———. Spring 1979. "The Early Efforts of the Oblate Missionaries in Western Canada." *Prairie Forum* 4: n.p.

Carriker, Robert C. 1985. "Joseph M. Cataldo, S.J.: Courier of Catholicism to the Nez Percés." In *Churchmen and the Western Indians, 1820–1920*, ed. Clyde A. Milner II and Floyd A. O'Neil, 109–139. Norman: University of Oklahoma Press.

———. 1995. *Father Peter John De Smet: Jesuit in the West*. Norman: University of Oklahoma Press.

Carriker, Robert C., and Eleanor R. Carriker. 1987. *Guide to the Microfilm Edition of the Pacific Northwest Tribes Missions Collection of the Oregon Province Archives of the Society of Jesus*. Wilmington, Del.: Scholarly Resources.

Cavanaugh, (Sister) Pierre. January 9, 1987. "Pottawatomies Appreciate Reopening of Old Indian Shrine in Mayetta." *The Leaven*, n.p.

Chamberlain, Alexander F. 1901. "Kootenay 'Medicine-Men.'" *Journal of American Folklore* 14:95–99.

Champagne, (Rev.) Joseph-Etienne, O.M.I. 1949. *Les Missions Catholiques dans l'Ouest Canadien, 1818–1875*. Publications de l'Institut de Missiologie. Ottawa: L'Université Pontificale d'Ottawa.

Charlevoix, Pierre de. 1966. *Journal of a Voyage to North-America*. 2 vols. Ann Arbor, Mich.: University Microfilms. Original publication 1744.

Chittenden, Hiram Martin, and Alfred Talbot Richardson, eds. 1905. *Life, Letters and Travels of Father Pierre-Jean de Smet, S.J., 1801–1873*. 4 vols. New York: Francis P. Harper.

Choquette, Robert. 1995. *The Oblate Assault on Canada's Northwest*. Ottawa: University of Ottawa Press.

Clements, William M. 1994. "The Jesuit Foundations of Native North American Literary Studies." *American Indian Quarterly* 18:43–59.

Clifton, James A. 1977. *The Prairie People: Continuity and Change in Potawatomi Indian Culture, 1665–1965*. Lawrence: The Regents Press of Kansas.

———. 1984. *The Pokagons, 1683–1983: Catholic Potawatomi Indians of the St. Joseph River Valley*. Washington, D.C.: The University Press of America.

———. 1985. "Leopold Pokagon." *Michigan History* (September–October), pp. 17–23.

Clinton, Catherine. July 8, 1977. "Indian Beliefs, Catholic Faith Blend as One." *Kansas Register*, p. 3.

———. 1987. "Our Lady of Snows Potawatomi Indian Mission," St. Dominic.

———. November 24, 1991. Interview by author, Topeka, Kansas.

Cloud-Morgan, Larry. October 16–19, 1990. Interviews by author, Madison, New York.

———. July 19–21, 1991. Interviews by author, Ball Club, Minnesota.

———. January 26–28, 1992. Interviews by author, Hamilton, New York.

———. October 15–16, 1995. Interviews by author, Burlington, Vermont.

Coleman, (Sister) Bernard. 1947. *Decorative Designs of the Ojibwa of Northern Minnesota*. Washington, D.C.: The Catholic University of America Press.

Collins, June McCormick. 1980. *Valley of the Spirits: The Upper Skagit Indians of Western Washington*. Seattle: University of Washington Press.

Conard, E. Laetitia Moon. 1901. *Les Idées des Indiens Algonquins Relatives a la Vie D'Outre-Tombe*. Paris: Ernest Leroux, Editeur.

Conkling, Robert. 1974. "Legitimacy and Conversion in Social Change: The Case of French Missionaries and the Northeastern Algonkian." *Ethnohistory* 21:1–24.

Cook, Elaine. August 7, 1993. Interview by author, Seattle, Washington.

Cooper, (Rev.) Leo. November 26, 1991. Interview by author, Kansas City, Kansas.

Craker, Ruth. 1935. *First Protestant Mission in the Grand Traverse Region*. Leland, Mich.: The Leelanau Enterprise.

Cuny, (Sister) Genevieve, O.S.F. August 8, 1986. Interview by author, Bozeman, Montana.

Curry, Janel. February 1979. "A History of the Houma Indians and Their Story of Federal Nonrecognition." *American Indian Journal* 5:8–28.

Curry-Roper, Janel, and Greg Bowman. 1982. *The Houma People of Louisiana: A Story of Indian Survival*. Houma, La.: United Houma Nation.

Dan, Morris. October 29, 1977. "Indian Teaching." Video, translated and transcribed by Vi Hilbert, Lushootseed.

Dana, Joan. August 23, 1992. Interview by author, Grand Lake Stream, Maine.

Danziger, Edmund Jefferson, Jr. 1978. *The Chippewas of Lake Superior*. Norman: University of Oklahoma Press.

Davidson, John Nelson. 1892. "Missions on Chequamegon Bay." *Collections of the State Historical Society of Wisconsin* 12:434–452.

Davis, (Sister) Wilma, O.S.B. 1988. "The Turtle Mountain People: A Special Faith." In *Scattered Steeples. The Fargo Diocese: A Written Celebration of Its Centennial*, ed. Jerome D. Lamb et al., 176–178. Fargo: Burch, Londergan & Lynch Publishers.

Degand, Mercedes, Cheryl Gillespie, and Donna Holstein. November 24, 1991. Interview by author, Potawatomi Reservation, Kansas.

Delâge, Denys, and Helen Hornbeck Tanner. 1994. "The Ojibwa-Jesuit Debate at Walpole Island, 1844." *Ethnohistory* 41:295–321.

Delanglez, (Rev.) Jean, S.J. 1935. *The French Jesuits in Lower Louisiana (1700–1763)*. Washington, D.C.: The Catholic University of America.

Densmore, Frances. 1938. "The Influence of Hymns on the Form of Indian Songs." *American Anthropologist* 40:175–177.

Devens, Carol. 1992. *Countering Colonization: Native American Women and Great Lakes Missions, 1630–1900*. Berkeley: University of California Press.

Devine, (Rev.) E. J., S.J. 1922. *Historic Caughnawaga*. Montreal: The Messenger Press.

Donnelly, (Rev.) Joseph P., S.J. 1967. *Thwaites' Jesuit Relations. Errata and Addenda*. Chicago: Loyola University Press.

——. 1968. *Jacques Marquette, S.J., 1637–1675*. Chicago: Loyola University Press.

——. 1975. *Jean de Brébeuf, 1593–1649*. Chicago: Loyola University Press.

Donnelly, William P. April 1935. "Nineteenth Century Jesuit Reductions in the United States." *Mid-America* 17:69–83.

Donohoe, (Rev.) Thomas, D.D. 1895. *The Iroquois and the Jesuits*. Buffalo, N.Y.: Buffalo Catholic Publication Co.

Ducatel, I. I. 1877. "A Fortnight among the Chippewas of Lake Superior." In *The Indian Miscellany*, ed. William Wallace Beach, 361–378. Albany, N.Y.: J. Munsell.

Duchaussois, (Rev.) Pierre, O.M.I. 1919. *The Grey Nuns in the Far North*. Toronto: McClelland & Stewart Publishers.

——. 1937. *Mid Snow and Ice: The Apostles of the North West*. Trans. Thomas Dawson. Ottawa: The University of Ottawa.

Duignan, Peter. 1958. "Early Jesuit Missionaries: A Suggestion for Further Study." *American Anthropologist* 60:725–732.

Dyer, Patricia A. 1994. "Ottawa/Odawa." In *Native America in the Twentieth Century: An Encyclopedia*, ed. Mary B. Davis, 413–415. New York: Garland Publishing.

Egan, (Rev.) Thomas F., S.J. July 8–10, 1989. Interviews by author, St. Regis, Quebec.

——. June 5, 1991. Telephone interview by author.

Egan, Timothy. April 21, 1992. "Chief's 1854 Lament Linked to Ecological Script of 1991." *The New York Times*, pp. A1, A17.

Elliott, Richard R. April 1896. "The Chippewas of Lake Superior." *The American Catholic Quarterly Review* 21:354–373.

——. January 1897. "The Chippewas and Ottawas: Father Baraga's Books in Their Language." *The American Catholic Quarterly Review* 22:18–46.

Ewers, John C. 1963. "Iroquois Indians in the Far West." *Montana: The Magazine of Western History* 13:2–10.

———. 1971. "A Unique Pictorial Interpretation of Blackfoot Indian Religion in 1846–1847." *Ethnohistory* 18:231–238.

Faber, Harold. May 4, 1980. "Vatican to Beatify Upstate Indian Maiden Who Died 300 Years Ago at 24." *The New York Times*, p. 69.

Fagan, (Rev.) Bernard, S.J. August 4, 1995. Interview by author, Kahnawake, Quebec.

Fargo, North Dakota. August 2–6, 1989. Author's fieldnotes, Tekakwitha Conference.

Farmer, John. August 7, 1992. Interview by author, Orono, Maine.

Fisher, Ann. 1968. "History and Current Status of the Houma Indians." In *The American Indian Today*, ed. Stuart Levine and Nancy Oestreich Lurie, 133–147. Deland, Fla.: Everett/Edwards.

Fonda, New York. July 14–16, 1989. Author's fieldnotes, Northeastern Tekakwitha Conference.

Foret, Noah. November 21, 1990. Telephone interview by author.

Forsman, Leonard. January 16, 1990. Interview by author, Suquamish, Washington.

Fox, (Rev.) Robert J. Paul. December 24–31, 1988. "Catholic Native Americans: A Church in Renewal." *America* 159:541–543.

Francis, John. November 21, 1990. Interview by author, Grand Caillou, Louisiana.

Freeman, John F. Spring 1965. "The Indian Convert: Theme and Variation." *Ethnohistory* 12:113–128.

Frideres, James S. 1988. *Native Peoples in Canada: Contemporary Conflicts*. Scarborough, Ontario: Prentice-Hall Canada.

Fruth, (Rev.) Alban. 1958. *A Century of Missionary Work among the Red Lake Chippewa Indians, 1858–1958*. Redlake, Minn.: St. Mary's Mission.

Furlan, William P. 1952. *In Charity Unfeigned: The Life of Father Francis Xavier Pierz*. [St. Cloud, Minn.:] Diocese of St. Cloud.

Gabriel, Joseph, Lillien Gabriel, and Simon Gabriel. August 23, 1992. Interview by author, Indian Township, Maine.

Gagnon, François-Marc. 1975. *La Conversion par l'Image. Un Aspect de la Mission des Jésuites auprès des Indiéns du Canada au XVIIe Siècle*. Montreal: Les Éditions Bellarmin.

Garraghan, (Rev.) Gilbert J., S.J. 1938. *The Jesuits of the Middle United States*. 3 vols. New York: America Press.

George, Doug. November 19, 1996. Lecture, Hamilton, New York.

Gilfillan, (Rev.) J. A. c. 1911. "Miscellaneous Lots of Notes." Smithsonian.

Giraud, Marcel. 1986. *The Métis in the Canadian West*. Trans. George Woodcock. 2 vols. Lincoln: University of Nebraska Press.

Goutier, (Rev.) M., O.M.I. N.d. " 'Come to Me . . . I am the Way.' " Mimeograph in author's possession.

Graham, Hugh. January 1931. "Catholic Missionary Schools among the Indians of Minnesota." *Mid-America* 13:199–206.

Grant, John Webster. 1985. *Moon of Wintertime: Missionaries and the Indians of Canada in Encounter since 1534*. Toronto: University of Toronto Press.

Gregoire, Frances Carlos. November 20, 1990. Telephone interview by author.

Gregoire, Mary, Lydia Gregoire Duthu, and Ted Duthu, Sr. November 20, 1990. Interview by author, Dulac, Louisiana.

Gregorich, Joseph. 1932. *The Apostle of the Chippewas: The Life Story of The Most Rev. Frederick Baraga, D.D., the First Bishop of Marquette*. Chicago: The Bishop Baraga Association.

Gresco, Jacqueline Kennedy. July–September 1973. "Missionary Acculturation Programs in British Columbia." *Études Oblates* 32:145–158.

——. 1982. "Roman Catholic Missions to the Indians of British Columbia: A Reappraisal of the Lemert Thesis." *The Journal of the Canadian Church Historical Society* 24:51–62.

Grim, John A. August 27, 1991. Telephone interview by author.

——. 1991a. "From Conversion to Inculturation: 'New Evangelization' in the Dialogue of Native American and Catholic Spiritualities." Unpublished ms. in author's possession.

——. 1991b. "Relations between Native American Religions and Roman Catholicism." Unpublished ms. in author's possession.

Gualtieri, Antonio R. 1980a. "Canadian Missionary Perceptions of Indian and Inuit Culture and Religious Tradition." *Studies in Religion* 9:299–314.

——. 1980b. "Indigenization of Christianity and Syncretism among the Indians and Inuit of the Western Arctic." *Canadian Ethnic Studies* 12:47–57.

Hallowell, A. Irving. 1971. *Culture and Experience*. New York: Schocken Books.

Hanley, Philip M. 1965. "The Catholic Ladder and Missionary Activity in the Pacific Northwest." M.A. thesis, The University of Ottawa.

——. April–June 1973. "Father Lacombe's Ladder." *Études Oblates*: 82–99.

Hanzeli, Victor Egon. 1969. *Missionary Linguistics in New France. A Study of Seventeenth- and Eighteenth-Century Descriptions of American Indian Languages*. The Hague: Mouton.

Harper, J. Russell, ed. 1971. *Paul Kane's Frontier*. Fort Worth, Tex.: The Amon Carter Museum.

Harrod, Howard L. 1971. *Mission among the Blackfeet*. Norman: University of Oklahoma Press.

——. 1984. "Missionary Life-world and Native Response: Jesuits in New France." *Studies in Religion* 13:179–192.

Healy, George R. 1958. "The French Jesuits and the Idea of the Noble Savage." *The William and Mary Quarterly* 15:143–167.

Hebert, (Rev.) Donald J. 1978–1985. *South Louisiana Records. Church and Civil Records of Lafourche-Terrebonne Parishes*. 12 vols. Cecilia, La.: Rev. Donald J. Hebert.

Hemauer, (Rev.) Gilbert F., O.F.M.Cap. August 9, 1986. Interview by author, Bozeman, Montana.

Hennepin, (Rev.) Louis. 1966. *A Description of Louisiana*. Trans. John Gilmary Shea. Ann Arbor, Mich.: University Microfilms. Original publication 1683.

Henry, Alexander. 1966. *Travels and Adventures in Canada and the Indian Terri-tories, between the Years 1760 and 1776.* Ann Arbor, Mich.: University Microfilms. Original publication 1809.

Hermant, (Rev.) Leon, O.M.I. 1948. *Thy Cross My Stay: The Life of the Servant of God, Vital Justin Grandin.* Toronto: The Mission Press.

Hickerson, Harold. 1962. "Notes on the Post-Contact Origin of the Midewi-win." *Ethnohistory* 9:404–426.

——. 1970. *The Chippewa and Their Neighbors: A Study in Ethnohistory.* New York: Holt, Rinehart & Winston.

Hilbert, Vi. 1985. "When Chief Seattle (*SI'Ał*) Spoke in 1855." Ms. and related documents, Lushootseed.

——. April 4, 1987. Interview by author, Hamilton, New York.

——. April 27–29, 1989. Interviews by author, Madison, New York.

——. January 9–23, 1990. Interviews by author, Seattle, Washington.

——. 1991. "When Chief Seattle (SI'Ał) Spoke." In *A Time of Gathering: Na-tive Heritage in Washington State,* ed. Robin K. Wright, 259–266. Seattle: University of Washington Press.

——. N.d. "Some Lushootseed Vocabulary." Ms., Lushootseed.

Hilger, (Sister) M. Agnes, O.S.B. June 1936. "In the Early Days of Wisconsin. An Amalgamation of Chippewa and European Cultures." *The Wisconsin Archeologist* 16:32–49.

——. December 1936. "Letters and Documents of Bishop Baraga Extant in the Chippewa Country." *Records of the American Catholic Historical Society of Philadelphia* 47:292–302.

——. 1939. *A Social Study of One Hundred Fifty Chippewa Indian Families of the White Earth Reservation of Minnesota.* Washington, D.C.: The Catholic Uni-versity of America Press.

——. 1951. *Chippewa Child Life and Its Cultural Background.* Smithsonian In-stitution, Bureau of American Ethnology Bulletin 146. Washington, D.C.: United States Government Printing Office.

Hoffman, Matthias M. July 1930. "The Winnebago Mission; A Cause Célèbre." *Mid-America* 13:26–52.

Holand, Hjalmar R. December 1933. "The Sign of the Cross." *The Wisconsin Magazine of History* 17:155–167.

Holy Family Mission (Montana) Diary. 1908–1917. Notre Dame.

Houma Indian Communities, Louisiana. November 18–22, 1990. Author's fieldnotes.

Hoxie, Frederick E. 1995. *Parading through History: The Making of the Crow Nation in America.* Cambridge: Cambridge University Press.

Hughes, Katherine. 1911. *Father Lacombe: The Black-Robe Voyageur.* New York: Moffat, Yard and Company.

Hultkrantz, Åke. 1981. *Belief and Worship in Native North America,* ed. Christo-pher Vecsey. Syracuse, N.Y.: Syracuse University Press.

Hutchinson, Gloria. August 12, 1982. "An Open, Affectionate People." *Church World* 53:14–15.

——. September 9, 1982. "Living a Faith Tradition." *Church World* 53:6.

Indian Sentinel, The. 1902–1962.

Indian Township, Maine. August 22–24, 1992. Author's fieldnotes.

Jacko, Ursula. October 12–14, 1990. Interviews by author, Toronto-Anderson Lake, Ontario.

Jacobs, (Rev.) Michael, S.J., and (Rev.) Thomas Egan, S.J. 1973, 1989. "The St. Regis Reserve . . . Baptisms, Marriages, Deaths . . . ," St. Regis.

Jacobs, (Rev.) Peter (Pah-tah-se-ga). 1855. *Journal from Rice Lake to the Hudson's Bay Territory, and Returning. Commencing May, 1852.* New York: Carlton and Phillips.

Jaenen, Cornelius J. 1969. "The Frenchification and Evangelization of the Amerindians in the Seventeenth Century New France." *Canadian Catholic Historical Association* 35:57–71.

———. 1974. "Amerindian Views of French Culture in the Seventeenth Century." *Canadian Historical Review* 55:261–291.

———. 1976a. *Friend and Foe: Aspects of French-Amerindian Cultural Contact in the Sixteenth and Seventeenth Centuries.* New York: Columbia University Press.

———. 1976b. *The Role of the Church in New France.* Toronto: McGraw-Hill Ryerson.

James, Bernard J. 1961. "Social-Psychological Dimensions of Ojibwa Acculturation." *American Anthropologist* 63:721–746.

Johnson, Marilyn E. 1983. "My Apprenticeship with a Modern Ojibwa Shaman: A Personal and Comparative Analysis of Shamanic Flight." M.A. thesis, York University, Toronto.

Jones, (Rev.) Peter (Kahkewaquonaby). 1861. *History of the Ojebway Indians; With Especial Reference to Their Conversion to Christianity.* London: A. W. Bennett.

Jung, A. M. 1925. *Jesuit Missions among the American Tribes of the Rocky Mountain Indians.* Spokane, Wash.: Gonzaga University.

Kahnawake, Quebec. August 4, 1995. Author's fieldnotes.

Karol, (Rev.) Joseph, S.J. 1953. "What Happened to the Potawatomi?" *American Ecclesiastical Review* 129:361–367.

Kateri, no. 185. Autumn 1995.

Kellogg, Louise Phelps. 1917. *Early Narratives of the Northwest, 1634–1699.* New York: Charles Scribner's Sons.

———. 1925. *The French Regime in Wisconsin and the Northwest.* Madison: State Historical Society of Wisconsin.

Kennedy, J. H. 1950. *Jesuit and Savage in New France.* New Haven: Yale University Press.

Kerygma (Mission: Journal of Mission Studies). 1967–1996.

Kidwell, Clara Sue. 1995. *Choctaws and Missionaries in Mississippi, 1818–1918.* Norman: University of Oklahoma Press.

Killoren, (Rev.) John J., S.J. 1994. *"Come, Blackrobe." De Smet and the Indian Tragedy.* Norman: University of Oklahoma Press.

Kinietz, W. Vernon. 1947. *Chippewa Village: The Story of Katikitegon.* Bloomfield Hills, Mich.: Cranbrook Institute of Science.

Klepac, (Sister) Therese, S.C.L. November 24, 26, 1991. Interviews by author, Topeka, Kansas.

Kohl, J. G. 1860. *Kitchi-Gami: Wanderings Round Lake Superior*. Ed. and trans. Lascelles Wraxall. London: Chapman and Hall.

Koppedrayer, K. I. 1993. "The Making of the First Iroquois Virgin: Early Jesuit Biographies of the Blessed Kateri Tekakwitha." *Ethnohistory* 40:277–306.

Kozak, David. 1991. "Ecumenical Indianism: Kateri and the Invented Tradition." Unpublished ms. in author's possession.

Krieger, Carlo. 1993. "The Micmac and the Question of Discourse." In *Re-Discoveries of America*, ed. Johan Callens, 87–101. Brussels: VUBPress.

Kurath, Gertrude Prokosch. 1954. "Chippewa Sacred Songs in Religious Metamorphosis." *Scientific Monthly* 79:311–317.

———. 1957. "Catholic Hymns of Michigan Indians." *Anthropological Quarterly* 30:31–44.

———. 1959. "Blackrobe and Shaman: The Christianization of Michigan Algonquians." *Papers of the Michigan Academy of Science, Arts, and Letters* 44:209–215.

Kurath, Gertrude, Jane Ettawageshik, and Fred Ettawageshik. 1955. "Religious Customs of Modern Michigan Algonquians," APS.

LaClair, Milton. November 27, 1991. Interview by author, Potawatomi Reservation, Kansas.

Lacombe, (Rev.) Albert. [1896]. *Pictorial Catechism*. Montreal: C. O. Beauchemin, & Fils.

Laflèche, Guy. 1980. "Le Chamanisme des Amérindians et des Missionnaires de la Nouvelle-France." *Studies in Religion* 9:137–160.

Lahontan, Baron de. 1905. *New Voyages to North-America*. 2 vols. Ed. Reuben Gold Thwaites. Chicago: A. C. McClurg & Co. Original publication 1703.

[Lalemant, (Rev.) Jérôme and François-Joseph LeMercier]. 1973. *Le Journal des Jesuites*. Montreal: Éditions François-Xavier.

Lalonde, Y. Renee. June 21, 1978. "Overcoming Divisions on the St. Regis Reservation." *North Country Catholic*, pp. 8–9, 16.

Landes, Ruth. 1970. *The Prairie Potawatomi: Tradition and Ritual in the Twentieth Century*. Madison: University of Wisconsin Press.

Laveille, (Rev.) E., S.J. 1981. *The Life of Father De Smet, S.J. (1801–1873)*. Trans. Marian Lindsay. Chicago: Loyola University Press. Original publication 1915.

Leach, (Rev.) George P., S.J., and (Rev.) Greg J. Humbert. [1989]. *Beedahbun. First Light of Dawn*. Espanola, Ontario: Anishinabe Spiritual Centre.

Leacock, Eleanor, and Jacqueline Goodman. 1976. "Montagnais Marriage and the Jesuits in the Seventeenth Century: Incidents from the Relations of Paul Le Jeune." *The Western Canadian Journal of Anthropology* 6:77–91.

Le Clercq, (Rev.) Christian. 1881. *First Establishment of the Faith in New France*. 2 vols. Trans. John Gilmary Shea. New York: John G. Shea. Original publication 1691.

Ledet, Laïse Marie. 1982. *They Came They Stayed: Origins of Pointe-aux-chênes and Ile à Jean Charles. A Genealogical Study 1515–1982*. Montegut, La.: Ledet.

——. November 18, 1990. Interview by author, Montegut, Louisiana.

Leger, (Sister) Mary Celeste. 1929. *The Catholic Indian Missions in Maine (1611–1820)*. Washington, D.C.: The Catholic University of America.

Lemert, Edwin M. 1954. "The Life and Death of an Indian State." *Human Organization* 13:23–27.

Lenz, (Msgr.) Paul A. August 7, 1986. Interview by author, Bozeman, Montana.

——. November 19, 1993. Interview by author, Washington, D.C.

Lequin, (Rev.) Thomas. June 17, 1992. Telephone interview by author.

——. August 8, 1992. Interview by author, Orono, Maine.

——. August 22, 1992. Interview by author, Indian Township, Maine.

Levi, (Sister) M. Carolissa. 1956. *Chippewa Indians of Yesterday and Today*. New York: Pageant Press.

Lickers, Henry. May 4, 1989. Interview by author, Hamilton, New York.

Linton, Ralph, ed. 1940. *Acculturation in Seven American Indian Tribes*. New York: D. Appleton-Century Company.

Long, John. 1904. *Voyages and Travels of an Indian Interpreter and Trader, 1768–1782*. Ed. Reuben Gold Thwaites. Cleveland, Ohio: The Arthur H. Clark Company. Original publication 1791.

Loyacono, Susan. February 23, 1990. "Native American Ministry Revived." *The Leaven*, p. 9.

Lucero, Sam M. April 26, 1990. "Spruce Returns to Faith, Reservation after Absence." *Catholic Herald*, p. 3.

Lummi Indian Reservation, Washington. January 22, 1990. Author's fieldnotes.

Lunstrom, Richard H. 1973. "A Hard Look at American Catholic Folklore. Mohawks, Martyrs, and Myths," and "'For If the Indian Peoples Die, Who among Us Deserve to Live?'" *Akwesasne Notes*, reprints, Marquette.

"The Mackinac Register." 1910. *Collections of the State Historical Society of Wisconsin* 19:1–162.

Maeder, (Rev.) Tobias. 1962. "St. John's among the Chippewa." *The Scriptorium* 21:57–73.

Magnuson, Roger. 1992. *Education in New France*. Montreal: McGill-Queen's University Press.

Mahoney (Sister) Denis, O.S.U. 1964. *Marie of the Incarnation, Mystic and Missionary*. Garden City, N.Y.: Doubleday & Co.

Majerus, Yvette. 1967. *Le Journal du Père Dominique du Ranquet, S.J.* Sudbury, Ontario: Université de Sudbury.

Manuel, George, and Michael Posluns. 1974. *The Fourth World: An Indian Reality*. New York: The Free Press.

Marie de l'Incarnation. 1967. *Word from New France; The Selected Letters of Marie de l'Incarnation*. Trans. and ed. Joyce Marshall. Toronto: Oxford University Press.

Martin, Douglas. September 16, 1984. "Pope Urges Indians and 'Newcomers' to Reconcile." *The New York Times*, p. 16.

Martinez, Zelda, and Laura Thackery. November 24, 1991. Interview by author, Topeka, Kansas.

Mathes, Valerie Sherer. 1980. "American Indian Women and the Catholic Church." *North Dakota History* 47:20–25.

McCarty, (Rev.) Paul, S.J. August 21, 1992. Interview by author, Pleasant Point, Maine.

McDonald, (Sister) Grace. 1929. "Father Francis Pierz, Missionary." *Minnesota History* 10:107–125.

McDonnell, Claudia. July 1987. "Kateri Tekakwitha. Native Americans' Gift to the Church." *St. Anthony Messenger* 95:19–23.

McKenney, Thomas L. 1827. *Sketches of a Tour to the Lakes, of the Character and Customs of the Chippeway Indians, and with Incidents Connected with the Treaty of Fond du Lac*. Baltimore: Fielding Lucas, Jun'r.

McMullen, (Rev.) John, O.S.B., M.S.L.S. 1969. *A Guide to the Christian Indians of the Upper Plains (An Annotated, Selective Bibliography)*. Marvin, S.Dak.: Blue Cloud Abbey.

McNamara, (Rev.) William, C.S.C. 1931. *The Catholic Church on the Northern Indiana Frontier, 1789–1844*. Washington, D.C.: The Catholic University of America.

Means, Philip Ainsworth. 1917. *Preliminary Survey of the Remains of the Chippewa Settlements on La Pointe Island, Wisconsin*. Smithsonian Miscellaneous Collections 66, no. 14. Washington, D.C.: The Smithsonian Institution.

Mello, Kenneth B. 1993. "Notes on the Jesuit Relations and Allied Documents." Unpublished ms. in author's possession.

Mengarini, (Rev.) Gregory, S.J. 1977. *Recollections of the Flathead Mission*. Trans. Gloria Ricci Lothrop. Glendale, Calif.: The Arthur H. Clark Company.

Metcalf, Leon. 1954a. "Memories of Ruth Shelton." Trans. Vi Hilbert. Transcripts of audiotapes, Lushootseed.

———. 1954b. "Messages." Trans. Vi Hilbert. Transcripts of audiotapes, Lushootseed.

Miller, Jay, and Vi Hilbert. 1989. "Caring for Control: A Pivot of Salishan Language and Culture." Lushootseed.

Mitchell, Delia. August 22, 1992. Interview by author, Indian Township, Maine.

Mitchell, (Sister) Kateri, S.S.A. August 7, 1986. Interview by author, Bozeman, Montana.

Mittelholtz, Erwin F. 1957. *Historical Review of the Red Lake Indian Reservation*. Bemidji, Minn.: Beltrami County Historical Society.

Monahan, David. June 14, 1987. "Old Sacred Heart: Birthplace of Church in State." *The Sooner Catholic*, p. 13.

———. September 18, 1988. "Traditional Tribal Religion Continues among Kiowa." *The Sooner Catholic*, n.p.

Moore, James T. 1982. *Indian and Jesuit: A Seventeenth-century Encounter*. Chicago: Loyola University Press.

Morice, (Rev.) A. G., O.M.I. 1904. *The History of the Northern Interior of British Columbia*. Toronto: William Briggs.

———. 1910. *History of the Catholic Church in Western Canada, From Lake Superior to the Pacific (1659–1895)*. 2 vols. Toronto: The Musson Book Company.

Morissonneau, Christian. 1978. "Huron of Lorette." In *Handbook of North American Indians,* vol. 15, *Northeast,* ed. Bruce G. Trigger, 389–393. Washington, D.C.: Smithsonian Institution.

Morrison, Kenneth M. 1979. "Towards a History of Intimate Encounters: Algonkian Folklore, Jesuit Missionaries, and Kiwakwe, the Cannibal Giant." *American Indian Culture and Research Journal* 3, no. 4:51–80.

———. 1981. "The Mythological Sources of Abenaki Catholicism: A Case Study of the Social History of Power." *Religion* 11:235–263.

———. 1984. *The Embattled Northeast: The Elusive Ideal of Alliance in Abenaki-Euroamerican Relations.* Berkeley: University of California Press.

———. 1985. "Discourse and the Accommodation of Values: Toward a Revision of Mission History." *Journal of the American Academy of Religion* 53:365–382.

Mrak, (Rev.) Ignatius. 1848–1894. Correspondence, Notre Dame.

Mulhall, David. 1986. *Will to Power: The Missionary Career of Father Morice.* Vancouver: University of British Columbia Press.

Mulvey, (Sister) Mary Doris, O.P. 1936. *French Catholic Missionaries in the Present United States (1604–1791).* Washington, D.C.: The Catholic University of America.

Murphy, (Sister) Carolyn, S.N.J.M. August 5, 1995. Interview by author, St. Regis, Ontario.

Murphy, Joseph F. 1974. *Tenacious Monks, The Oklahoma Benedictines 1875–1975: Indian Missionaries, Catholic Founders, Educators, Agriculturalists.* Shawnee, Okla.: Benedictine Color Press.

Naquin, (Rev.) Roch R. November 18, 20, 1990. Interviews by author, Grand Caillou, Louisiana.

Nolan, Charles. July 5, 1990. Telephone interview by author.

Norton, Mary Aquinas. 1930. *Catholic Missionary Activities in the Northwest, 1818–1864.* Washington, D.C.: The Catholic University of America.

Notices & Voyages of the Famed Quebec Mission to the Pacific Northwest. 1956. Portland: Oregon Historical Society.

Nute, Grace Lee. 1942. *Documents Relating to Northwest Missions, 1815–1827.* Saint Paul: Minesota Historical Society.

———. 1944. *Lake Superior.* Indianapolis: The Bobbs-Merrill Co. Publishers.

Office of Indian Ministry *Newsletter,* Archdiocese of St. Paul and Minneapolis. 1989–1992.

Office of Minority Ministries. 1987. "An Overview of Information and Activities on the Minority Communities within the Archdiocese of Seattle, Fiscal Year 1986–87," OMMS.

———. 1988. "Pastoral Ministry to Native Americans, Archdiocese of Seattle," OMMS.

———. 1989. "Activity Report," OMMS.

Order of St. Benedict. 1887. *Schools for the Chippewa Indians.* St. Paul: Wanderer Printing Co.

Orono, Maine. August 5–9, 1992. Author's fieldnotes, Tekakwitha Conference.

Our Negro and Indian Missions. 1926–1976.

Palladino, (Rev.) Lawrence B., S.J. 1922. *Indian and White in the Northwest: A History of Catholicity in Montana, 1831–1891*. Lancaster, Penn.: Wickersham Publishing Company.

Paper, Jordan. 1983. "The Post-Contact Origin of an Amerindian High God and the Suppression of Feminine Spirituality." *American Indian Quarterly* 7:1–24.

Paredes, J. Anthony, Timothy G. Roufs, and Gretel H. Pelto. 1973. "On James's 'Continuity and Emergence in Indian Poverty Culture.'" *Current Anthropology* 14:158–167.

Parkman, Francis. 1901. *The Jesuits in North America in the Seventeenth Century*. 2 vols. Boston: Little, Brown & Co.

Paul, Joan. August 21, 1992. Interview by author, Pleasant Point, Maine.

Peabody, B. O. 1877. "The Early Jesuit Missionaries of the North Western Territories." In *The Indian Miscellany*, ed. William Wallace Beach, 102–119. Albany, N.Y.: J. Munsell.

Peelman, (Rev.) Achiel, O.M.I. 1995. *Christ Is a Native American*. Ottawa: Novalis-Saint Paul University.

Pelotte, (Most Rev.) Donald E., S.S.S. August 6, 1993. Interview by author, Seattle, Washington.

Perkins, Rosemary. July 2, 1972. "St. Regis Indian Mission Was Established 120 Years before Founding of Diocese." *North Country Catholic*, pp. 14–15.

Peterson, Jacqueline. 1993. *Sacred Encounters: Father De Smet and the Indians of the Rocky Mountain West*. Norman: University of Oklahoma Press.

Petius (Isadore Tom). August 23, 1976. Conversation with Vi Hilbert, transcript of audiotape, Lushootseed.

———. May 20, 1977. Lecture, translated transcript of videotape by Vi Hilbert, Lushootseed.

———. August 11, 1978. "The Gifts of the Spirit," transcript of audiotape, Lushootseed.

Phoenix, Arizona. September 12–14, 1987. Author's fieldnotes, Tekakwitha Conference.

Pierz, (Rev.) Francis. 1837–1852. Correspondence, Notre Dame.

———. 1947–1948. "The Indians of North America." *Social Justice Review*, vol. 40: 24–27, 59–62, 96–98, 130–133, 167–170, 207–209, 243–245, 279–282, 316–318, 353–355, 388–390; vol. 41: 24–27, 60–64, 97–100, 132–134, 168–170. Original publication 1855.

Pillar, James J. 1988. "The Catholic Church's Ministry to the Choctaws of Mississippi in the Nineteenth Century." *Journal of Mississippi History* 50:287–315.

Pizzorusso, Giovanni. 1990. "Roman Ecclesiastical Archives and the History of the Native Peoples of Canada." *European Review of Native American Studies* 4:21–26.

Placilla, (Sister) Mary Hugh, I.H.M., and (Sister) Therese Culhane, I.H.M. August 5, 1992. Interview by author, Orono, Maine.

Pleasant Point, Maine. August 21, 1992. Author's fieldnotes.

Point, (Rev.) Nicolas, S.J. 1967. *Wilderness Kingdom, Indian Life in the Rocky Mountains: 1840–1847*. Trans. (Rev.) Joseph P. Donnelly, S.J. New York: Holt, Rinehart & Winston.

"Politicization of the Dead: The Case of Hammonds Meadow." 1992. Unpublished ms. in author's possession.

Pompedli, Michael. 1987. "Beyond Unbelief: Early Jesuit Interpretations of Native Religions." *Studies in Religion* 16:275–287.

Potawatomi Indians. 1939. Correspondence, Notre Dame.

Potsdam, New York. August 2–6, 1995. Author's fieldnotes, Tekakwitha Conference.

Pouliot, (Rev.) Léon, S.J. 1940. *Étude sur les Relations des Jesuites de la Nouvelle-France (1632–1672)*. Paris: Desclée de Brouwer & Cie.

———. 1967. "American Indian Missions (Canada)." *New Catholic Encyclopedia* 1:401–402.

Preston, James J. 1989. "Necessary Fictions: Healing Encounters with a North American Saint." *Literature and Medicine* 8:42–62.

———. April 6, 1991. "The Politics of Sainthood: Blessed Kateri Tekakwitha." Paper presented at conference, "The Secular Becomes the Sacred," Colgate University, Hamilton, New York.

———. 1991. "The Reinterpretation of Tradition: Catholic Devotions among Native Americans." Unpublished ms. in author's possession.

———. 1993. "The Canonization of a Native American Saint." Paper presented at the American Academy of Religion annual meeting, Washington, D.C.

———. August 4, 1995. Interview by author, Kahnawake, Quebec.

Puckkee, Jane, and Sarah Patterson. November 24, 1991. Interview by author, Potawatomi Reservation, Kansas.

Radin, Paul. c. 1926. "Ojibwa and Ottawa Indians, Notes," APS.

———. 1936. "Ojibwa and Ottawa Puberty Dreams." In *Essays in Anthropology Presented to A. L. Kroeber*, 233–264. Berkeley: University of California Press.

Reardon, James Michael. 1955. *George Anthony Belcourt: Pioneer Catholic Missionary of the Northwest, 1803–1874*. St. Paul, Minn.: North Central Publishing Company.

Rhodes, Willard. 1960. "The Christian Hymnology of the North American Indians." In *Men and Cultures*, ed. Anthony F. C. Wallace, 324–331. Philadelphia: University of Pennsylvania Press.

Richter, Daniel K. 1983. "Jesuit Missions and Iroquois Polities, 1642–1687." Paper presented at the American Academy of Religion annual meeting, Dallas, Texas.

———. 1984. "The Ordeal of the Longhouse: Change and Persistence on the Iroquois Frontier, 1609–1720." Ph.D. dissertation, Columbia University, New York.

———. 1985. "Iroquois Versus Iroquois: Jesuit Missions and Christianity in Village Politics, 1642–1686." *Ethnohistory* 32:1–16.

Ritzenthaler, Robert E., and Pat Ritzenthaler. 1970. *The Woodland Indians of the Western Great Lakes*. Garden City, N.Y.: Doubleday & Co.

Roark-Calnek, Sue N. November 12, 1991. Interview by author, Hamilton, New York.

Roderick, M. Grace. August 21, 1992. Interview by author, Pleasant Point, Maine.

Rogers, Edward S. 1962. *The Round Lake Ojibwa*. [Toronto]: Ontario Department of Lands and Forests.

Ronda, James P. 1972. "The European Indian: Jesuit Civilization Planning in New France." *Church History* 41:385–395.

——. 1977. "'We Are Well as We Are': An Indian Critique of Seventeenth-Century Christian Missions." *The William and Mary Quarterly* 34:66–82.

——. 1979. "The Sillery Experiment: A Jesuit-Indian Village in New France, 1637–1663." *American Indian Culture and Research Journal* 3:1–18.

Rouquette, (Rev.) Adrian. 1842–1885. Papers, Notre Dame.

Rousseau, Jacques. 1952. "Persistances païennes chez les Amérindians de la forêt boréale." *Les Cahiers Des Dix* 17:183–208.

Sampson, Martin J. 1972. *Indians of Skagit County*. Mount Vernon, Wash.: Skagit County Historical Society.

——. 1977. Lecture, translated and transcribed by Vi Hilbert, Lushootseed.

Schaeffer, Claude. 1937. "The First Jesuit Mission to the Flathead, 1840–1850: A Study in Culture Conflicts." *Pacific Northwest Quarterly* 28:227–250.

Schoenberg, (Rev.) Wilfred P., S.J. 1957. *Jesuit Mission Presses in The Pacific Northwest: A History and Bibliography of Imprints, 1876–1899*. Portland, Ore.: The Champoeg Press.

——. 1960. *Jesuits in Montana, 1840–1960*. Portland, Ore.: The Oregon-Jesuit.

——. 1962. *A Chronicle of the Catholic History of the Pacific Northwest, 1743–1960*. N.p. Gonzaga Preparatory School.

——. 1982. *Paths to the Northwest: A Jesuit History of The Oregon Province*. Chicago: Loyola University Press.

Schoolcraft, Henry R[owe]. 1853–1857. *Information, Respecting the History, Condition and Prospects of the Indian Tribes of the United States*. 6 vols. Philadelphia: Lippincott, Grambo & Company.

Scott, Hugh L. 1919–1931. "Reports and Correspondence from Chippewa Agency, Minnesota." Smithsonian.

Seattle, Swinomish, Lummi, Washington. August 4–8, 1993. Author's fieldnotes, Tekakwitha Conference.

Seliskar, John. 1911. "The Reverend Francis Pirec, Indian Missionary." *Acta et Dicta* 3:66–90.

Shea, John Gilmary. 1855. *History of the Catholic Missions among the Indian Tribes of the United States, 1529–1854*. New York: Edward Dunigan & Brother.

Shillinger, Sarah. August 5–6, 1993. Interviews by author, Swinomish, Seattle, Washington.

Shimpo, Mitsuru, and Robert Williamson. 1965. *Socio-cultural Disintegration among the Fringe Saulteaux*. Saskatoon: University of Saskatchewan.

Sieber, S. A. 1950. *The Saulteaux Indians*. Techny, Ill.: The Mission House.

Skolla, (Rev.) Otto. 1936. "Father Skolla's Report on His Indian Missions." Trans. Thomas J. Shanahan. *Acta et Dicta* 7:217–268.

Slind-Flor, Victoria. February 24, 1985. "'If I Can Help My People, That's What I Want to Do.'" *West Bank Guide*, pp. 1A–2A.

Smet, (Rev.) Pierre Jean de, S.J. 1847. *Oregon Missions and Travels over the Rocky Mountains in 1845–46*. New York: n.p..

———. 1851–1865. Correspondence, Notre Dame.

———. N.d. *New Indian Sketches*. New York: n.p.

Smith, Donald B. 1985. "Kahgegagahbowh (George Copway): Canada's First Indian Author." Unpublished ms. in author's possession.

Smith, John. [1919]. *Being the Life History of Chief John Smith, as Narrated by Himself and Interpreted by His Adopted Son, Thomas E. Smith*. Walker, Minn.: The Cass County Pioneer.

Smith, Nicholas N. 1976. "Christian Holidays Important to the Wabanaki." In *Papers of the Seventh Algonquian Conference, 1975*, ed. William Cowan, 115–128. Ottawa: Carleton University.

Smith, Theresa S. 1993. "The Church of the Immaculate Conception: Integration or Appropriation of Anishnaabe Traditions." Paper presented at the American Academy of Religion annual meeting, Washington, D.C.

Snow, Dean. 1994. *The Iroquois*. Cambridge, Mass.: Blackwell Publishers.

Solet, Pierre, and Mary Solet. August 5, 7–8, 1992. Interviews by author, Orono, Maine.

Spier, Leslie. 1935. *The Prophet Dance of the Northwest and Its Derivatives: The Sources of the Ghost Dance*. Menasha, Wisc.: George Banta Publishing Company.

"Spirit in the Wind." 1988. Videotape, Archdiocese of Oklahoma City.

Spitzer, Allen, and Mary L. Spitzer. 1960. "Religious Reorganization among the Montana Blackfeet." *Review of Religious Research* 2:19–35.

Ste.-Anne-de-Beaupré, Quebec. July 26, 1990. Author's fieldnotes.

St. Hilaire, George P. 1976. "Indian Sacraments: A Sanpoil Model." *Cross Currents* 26:172–188.

St. Louis, A. E. 1951a. "St. Regis Reserve," St. Regis.

———. 1951b. "The St. Regis Reserve and St. Regis Band of Indians," St. Regis.

———. 1952. "The Foundation of St. Regis Mission," St. Regis.

St. Lucy's Church, Syracuse, New York. November 6, 1993. Author's fieldnotes.

St. Regis, Ontario. August 5, 1995. Author's fieldnotes.

St. Regis Parish Council. 1977–1985. Minutes and Correspondence, St. Regis.

Starkloff, (Rev.) Carl F., S.J. 1982. *A Theological Reflection: The Recent Revitalization of the Tekakwitha Conference*. Great Falls, Mont.: Tekakwitha Conference National Center.

———. 1985. "The Anishinabe Ministry Training Project: Scriptural-Theological Formation." *Kerygma* 19:71–81.

———. March 18, 1985. Personal communication with author.

———. August 7, 1986. Interview by author, Bozeman, Montana.

———. 1989. "Keepers of Tradition: The Symbol Power of Indigenous Ministry. *Kerygma* 52:3–120.

———. August 24, 1990. Personal communication with author.

———. October 11–14, 1990. Interviews by author, Toronto-Anderson Lake, Ontario.

———. 1991. "'Good Fences Make Good Neighbors'? or 'The Meeting of the Two Rivers'?" Unpublished ms. in author's possession.

Steckley, John. 1992. "The Warrior and the Lineage: Jesuit Use of Iroquoian Images to Communicate Christianity." *Ethnohistory* 39:478–509.

Stevens, George, Jr. August 23, 1992. Interview by author, Indian Township, Maine.

Stevens, Michael E. 1974–1975. "Catholic and Protestant Missionaries among Wisconsin Indians: The Territorial Period." *Wisconsin Magazine of History* 58:140–148.

Stogre, (Rev.) Michael, S.J. October 13, 1990. Interview by author, Anderson Lake, Espanola, Ontario.

Suquamish Indian Tribe. 1982–1983. Suquamish Tribal Oral History Project, Suquamish.

Swinomish Indian Reservation, Washington. January 14, 1990. Author's fieldnotes.

Talbot, (Rev.) Francis Xavier, S.J. 1956. *Saint among the Hurons: The Life of Jean de Brébeuf*. Garden City, N.Y.: Doubleday & Co.

———. 1961. *Saint among Savages: The Life of Isaac Jogues*. Garden City, N.Y.: Doubleday & Co.

Taylor, (Sister) Mary Christine, S.S.J. 1976. *A History of the Foundations of Catholicism in Northern New York*. New York: United States Catholic Historical Society.

Tekakwitha Conference Newsletter. 1981–1996.

Tennelly, (Rev.) J. B. 1935. "Father Pierz, Missionary and Colonizer." *Acta et Dicta* 7:104–130.

Terrell, John Upton. 1964. *Black Robe: The Life of Pierre-Jean De Smet, Missionary, Explorer & Pioneer*. Garden City, N.Y.: Doubleday & Co.

Thibodeau, (Rev.) Norman. August 7, 1992. Interview by author, Orono, Maine.

Thomas, George L. 1986. "Catholics and the Missions of the Pacific Northwest—1826–1853." Ph.D. dissertation, University of Washington.

Thornton, Russell. "Population." In *Native America in the Twentieth Century: An Encyclopedia*, ed. Mary B. Davis, 461–464. New York: Garland Publishing.

Thwaites, Reuben Gold, ed. 1896–1901. *The Jesuit Relations and Allied Documents*, 73 vols. Cleveland: The Burrows Brothers Company.

Tinker, George. 1993. *Missionary Conquest: The Gospel and Native American Cultural Genocide*. Minneapolis: Fortress Press.

Topash, Thomas W., and James M. McClurken. 1994. "Pokagon Potawatomi." In *Native America in the Twentieth Century: An Encyclopedia*, ed. Mary B. Davis, 468. New York: Garland Publishing.

Trigger, Bruce G. 1965. "The Jesuits and the Fur Trade." *Ethnohistory* 12:30–53.

———. 1976. *The Children of Aataentsic*. 2 vols. Montreal: McGill-Queen's University Press.

Turtle Mountain Indian Reservation, Belcourt, North Dakota. [1985]. *St. Ann's Centennial: 100 Years of Faith, 1885–1985*. Rolla, N.Dak.: Star Printing.

Twohy, (Rev.) Patrick J., S.J. 1984. *Finding a Way Home: Indian and Catholic Spiritual Paths of the Plateau Tribes*. Inchelium, Wash.: St. Michaels [*sic*] Mission.

Twohy, (Rev.) Patrick J., S.J. et al. May 1987. "Statement in Support of the Native People from California." *Tekakwitha Conference Newsletter* 6:17.

Unity Grapevine, The. 1994–1995.

Vanderburgh, R. M. 1977. *I Am Nokomis, Too: The Biography of Verna Patronella Johnston*. Don Mills, Ontario: General Publishing Co.

Vecsey, Christopher. 1983. *Traditional Ojibwa Religion and Its Historical Changes*. Philadelphia: American Philosophical Society.

———. 1992. "Vi Hilbert, Translator." In *Writings about Vi Hilbert, by Her Friends*, ed. Janet Yoder, 50–54. N.p.: Lushootseed Research.

Veillette, John, and Gary White. 1977. *Early Indian Village Churches: Wooden Frontier Architecture in British Columbia*. Vancouver: University of British Columbia Press.

Verret, Kirby. November 18–22, 1990. Interviews by author, Grand Caillou, Dulac, Louisiana.

Verwyst, (Rev.) Chrysostom. 1886. *Missionary Labors of Fathers Marquette, Menard and Allouez, in the Lake Superior Region*. Milwaukee and Chicago: Hoffmann Brothers.

———. 1900. *Life and Labors of Rt. Rev. Frederic Baraga, First Bishop of Marquette, Mich*. Milwaukee: M. H. Wiltzius & Co.

———. 1914. "A Short Account of the Fond du Lac Indian Mission." *Acta et Dicta* 3:236–252.

———. 1971. *Chippewa Exercises, Being a Practical Introduction into the Study of the Chippewa Language*. Minneapolis, Minn.: Ross & Haines. Original publication 1901.

Vogel, (Rev.) Claude L., O.M.Cap. 1928. *The Capuchins in French Louisiana (1722–1766)*. Washington, D.C.: The Catholic University of America.

Walker Art Center and the Minneapolis Institute of Arts. 1968. *American Indian Art: Form and Tradition*. New York: E. P. Dutton and Co.

Walker, Deward E. 1968. *Conflict and Schism in Nez Perce Acculturation, A Study of Religion and Politics*. N.p.: Washington State University.

Wallace, Paul A. 1945. *Conrad Weiser, 1696–1760. Friend of Colonist and Mohawk*. Philadelphia: University of Pennsylvania Press.

Walworth, Ellen Hardin. 1893. *The Life and Times of Kateri Tekakwitha: The Lily of the Mohawks, 1655–1680*. Buffalo, N.Y.: Peter Paul.

Warner, Mikell de Lores Wormell, and Harriet Duncan Munnick, trans. and eds. 1972. *Catholic Church Records of the Pacific Northwest: Vancouver, Volumes 1 and 2 and Stellamaris Mission*. St. Paul, Ore.: French Prairie Press.

Watembach, Karen. 1983. "The History of the Catechesis of the Catholic Church on the Crow Reservation." M.A. thesis, Montana State University.

Weiser, (Rev.) Francis X., S.J. 1972. *Kateri Tekakwitha*. Montreal: Kateri Center.

Whitehead, Margaret. 1981. *The Cariboo Mission: A History of the Oblates*. Victoria, B.C.: Sono Nis Press.

———. July 1981. "Christianity, a Matter of Choice: The Historical Role of Indian Catechists in Oregon Territory and British Columbia." *Pacific Northwest Quarterly* 72:98–106.

Whitehead, Margaret, ed. 1988. *They Call Me Father: Memoirs of Father Nicolas Coccola*. Vancouver: University of British Columbia Press.

Winchell, N. H. 1911. *The Aborigines of Minnesota*. St. Paul: The Minnesota Historical Society.

Wind River Rendezvous, The, vol. 9. May–June 1979.

Woodward, Kenneth L. 1990. *Making Saints*. New York: Simon & Schuster.

Woolworth, Nancy L. 1965. "The Grand Portage Mission: 1731–1965." *Minnesota History* 39:301–310.

Works Progress Administration. 1936–1940, 1942. *Chippewa Indian Historical Project Records*, 2 reels microfilm, Wisconsin.

Wren, Christopher S. March 10, 1985. "Pope's Cancelled Visit Makes Mark in Canada." *The New York Times*, p. 20.

Wyne, Mike. October 4, 1968. "Swinomish Indians' Woe." *The Catholic Northwest Progress*, p. 6.

———. October 25, 1968. "Something Better for Their Children, Too." *The Catholic Northwest Progress*, pp. 6–7.

Yokules, Elaine, and Suzanne Hess. [1965]. "Names," St. Dominic.

Zaplotnik, (Rev.) J. L. 1917. "A Lecture Delivered by Bishop Baraga, 1863." *Acta et Dicta* 5:99–110.

———. 1934. "Rev. Lawrence Lautishar in Minnesota." *Acta et Dicta* 6:258–287.

Zuern, (Rev.) Ted, S.J. August 4, 1995. Interview by author, Kahnawake, Quebec.